INVITATION TO THE THEATRE

THIRD EDITION

INVITATION TO THE THEATRE

THIRD EDITION

GEORGE KERNODLE
EMERITUS, UNIVERSITY OF ARKANSAS

PORTIA KERNODLE

EDWARD PIXLEY
STATE UNIVERSITY OF NEW YORK AT ONEONTA

HARCOURT BRACE JOVANOVICH, PUBLISHERS
San Diego New York Chicago Atlanta Washington, D.C.
London Sydney Toronto

ISBN: 0-15-546924-X

Library of Congress Catalog Card Number: 84-81519

Printed in the United States of America

Cover: Photograph, by Yann Arthus-Bertrand, first published in GEO magazine, March 1984.

Copyrights and Acknowledgments

The authors are grateful to the following publishers and copyright holders for permission to reprint excerpts from the indicated plays and musicals:

CHAPPELL MUSIC COMPANY *My Fair Lady:* Copyright © 1956 by Alan Jay Lerner and Frederick Loewe. Chappell & Co., Inc., owner of publication and allied rights throughout the world. International copyright secured. All rights reserved. *South Pacific:* Copyright © 1949 by Richard Rodgers and Oscar Hammerstein II. Copyright renewed, Williamson Music Co., owner of publication and allied rights throughout the Western Hemisphere and Japan. International copyright secured. All rights reserved.

FRANK MUSIC CORP. *Guys and Dolls:* Music and lyrics by Frank Loesser. © 1950 Frank Music Corp.; © renewed 1978. International copyright secured. All rights reserved. Used by permission.

GROVE PRESS, INC. *Waiting for Godot:* Copyright © 1954 by Grove Press, Inc.; renewed 1982 by Samuel Beckett. *The Homecoming:* Copyright © 1965 and 1966 by H. Pinter Ltd. *The Elephant Man:* Copyright © 1979 by Bernard Pomerance.

THE STERLING LORD AGENCY *Dutchman:* Copyright © 1964 by LeRoi Jones.

RANDOM HOUSE, INC. *A Raisin in the Sun:* Copyright © 1958, 1959 by Robert Nemiroff as executor of the Estate of Lorraine Hansberry.

FLORA ROBERTS, INC. *West Side Story:* Copyright 1957 by Stephen Sondheim.

ST. MARTIN'S PRESS, INC. *Spell #7:* Copyright © 1981 by Ntozake Shange.

THE SOCIETY OF AUTHORS *Pygmalion:* Reprinted by permission of The Society of Authors on behalf of the Bernard Shaw Estate.

Picture credits appear on page 447, which constitutes a continuation of the copyright page.

PREFACE

When *Invitation to the Theatre* first appeared in hardcover nearly twenty years ago, it quickly became one of the most widely used introductory texts in the field, retaining its considerable popularity through two paperback editions. By emphasizing the impulses that cause people to create and go to the theatre, *Invitation* made it possible for the theatre novice to appreciate a wide variety of theatre genres while discovering the links that connect theatres of the past to those of our time. This new edition retains the core of the earlier editions (the historic-generic chapters, updated and revised), but in keeping with recent teaching trends it places added emphasis on an experiential approach.

Two entirely new chapters in Part I introduce the reader to the theatre from the point of view of the audience. Chapter 1 shows the kinds of configurations in which theatre occurs and the kinds of experiences theatregoing evokes, while Chapter 2, using *The Elephant Man* for detailed illustration, shows the ways in which both play and production structures invite audiences to share the theatre event. Part II, consisting of the historic-generic chapters, reduces somewhat the number of examples, allowing for a more detailed treatment of one play in each chapter to illustrate the ideas developed in the chapter.

In Part III of this edition, a separate chapter is devoted to each of the major theatre artists: playwright, director, designer, and actor. The purpose here is not to provide introductory training in the methods of these artists, but to help the reader appreciate what theatre artists do in bringing the play from the first imaginings of the playwright to the realized performance of actors in the presence of an audience. As in the earlier historic-generic chapters, each chapter focuses on a single play to show just how the artists go about bringing the play to life.

After Chapters 1 and 2, which should be read first, the chapters can be assigned independently—in or out of order—to suit the preferences of individual instructors. Moreover, the chapters of Part III are designed so that they may be assigned along with chapters in Part II, thus heightening the experiential approach. For example, while reading about tragedy in Elizabethan England in Chapter 4, the students may also study the process of directing *Hamlet* in Chapter 12. Or by reading either Chapter 5 or 7 in tandem with Chapter 14, they may learn about the comic or the realistic theatre and, at the same time, see what an actress might go through in creating the realistic comic role of Eliza Doolittle in *Pygmalion*. Similarly Chapter 11 (on playwriting) coordinates with Chapter 6 (romantic theatre), and Chapter 13 (the designer) could coordinate with either Chapter 8 or 10 (disruption or liberation).

Finally, a glossary has been added in this edition, so that students may quickly find definitions of unfamiliar theatre terms that are used in the text.

To George and Portia Kernodle, for trusting me with this revision and for generous encouragement and suggestions along the way, my indebtedness can hardly be put into words. Being asked to do the revision was an honor; doing it was a joy. I am grateful to Dolly Beechman, Pennsylvania State University, Ogontz; LeRoy D. Haberman, Ventura College; James W. Hawes, Radford University; and Wallace Sterling, University of Akron, for their careful review of the Second Edition and their suggestions for revision; and to William Kuhlke, University of Kansas, Lawrence, and Robert H. Wilcox, Blackburn College, for their thoughtful and perceptive reviews of the manuscript. I am particularly indebted to Fred Miller, Richard Siegfried, Josef Elfenbein, Esther Elfenbein, Muriel Kellerhouse, and Theodore Kottke, my theatre colleagues at the State University College at Oneonta, for advice on individual chapters. Most of all, thanks go to my friend and colleague Junius Hamblin, whose insightful suggestions at the beginning of the project and whose close critical reading of the entire manuscript have been invaluable. Finally, a special thank you to my wife, Kathryn, for her encouragement and her patient insistence on clarity as she read and reread every word at each stage of revision.

Edward Pixley

CONTENTS

THE PLAY IN ITS TIME

INVITATION TO THE THEATRE

THIRD EDITION

MY ONE AND ONLY
THE NEW GERSHWIN MUSICAL
TOMMY TUNE AND TWIGGY ARE TOPS IN TAPS!

PROLOGUE: THE THEATRE INVITES YOU

The lure of Broadway—the marquee of the St. James Theater, New York City.

Night after night, year in and year out, blazing marquees and tantalizing advertisements throughout the world extend their invitation: Come To The Theatre! For more than twenty-four centuries, ever since the ancient Greeks began exporting culture to the rest of the Mediterranean world, theatres of one form or another have been sending out their invitations, and willing audiences have gladly responded to their call.

For the citizens of Athens in the fifth century B.C., there must have been a special magic in going to the theatre. They had often heard poets recite the stories of the ancient battles of Troy and marveled at the days when gods talked with men and men walked like heroes over the land. For the annual festival of drama, the shops would close, all government business would cease, and the priests would lead the procession to the magnificent theatre, carved out of a hillside, with its altar dedicated to the life-renewing spirit of the god Dionysus. For months the best poets had been polishing their work, the most gifted actors, singers, and dancers had been rehearsing, and now they would don heroic robes and tragic or comic masks to recreate before the eyes of the entire city the inspiring legends of their ancestors.

Or imagine the excitement in a sixteenth-century rural French cottage at the

Theatre comes to the audience—a *commedia dell'arte* group of Players arriving in town.

news that the Players have come to town. The year has been backbreaking routine—hoeing the landlord's fields, harvesting the landlord's crops, while trying to eke out some fresh food for the table from the tiny space behind the cottage. But the arrival of the Players breaks the routine. The family, gathering for supper, already begins to smile at the thought of Harlequin, that patched scamp who romps through the plays, happily and irreverently making fools out of the learned Doctor, the stuffy businessman, Pantalone, and even the bragging soldier, Il Capitano, who is always the greatest coward of them all. And when Harlequin gets caught, as he always does, he gets his inevitable beating from the ever-present slapstick but always comes up smirking, humbled only long enough to plan his next defiance of the authority figures in his life. However momentary, however illusory, what freedom, what joy those audacious Players bring to the little village!

Now leap ahead to 1848 and the simmering heat of a Manhattan summer. The fashionable boxes are filled with the carriage trade from the brownstone mansions around Washington Square, while laborers from the garment district and the waterfront docks pack the pit and galleries. For Saturday night means the theatre, and what a theatre it is! Both high class and low come to live out their fantasies of frontier America with the heroic Edwin Forrest, whose powerful voice and body might challenge the forest primeval one night or high-society

F.S. CHANFRAU IN THE CHARACTER OF "MOSE"

Mose, the Bowery Boy, a well-loved hero of nineteenth-century melodrama on the New York stage, played by Frank S. Chanfrau.

snobs the next. Or perhaps they can watch the noble Junius Brutus Booth bring to life the great romantic roles—Othello, Hamlet, Romeo—and lift them to heights of poetic glory or inspire them with the terrors of tragic death.

It's easy, of course, to glorify the importance of live theatre for audiences of the past who had little else for entertainment, but with the rise of film in our own era, then of radio and at last television, voices of dire prophecy arose. Each of these media could reach larger audiences with more varied material and at greater cost effectiveness; thus, each in turn was destined to bury the theatre. The fragile theatre could survive, if at all, only for the elite with money and leisure enough to indulge in antiques and nostalgia. Yet today it is those prophecies that are buried, not the theatre. Despite the easy access to television, despite the scope of film, with its on-location realism and its quick cutting across time and space, the live theatre continues to flourish. In the 1982 season, an estimated 40,000 people per day attended the theatre in New York City alone. One need only couple this figure with the vast audiences in such theatre centers as Los Angeles, Toronto, London, Milan, and Tokyo (to name just a few), and then imagine the thousands who attend the countless educational, regional, community, dinner, and arts theatres the world over to realize how far our love for theatre extends.

But there is no need in these pages to put theatre into competition with television and film. In fact, drama in the live theatre has so much in common with drama in film and television that this book will draw examples from all three whenever appropriate.

THE ATTRACTION OF THE THEATRE

So let's set aside comparison and start exploring the ongoing attraction of the theatre. What is it that irresistibly drew the ancient Greek citizens, the Renaissance peasant families, and the nineteenth-century New York laborers and socialites to the theatre? Why do audiences by the tens of thousands continue to accept the theatre's invitation, taking the trouble and expense of going to a play?

The ads on the theatre page of the newspaper provide some clues, ads such as "Dorothy Loudon in *Noises Off*" or "*My One and Only*, starring Twiggy and Tommy Tune." We are invited to see not only the play but the actors—not only the drama in the lives of the characters but the actors who impersonate those characters. All human beings, just like actors, play roles in daily life; moreover, the patterns that shape these plays—conflict, confrontation, crisis, resolution—are the very patterns of life itself. In Shakespeare's *As You Like It*, Jaques says:

> All the world's a stage
> And all the men and women merely players:
> They have their exits and their entrances;
> And one man in his time plays many parts.

Yet life in the world and life on stage are not the same. Everyone knows that the theatre, with its false front and painted canvas, its masks and disguises, is illusion created by sleight of hand. But everyone is glad to make believe, to participate in the deception that deceives no one, because the theatre, in spite of its illusion—perhaps even because of its illusion—can offer us the patterns and characters of life more intensely than life itself can.

THE ELEMENTS OF THEATRE

In the theatre we expect actors and actresses to play roles. Because we know that they are roles, artificial constructs created for our pleasure, we can view those characters with sympathetic detachment, enter into their lives with a protected intimacy impossible in life itself. We expect the conflicts and crises of life to be set before us, but not in the drab reality and uncertainty that shape our daily lives. We look for vivid characters, heightened language, clearly defined problems for the characters to resolve, and obstacles that we can recognize. Hamlet must avenge his father's death without destroying his own soul; Oedipus must save his people from the plague by tracking down the murderer of King Laius; and the miserly Harpagon must preserve his lovely money while he finds suitable marriages for his reluctant son and daughter. And so the drama concentrates its effects and presents the patterns of life—intensified.

For centuries, the elements of theatre were identified in this two-part model: the play itself and the means of performance. Aristotle, in ancient Greece, identified six parts to the drama, ascribing plot, character, and thought, which he considered the most important parts, to the play itself, and relegating language, music, and spectacle (the means of performance) to a secondary status. In Renaissance Spain, Lope de Vega, who wrote more than eighteen hundred plays himself, said that all the theatre needed were "three boards, two actors, and a passion," thus giving top billing to the means of performance (the stage and the performers), and putting that which is performed (the "passion") into third position. Aristotle and Lope may disagree on which is the more important, but they share the two-part breakdown—the dramatic elements and the performance elements—and have passed their perception on to posterity.

Yet a third element had always been present, an element that everyone knew about but never acknowledged as part of the event. This third element was the *audience*, considered to be mere spectators, passive receivers of the performed event. When their participation was acknowledged, it was seen as a distraction. Shakespeare's Hamlet even blamed the clowns for speaking "more than is set down for them" in order to make the crowds laugh, for by such actions they may lose "some necessary question of the play."

Not until film and television actors found themselves performing without live audiences out front did the audience's full share in the event begin to get credit. Radio and television soon introduced laugh tracks to simulate that nec-

The final ingredient of theatre, without which there would be no theatre—an attentive, absorbed audience. Here, at the Park Theater, New York.

essary third element, and "filmed before a live audience" became a standard criterion for quality television comedy once Tony Randall and Jack Klugman insisted on its use in filming *The Odd Couple* episodes in the late 1960s.

So when a young Polish theatrical innovator, Jerzy Grotowski, set out to discover the essence of a theatre for our time, he looked first at the lavish theatrical presentations he saw around him; then he began to strip away, one by one, all the elements that could be dispensed with and still leave something that could be called theatre. He found that costumes, makeup, settings, lights, music—even language—could go. Thus he arrived at a new model, what he called "the poor theatre," theatre reduced to its essence. What was left were the actor and the audience. The play itself received only passing acknowledgment in Grotowski's model.

If by some miracle of imagination and technology we could join the citizens of ancient Athens in the Theatre of Dionysus to see a full-scale production of Sophocles' *Oedipus the King*, with every word, movement, and special effect of the original intact, we would doubtless find it a moving experience. But would our experience be the same as that of the Athenians? How could we put our-

"Vivid characters and heightened language"—the Chorus of Theban Elders pleading with their king, Oedipus. The Guthrie Theatre production of Sophocles' *Oedipus the King*, directed by Michael Langham.

selves into the spirit of those citizens who came to the theatre filled with the pride of their city, the glory of the civilized world, who shared with their neighbors in this theatre one of the crowning achievements of their people? The story of King Oedipus they had known since childhood. His secret burial place was a symbol of their city's hospitality and security. With pride they watched him try to save his people from the plague by seeking out the murderer of the man who was king before him. With growing horror they watched him become obsessed to know the truth, usurp the role of the gods themselves, defy their priests, and blindly refuse to call off the search that must finally bring him to his knees, a supreme penitent, when he finally learns that he himself is the murderer he seeks, that he had killed the former king not knowing he was king, not knowing that that very king was his own father and that the woman he now calls wife and queen is his own mother. That horror would mount as they watched Oedipus gouge out the eyes that had so long deceived him with the lure of earthly triumphs and forever leave his native city, a wandering exile, suffering alone the punishment for his pride. Those citizens would also share the inspiring transformation that makes him face his penance and prepares him for the destiny that ultimately protects their own city from its enemies. Certainly we can find much in this incredible enactment of human striving and human destiny to relate to our own world. But that special relationship that the Athenian citizens had to the play is not ours to share. Our experience of *Oedipus the King,* powerful as it may be, will not be the Athenian experience. It will be our own, informed by our knowledge of the past and our own contemporary world.

We need only look back to the rock musical *Hair* that packed theatres in new York, Los Angeles, Toronto, and as far away as London and Sydney in the late sixties to see how ephemeral a thing this third element of the theatre experience is. Now, less than two decades later, where would we find the audience of the sixties, those freedom-seeking young people bent on "doing their own thing"? Today, no one is rushing to produce *Hair;* we couldn't cast the audience, one of the most essential elements of that play.

Thus, we arrive at a point of distinction often overlooked. Undoubtedly, audiences are attracted to the live theatre by the intensification of life found in the stories and the plots; surely they are attracted to the productions of those plots and stories by skilled performances and electrifying displays of the scenic artists. But the ingredient that makes the final difference is the actual presence of the audience, without whom theatre does not, cannot exist. When the theatre invites you, it does not simply ask you to come and be entertained; it invites *you*—to bring something of yourself along, to share and to participate in the event.

THE
AUDIENCE

I

THE AUDIENCE

Audiences come to the theatre, as they do to any work of art, seeking a more intense experience of life than life itself affords. "Exciting," "thrilling," "marvelous" are the terms they hope will describe the experience, never merely "adequate" or "interesting." "Adequate" could come from reading the play at home, imagining a performance in their own minds; "interesting" could apply as easily to a newspaper item. But theatrical intensification is spellbinding, and to be spellbound is to be superconscious, to be involved so completely that all else slips into the background and disappears while our total being is concentrated in the immediate event. When we are spellbound, we are able to respond to the smallest detail of a character's movement, the subtlest shading of a vocal inflection; yet at the same time we are sensitized to the event as a whole, able to grasp the absolute rightness of all the parts working together to lift us out of ourselves and into the realm of art. Such intensity is invigorating; it makes us feel alive in ways that life itself rarely does, and when it is over, we come away feeling transformed by the event. Watch the audiences emerge from a hit musical. The smiles on their faces, melodies on their lips, and lightness in their step result from total involvement in the magical world of the play. From a tragedy we may emerge exhausted, physically and emotionally drained, yet irresistibly exhilarated from having spent two hours in passionate intimacy with people living on the brink of triumph or disaster. Though not all theatre events achieve such intensity, it is surely the goal toward which they aspire and for which all audiences hope.

In the next two chapters, we shall look at some of the elements that help to shape such intense experiences. Chapter 1 will focus on the performance place and on the audience; Chapter 2 will show how the playscript and the production set the imagination of the audience to work. Thus, within a particular performance place, the playscript, the production, and the audience all join together to complete the theatre experience.

THE AUDIENCE IN THE THEATRE

1

An outdoor festival theatre for Shakespeare.
The auditorium is a variant of the Greek theatre, but the stage is based on early twentieth-century reconstructions of the Elizabethan
theatre. The Oregon Shakespeare Festival
Theatre, Ashland, Oregon, founded by Angus
Bowmer.

THE PERFORMANCE PLACE

*T*he great performer can arouse an audience to intense experiences any-where—in street or field—but once theatre found its place in a nation's culture, specific areas were soon designated or built for performance, thus providing continuity to theatre as an institution. The shape of these areas took into account the needs of the audience—that is, it ensured that all could hear and see; equally important, it established whatever relationship each culture expected its audience to have toward the performance. At the same time, the performance spaces had to accommodate the produced play, including scenic effects, appropriate entrances and exits, and space for costume changes.

Theatre groups have always used and probably always will use whatever improvised or "found" space is available. That space will usually be either an *arena*, a *thrust*, or a *proscenium* stage, the three major forms in which theatres today are constructed. Although almost any play can be adapted to any of these three, each evolved out of a different audience-performer relationship, and each has its own set of conventions.

The simplest form is the *arena* or *theatre-in-the-round*, with the audience in a circle or rectangle surrounding the playing area. It is the form of the natural

A well-equipped, fairly large arena theatre, seating 752 in steeply banked rows. The Arena Stage, Washington, D.C.

A throne with formal entrances and upper stage serves as the symbolic backing for a thrust stage that allows audience seating on three sides. Set up in the Presbyterian Assembly Hall for the Edinburgh Festival, the stage accommodates a production of Lindsay's *The Satire of the Three Estates*. Directed by Tyrone Guthrie. Drawing by Richard Leacroft, from Helen and Richard Leacroft, *The Theatre.*

setting of most primitive villages, and when the village was small enough, all the people sat or stood in a circle close around the performers. For sports events and dramatic war games, the ancient Romans built huge arenas seating many thousands. But today it is the small arena that is popular, first, because its small size and use of imaginary walls keeps down the cost of production and, second, because it brings the spectators close to the actors, increasing the intimacy of performance.

Because the audience is so close to the stage, with no physical separation, the actors can perform with a naturalness that they might use in their own living rooms, giving the audience the illusion of actual reality. But, paradoxically, the shape of the space can also remind them that it *is* theatre, since directly across the arena they see other audience members watching the performance just as they are. And when an actor comes to the edge of the playing space and looks through an imagined window, the audience, sitting only a few feet away, is asked to believe that the actor is seeing, not them, but perhaps a storm raging or a stranger approaching from outside the house, thus increasing the shared feeling that they are using their imaginations to help create the event. This paradoxical mixing of the real and the theatrical can even extend to the tidy spectator who

A large nineteenth-century example of the traditional proscenium theatre: Covent Garden Theatre, 1804. The stage set—for Sheridan's romantic *Pizarro*—includes realistic detail painted on easily changed wings and backdrops.

reaches onto the set to replace some small object *(prop)* that has fallen to the floor. If a character is supposed to replace the prop later, as part of the action, such helpfulness may force the actors to rewrite some lines on the spot.

The second form of theatre, variously called *thrust, apron,* or *open* stage, seats the audience around three sides of an open platform. At the back of the platform is usually a scenic unit, often symbolic, containing two or more entrance doors and frequently more than one level. The origin of this form was a temple stage with sacred doorways through which figures could enter from the "other world" of gods, demons, ghosts, and ancestors. The thrust stage remains popular for several reasons. It brings actors and audience close together in a dynamic relationship because, like the arena stage, it puts no physical separation between audience and play. This gives the characters freedom, at one moment, to be totally involved with other characters on stage and, at the next, to speak directly to the audience in asides and soliloquies. Yet it permits more scenic and lighting effects than are possible in the arena circle. It appeals most, however, because, like its sacred ancestor, it easily suggests the symbolic, the mysterious, and the mystical.

The third form of theatre today is the *proscenium* stage. It was invented by Italian dukes in the sixteenth century and independently in Japan in the seventeenth century, when a new bourgeois merchant class wanted to see a complete painted picture, framed and revealed by a front curtain, creating the illusion of the streets, houses, and rooms of the world they knew. In the proscenium theatre, audience members, all facing the same way, watch the play as through a picture frame. The convention of the missing "fourth wall" between stage and audience requires the actors to be completely immersed in their characters and to make no contact with the audience.

Since its beginning, the proscenium stage has dominated the Western theatre and remains the standard form. It has been under attack for decades, however, and new theatres today are usually more open. Many resident companies and most university drama programs use at least two theatres: a proscenium theatre and a flexible room that permits different arrangements of chairs and

An environmental-theatre approach to Henrik Ibsen's *Peer Gynt* in which the audience must choose which action to follow. Trinity Square Repertory Company production, directed by Adrian Hall.

playing areas. Such a room, sometimes called a "little black box," can easily be shaped into an arena or a thrust stage.

In addition, the flexibility of the little black box permits new audience-performer relationships that have been developed by recent experimental groups. In the forms already discussed, the audience members sit in designated spots and then watch the single stage on which the action takes place, where their focus remains throughout the performance. However, in an attempt to make theatre more like life itself, *environmental* theatre uses multiple focuses, several acting areas spaced around the room, with the audience interspersed throughout the space. The action may shift from one area to another or may occur simultaneously in more than one space at once, requiring the members of the audience to shift their focus and even choose where to focus, as they would have to do in watching events in real life. In what the English call *promenade* theatre, the audience has no designated space, but simply moves wherever the play moves, standing or sitting around the actors until the actors move to a new area, sometimes even joining in the action with the characters, as though sharing in a community creation of the play.

THE INTENSITIES OF THEATRE

Each performing place brings audience and actors together in its own special relationship, but what occurs in the performing place is what intensifies normal experience and holds the audience spellbound. What exactly causes such intensification? Teachers of dramatic literature are likely to point to the great stories, characters, and themes in the plays. Producers and managers might emphasize the appeal of a popular actor or the lure of sets, music, and costumes. Actors, directors, and designers have good reason to believe that their artistic skills bring out the intensities of the stage life.

In live theatre, the intensities come from all these and more. As members of an audience, in fact, we respond to many kinds of experience at once. During a performance, we rarely separate them consciously, but for analysis, it will be useful to identify some of the many aspects of the theatre experience that combine to produce its intensities.

Sensory Experience

"I'm going to see a play." That's what most of us announce when we go to the theatre, and the word *theatre* itself comes from a Greek word meaning "seeing place." This is no mere figure of speech; it defines what we expect at the theatre—a "good show." Goethe once said of the theatre, "It is corporeal man who plays the leading role there—a handsome man, a beautiful woman," and the modern critic, Eric Bentley, adds to this perception: "The art of theatre starts in the simple sensuousness of direct physical attraction . . . in the beautiful bodies

Alluring spectacle—the direct appeal to the senses—in the Brown University production of *The Beggar's Opera*, directed by Don B. Wilmeth.

of performers." Direct appeal to our senses also accounts for the pleasure we get from colorful sets, stimulating music, and dynamic patterns of movement. Although sensory experience may not be the most important intensity of theatre, without it there would be no show at all. When all the elements "click"—the combined power of the live performers and the continuously evolving patterns of sound, movement, lights, colors, shapes, and rhythms—we can be swept to dazzling heights or suspended in quiet anticipation and reflection.

Artistic Appreciation

Sensuous beauty alone, alluring as it may be, will not hold our attention for long. The handsome body must *do* something. After all, drama is action. As with athletes, we are finally less interested in how performers look than in what they do, and in the skills they display in doing it. "Astonish me," the Russian impresario Sergei Diaghilev reportedly said to Jean Cocteau. For theatre must give us something to admire, to marvel at. A baseball fan may get as much pleasure from a well-executed double play as from the final score; so may a theatregoer be delighted by a skillful double-take, regardless of the outcome of the play. Beginning actors are often dismayed when "naive" audiences are amazed, not at the subtlety of their characterizations but at their ability to "memorize all those

The skill and energy of actors invite the audience's artistic appreciation. From left: Don Perkins, Victor Eschbach, Jon Voight (as Romeo), and Anthony Zerbe in a dueling scene from Shakespeare's *Romeo and Juliet*. Old Globe Theatre, San Diego, 1966.

lines." But their amazement is appropriate, for audiences will admire those skills they recognize as beyond their own powers.

Several seasons ago, when England's Old Vic Company toured Shakespeare's *Twelfth Night* in the United States, audiences watched the pompous lover, Malvolio, untie his gartered stockings and quickly retie them when he heard someone coming. As he hurriedly tied them in the cross-gartered fashion that he had been told would please his lady-love, the actor had Malvolio unknowingly tie his legs together. Seeing this, the audiences waited expectantly for the inevitable moment when he would rise and clumsily trip himself up. But as he rose, Malvolio instantly realized his problem, too late to repair the damage, and proceeded to move around the stage in an ungainly hopping motion, trying to preserve his puritanical dignity while concealing from his tormentors the fact that anything was wrong. The audience broke into gales of laughter, appreciating the inventiveness of the actor at the same time they enjoyed the plight of the character.

Plays we have seen before invite artistic comparisons. Many Shakespeare fans have seen as many as a dozen different *Hamlets,* always enjoying the new insights from each production, but also ready to be thrilled or disappointed by ways that this production may surpass or fall short of previous experiences. Opera-goers are famous for detailed recollection of stage business, musical climaxes, and even the way that a particular soprano they heard fifteen years ago approached the high C in her dying aria. Likewise, new treatments of old stories bring out our artistic appreciation, as with the film buff who can't resist comparing the film to the book. In ancient Greece, where playwrights used the same few subjects year after year, a major part of the audience pleasure apparently came from comparing this season's treatment of the story with those of previous years.

Even in plays we have never seen or read, we often compare what we see on stage with some ideal production we imagine even as we watch. Few things give more pleasure in the theatre than a performance that exceeds what we expect; likewise, few things are more disappointing than a production falling short of the possibilities that we ourselves imagine.

Sympathetic Identification

The intensities discussed so far result largely from the skills of the theatre artists, but the theatre invites another sort of pleasure as well. In the theatre, artists present human characters striving for human goals, undergoing terror and

Both Walter Lee (Ossie Davis) and his Mama (Claudia McNeil) invite sympathetic feelings from the audience in Hansberry's *A Raisin in the Sun*.

anguish, achieving triumph and joy, and audiences come to share the emotional world of the characters, striving with them and caring about what happens to them. We begin by admiring the swashbuckling hero Cyrano de Bergerac, with his daring wit and his swift sword. Then we discover that his heroics are only to make himself worthy of the beautiful Roxane, whom he knows he can never win because of his grotesque nose. Only then do we start to identify, to sympathize. We experience his anguish in vowing to protect his handsome rival in order to please the unattainable Roxane, and our sympathy is mixed with astonishment as we see him set out to make her love his soul (though not his person) through the poetry he teaches his handsome, but tongue-tied, rival. We experience *sympathetic identification* when we discover something of ourselves in the characters of a play. Our sympathy is intensified when those characters come up against obstacles (both inside and outside themselves) that threaten their well-being.

Walter Lee and Mama, in *A Raisin in the Sun*, capture our sympathetic identification, while Mama's plant creates an ironic awareness of the family's need for nurturing care and a compatible environment.

In Lorraine Hansberry's prize-winning play, *A Raisin in the Sun*, young people may identify with Walter Lee, a young black who has never had enough control over his life to earn respect from his mother, his employer, his wife, or even his son, and now that his father's life insurance money might provide him his chance, he sees his mother making the decisions as though he were still a boy. Older people might relate to the mother, Mrs. Younger, who has devoted her whole life to the good of her children. Now she sees the new wealth that might help lift them out of the ghetto tearing her children from each other, destroying their values, and possibly their lives. Or more likely, the audience will sympathize with both characters at once, as well as with other members of the family, and share their common plight as they try to discover or retain their dignity in a society that denies them the means of earning the respect they so desperately need.

Ironic Experience

Sympathetic identification with the central characters may be our basic emotional reaction to a play, but we rarely sympathize with characters on a one-to-one basis, feeling exactly as they do. Not only do we shift our sympathies from one character to another, we also see the characters' errors and weaknesses even as we share their hopes. In comedy, even when we want the character to come out on top, his or her methods may be so foolish and inept that all we can do is laugh at the silly predicaments. In such cases, our superior knowledge gives us an *ironic perspective* on the action. Even in tragedy, where we often want what the hero or heroine wants, we can see the actions leading to disaster, not success. Our ironic position allows us to experience the tragedy more intensely because we see it coming step by step, yet can do nothing to stop it. Drama provides the opportunity to become emotionally attached to a character, sharing his or her emotions, but also to stand back and experience those emotions from a larger point of view. In this dual position of participant and observer, we can experience life more intensely in the theatre than we can in the real world.

In Tennessee Williams' modern classic, *A Streetcar Named Desire*, there is a scene in which Blanche DuBois, a Southern belle who has fallen on hard times, believes that she at last has found a home, security, and a man to respect and protect her. The audience shares her passionate desire for peace. In the scene in question, she is offstage taking a bath, preparing for her birthday party. We hear the water running and we hear her singing "Paper Moon," a haunting song of hope. But onstage, her spiteful brother-in-law, Stanley, is disclosing the shabby details he has dug up about Blanche's shady past and preparing to present her with his birthday gift, a one-way bus ticket back to the town she escaped from in her search for refuge. We fully share her desires, but hardly her joy. Instead, we anticipate in fascinated suspense the moment when the disaster will break on her, and the more joyful her singing, the more terrifying the impending crisis.

By contrast, if the disaster is to happen to a character we dislike, we watch with delicious pleasure as the person moves confidently toward well-earned defeat. In one sense, then, we move through the action of the play, sympathetically relating to one or more of the characters in their actions; in another sense, we move with the play itself, judging the characters, weighing one against the other, and observing the twists and turns which they follow toward their destiny. Finally, it is because we experience plays ironically that we can be dramatically and artistically satisfied even when the play ends in defeat for characters with whom we sympathized.

Synthesizing Experience

No matter how our senses have been stimulated, no matter how great our appreciation of the artists' skills, no matter how intensely we have followed the fortunes of a character or the twists and turns of the plot, many of us finally value a play for yet another kind of intensity: the way that it directs our attention or our feelings back into the world outside the play, causing us to synthesize the play's insights with our own experience of reality. All plays that please their audiences provide sensory stimulation, artistic appreciation, and emotional gratification, but great works of art do these things, and more. A play that we remember leaves us changed in some way, perhaps wiser, more tolerant, more compas-

Friendship, love, trust, jealousy, and deceit— these are themes we come to know intimately in Shakespeare's *Othello*. Here, Othello (James Earle Jones) drinks in the poisonous lies of his trusted aide, Iago (Anthony Zerbe).

sionate, more sensitive to our common humanity, and more deeply aware of our own strengths and frailties.

We laugh uproariously at Moliere's foolish hypochondriacs, misers, and possessive husbands or at Neil Simon's middle-class playboys, divorcees, and newlyweds; but we find them most appealing because they remind us of our own weaknesses and dreams, and boldly call our attention to the universal follies that are part of being human. We may be moved to compassionate tears by Shakespeare's or Tennessee Williams' suffering heroes, but we also experience something of the terror that comes as they hold on too staunchly against overwhelming odds to what they believe right and true. Though we admire their persistence, we also recognize the danger that may await us should we carry our noblest convictions to their limit. Drama can make us test the beliefs that in life we take for granted.

No wonder that drama has often been used as the ultimate teacher, as a device for instilling in its audiences, not only knowledge and ideas, but entire value systems. Likewise, it is no wonder that the free use of drama has been seen by many societies as dangerous, as revolutionary and undermining to the status quo. When skillfully used, its methods are more enticing and its expression more persuasive than those in any other art form.

THE PLAY AND THE CREATIVE AUDIENCE

2

Audience and actors mingle in the same space in a promenade-theatre production of Keith Dewhurst's *Lark Rise* at the Cottesloe Theatre in England's National Theatre complex. The audience becomes a part of the community activities of a nineteenth-century Oxfordshire village.

*T*he prologue defined the theatre experience by a three-part model: the play, the performance or production elements, and the audience. This chapter will draw examples from several well-known plays and then concentrate on a single contemporary play, Bernard Pomerance's *The Elephant Man*, to show how the script, together with the production elements, invites the audience to become creative participants, not merely spectators, through their own imaginative involvement in the theatrical event.

Watching a play is, above all, an activity. Each piece of information or *cue* that we receive from the stage, whether verbal or nonverbal, actively engages us in the play. Each cue we observe we store away to combine with other cues, weigh one against another, and out of them build our own experience of the play. This process can be illustrated in a series of incidents from the first scene of *A Streetcar Named Desire*, all built around a single hand prop—a whiskey bottle.

Blanche DuBois, the Southern lady down on her luck whom you encountered in Chapter 1, comes to visit her younger sister Stella in a working-class neighborhood of New Orleans. The apartment is empty when Blanche arrives, and she appears to be emotionally shaken by the unexpected commonness of her sister's home. While she waits for Stella to return home from bowling, Blanche sits stiffly clutching her purse. "Suddenly she notices something in a half opened closet. She springs up and crosses to it, and removes a whiskey bottle. She pours a half tumbler of whiskey and tosses it down. She carefully replaces the bottle and washes out the tumbler at the sink." The urgency to get the drink, the amount poured, the way it is tossed down, and the cleaning up are all noted by the audience, and out of this information they begin to form impressions and attitudes about Blanche.

Stella arrives soon and, in the midst of an emotional reunion, Blanche suddenly interrupts:

> I know you must have some liquor on the place! Where could it be, I wonder? Oh, I spy, I spy!
> *(She rushes to the closet and removes the bottle; she is shaking all over and panting for breath as she tries to laugh. The bottle nearly slips from her grasp.)*
> STELLA *(noticing):* Blanche, you sit down and let me pour the drinks. I don't know what we've got to mix with. Maybe a Coke's in the icebox. Look'n see, honey, while I'm—
> BLANCHE: No Coke, honey, not with my nerves tonight!

Built out of the previous incidents, we see in Blanche a growing urgency—almost desperation—and deception. But we also note how differently Stella reacts. She does not exhibit the same urgencies as Blanche; she has nothing to hide. Already the audience can put together one of the major personality differences from which the play will be built. Stella offers Blanche a second drink, but Blanche declines—"No, one's my limit"—and we begin to wonder whether Blanche is not also deceiving herself.

Having prepared us so carefully, Williams uses the bottle once more. Stanley, Stella's low-class husband, arrives home, and he and Blanche meet for the first time. Stanley offers her a shot, and she turns it down: "No, I—rarely touch it." But we have already seen Stanley measure the level of remaining whiskey with his eye, and his reply is loaded: "Some people rarely touch it, but it touches them often." Another deception—but this time no one has been deceived. Through this brief encounter over a single shot of whiskey, offered and refused, we know that the drama is in motion—that the struggle is on between Stanley's macho control by intimidation and Blanche's attempt at refinement and respectability. We know also that Stanley has won the first round.

Perhaps we're even pleased to see Blanche's deception so skillfully checked. But the scene ends on a different note when Stanley asks Blanche about her former husband. She responds, "The boy—the boy died. *(She sinks back down.)* I'm afraid I'm—going to be sick! *(Her head falls on her arms.)*" Suddenly a new ingredient is added. Was her husband's death that traumatic? Is her temporary defeat by Stanley that disastrous? Or perhaps she's sick from the two drinks. Perhaps, after all, she does rarely touch liquor, and today was just unusually nerve-wracking for Blanche.

In any case, Williams, like other playwrights, clearly expects an active audience alert to small details, alert to patterns among those details—an audience that makes connections, weighs the information, and begins to raise questions. In addition, he expects his audience not to jump to conclusions from the first few cues, but to remain alert, prepared to be surprised by unexpected turns as new combinations of detail gradually shape the total experience of the play. Several key terms can help explain how plays and their productions invite this kind of creative participation from audiences: *dramatic action, theatrical convention, plot, character, language, production format, subtext, dramatic irony,* and *theme.*

As we saw in Chapter 1, in the theatre we identify with characters and become involved in the fictional world they inhabit. But a character expresses human personality through action. In contrast to a painted portrait or even to real people, we come to know dramatic characters by what they do, not by how they look. What does Lady Macbeth look like? The only possible answer is that she looks like someone who would do the kinds of things she does. In other words, her actions define her looks, not the other way around, and any actress who convincingly portrays those actions, no matter what she looks like, will give Lady Macbeth life on the stage. Therefore, our discussion must begin with *dramatic action.*

DRAMATIC ACTION

Dramatic action is not physical movement; rather, it has to do with the movement we associate with *process*—the movement toward some predetermined goal. In any play, each character's action is, in fact, to strive for a goal. In *The*

Glass Menagerie, Amanda Wingfield tries to get a Gentleman Caller to court her daughter, Laura. Harpagon, in Moliere's *The Miser*, tries to marry his daughter off to a rich widower. Dr. Dysart in *Equus* tries to salvage the life of an emotionally disturbed boy. Annie Sullivan in *The Miracle Worker* tries to communicate with the deaf and blind Helen Keller. Each character has a goal, something to work toward. But each character also encounters complications and obstacles. Laura Wingfield refuses to come to the table when the Gentleman Caller arrives—a complication. The Miser's daughter already has a suitor—an obstacle. Dr. Dysart discovers that he may destroy the boy even while he tries to cure him—a complication, and Annie Sullivan must overcome interference from Helen's overprotective family—an obstacle. *The process of overcoming obstacles and adjusting to complications while striving toward a goal is the dramatic action of each character;* it gives the illusion that what we are watching on stage are the processes of life itself. On stage the process occurs in a set time framework and moves toward an end that the script has already defined; yet it always creates the illusion that it is now occurring for the first time.

Like any good play, *The Elephant Man* (1979), by Bernard Pomerance, offers such an action. The play covers the last six years in the life of John Merrick, a

Annie Sullivan trying to reach her deaf and blind pupil, Helen Keller. University of Texas production, directed by James Moll.

An actual photograph of John Merrick (the Elephant Man), taken when he was first examined by Dr. Fredrick Treves.

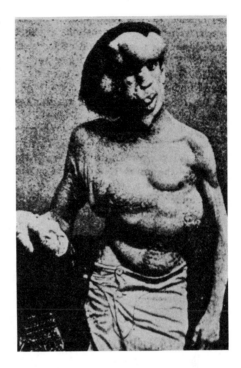

young nineteenth-century Englishman whose body had been grotesquely deformed by an "unknown" skin disorder, so that he looked like a monster. Merrick's head was disfigured by large bony masses and spongy growths that rendered normal speech and facial expression impossible; huge sack-like growths hung from his back and chest. Though his left arm and hand were normal, his enormous right arm had a useless fin-like hand hanging from it, and misshapen legs and feet and a hip defect forced him to walk with a cane. In the play the early scenes depict Merrick's condition as hopeless; his misshapen body, grotesque face, and incomprehensible speech make people think him an imbecile. He survives only by displaying himself as a carnival freak, but the police close the show down as an obscenity, and his manager, Ross, finally abandons him as a liability, leaving him desperate and destitute.

At this point the play's second central character, Dr. Frederick Treves, an up-and-coming young physician at the London Hospital, rescues Merrick, provides him with a home in a private ward, and tries to help him lead a normal life. Once Treves settles Merrick in his new hospital-ward "home," he finds him to be highly intelligent, with the sensitivity of an artist, aspirations toward religious fulfillment, a love of beauty, and a highly developed set of ethical values. To help Merrick live normally, Treves tutors him carefully in the rules of his new home, provides him with books, and brings in visitors to converse with him. The first of these visitors, Mrs. Kendal, one of London's leading actresses, is so taken with Merrick's extraordinary mind that she turns him into a *cause célèbre*, visited by the Bishop of London, duchesses and lords, and even the Princess of Wales.

Merrick's action is to become "a man like others." To do so he must overcome the obstacles of his own physical deformities as well as the fear that others show toward him. In the safety of his new home, he must deal with the added complication of a Victorian value system imposed on him, but unrelated to the life he is forced to live. To his benefactor, Dr. Treves, to be a man means following Victorian social rules, which "make us happy because they are for our own good." To his tormentor, Ross, it means having a woman. Thus, to be "a man like others," Merrick must learn to define manhood on different terms than others do. He finds his definition in the creative power of imitation, but not just in imitating other men. He builds a model of St. Philip's Church: "not stone and steel and glass," but "an imitation of grace flying up and up from the mud. So I make my imitation of an imitation. But even in that is heaven to me."

Dr. Treves, too, has an action and a goal. His goal is to help Merrick lead as normal a life as possible, for which he must help others overcome their "fear and loathing" of him. But Treves' real action results from unexpected complications. He begins the play with complacent confidence in himself and the system:

> A scientist in an age of science.
> In an English age, an Englishman. A teacher and a doctor at the London. Two books published by my thirty-first year. A house. A wife who loves me, and my god, 100 guinea fees before I'm forty.

Though Treves' own success brings him knighthood, and royalty as clientele, his values make no sense when applied to Merrick. Soon Merrick's disconcerting questions begin to chip away at the edges of Treves' self-complacency, particularly at his belief in the supremacy of science and the glory of Victorian order and morality. The turning point in his confidence is set off by an incident that shocks his Victorian sensibilities. Mrs. Kendal gratifies Merrick's ingenuous desire to experience the full beauty of womanhood by delicately exposing her body to his view. At that moment Treves walks in. He is appalled and breaks off further contact between the two. Later, realizing the innocence of the event, he begins to doubt his own moral values.

Scientific success, however, has raised even greater doubts. Though he has helped his patient achieve social normality, Treves, the medical scientist, is helpless to prevent his dying: "So—a parable of growing up? To become more normal is to die? More accepted to worsen? He—it is just a mockery of everything we live by." As is so often true in drama, the action of each central character forms the major complication for the other's goal, while their actions intertwine and motivate each other.

While each character has a dramatic action, the play has its own action, built from those of all its characters. It is to this larger action that the audience is finally drawn. In *The Elephant Man*, we may sympathize with Merrick's desire to become "a man like others" and be awed by his aspirations toward beauty. We may admire Treves' efforts to help Merrick and sympathize as he tries to reconcile the contradictions that he finds in both success and failure. But midway through the play, one scene focuses audience attention on yet another action. Seven of the characters who have observed and befriended Merrick report briefly on how they see themselves in Merrick. Treves later concludes: "We have polished him like a mirror, and shout hallelujah when he reflects us to the inch."

In the latter part of the play, characters come more and more to see themselves through Merrick. Treves, for example, dreams that he is the freak and Merrick the scientific observer; Mrs. Kendal responds to Merrick's trust by trusting him with a view of her body; the Bishop sees in Merrick a "happy example" of religious consolation; even Ross, Merrick's former exploiter, is reduced by age and illness to beg Merrick to be exploited once again, thus defining himself as the "pimp" he has always been. As the characters observe Merrick through these multiple perspectives, audience members are gradually invited to discover their own perspectives, either sharing the characters' observations or making their own. At the end of the play, following Merrick's death, the hospital administrator, Gomm, prepares Merrick's obituary, the ultimate observation on a person's life. When Treves tries to add a personal touch to Gomm's coldly objective prose, he fails to find the right words; then, at the last moment, thinks of "one small thing." But Gomm's last line before the curtain, "It's too late, I'm afraid. It is done," leaves the audience to define for itself that "one small thing" that might express the reality of John Merrick, the elephant man, as they have come to know him. Though each character has completed his or her action, we, the audience, must complete the action of the play: to find in Merrick the reflection of ourselves.

THEATRICAL CONVENTIONS

In *The Elephant Man*, audiences see more than the struggle to help John Merrick lead a normal life; they are exposed to the struggle that his example mirrors in the lives of the "normal" people who surround him. They actually see far more than a real-life witness could have seen. This intensified view of drama on stage is made possible in part by *theatrical conventions*, which have to do with the expectations we bring to the theatre. They are agreed-on falsehoods, so to speak, the rules of the game that form a kind of contract between production and audience. They make full communication possible, unhampered by the restrictions that normal reality would impose. Examples are the *soliloquy*, a convention Shakespeare used to allow his characters to share their private thoughts with the audience, and the *aside*, a convention that allows an audience member fifty feet away to hear plainly what a character standing five feet away does not hear. Conventions require that audiences cooperate to make the theatrical experience occur.

The Elephant Man uses such standard conventions as dividing the play into scenes and changing lights to indicate elapsed time or a change in location. In addition, two unusual conventions help to shape its unique dramatic form: first, except for the actor playing Merrick, everyone plays two or more roles in the play. Though the script does not insist on what combinations to use, both the London and New York productions cast a single actor in the roles of Dr. Treves, Merrick's chief benefactor, and a policeman who beats him and drives him out of Belgium. In another production, the actor who beat Merrick as the Belgian policeman later blessed Merrick in the role of the Bishop. One actor who played the role of Merrick noticed a surprising effect resulting from this multiple casting. Because the relationship of each actor to him kept changing as the actors moved from role to role, he found that his character should not quite rely on human relationships, not even on those that seemed most dependable. Merrick had to find consolation in his concept of something higher, defined in the play by the phrase, "I believe in heaven." The multiple casting also reinforces for the audience the constantly shifting perspectives of those who relate to Merrick. As the

The actor simulates Merrick's deformities while Dr. Treves lectures his class in this 1983 production of Pomerance's *The Elephant Man* at State University College, Oneonta, N.Y., directed by Edward Pixley.

actors change their perspectives in moving from role to role, we as audience are reminded of the multiple ways in which Merrick reflects society—both Victorian London's and our own.

Even more important are the multiple perspectives in the portrayal of Merrick himself. Pomerance has introduced a most unusual convention—one that is uniquely appropriate to the theatre, in that it constantly calls attention to its own theatricality. When we first see the actor who plays Merrick, he is just that—an actor. He is, moreover, a very normal-looking, even handsome, actor, his trim body costumed only in a loincloth. Then Dr. Treves begins to lecture on Merrick's disorder, illustrating his points with slide pictures of the actual elephant man. As he describes, one by one, the grotesque deformities that Merrick suffered, the actor playing Merrick begins to contort his face and body to approximate the images described and displayed through the slides. As audience we see the photographic portraits of the real Merrick; at the same time we watch the transformation of the actor into an artistic portraiture, an abstraction, of Merrick. The effect is among the most remarkable the theatre has to offer. Through the rest of the play, the audience has a dual image. The normal body of the actor is always before us, a visual symbol of the inner beauty of the character, while its contorted appearance also calls to our minds the photographs—the real Merrick—the grotesque body in which the inner self is trapped. Thus, the character's struggle to externalize his inner being is dramatized through this unique convention, allowing the audience to perceive both aspects of the character at once.

Having chosen this convention for portraying Merrick, Pomerance uses the character in yet another way. Late in the play, when Dr. Treves begins to doubt his own view of reality, he dreams that Merrick is the normal one and he himself the freak. In the dream, a normal-looking Merrick delivers a lecture on the psychological anatomy of Treves. As Treves awakens, Merrick, before the audience's eyes, resumes his contorted shape. But which of the two characters, Treves or Merrick, has the truest view of normality is a haunting question that reverberates from the visual transformations we have just beheld.

PLOT

While dramatic action gives the play its illusion of life, theatrical conventions show that the illusion does not result simply from transferring segments of life to the stage. Playwrights are artists and, far from simply copying life, they artfully select and arrange the materials of life—that is, they *plot* the dramatic action. Centuries ago the Greek philosopher Aristotle defined plot as the imitation of an action, not as a copy of life. If we begin by thinking of "plot" as a verb rather than a noun, we might come to a truer understanding. It is something that playwrights *do*—that is, they select the incidents and information they want the audience to see and know; then they strategically organize them into a structure, called "the plot," in order to draw the audience into the actions of the play.

Many stories have been used in plays over and over again. Shakespeare ransacked stories and plays from the Italians, the Romans, and the Germans and replotted them to create his own great dramas. At least four major plays have been plotted out of the Joan of Arc story, no two alike, yet all based on the same historical event. Orestes and Electra, the legendary brother and sister who executed their own mother, formed the basis of a play by each of the ancient Greek tragedians, and both Eugene O'Neill and Jean-Paul Sartre created modern plays from the same story, the first employing a Freudian, the second an existential view of reality.

Bernard Pomerance could have plotted *The Elephant Man* to begin with Merrick suffering the indignities of his carnival life. Instead, he starts the play with Dr. Treves first arriving at the London Hospital, where Gomm, the hospital administrator, admires his past record and assures him that he will soon be rich and famous. "You'll find it is an excellent consolation prize." It is at this point that Treves, left alone on stage, recounts the signs of success quoted earlier that now fill his life: "Consolation for what?" he asks. "As of the year A.D. 1884, I, Freddie Treves, have excessive blessings. Or so it seems to me." In this way, the playwright sets up the initial dramatic question of the play as that of Treves, not of Merrick. A quick blackout ends the scene and lights come up abruptly on Ross, a carnival-like barker, luring passersby "to pay to gape and yawp at this

The carnival barker, Ross (John Clarkson), trying to persuade Dr. Treves (Edwin J. McDonough) to come in and view the Elephant Man. Alaska Repertory Theatre, 1981.

freak of nature, the Elephant Man." The audience, however, sees only a large advertising sign of "a creature with an elephant's head" and hears Ross's tantalizing appeal to "step in and see . . . a despised creature . . . with his physical hideousness, incapacitating deformities and unremitting pain," while Dr. Treves, the medical scientist, actually enters to get a look at Merrick. Then, for five bob, Ross agrees to release Merrick to Treves to examine "in the interests of science." The lights black out on Ross, viciously ordering Merrick out: "Out here, Merrick. Ya bloody donkey, out!" When they come up next, it is on Treves' slide lecture. Now the audience finally sees Merrick, first as the actor, then simultaneously in the slides and in the actor's physical transformation into the character of Merrick.

Though Pomerance contrasts these two scenes, the one a vicious exploitation of the deformed man, the other a clinically objective description of Merrick's disorder, the audience is likely to notice some surprising parallels. Both Ross and Treves describe Merrick's plight in the most vivid terms. Ross describes mainly his mental anguish and humiliation in the interest of financial gain, while Treves graphically describes his physical deformities in the interest of science. But all we see of Merrick during Ross's pitch is the picture on the advertising poster. On the other hand, while Treves lectures, we watch a normal actor transform himself into the physical monster, who is soon sent back to the "disgrace" and "indecency" of his exhibition again. After all, Treves points out, "I am a doctor. What would you have me do?" Thus, it is Treves' lecture, not Ross's pitch, that evokes the first direct sympathy for Merrick as Treves abandons him to his former exploitation.

Plot then engages us in the process of the play, makes us creative participants as we notice that neither Ross's carnival approach nor Treves' clinical approach offers Merrick any consolation. Ross at least has the advantage of helping Merrick earn a living. But in a quick series of short scenes that follow, Merrick goes from bad to worse. He and Ross, after being driven out of London, try their luck in Belgium. There Merrick is beaten by the police, rejected by his fellow freaks, the Pinheads, robbed and abandoned by Ross, and sent back to London where he is mobbed by outraged citizens and threatened by an unsympathetic policeman. By good fortune, Treves' card is found in Merrick's pocket. The powerful momentum of Merrick's cascade toward disaster is finally broken when Treves enters and recognizes Merrick, and the scene ends with Merrick's desperate appeal to the doctor: "Help me!"

One major plot device in *The Elephant Man* is its fragmentation. Twenty-one brief scenes make up the play. Each one quickly zeroes in on an incident in the Treves-Merrick relationship, makes its point, then abruptly ends—no elaboration, no transitions, no winding down—just the incident itself, terse and simple. Like the anatomy lecture, with its abrupt rhythm of slide replacing slide, the play takes on a demonstration rhythm of scene replacing scene, helping the audience to notice the similarities and contrasts between such things as Ross's sideshow

Merrick entertaining his guests in the 1983 Oneonta production of *The Elephant Man*.

pitch with its poster and Treves's anatomy lecture with its slides. Thus, we are ready to see the parallel late in the play when Treves dreams that Merrick delivers a lecture on Treves's psychological anatomy, and the further parallel when Treves, now morally disoriented as Merrick had been socially disoriented, makes his appeal to the Bishop: "Help me."

CHARACTER

It is the plotting that helps the audience notice the many connections and contradictions that are set forth in the actions of its characters. Perhaps even more important is the way the playwright plots his material so as to engage us in the lives of the characters themselves. *Character* provides the most noticeable point of audience involvement, since sympathetic identification with character is perhaps the most widely acclaimed experience we have in the theatre. Every theatregoer enjoys identifying with characters we can admire: the brave heroes, witty hero-ines, passionate lovers, impudent servants, and uncompromisingly honest men and women who dare to stand firmly for goodness and truth. Few of us can resist the pleasure of aligning with righteousness against evil, cleverness against incompetence, wisdom against stupidity, or honesty against hypocrisy, the ingredients of most dramatic conflict. All these confrontations are what we call *external conflicts:* a *simple character*—that is, a brave, honest, clever, or wise *hero*—pitted against an enemy, a rival, an unbending parent, or perhaps just impossi-ble odds. Such simple characters are narrowly drawn, with one or two dominant qualities that govern all their actions. Luke Skywalker and Princess Leia are brave and honest and good. Darth Vader is evil, and when goodness wins him over at the end of *Return of the Jedi,* he has to die; a good Darth Vader could serve no function for future plots. *Superman III* was vehemently criticized, you may remember, precisely because it made its hero too complex and lost the simple pleasure of a good hero triumphing over evil.

In *complex characters* the conflicts are *internal.* A character begins by confront-ing an external obstacle but gradually finds the real enemy to be within. Thus, the internal dilemma must be resolved before meeting the external challenge. Hamlet has a simple external goal: kill the king who murdered his father. After procrastinating for four acts, he knows his problem is not so simple. By Act II he begins to wonder whether he is a coward or whether he doesn't trust the ghost who told him of the murder. Even after proving to himself that the king is guilty, he tells the audience in Act IV:

> I do not know
> Why yet I live to say, "This thing's to do,
> Sith I have cause, and will, and strength, and means
> To do't. Examples gross as earth exhort me.

For more than a century, Hamlet's failure to act has fascinated literary critics and psychologists, who have attributed it to everything from a death wish to a per-verted love for his mother. Whatever the cause, he cannot act against the exter-nal enemy until he resolves his internal conflict.

Other complex characters may appear to have a simple conflict, but deeper motives soon emerge. Cyrano de Bergerac pits his sword and wit against pomp-ous fools, but we soon discover beneath his brave exterior an insecure romantic trying to make himself worthy of the most beautiful woman in Paris. In both Hamlet and Cyrano, the discovery of the internal conflict, the deeper motive, invites the audience to enter more intimately into the characters' lives, to share desires and uncertainties of which the plays' other characters know nothing.

Identification with characters, either simple or complex, brings the audience emotionally into the theatre experience—what Eric Bentley refers to as encoun-tering ourselves in the theatre, noticing first that "this concerns me," and then that "this *is* me." In *The Elephant Man*, we as audience acquire a sympathetic identification with Merrick—not merely as a simple character to be pitied, but as a complex character whom we can relate to on an equal basis—through several fascinating plot devices. First, because we watch the actor transform himself into Merrick, we already have a basis for connecting to his normality as well as to his deformity. Second, when we first encounter Merrick as a character, he is alone with the Pinheads and begins to speak to them as equals. But each attempt at conversation results in the same mindless response from the girls: "Allo! Allo!" At last Merrick recognizes their lack of comprehension: "Little vocabulary problem, eh?" he quips. This is the first line of the play designed to draw a laugh, attracting the audience to Merrick's wit. His first line in his new hospital-ward home is equally attractive. Treves has hired Nurse Sandwich, an overconfident former missionary, to help care for Merrick. For their first meeting, Nurse Sandwich offers to carry in Merrick's lunch tray, but Treves chooses—wisely—to carry it himself, for as soon as the nurse sees Merrick, she bolts from the room, screaming. Treves begins to apologize to Merrick, but Merrick interrupts—not with self-pity, but to thank Treves "for saving the lunch this time."

From this bit of plotting we begin to look for the moments in the play when others will start to recognize in Merrick the wit and the humanity that we have begun to see. Thus, by the time we get to Scene 10 where he meets Mrs. Kendal, the audience can share in the joy that comes as the actress, in a scene that parallels the Sandwich scene, discovers the depth and sensitivity of Merrick's mind.

In addition to the central characters that audiences identify with (or against), most plays also have a variety of *supporting characters,* all with different points of view to reveal new dimensions in the central characters. Through Ross we see Merrick as a despised creature, without consolation, and later as a character affirming his manhood on his own terms; through Mrs. Kendal, we see him aspiring toward beauty and close personal relationships; through the Pinheads we see a character of compassion and wit; through the Bishop we see him seeking salvation beyond the body in which he is trapped; and through his complex relationship with Dr. Treves, we see Merrick seeking to become like others, but always evaluating those others on his own terms. If the central character is the "me" that we relate to, these supporting characters make up the many aspects of the "non-me," and through their multiple interactions with the central character we construct our sense of the whole character, not only as an emotional being, but as a social and moral entity whom we identify with, understand, perhaps pity, admire, and even judge, all at the same time.

All characters in plays are merely constructs, designed to serve a function. They are not real people, and playwrights provide them with only those qualities needed for the function they serve. Any more would be distracting. The messenger who enters in Act II might be tongue-tied from excitement or from fear about how his message will be received, but audiences are not interested in his sick mother at home or his troubles with his wife. The Pinheads in *The Elephant Man* are such characters; in fact they change character to suit the needs of the play. In the early carnival scene, they are mindless freaks, delighted by signs of friendship from Merrick and terrified when attacked. They are used to show how bad Merrick's situation is and also to show his compassion toward those who are exploited. Later the Pinheads appear in Treves' dream as intelligent beings, appalled by the psychological conditions that Merrick the lecturer describes. Finally, they appear as dreamlike figures who straighten out Merrick's body as he dies. Their past or whether they even have a past is irrelevant. They function in the play to reveal qualities in the characters of Merrick and Treves. Through them we come to see abnormality in the normal and normality in the abnormal. It is their changing function that is important to the play, not their internal consistency as human beings.

LANGUAGE

The playwright's most powerful tool for helping audiences get to know the characters is language. Like people in real life, characters in a play, who are imitations of people, communicate with language that reflects their personalities, provides insights into their social and cultural background, and indicates attitudes and emotional states. Choice of vocabulary, images, syntax, rhythmic patterns, and even sounds all play their part. When Maggie in Tennessee Williams' *Cat on a Hot Tin Roof* refers to her nieces and nephews as "no-neck monsters," she gives a vivid image of the children, an unmistakable picture of her feelings toward them, and hints of an underlying coarseness in her own character. When Hamlet complains about his widowed mother's hasty remarriage, he does not simply accuse her of running quickly to her brother-in-law's bed, though that is his literal meaning. His charge is that she did "post with such dexterity to incestuous sheets," and the words fairly hiss with his contempt.

Playwrights also use language to cue the audience to the nature and progress of the play's action. Edward Albee, in *Who's Afraid of Virginia Woolf?*, puts two faculty couples from an Eastern college through a torturous night in which they force each other to give up the fictions that they use to keep from looking honestly at themselves and their relationships. The language is contemporary and conversational, but Albee couches it in images of the games the characters play to attack each other. The game motif reminds us that the characters, though outwardly vicious, are trying to keep aloof from their own actions. The series of games they play also helps us keep track of the progress of the action: "Humiliate the Host," "Get the Guests," "Hump the Hostess," and "Bringing up Baby." Dawn starts to break with the four characters laying the last illusion to rest, while the host, in the background, recites a Latin litany for the dead, casting a sense of finality over the foursome.

A scene from the torturous night of truth in the 1962 New York production of Albee's *Who's Afraid of Virginia Woolf?* At right, Arthur Hill and Uta Hagen as George and Martha.

Language in *The Elephant Man* also appears to be simple conversational realism. Yet it constantly reveals character and guides audience involvement in subtle ways. Dr. Treves' preparing of Mrs. Kendal for her first meeting with Merrick provides a good example. Mrs. Kendal, attempting to cover her fears with light, almost frivolous observations, contrasts sharply with Treves' attempt at serious objectivity. Treves tells her that women are critical in helping Merrick toward a normal life:

> I will explain. They have always shown the greatest fear and loathing of him. While he adores them of course.

MRS. KENDAL: Ah. He is intelligent.

TREVES: I am convinced they are the key to retrieving him from his exclusion. Though, I must warn you, women are not quite real to him—more creatures of his imagination.

MRS. KENDAL: Then he is already like other men, Mr. Treves.

TREVES: So I thought, an actress could help. I mean, unlike most women, you won't give in, you are trained to hide your true feelings and assume others.

MRS. KENDAL: You mean unlike most women I am famous for it, that is really all.

TREVES: Well. In any case. If you could enter the room and smile and wish him good morning. And when you leave, shake his hand, the left one is usable, and really quite beautiful, and say, "I am very pleased to have made your acquaintance, Mr. Merrick."

MRS. KENDAL: Shall we try it? Left hand out please.

Mrs. Kendal, in this sequence, keeps turning Treves' clinical observations into personal images she can connect to, while Treves, not quite knowing how to take her seeming flippancy, hesitates and then continues in his same objective vein. Language vividly differentiates the characters and prepares the audience to anticipate dramatically what will happen when Mrs. Kendal actually meets Merrick.

But Mrs. Kendal's lines provide an equally sharp contrast to those of Nurse Sandwich two scenes earlier. Whereas Mrs. Kendal clearly tries to shape some image of the person she is about to meet, Nurse Sandwich is sure that she already knows.

TREVES: You have had experience in missionary hospitals in the Niger.

SANDWICH: And Ceylon.

TREVES: I may assume you've seen—

SANDWICH: The tropics. Oh those diseases. The many and the awful scourges our Lord sends, yes, sir.

TREVES: I need the help of an experienced nurse, you see.

SANDWICH: Someone to bring him food, take care of the room. Yes, I understand.

Then, when Treves tries to prepare her for Merrick's hideous appearance, Sandwich lectures him: "Let me put your mind to rest. Care for lepers in the East, and you have cared, Mr. Treves. . . . Appearances do not daunt me." The result is not only a contrast in the two women, but a contrast in audience sympathy toward them. Audiences are almost delighted when the overconfident Nurse Sandwich runs from the room in terror, whereas Mrs. Kendal's more cautious, yet highly personal, observations inspire the wish that her meeting with Merrick will succeed. Since she and Merrick are the only two characters who have displayed some wittiness in their language, success may even be within reach.

Perhaps the most important language quality in *The Elephant Man* is repetition—lines and phrases that keep recurring in new contexts to help the audience draw connections among the actions and ideas of the play. The example of Merrick and Treves, each crying out, "Help me," at different points in the play, has already been cited. When Treves first brings Merrick to his new home, he coaches him in the ways of Victorian manhood as he sees them, makes him repeat key ideas. "Rules make us happy because they are for our own good," is the culminating truism of this lesson. Late in the play, as Treves begins to doubt his own value system, Merrick tests him with his own words: "They make us happy because they are for our own good," to which Treves confesses, "Well. Not always." Sometimes the shape of an entire speech is repeated in a later scene, like a variation on a theme, until the play begins to take on the intricacy of repeated motifs in a musical composition. The most obvious example is Treves' anatomy lecture which Merrick repeats in the dream. Treves begins his lecture by saying, "The most striking feature about him was his enormous head." Merrick begins the dream-lecture with, "The most striking feature about him, note, is the terrifyingly normal head." The Merrick of the dream then describes each anatomical feature as Treves had done, but he applies psychological and moral values to what Treves had described as physiological abnormalities: "Due also to the normal head, the right arm was of enormous power; but so incapable of the distinction between the assertion of authority and the charitable act of giving, that it was often to be found disgustingly beating others—for their own good." "For their own good" becomes a disturbing refrain accentuating the dramatic change that is occurring in the character of Treves, who is, of course, both the dreamer and the subject of the lecture in the dream. Thus, language helps to define character, invites audience sympathy, draws sympathetic connections and contrasts among characters, and, most strikingly, focuses attention on the dramatic changes that the characters undergo through the play.

PRODUCTION FORMAT

So far we have considered how audiences use materials structured by the playwright to enter into the experience of the play. Directors, actors, and designers also help shape the theatre experience. Just as playwrights create through the artistic structure of plot, these artists create through a comparable structure—the *production format*, the producing artists' counterpart of plot. They select and arrange the scenic and performance elements of the play so as to draw the audience into the action of the characters and the play during performance. To people who have not worked backstage, this process is relatively unknown. Yet the designing, directing, and rehearsing are what finally give the play its life for a theatre audience. When the show is closed, the sets dismantled, the costumes cleaned and stored, and when the actors move on to other roles, the play becomes only a memory for its audiences. Once again it is a script ready to be recreated by a new set of artists for yet new audiences.

Many modern scripts have a partial production format built right in as stage directions, though such stage directions are often a stage manager's record of the first production or the work of a helpful editor, not the words of the playwright. The nineteenth-century Norwegian playwright Henrik Ibsen, however, elaborately suggests a production format at the opening of the second act of *A Doll's House*:

In the corner, beside the piano, stands the Christmas tree, stripped, and with the candles burnt out. Nora's outdoor things lie on the sofa. (Nora, alone, is walking about restlessly. At last she stops by the sofa, and takes up her cloak.)

NORA. *(Dropping the cloak.)* There's somebody coming! *(Goes to the hall door and listens.)* Nobody; of course nobody will come today, Christmas-day; nor tomorrow either. But perhaps . . . *(Opens the door and looks out.)* . . . No, nothing in the letter box; quite empty. *(Comes forward.)* Stuff and nonsense! Of course he won't really do anything. Such a thing couldn't happen. It's impossible! Why, I have three little children.

With this description Ibsen sets the "after Christmas" visual atmosphere of the room, and also shows a reader the kind of nervous movement an audience would see the character making on stage. From Nora's business with the door and letter box, the audience-reader notices her fear of something beyond the room.

Though helpful, such directions barely scratch the surface of the producing

A fight from Shakespeare's *Romeo and Juliet* at New Haven's Long Wharf Theatre as worked out by the fight master, B. H. Barry.

artists' work. Texts from earlier periods are even less helpful. A typical stage direction in Shakespeare's *Romeo and Juliet* is this one from Act III: *"They fight. Tybalt falls."*—this to describe an elaborate sword fight in which the hero, Romeo, kills the cousin of his new bride, forcing him to flee the country without getting a message to Juliet. It is up to the director and actors to stage the fight so that its visual impact on the audience matches the emotional power of this major catastrophe in the lives of the characters. Students, reading Shakespeare's scant directions and then experiencing the breathtaking theatricality of the plays in production, sometimes ask whether directors have special scripts telling how to stage them. Of course, they don't. Directors and designers start from the same script as the reader, and then, using the language, plot, and action as guides, invent appropriate ways to translate the play from the printed page to living productions.

The differences among productions are often quite astonishing. Imagine seeing three different *Julius Caesars:* first the Marlon Brando film of the 1950s, complete with togas, Roman hair styles, and on-location shots of ancient Rome's magnificent architecture (this is how we might imagine the play in reading it); second, a production on a thrust stage, backed by a wall of carved and paneled wood, with costumes of the sixteenth-century English court (the way Shakespeare himself probably produced the play); or, third, set in Nazi Germany in the 1930s, with modern armaments of war, jackbooted soldiers, and spies in trench-coats (the style of Orson Welles' 1937 Mercury Theatre production). The script in each case is essentially the same, yet each production format creates a totally different experience for its audience. Critics might argue the validity of these varied approaches, but the fact that they can be and have been done reveals a fundamental truth about how plays work in the theatre.

In the script of *The Elephant Man,* only minimal stage directions guide a production format, leaving each design-directing team considerable freedom of choice. David Jenkins, who designed sets for the New York production, commented that "Shakespeare gave you more hints."* Jenkins, working with director Jack Hofsiss, used a proscenium staging approach, so that all audience members could see the slides in Treves' lecture from the same angle. The basic setting was the institutional world of a Victorian hospital, made of bricks and pillars, with a set of clerestory windows above. Using curtains that could be opened or closed between pillars and the addition or subtraction of simple props—a bed, a bathtub, a desk, a carnival poster—the action could move quickly—almost dissolve—from scene to scene.

A vastly different production format was used for a 1983 production by the State University College at Oneonta, New York. Here, environmental staging was used, suggested by the fragmented style of the script, with its twenty-one

---

*For Jenkins' design format, see *Theatre Crafts,* January/February 1980, pages 27, 97.

different scenes, by the multiple casting of roles, which constantly put actors into the new relationships as they played different characters, and by the constantly shifting perspective of characters being observed or on display. Several playing areas in front of, behind, and even in the midst of the audience caused the audience to shift its own perspective from one scene to the next, sometimes even having to choose which of two or more areas to look at within a scene. In this way, audience members were often in the same positions as the characters who were doing the observing, and frequently they found themselves adjacent to a character who was being observed. Some audience members found themselves watching other audience members, and then became aware that they themselves were being watched, drawing them more fully into the observed/observer motif that shaped the entire production. For a fuller description of this production format, see Chapter 13.

The playwright, of course, plotted the action that sets one scene against another to draw connections between the lives of John Merrick and Dr. Treves, but the combined inventions of creative designers and directors found two different production formats to make these actions work in the theatre. Every produced play involves such collaboration, though most audiences are never aware of how the process works.

THE ACTORS: TEXT AND SUBTEXT

The final step of the producing artists, the one to which audiences react most directly, is the work of the actor. The playwright provides the lines that actors speak, the *text*, but actors give them life by the way they speak the lines and by the ways they visually react to other characters. Their ways of speaking and reacting result from the thoughts that accompany the lines, what actors usually call their *subtext*. Subtext grows directly out of the lines of the text, but actors actually invent it as they search out the emotional context for those lines. The real-life greeting "How are you?" may express genuine concern for someone's health, but usually it simply expresses pleasure at seeing the person or, sometimes, impatience and a desire to get away. These varied reactions suggest three very different subtexts for the same simple greeting. Early in Arthur Miller's play *Death of a Salesman*, Willy Loman, the down-and-out salesman of the play, turns to his wife "guiltily," according to a stage direction, and asks, "You're not worried about me, are you sweetheart?" The word "guiltily" is the playwright's clue to the subtext, and the actor playing Willy might be thinking, "She knows that I've let her down," to help give the proper guilty feeling to the line. If he had had to say the line "confidently," he would have invented a different thought, such as, "Everyone else is worried, but we know better, don't we?" thus using his subtext to change the meaning of the line. One could have fun inventing subtexts for saying that same line "comfortingly," "pitifully," "menacingly," or even "sarcastically."

Plays from earlier periods often used *asides* to reveal a character's subtext. We're all familiar with this sort of thing, as when Joseph Surface, the villain in Richard Brinsley Sheridan's *The School for Scandal*, learns that his uncle has unexpectedly arrived in town. He says, "Well, I am strangely overjoyed at his coming," and then in an aside to the audience announces, "Never, to be sure, was anything so damned unlucky!" The aside allows the audience the fullest enjoyment of Joseph's conflict between his public sentiment and his private fears.

In the theatre, we almost never focus on the speaking character alone, but involve ourselves fully as much in the characters who are listening. In another scene from *The School for Scandal*, Sheridan admirably focuses audience attention on the nonspeaking characters without using asides. This time, Joseph Surface has been trying to seduce the wife of his best friend, Sir Peter Teazle. When Sir Peter and Joseph's brother, Charles, arrive unexpectedly, Lady Teazle quickly

George C. Scott as Willy Loman reveals his inner sense of exhaustion through posture and facial expression in this 1975 production of Miller's *Death of a Salesman* at Circle in the Square, New York City.

hides behind a screen. Charles pulls it down for a joke, exposing the compromised lady:

CHARLES: Egad, you seem all to have been diverting yourselves here at hide and seek—
and I don't see who is out of the secret. Shall I beg your ladyship to inform me?—
not a word!—Brother, will you please to explain this matter? What! Morality
dumb too! Sir Peter, though I found you in the dark, perhaps you are not so now!
All mute! Well—though I can make nothing of the affair, I suppose you perfectly
understand one another; so I'll leave you to yourselves.

Though the other characters remain silent through this speech, Charles speaks to
each in turn, seeking an explanation. Thus, the audience is invited to enjoy each
of their reactions separately and the group reaction together for a full involvement in all of their subtexts, though none of them says a word.

Like any good play, *The Elephant Man* constantly engages its audience in the
characters' subtexts. We have already seen how language suggested two conflicting internal attitudes in Dr. Treves and Mrs. Kendal when he prepared her
for meeting Merrick. As the scene continues, she practices on Treves four different ways to shake his left hand and say the line that Treves had given her: "I
am very pleased to have made your acquaintance, Mr. Merrick." After weighing
and rejecting each of the first three, Mrs. Kendal finally settles on her fourth
method. Dr. Treves, on the other hand, becomes more and more awed by Mrs.
Kendal with each variation: "By god, they are all splendid. Merrick will be so
pleased." The audience not only enjoys Mrs. Kendal's personalized decision
process; they can also enjoy the subtextual awareness of Treves' reactions as she
shakes his hand four times in a row.

The effect that Merrick has on Mrs. Kendal is even more strikingly revealed
through her subtext in the scene that follows. As they first come together, we
watch two people trying delicately to start a meaningful conversation. Merrick is
awed by her beauty and can't quite find the opening to make her relax. She is
impressed by his grace and charm, but can't quite see beyond his physical ugliness. At last, after one interminable silence, Merrick says, "Well. You are a
famous actress," which she modestly affirms. But Merrick's next line catches her
off guard. "You must display yourself for your living then. Like I did." She
quickly recovers: "That is not myself, Mr. Merrick. That is an illusion. This is
myself." When he replies, "This is myself too," she is once again at a loss and so
changes the subject—to books.

Books they have in common. Merrick is reading *Romeo and Juliet*, and Mrs.
Kendal, having played Juliet many times, is now on familiar ground and can
even joke about playing the role opposite a certain "scene-stealing" Romeo, who
always seems to lament excessively while she lies "dead dead dead." "Romeos,"
she concludes, "are very undependable."

Mrs. Kendal offers to shake Merrick's right hand instead of his normal left hand. *The Elephant Man*, Trinity Square Repertory Company. Directed by Peter Gerety.

MERRICK: Because he does not care for Juliet.

MRS. KENDAL: Not care?

MERRICK: Does he take her pulse? Does he get a doctor? Does he make sure? No. He kills himself. The illusion fools him because he does not care for her. He only cares about himself. . . . That is not love. It was all an illusion. When the illusion ended he had to kill himself.

MRS. KENDAL: Why. That is extraordinary.

Though Mrs. Kendal thought herself on her own territory with the most famous love story in all drama, she suddenly hears the story as though for the first time. Quite unexpectedly, she no longer thinks of Merrick as a physical monster, but as an extraordinarily sensitive human being. As audience, we too know *Romeo and Juliet* as a great love story, and, perhaps because we have never quite trusted what our teachers have imposed on us as greatness, we become fascinated by this remarkable perception along with Mrs. Kendal, and we share her subtext at a personal level. Thus, when she says, "That is extraordinary," she provides the line that completes both her thoughts and our own.

One of the most striking examples of subtextual involvement in the modern theatre occurs at the end of this scene when Mrs. Kendal takes her leave of Merrick and at last shakes his hand and gives the line she had practiced on Treves. But the line she delivers is not quite what she had rehearsed four times. The slight variation, which places emphasis on the pleasure rather than on herself, shows the genuineness of her feeling: "Mr. Merrick, it has been a very great pleasure to make your acquaintance." The New York production added one other element which has since become a standard ingredient of the scene. Mrs. Kendal raises not her left hand, but her right. Then as Merrick raises his good left hand toward her, she delicately pulls back, and in the silence, Merrick, almost in disbelief, realizes that she wishes to shake the deformed hand that hangs useless at his right side. The raising of the right hand, for which there is no text, creates a communion between the two of them that no words could possibly accomplish. Though the moment has been carefully prepared through the text, the audience shares in the communion precisely because its climax occurs at the subtextual level.

The words spoken are essential to the scene, of course. There would be no scene without them. But the real drama is what the playwright has set up to occur between and under the lines, in the subtext which the actors reveal and the audience shares, creating what we call *empathy*, a "feeling with" the characters.

AUDIENCE SUBTEXT AND DRAMATIC IRONY

Often subtextual involvement results in empathy with two different characters at once, or our private knowledge of each character causes us to relate to the situation as a whole from the perspective of *dramatic irony*. Then, instead of empathizing with the characters, we judge them and anticipate their next moves; thus, we the audience begin to have a subtext of our own, carrying on a personal dialogue with the play and with our own thoughts.

Late in *The Elephant Man*, when Mrs. Kendal reveals her body to Merrick, this type of subtextual dialogue helps to shape our ironic experience of the play. Alone with Mrs. Kendal on a rainy afternoon, Merrick cautiously introduces a forbidden subject—sex. He would like to have a mistress, since "everyone seems to. Or a wife. Some have both." Though he concludes that such a wish "is hopeless," he goes on to confess that he has never "seen a naked woman," and he begins to describe the ideal woman he envisions. It quickly becomes apparent that he is describing Mrs. Kendal—"A lady. Someone kept up. Respectful of herself."—but she keeps eluding the comparison.

MRS. KENDAL: You mean someone like Princess Alexandra?
MERRICK: Not so old.
MRS. KENDAL: Ah. Like Dorothy.
MERRICK: She does not look happy. No.
MRS. KENDAL: Lady Ellen?
MERRICK: Too thin.
MRS. KENDAL: Then who?
MERRICK: Certain women. They have a kind of ripeness. They seem to stop at a perfect point.

The tension of the separate subtexts builds through the scene, as each character strives to avoid the hidden dialogue that lies just below the surface, and we as audience watch and wait expectantly for the hopeless conclusion that seems imminent. Then at the point where some culmination must occur, Mrs. Kendal unexpectedly relieves the tension with an almost lighthearted denial of Merrick's dream: "My dear she doesn't exist." Merrick grasps her easing of the tension with equal lightheartedness: "That is probably why I never saw her."

The next movement of the scene takes the two subtexts even further apart before bringing them back together for the climax of the scene. Mrs. Kendal is flattered that Merrick has trusted her with his secret desires, though he has never told Dr. Treves, for fear of shocking him. "Too little trust has maimed my life," she confesses. Then, while Merrick, abandoning his dream of feminine perfection, changes the subject back to books, we watch Mrs. Kendal working out her decision to offer Merrick a glimpse of her femininity.

MERRICK: What are we going to read?
MRS. KENDAL: Trust is very important you know. I trust you.
MERRICK: Thank you very much. I have a book of Thomas Hardy's here. He is a friend of Frederick's. Shall we read that?
MRS. KENDAL: Turn around a moment. Don't look.
MERRICK: Is this a game?
MRS. KENDAL: I would not call it a game. A surprise. *(She begins undressing.)*

When Merrick is allowed to turn around again, he is overwhelmed by what he sees: "It is the most beautiful sight I have seen. Ever." Mrs. Kendal, suddenly cautious, warns him that he must never tell. Then, relaxing once again, she lets her hair fall down around her shoulders. "There. No illusions. Now. Well? What is there to say? 'I am extremely pleased to have made your acquaintance.' "

The audience has a moment to share in this new level of communion that Merrick and Kendal have reached, while enjoying the ironic recollection of the line that had been rehearsed to end their first meeting. But the irony is to be extended one more step—an unpleasant step. Suddenly Treves appears. "For God's sakes," he explodes. "What is going on here?" Mrs. Kendal tries to help him see the innocence: "For a moment, Paradise, Freddie," then quickly begins dressing to protect her modesty. Treves, however, sees only the surface indecency: "Are you not ashamed? Do you know what you are? Don't you know what is forbidden?" Mrs. Kendal's innocent offering and Treves' Victorian prudery are countered by yet another element: Merrick places one more piece on his church model.

In the above scene, the audience has been able to share empathically Mrs. Kendal's subtext as she overcomes her modesty to offer herself to someone she cares for, as well as Merrick's subtext as he overcomes his inner desires out of respect for her person. We do not want Mrs. Kendal's modesty violated; yet we do not want Merrick denied that image of beauty that seems important to his manhood. Thus, it is deeply satisfying to watch Mrs. Kendal delicately resolve the dilemma. And it is with shock, perhaps indignation, that we watch Treves break in, judging them in ways that violate their relationship. The ironic perspective the audience has gained is completed by the three-part image that lingers at the end of the scene: Treves in violent accusation; Mrs. Kendal covering her modesty with her clothing; and Merrick affirming his vision of paradise with one new piece on his church model.

One more subtextual experience remains in the scene. Our private subtext may direct us toward a synthesizing experience as we recognize in the three-part relationship the fragile levels of communication that exist between people—even between people who care deeply for each other. We see true communication come only when mutual respect and trust are at such a level that no misunderstandings can occur. Then, even when communion is complete, the breaking of the spell leaves each person again alone, having to deal with the experience in his or her own personal manner. Even as we follow the action, identifying empathically with the characters, anticipating ironically how their dilemma will be resolved, breathlessly watching the fragile communication that grows, only to be jolted by the inevitable interruption, we also note how the scene echoes those delicate attempts at communication we have experienced in our own lives.

This synthesizing dialogue, often referred to as the *thought* or *thematic structure*, is part of all plays of any substance, and it always occurs as the audience, often unconsciously, recognizes what it is watching as true. Many plays go much further in encouraging such dialogue, using lines that actually force the audience to step back from the play and notice its connections to their own world. The French comedy master, Moliere, frequently had one of his characters refer disdainfully to the plays of Moliere. The English satirist George Bernard Shaw loved to insert some sarcastic jab at the attitudes and habits of Englishmen, whether the play was set in modern Bulgaria, medieval France, ancient Egypt, or in Shaw's own version of Hell.

In *The Elephant Man*, Pomerance uses a variety of techniques to draw audience attention to connections outside the play. One of the most obvious occurs in Scene 12, when the other characters gather on the stage to describe individually how they see themselves reflected in Merrick, inviting the audience to note reflections of their own. Pomerance appropriately titled the scene, "Who Does He Remind You Of?" Time and again in the play, as Merrick tries to become a man like others, the audience is invited to note what qualities of humanity Merrick is striving for—what things he sees in us to emulate or reject as he strives toward normality. Is normality, as Ross maintains, the fact that we are all whores, selling ourselves for whatever benefits we can get? Is it following the rules of society in order to be happy, as Treves argues? Is it to be practical, to accept the "daily evil" and "be thankful for small goods," as Gomm, the hospital administrator, claims? Is it to seek salvation, as the Bishop affirms? Or is it to be "rather odd. And hurt. And helpless not to show the struggling," as Mrs. Kendal confesses?

As we have already seen in the section on plot, the play extends one final invitation for the audience to relate personally to the significance of Merrick's life. When it is too late for Dr. Treves to add "one small thing" to Mr. Gomm's coldly objective obituary-letter about Merrick, the final dialogue of the play is left hanging. The audience's creative imagination must supply whatever final statement is to be made. A great deal of the audience's appreciation of a play comes from this dialogue between the play and our own experience, and we come to know and understand more of our own world as we find it informed by the world of the play.

THEATRE: A LINK ACROSS HUMANITY

All great plays can stimulate such dialogue. This book assumes that people have certain impulses in common, impulses that have found their expression in the theatre from the earliest times, that people, no matter what their background, share basic desires and concerns that time and place have not altered. Thus, whenever the theatre has expressed and illuminated such basic human concerns, it has the potential to speak to us as well.

A little orientation, of course, can make the great drama of other times and cultures more accessible. Being introduced to the conventions of these plays of the past and acquiring some of the background knowledge that informed them in their first productions can make them clear and meaningful for us. Theatre does have power *to make the familiar strange*. That is, it allows us to glean new perspectives on our own actions by thrusting those actions out of their normal context to be played by people different from ourselves. It also has the power *to make the strange familiar*, allowing us to discover sympathetic connections to other human beings who had before been alien to us, thereby increasing awareness of what it is to be human.

An invitation to the theatre is not simply a matter of putting out the welcome mat, allowing all to enter who wish and then leaving them to fend for themselves. An invitation into this world of marvels, of pleasure and tears, of tragic suffering and uproarious laughter, of passionate feeling and cool control, of heroics and knavery, of struggle and defiance, and, most of all, of astonishing delight, suggests that the guests be introduced around. Who have we come to meet? What wonders can they share with us? What illuminations can appear as together we create a living threatre experience? Accepting the invitation means coming prepared to share in the fun and joy of creating together once the introductions have been made.

In the next few chapters of this book, as you are invited into theatres both past and present, you will be introduced to impulses that inspired and continue to inspire those who created those theatres and to the plays that they presented in them. You will be introduced to the conventions used to create those theatre events. And you will be shown how those same impulses have moved through the ages, shifting and reshaping themselves to speak to the ever changing situations in which people find themselves.

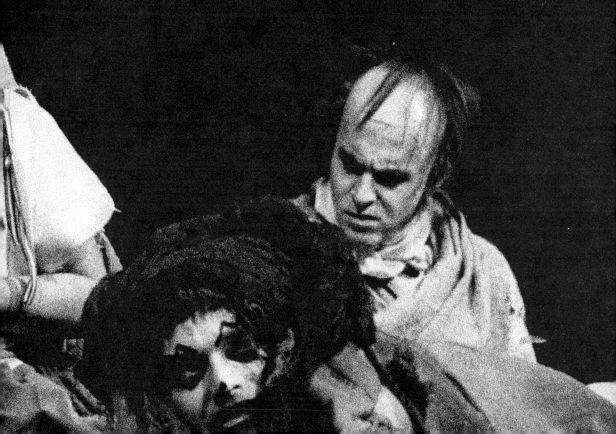

THE PLAY
IN ITS
TIME

II

THE PLAY IN ITS TIME

Each kind of play presents a different attitude toward life, a different way of responding to the problems and questions of life. Some plays can be called comedy, tragedy, melodrama, or farce, to use the favorite classifications of our textbooks and theatre marquees; but most plays do not fit neatly into these categories. In one sense every good play is a category in itself, expressing a particular attitude in its own manner. Nevertheless we do like some classifications, imperfect and tentative as they may be. This part of the book will describe six different kinds of plays, distinguishing them according to six different purposes for which people create theatre and six different impulses that attract people to the theatre—tragedies and festival dramas for inspiration and exaltation;

knockabout farces for a good belly laugh; high comedies for more thoughtful laughter; romantic plays, operas, musicals, and dance for variety, charm, and escape from drab reality; realistic dramas for a practical look at the everyday world; and a whole range of experimental twentieth-century dramas for an understanding of the disruption and chaos of modern living.

Whatever impulse attracts us to theatre, it cannot be fulfilled without a form—an engaging character, a compelling story, a plot—in short, a play. Though it must seem fresh and improvised, the play needs a structure and a point of view or it vanishes with the performance, leaving only memories behind. The continuity of the theatre depends on a finished play, either handed down by memory in oral cultures or written down to be performed again.

In this continuity, the theatre is like a flower and its seed. The performance is the flower, a colorful blossoming, the climax of long, unseen growth. It is enjoyed in its brief perfection and vanishes forever. But it leaves a seed—the play—from which another flower may be grown. Readers of a play get substance from the seed, especially if they know enough about theatre to create a performance in their imaginations. But a richer experience is to see the fine blossoming itself, an actual performance on some kind of stage, where talented actors, creating their roles in a well-written play, cast a spell upon a responsive audience.

THE THEATRE OF EXALTATION: GREEK TRAGEDY

3

A tragic hero enhanced by a large mask, a costume that adds size, and boots that add height. Sophocles' *Oedipus the King*. Stratford Festival production, directed by Tyrone Guthrie, with costumes and masks by Tanya Moiseiwitsch.

*F*rom the earliest remnants of drama, audiences have been attracted to theatre experiences that help them to explore their own relation to divine purpose, to great moral challenges, and to the infinite. Whether they went to see Greek heroes like Agamemnon or Creon divinely punished for usurping the roles of the gods themselves, or whether they go to see modern characters coming to terms with their own deaths in such plays as *Endgame* or *The Shadow Box,* whether they watch Shakespeare's Macbeth daring damnation in order to crown his own human achievements, or whether they watch heroes from their own past challenging history's frontiers, audiences have always sought out plays that both affirm and challenge their own beliefs and values. Confronted by heroic deeds, by death, by the gods, or even by sublime emptiness, they take a look beyond the limits of their everyday world.

The principal subject of prehistoric drama was the coming of the gods into the life of humankind, the conflict with the evil demon of destruction and chaos, and the rebirth of the spirit in eternity. The earliest records of dramatic-like ritual come from ancient Egypt. One of these dating from about 2500 B.C. suggests that each new king performed the central role in a coronation drama, to celebrate his own rebirth as son of the Divine Spirit following the victory of the young god Horus over the evil spirit Seth.

The Greeks, though influenced by the Egyptians, kept the gods in the background and placed at the center of their drama a human hero, who often set himself against the old customs of the gods. The occasion for this new approach was a religious event, the annual festival of Dionysus, god of wine and fertility, which celebrated the resurrection of living spring out of dead winter. The festival began with an ecstatic procession bringing the statue of Dionysus into his theatre. There the Greeks presented their unique addition to theatre, *tragedy*, which combined the pain and humiliation of sacrificial death with the exaltation of resurrection. Though profoundly religious, tragedy put the emphasis on human beings and the values of the world. In this first age of skepticism, the Greek heroes were free to question the gods, though death might well be the punishment. Even while accepting the inevitable death and defeat, the audience could relate with pride to a hero or heroine who had challenged the universe and measured the human reach against the infinite. As Nietzsche pointed out in the nineteenth century, tragedy is our greatest affirmation of life, and since it is the most acclaimed form of theatre of exaltation, it will command the bulk of our attention in these chapters.

THE TRAGIC VISION

The popular idea of tragedy is what we find in such newspaper headlines as Tragic Nursing Home Fire Leaves 10 Dead. But catastrophic disasters such as fires, tornadoes, and floods, while they may arouse great feelings of pathos, have little to do with tragic form in the theatre. Tragedy does deal with irrational forces to which our lives and deaths as human beings are bound, but it focuses its attention on the human hero who takes an ethical stand, who defies the overwhelming odds, challenges the irrational, and tries to impose human understanding upon the infinite. Thus, even though its subject is death and defeat, tragedy provides the theatregoer with profound pleasure, a paradox that never ceases to puzzle and intrigue students of drama.

Numerous theories have been advanced to explain this paradox, theories that involve problems of aesthetics and audience psychology, as well as philosophy. For tragedy asks that we ponder the profoundest kinds of questions: What is our relation to the world, to ourselves, and to God? What is the meaning of evil and suffering, of choice and responsibility? How can we be both individuals exercising free will and a part of society and the universe? Those who are shaken deeply by seeing tragedy often find that if the first part of the play strengthens their sense of rebellious individualism, the ending and the import of the play reconcile them to the mystery at the heart of the universe.

Especially helpful for understanding the many possible patterns in tragedy is Kenneth Burke's exploration of tragic rhythm in *Philosophy of Literary Form*. He defines three moments in the rhythm, which Francis Fergusson in his book, *The Idea of a Theatre*, designates as a sequence of three P's: *purpose*, *passion*, and *perception*.

Purpose

The sympathetic identification audiences feel for the tragic hero begins as the character takes up some overwhelming burden that will test human power to the utmost. As Aristotle said, tragedy imitates men pursuing their better nature, that is, human beings testing their power against the gods, against all nature, or against the very bonds that hold their society together. Most of us when confronted with such challenges retreat to the security of conventional wisdom or to the established rules of society and religion, but we have all felt the urge to strike out with indignation or with idealistic fervor, to demand our rightful place, or to make the universe submit to our sense of justice and truth. Thus, the tragic hero taking up the challenge, though he or she may face death as a result, is a figure of uncommon attraction.

Oedipus, who had refused to submit to the terrible prophesy that he would kill his father and marry his own mother, singlehandedly takes on the burden of his people—to cleanse the land from the fearful blight that has fallen on it. Macbeth is stirred to ambition by the witches' promise that he will be king. He knows that to "catch the nearest way," he must murder his king and guest, the most heinous of crimes; yet he is lured on against his nature to begin the journey from which he cannot return.

Isolation is the immediate price the tragic hero pays for taking up the burden, but the isolation gives him identity. Beginning with Aeschylus's Prometheus, who stole fire from heaven to succor mankind in defiance of Zeus, the heroes and heroines of tragedy have taken a stand against the accepted order, whether of man or of the gods. Such defiance may destroy them, but not before they have had their say. Out of the solid rock of necessity they hew a space for freedom. It is a perilous freedom, gained at a terrible price, but for a moment the hero or heroine holds it, becoming one with the gods, exercising choice and free will, transcending the finite even while sinking, lost in the infinite. And we as audience witnessing their deeds share a peculiar triumph, knowing that that particular battle has marked out one little plot of freedom for humanity.

Passion

Before they reach a reconciliation, most tragic heroes undergo tremendous suffering in which they question the basis of their own being and see the foundations of the world shaken. Terrifying enough when there is utmost faith in a benevolent god, the glimpse over the edge often comes when the hero is in deepest conflict and acutely aware of the hideous cruelty in the world. Prometheus, chained forever to a rock for his defiant theft of fire from the gods, cries

In this scene from Friedrich Dürrenmatt's *The Visit*, Alfred III speaks hopefully to a skeptical Clair Zachanasian, while the Chorus and two blind eunuchs in the background portend the disastrous future that awaits Alfred.

out against Heaven's crackling thunderbolts that he is "wronged." Macbeth, seeing his path to power steeped in blood, is haunted by visions of those whom he has slain. Most protagonists ultimately find religious meaning or moral order in the universe, but not until they have fully faced the indifference, the malignity, and the devastating play of chance and accident.

Perception

Tragedy achieves its full significance in its final phase, that is, when meaning becomes clear, when the sacrifice is followed by resurrection, when the isolated hero is reconciled to the world, having learned through suffering to be both an individual and a part of the mysterious larger entity. At last the world that seemed capricious, malignant, and unjust is revealed as moral, meaningful, and ordered, though the finite human being may never completely understand that order. Only the hero, whose passion has forced him to look into the abyss, seems to fully comprehend the meaning, and in doing so, achieves a serenity that is awesome to those of us still tied to the values of the world. Having faced the worst that the universe has to offer, the tragic hero reconciles himself to a higher order and is no longer troubled by the petty burdens of ordinary mortals. In the tranquil but determined affirmation of his destiny, he provides us with a glimpse into the unknown.

On the simplest level, the hero faces the result of his own actions. Even the melodramas of the nineteenth century show the fitness of retribution. In Verdi's opera *Rigoletto*, the hunchback jester plots to kill his enemy but kills his own daughter instead. A more complex retribution plot is that of Friedrich Dürrenmatt's modern play, *The Visit*, where Alfred Ill finally comes to accept the collective murder that his fellow townspeople plan against him as just punishment for the crimes of his youth. Ethical judgment, not mere survival, shapes his personal destiny, but the townspeople will have to work out their own guilt after they murder him, not for justice but for greed. Most tragedies suggest that the hero is at least partially responsible for his fate, and when the verdict is clear, there is relief in the assurance of a dependable moral order.

Another partial explanation of the satisfaction that tragedy brings is suggested by a pattern of primitive ritual. Among tragic heroes, Oedipus is the most conspicuous prototype of the scapegoat. He bears the sins of the city, and when he is expelled, the city is cleansed. Even Willy Loman's sacrificial suicide in *Death of a Salesman* clears the way for his son and heir, Biff, to free himself at last from his father's debilitating dream.

Instead of a ritual purging, Aristotle suggested a metaphor of medical purging to explain the tragic effect. He maintained that tragedy arouses "pity and terror to provide a catharsis for such emotions." The literal meaning of catharsis is "purging" or "purification"; but since we cannot know exactly what Aristotle meant, the term has been variously interpreted to mean every kind of emotional release, from the repose of "all passions spent," to a cleansing from all selfish and petty emotions, to an understanding of emotions that frees one from their enslaving power.

The tragic hero's reconciliation may be metaphysical or psychological, or both. Tokens of a wider, metaphysical justice break into the tragic world in many ways. The Furies in Aeschylus's *Oresteia,* the Ghost in *Hamlet,* and the witches in *Macbeth* are vivid supernatural forces that find immediate echoes in the psychological. In *Oedipus the King* the oracles and the old soothsayer with their dark forebodings of future disaster remind us of a larger-than-human framework for the action, and in many Greek plays, the gods come directly on stage as symbols of forces beyond human control. Romantic writers skillfully use Gothic settings and grotesque characters to build an atmosphere of terror and superstitious dread that suggests impending disaster and unaccountable fate. For many realistic writers, the environment is all-important, and its inescapable influence is suggested by storms, floods, decay, and disease. Eugene O'Neill begins *Long Day's Journey into Night* on a bright sunlit morning, but by Act II the fog has begun to move in, and the passionate raging in the last act is punctuated by the foghorn's mournful sounds.

In psychological terms, the reconciliation is with the self. All pretense has been removed and pride exhausted. Oedipus works out his self-loathing by blinding himself. He finds his identity and accepts responsibility for his deeds. Broken as he is, he takes up his burden with dignity and serenity. As is common in tragedy, the Chorus who witness the deep humility of his suffering discover in it a new bond of sympathy that connects to all suffering humanity: "Count no man happy until he is dead. For the dead are free from pain."

THE CLASSIC AGE OF TRAGEDY

Tragedy was the invention of the Greeks, and Thespis, winner of the first contest for a tragedy in Athens in 534 B.C., has traditionally been credited with being both the first actor and the first tragedian. During the following century, their Golden Age, the ancient Greeks produced four of the world's greatest dramatists, new forms of tragedy and comedy that have been models ever since, and a theatre to which every age returns to rediscover some basic principle. Their great tragedies can be better understood, however, by some knowledge of where and how they did those plays.

At that time the Athenians had just rid themselves of a series of dictators and established the world's first important democracy. When the Persian armies invaded Europe, the Athenians led the confederation of little city-states and drove them back. They rebuilt their burned city in marble and made Athens the artistic as well as the political center of Greece. On top of a fortified rock, the Acropolis, they built the Parthenon, a beautiful temple to Athena, goddess of wisdom, but down by the roadside on the southern slope, available to every-

Night performance of a Greek tragedy in the ancient theatre at Epidaurus. The chorus takes a formal position in the large circular orchestra. Euripides' *Hecuba*. The Greek National Theatre Company, 1955.

body, they built a theatre, seating around 17,000 people, a shrine to Dionysus.

The center of the theatre was a round space, the *orchestra* or "dancing place," so called because the drama was derived from the *dithyramb*, a hymn to Dionysus, danced and chanted by a chorus. The rows of seats, built up the slope of the hill, almost completely surrounded the orchestra. The earliest plays centered on an altar in the orchestra and had only one actor who carried on a dialogue with a chorus of fifty. Soon the chorus was reduced to fifteen, but two more actors were added and the actors' dressing hut, or *skene*, was moved up to the edge of the orchestra so that its three formal doors could serve as entrances into the action— hence the term *scene*. Eventually a raised stage was also built, but in classic times the actors were probably not separated from the chorus.

Since it grew up amid primitive religious rites, with mask and ceremonial costumes, and made use of music, dance, and poetry, the Greek drama was at

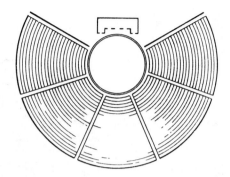

The general plan of the ancient Greek theatre. The actors entered from the *skene*, to meet the chorus in the circular *orchestra*, or dancing place, almost surrounded by the audience. Drawn by Don Creason.

the opposite pole from the modern realistic stage. In fact, probably no theatre in history has made fuller use of theatrical conventions to create its intensities. The chorus all together or in semi-choruses danced and sang their odes in unison. The actors, costumed in long tragic robes and artfully crafted masks, moved and gestured with dignified elegance and spoke their lines in the familiar cadences of the great epic poets. The masks, made of painted linen, wood, and plaster, brought into the theatre the primitive atmosphere of gods, heroes, and demons. For years it was believed that masks must have reduced believability and dramatic power, but recent Greek revivals as well as experiments in many modern plays have shown that a good actor can, by a shift in posture or a tilt of the head,

Tragic masks of the Greek theatre. The large, dignified masks made a strong facial expression visible in a vast theatre. Between episodes they could be changed to indicate a change of emotion. Drawn by Martha Sutherland.

cause astonishingly subtle variations in the attitude conveyed by a well-designed mask. Just recall the haunting power that a goblin's or witch's mask takes on when animated by an innocent child at Halloween. Moreover, the Greek actor, with a change of mask between episodes, could give for each episode an increasingly more intense expression than any human face could. When Oedipus came back with bleeding eyes, the new mask could be more terrible than any facial makeup the audience could endure, yet in its sculptured intensity be more beautiful than a real face.

The Chorus

Most essential to the tragic intensities, and hardest for us to understand, was the chorus. It is easy to see how, during the dramatic episodes played by the actors, the chorus could provide a background of group response, enlarging and reechoing the emotions of the characters, sometimes protesting and opposing,

Chorus reacting to an actor. Sophocles' *Oedipus at Kolonos*. The Greek National Theatre Company at Epidaurus, 1966.

Chorus in a formal semicircular gesture of horror. Sophocles' *Oedipus at Kolonos*. The Greek National Theatre Company at Epidaurus, 1958.

but usually serving as ideal spectators to stir and lead the reactions of the audience. We are familiar with such group responses in the crowds of our romantic plays and the choruses of operas and musicals. More difficult to imagine is the treatment of the choral odes, the long lyrical passages in which the chorus, alone on stage, reflects on the ideas and meaning of the action or on the meaning of human destiny. Since the action itself, in most Greek tragedies, seems complete without the odes, the modern reader often skips the odes and supposes that they served as some lyric punctuation, like intermissions between the acts of a play.

We know that the choral odes were complex performances, with sung or chanted words, musical accompaniment, and vigorous, sometimes even wild, dances and symbolic actions that filled orchestras sixty to ninety feet across. We know that the playwrights had sophisticated audiences and highly trained performers for their choruses because the dithyrambic contests had long been among the most important parts of the festival. In the plays the chorus sometimes expressed horror or lament. Sometimes it chanted and acted out, in unison and in precise formations, the acts of violence the characters were committing offstage. When Phaedra rushed offstage in *Hippolytus* to hang herself, all fifteen members of the chorus performed in mime and chanted the act of tying the rope and swinging from the rafters. Sometimes the chorus related or reenacted some incident of history or legend that paralleled and clarified the situation of the play. Sometimes it put into specific action what was a general intention in the mind of the main character. For example, when Oedipus resolved to hunt out the guilty person and cleanse the city, he spoke metaphorically, but when he was offstage the chorus invoked the gods of vengeance and danced a wild pursuit.

The audiences of ancient Greece may well have found the chorus, often depicted as citizens of the city, the main focus of their synthesizing experience with the play. Especially in the tragedies of Aeschylus and Sophocles, the action directly affects the general welfare of the people. The Chorus of Theban Elders in *Oedipus the King*, for example, sets the play in motion by appealing to Oedipus to

The homecoming of Agamemnon. Chorus of old men at the left. Aeschylus's *Agamemnon*. The Greek National-al Theatre Company at Epidaurus, 1966.

rid the city of the plague. It is the general populace who ultimately emerges cleansed by his sacrifice, and it is the Chorus that connects Oedipus's destiny to all mankind. When the plays of Euripides reduced the general welfare as a subject of the action, the chorus's role diminished, and by the fourth century B.C. it had all but disappeared.

Greek Tragic Dramatists

Three great writers of Greek tragedy had different visions of human destiny. Aeschylus, the earliest, caught the heroic mood of an Athens that had just defeated the invading Persians and was reshaping old institutions and loyalties for a new age of responsible public life. Sophocles reflected the ideals of the Golden Age of Pericles, when men of intelligence and reason were striving for a well-balanced life in a world where blind chance and old political loyalties were constant sources of danger. And Euripides wrote at a time when the old ideals were fading, as Athens was drawn deeper and deeper into war with Sparta. In a world of torture, madness, and violence, he denounced old superstitions and offered a deep compassion for the suffering of defeated mankind. While Aeschylus's characters are superhuman (Titans, gods, and primeval kings struggling

Agamemnon returning in triumph from the Trojan Wars in John Lewin's *The House of Atreus*. Directed by Sir Tyrone Guthrie at The Guthrie Theatre, Minneapolis.

to bring order out of primitive darkness), Sophocles' characters are very human, searching for private identities in the midst of public duties, and Euripides' characters are neurotic individuals, bursting into uncontrolled violence in response to the evil around them.

Of the works of Aeschylus that have come down to us, the most notable are the three plays of the *Oresteia*, the only example we have today of a complete Greek *trilogy*, or group of three plays that depict succeeding aspects of a continuous story-line. The *Oresteia* traces the emergence of a new social order through a series of horrible murders in a guilt-ridden royal family, until the goddess Athena comes down to help replace private hatreds with public order. In the first play, *Agamemnon*, Clytemnestra, the queen, conspires with her lover to murder the king on his triumphant return from Troy. Clytemnestra had never forgiven her husband for sacrificing their daughter, Iphigenia, in order to get favorable winds when he set sail ten years before. The guilty pair think that their act of revenge will bring peace, but in the next play, *The Libation Bearers*, the king's son, Orestes, goaded by his sister Electra, murders his mother and her lover. These avengers, in their turn, find no peace, for the Furies, primitive underground spirits of vengeance, come to punish Orestes. If history is nothing but neurotic violence in answer to violence, what hope is there for humanity? The last play, *Eumenides*, finds a solution. Orestes flees the avenging Furies and takes his case to Athena, the direct representative of Zeus. Knowing that a solution cannot be imposed from outside, she establishes a new human institution, trial by jury, to hear the case and consider the motives rather than order punishment by the old rules. Orestes is acquitted, but the old forces and instincts cannot be suppressed or destroyed—they must be transformed. Athena, goddess of wisdom, persuades the Furies to become Eumenides, "beneficent ones," and to dwell in open caves near the city, helping to preserve justice in Athens—a solution at once political, psychological, and metaphysical, thus exalting in its impact.

Aeschylus's story is a bloody tale of violence and vengeance. How is it that many of us who are horrified at the violence in film and television do not condemn these plays but revere them as classics? Is it all right for Clytemnestra in a primitive age to use an axe on her husband and his concubine and not right for cops in the streets of modern cities to shoot it out with punks and mobsters? Actually there are major differences in the treatment of violence. The modern screen often wallows in the blood and gore of explicit physical cruelty. The violence is for sheer excitement and satisfies the simplest impulse to hit back, rarely looking beyond the violence itself. In the Greek theatre, however, the murders were not shown on stage. They were described, vividly, by an official messenger, or revealed as the murderer looked on his victim, wheeled in on a platform machine called the *eccyclema*. The Greeks were more interested in reaction than simple action, as an example from Euripides' *Medea* will illustrate. After Medea sent exotic garments as gifts to the princess, rival for her husband's love, the Messenger describes how the girl puts them on and admires herself. Then the enchanted garments turn to flame, searing her flesh and clinging to her tortured body, as well as to her father's when he tries to smother the flame. No more gory description exists than the tearing of the gobs of flesh from the two bodies as they try to separate from each other. But by describing rather than by attempting to stage the scene, Euripides allows the audience the full play of their imagination to appreciate the horror, while at the same time they can watch the contrasting reactions of the appalled Messenger, the sickened Chorus, and the gloating Medea, triumphant over her enemies. Audience focus is more on reaction to the event than on the event itself.

The ironic effect of such description is supported by the entire production format to increase aesthetic distance, to create an atmosphere of artistic beauty rather than simple shock: the open-air theatre, the padded, larger-than-life actors, the large sculptured masks, the musical accompaniment, the chanting of much of the poetry, the formal odes of the chorus, and the constant reference to religious and philosophical principles. Even more important in Aeschylus's trilogy is that he shows how people can move out of the primitive age of violent revenge into a more civilized age of justice and order, with public trials before a jury. In Aeschylus's vision of history, human beings are not hopeless victims of their primitive emotions but are capable of transforming their emotions by spir-

Oedipus watches the Corinthian Messenger question the Shepherd about Oedipus's birth. The Guthrie Theatre, 1972, directed by Michael Langham.

itual understanding and of mobilizing them in support of public institutions of justice.

At the center of any discussion of Greek tragedy is Sophocles, for he has the clearest vision of men and women struggling mightily against fate, suffering greatly, and facing defeat with dignity. Though religion and the gods are always in the background, the decisions and choices are clearly made by human beings. Sophocles' heroes are royal leaders whose fate involves the health of the state, but their struggles are the inner conflicts of solitary souls. We have frequently referred in these pages to Sophocles' masterpiece *Oedipus the King*, a play that exemplifies how personal, human struggle intricately connects to the larger society and to the gods. When a blight falls on the land, leaving no crops and no new births, Oedipus pledges to find and eradicate the cause. The welfare of the state depends on the eternal laws of justice, and one man sets out to rectify the wrong. But Oedipus's search soon becomes a personal struggle when the accusing finger points at him. It does not matter that the audience knows the story already. More terrible than simple surprise is the suspense of watching Oedipus come nearer and nearer to the appalling discovery of his own guilt and then seeing him exile himself in order to cleanse his city and gouge out the eyes that had deceived him all his life.

Nineteenth-century critics regarded Oedipus as a victim of malevolent fate, already announced in a series of oracles. Waking to suffering that came on him from the past, Oedipus had no chance. But for the twentieth century his tragedy has new meanings. Above all, it is a study of the search for identity, an agonizing concern of our age. It is his need to find out who he is that drives Oedipus on, though his wife begs him not to ask, insisting that the world is chance and nothing can be predicted.

Unlike Sophocles, Euripides shocked his first audiences; they considered him too sensational in depicting abnormal states of mind. He used exotic foreign melodies and dwelt on the sordid topics of betrayal, cruelty, murder, and incest. In later centuries he became the most popular of all the Greek dramatists and in modern times has had the greatest influence. He portrayed the skepticism, rebellion, and desperation of an Athens drifting away from the high ideals and the religious devotion of earlier times. The democracy broke down in political corruption as the war with Sparta dragged on, and disease, superstition, and hysteria were rife in the crowded streets of Athens. Some Athenians could joke about the war and corruption; the comic poet Aristophanes lashed out at it in fantastical satires that are as funny now as they were at the end of the fifth century B.C. But Euripides could not laugh. He was haunted by images of Medea in hatred killing her own children, of Agave in religious ecstasy tearing off her own son's head, of Phaedra in madness causing the death of her stepson—of women helpless in the grip of violent emotion, goaded by the unforgivable cruelty and injustice of the world.

In Euripides' *The Trojan Women*, Queen Hecuba laments over the body of her slain grandson laid out on her dead son's shield. The Greek National Theatre Company at Epidaurus, 1966.

Euripides was shocked when Athens killed the men and enslaved the women and children of a small island that wanted to remain neutral in the war. Then when he saw Athenians building a fleet to conquer Sicily—an ill-fated expedition that led to Athens' defeat—he produced a play about ancient victims of Greek aggression, *The Trojan Women*, the most famous of all antiwar plays. The anguished women of Troy leave their burning city to be slaves to their arrogant conquerors. As the ultimate cruelty, the Greeks kill the little son of Hector and deliver his broken body on a shield to his grandmother, Queen Hecuba. A procession of doom, the play has enough indignation, enough compassion to hold the stage today. Its different episodes are arranged with strong contrast and variety, from a half-insane Cassandra whirling a torch, gloating in her prophetic knowledge that her new master, Agamemnon, is doomed when he arrives home, to the wily Helen of Troy, conniving to get back into the good graces of her husband, Menelaus.

Antigone: A Model Greek Tragedy

Though Sophocles wrote *Antigone* fourteen years before writing *Oedipus the King*, he used Oedipus's daughter, Antigone, and brother-in-law, Creon, as his tragic heroes. When Antigone's uncle, Creon, newly crowned as king, issues orders on

Ismene pleading for Antigone's life in the 1956 Festival production at the Theatre of Epidaurus.

pain of death that no one is to bury her brother Polyneices, who had attacked the city, while giving all honors to the body of her other brother, who had defended it, Antigone makes up her mind to disobey him. In the opening scene she tells her sister, Ismene, her purpose. She must perform the religious rites due the dead. Ismene warns her of the law and Creon's wrath, but Antigone looks to a higher law, "I know that those approve / Whom I most need to please," and defiantly looks forward to "death, with honor."

After this first episode, most of the play centers on Creon, but all his actions flow from Antigone's defiance and his own unbending pride. In his first scene, he pronounces his edict publicly: The traitorous brother's body shall be left to the dogs. If Antigone is unbending in upholding the laws of God, Creon is equally determined to enforce what he sees as "best for the state," with "death to anyone who interferes." Already as Creon sets forth his supreme law, the audience sees the conflict ahead. Then the Sentinel arrives—someone has performed the forbidden burial rites. The terrified Sentinel quakes before Creon's anger and leaves, promising never to return here again, but soon reappears, this time by choice. He has caught the culprit, Antigone. His change of heart serves as an ironic warning to Creon: "A man should never vow he will not do a thing, for second thoughts belie the purpose." But Creon is determined to maintain his vow, even though it means killing his own niece.

The battle of wills that follows increases both Creon's and Antigone's determination. She will answer only to the gods, while he will assert the power of the state. "Tempers too stubborn are the first to fail," he warns Antigone, but fails to recognize his own stubbornness and condemns her to death. The episode between Antigone and Creon was bound to end in confrontation, two opposing minds equally bullheaded in their determination. In the next episodes, Creon is given two chances to back off from his entrenched position. First his son, Haemon, Antigone's fiancé, uses every technique of persuasive art, a skill much admired in Athens where every citizen was his own lawyer. In contrast to Antigone, Haemon starts by honoring and praising Creon. Next, out of concern for Creon's welfare, he tells him confidentially how the people of the city are secretly praising Antigone's deed. Then, using the image of a tree that breaks when it will not bend before the hurricane, he begs his father to yield. But Creon only grows more adamant until Haemon finally loses control, accuses him of "trampling on Heaven's honor," and promises that Antigone "shall not die alone." Second, after Creon has sent Antigone to be entombed alive, so that the city will not be guilty of her blood, Teiresias, the blind soothsayer, comes to warn Creon of the omens he has had. At last Creon recognizes his impiety, and after much torment, finally agrees to bend, to acquit Antigone and to bury the brother's body. "O God, 'tis hard! But I quit . . . and yield; I cannot fight at odds with destiny." Creon's passion follows his change of heart, which comes too late, for his suffering lies ahead. The Messenger tells us how Creon went to the tomb himself, there to find Antigone hanged and Haemon maddened by her death. Seeing his father, Haemon attacked him with his sword and, missing, turned it on himself. Creon enters, mourning the son he carries in his arms, but he has still more to learn. His wife, mute witness to the Messenger's tale, heard the whole story, then quietly went to her altar and killed herself. The unbending man, upholder of stately power, perceives that he alone is guilty and that he has nothing now to look forward to but death: "Come quick, I pray; Let me not look upon another day!"

Creon undergoes the greatest change in a struggle to uphold his man-made laws, finally bringing himself and his family to destruction. But Antigone's defiance sets it all in motion, and the poet does not forget her struggle. Though she knows from the beginning she must die, never blind to her fate as Creon is, though step by step she moves consciously toward her certain doom, Antigone has one monumental struggle—to prepare to meet her death, to reason out the fate that has brought her to this end. In one of the most striking scenes of the play, Antigone pours out her farewells to the sun, reflects on the everlasting coldness and tears of Hades, and questions why she was destined to do this pious act that means her doom. Her song is a dance of death, and perhaps she moves down into the orchestra, where she and the Chorus together can dance and sing her passion, for only in this one scene does the Chorus, as a whole, interact with one of the characters.

Throughout the play, the Chorus Leader has been involved in each episode, serving as the objective observer, trying to help the characters become more moderate, trying to inject reason into their stubbornness. The Chorus, without speaking, may well have suggested both sympathy and horror through their movements while the episodes progressed, but it is in their choral odes that we find their true significance. Between each episode described above, a choral song and dance give pause for reflection. A few quotations from these odes will illustrate the variety of ways that the Chorus directs the audience's thoughts to larger issues implied in the actions of the characters.

The first ode is a joyous greeting to the sun, which briefly recalls the miseries that Thebes has suffered, then looks with hope toward a bright future:

> But now loud Victory returns at last
>   On Theban chariots smiling.
> Let us begin oblivion of the past,
>   Memories of the late war beguiling into
>   slumber sound.

Coming as this ode does immediately after Antigone's vow to bury her brother and right before Creon's public proclamation, it forms an ironic awareness of how short-lived human happiness is.

The second ode follows Creon's proclamation and Antigone's first defiance of that law. It celebrates the wonder of human cunning, of our conquests over nature, of our skills at language and the law, but it also rejects the impiety of the man who wrests "his country's law to his own will."

> He that will work the works of wickedness,
> Let him not house, let him not hold, with me!

These ambiguous words might sanction Creon's edict against burying the traitor; yet the warning could apply to Creon himself. So the Chorus makes us ponder the actions in a larger context: Man's cunning may overstep its bounds.

One might expect the choral ode that follows the Creon-Haemon episode to reflect on the dangers of excess and pride, to intensify the fear of Creon's growing wrath, as it encircles even those closest to him. But Sophocles' choruses are never that simplistic. Instead, the choral song that follows this painful rift between father and son is an ode to love, not to its sweet pleasures, but to its power to madden. Sophocles plucks from the father-son episode an unexpected theme, Haemon's theme, intensifying the audience experience by the variety of questions that the actions raise.

Following Creon's change of heart, the Chorus has one more ode, a hopeful prayer to the god Bacchus to rush to them to relieve their city of its pain. This ode creates an ironic joy, a belief that the gods can save people from their errors, but the die has been cast; the change of heart and the joyful prayer come too late. People had set themselves above the laws of the gods, and their actions must now pursue them to the end. The final ode which closes the play sums up the wisdom—the perception—of the play:

> There is no happiness where there is no wisdom;
> No wisdom but in submission to the gods.
> Big words are always punished,
> And proud men in old age learn to be wise.

The play *Antigone*, a new look at a story familiar to its Athenian audience, was performed as an offering at one of the most important religious celebrations

A modern version of a Greek Chorus. Andrei Serban's production of *Fragments of a Trilogy*, selections from Euripides. La Mama Experimental Theatre Club, New York, 1972.

of the city. In its passionate expression of the dangers people can suffer and the sufferings they can bring on others when they overstep the bounds set forth for mankind, it is no wonder that it won its author the coveted first prize.

GREEK TRAGEDY ON THE MODERN STAGE

To see an ancient Greek play in one of the ruined ancient theatres is a high point for summer travelers. There are no performances at the Dionysian theatre at Athens, but a few hundred feet west, in the ruins of the Roman theatre of Herodias Atticus, concerts and plays are frequently presented. The greatest adventure is to go to the beautifully preserved theatre at Epidaurus, where in midsummer companies from Athens or other cities perform the ancient plays in modern Greek several times a week.

The power of Greek drama lives in many kinds of modern productions. An unearthly intensity of voice and movement was achieved by the director Andrei Serban in his 1974 production of *Fragments of a Trilogy,* based on scenes from *Electra, The Trojan Women,* and *Medea,* under the auspices of that very experimental Off Broadway theatre, La Mama Experimental Theatre Club. *Fragments of a Trilogy* played several times in New York and, during a period of five years in the seventies, in more than forty festivals in fifteen countries. Serban used not a word of English, but phrases from the Greek and Latin versions of the tragedies and sounds and syllables that belonged to no language. The audience was brought into a dark room with only cushions and a runway around the sides of the hall. *Medea* was played in darkness except for one beam of light down the middle of the room. During Medea's passionate solo, only a pinspot lighted her face. Most extraordinary was the use of voices—crying, singing, wailing, cursing to primitive melodies and sound patterns composed and drilled by Elizabeth Swados. For *The Trojan Women* the hall was fully lighted, with the audience sitting around the edges, or standing and now dodging the fast-moving carts carrying the captive women, now watching wild attempted flights on the runway high above. Though all portions of the *Trilogy* had complicated patterns of energetic action and moved at a rapid, sometimes frantic, pace, the performance was beautifully controlled and retained the power, the feeling of exaltation we associate with ancient tragedy.

Among the most challenging attempts to bring Greek tragedy to the modern stage is the John Barton-Kenneth Cavender distillation of nine Greek tragedies into one stupendous trilogy called *The Greeks.* It required seven hours of performance time, plus lunch and dinner breaks, when performed by the Hartford Stage Company in the winter of 1982. Originally done in 1980 by England's Royal Shakespeare Company, *The Greeks* is a sweeping drama of the period of the Trojan war, a subject which preoccupied Greek writers and performers for centuries. Part I begins with the sacrificial murder of the young Iphigenia by her

Dame Judith Anderson as Medea in the Robertson Jeffers adaptation, 1947.

father Agamemnon for favorable winds to help the Greek ships to Troy, and takes in the terrible conclusion to that war itself. Then come the murderous acts of vengeance that followed the war as the Greeks returned to their homeland in Part II, followed in Part III by a series of godly interventions bringing stability back into the lives of the Greeks. The chorus of women who follow the relentless catapulting of the action from catastrophe to catastrophe, until only the gods can impose an order on the lives of the people, lends a strikingly feminine and peculiarly modern perspective to this ancient world of masculine arrogance, cowardice, and hypocrisy.

The great tragic roles of ancient Greece are, of course, an irresistible lure to modern actors, reaching new heights in Judith Anderson's unforgettable creation of *Medea* in 1947 in an adaptation especially made for her by the poet Robinson Jeffers. Dame Judith's snarling contempt for Medea's priggish and cowardly husband, the heroic Jason, thrilled audiences on both sides of the Atlantic for nearly two decades, and won her Broadway's highest honor for an actress, the coveted Tony award, in 1948. In 1982 she came out of retirement, this time to play the Nurse to the Medea of the Australian actress, Zoe Caldwell. Repeating her mentor's triumph, Caldwell won the Tony award for the same prodigious role, while Dame Judith, at the age of 84, won a Tony nomination herself.

The basic themes and characters of Greek tragedy have inspired many new versions, in which twentieth-century dramatists find modern solutions for the old dilemmas. Jean Anouilh's *Antigone*, first produced in 1944 in Paris during the German occupation, cuts the religious basis from Sophocles' play, but makes Antigone stubbornly keep her resolve to go against Creon's decree and bury her brother's body, even as she learns that her brother was not worth honoring and that her deed can have no meaning except in her own mind. This existential view—the character defining herself by her action—continues to make *Antigone* popular on American campuses.

In using the Greek story of Agamemnon in *Mourning Becomes Electra* (1931), set in New England just after the Civil War, Eugene O'Neill made a major attempt to recapture the Greek tragic pattern. Instead of a family curse passed down through the generations, he used the Freudian concept of the dangers of sexual repression. The trauma of her wedding night has created in General Mannon's wife a neurotic hatred for her husband that eventually leads her to murder him, after taking his cousin as a lover. Then the son and daughter murder the cousin and drive their mother to suicide. The mixture of love and hate, envy and anger, involves the brother and sister too closely with each other and leads to the brother's suicide. Lavinia, the Electra of this play, shuts herself inside the family mansion to live out the rest of her life with her ghosts: Mourning is indeed becoming to Electra. In the 1930s the play seemed a profound study of destructive psychological forces, perhaps the greatest play America had produced. Its thirteen acts were played in one evening, starting at five o'clock and running to midnight, with an intermission for dinner. When the film was made two decades later, the trilogy was compacted into one screenplay of ordinary length, and the story became a thin melodrama of no consequence. O'Neill had given the tale a scope that was lost in the condensation. One can understand why Aristotle demanded magnitude for tragedy.

THE MODERN FESTIVAL THEATRE

The Greek spirit lives most vividly today in the festival theatre, usually a large outdoor structure on a hillside at a sacred spot to which travelers make special pilgrimages. Since the seventeenth century travelers from around the world have gathered every ten years in the Bavarian mountain village of Oberammergau to witness the passion play put on with religious devotion by the villagers themselves. A descendant of Oberammergau is the Passion Play that is performed each summer in the Black Hills of South Dakota. England has a well-

Mother Nature is the backdrop for *Texas*, an American festival drama presented annually near Canyon, Texas.

established tradition of religious plays, usually presented in the great cathedrals. Near Palmyra, New York, Mormons and their friends see the Hill Cumorah come alive each July with hosts of devout performers reenacting the visions of Joseph Smith. Outdoor historical pageant-dramas, or "symphonic dramas," which exalt the traditions of American history, have drawn large audiences of vacation travelers over the last four decades. Of these the best-known are Paul Green's *The Lost Colony*, which has been presented annually since 1937 on the spot of the first English settlement in North America and *Unto These Hills*, the moving story of the Cherokee tribes, presented each year in the town of Cherokee near Asheville, North Carolina. Even more popular in recent years have been numerous summer festivals honoring the works of Shakespeare, of which the most famous are those in the three Stratfords—England, Ontario, and Connecticut—in Ashland, Oregon, and in New York City's Central Park. While a few festivals use some elements of painted scenery, most go back to the unity and simplicity of the formal architectural structure used by the Greeks.

The Greeks gave us the word *theatre* and the idea of a splendid building for the whole public to watch a play of religious, historical, and national importance. They gave us the idea of a play as the high point of a religious festival, performed at a sacred shrine. They gave us the word *drama* and the idea of a play as a work of art, complete in itself, to be looked at, felt, and thought about. Along with the words *poetry* and *poem,* they gave us the idea of a performing poet, competing with other poets, presenting his own personal view of the human condition, often in conflict with both the orthodox view and the views of other poets. They gave us tragedy and three great tragic writers. The Western world owes an enormous debt to the Greek example. Different as most modern plays are from those given in the Athenian theatre of Dionysus, it is hard to imagine how they could have existed at all without the splendid groundwork of the inspired ancients.

THE THEATRE OF EXALTATION: FROM MEDIEVAL DRAMA TO MODERN TRAGEDY

4

The spirit of tragedy is evoked by the prophetic
witches in this Utah Shakespearean Festival
production of *Macbeth*.

*A*round 240 B.C. the Romans began to imitate and adapt the classic tragedy of Greece and continued to do so for about three hundred years, reaching a high point in the writings of Seneca in the first century A.D. Several of Seneca's tragedies were to have great influence on Renaissance dramatists more than fifteen hundred years later, but during the lavish days of the Roman Empire, Rome's attempts to exalt human behavior and to explore man's relationship to the gods through tragedy were soon overwhelmed by spectacular entertainments. These ranged from elegantly danced pantomimes to gladiatorial contests, sham sea fights (with as many as 19,000 participants), vulgar comic mimes, and plays with explicit sexual acts and actual crucifixions. The young Christian church set itself squarely against such decadent theatre and by the sixth century had gained sufficient power to put an end to it. A thousand years were to pass before Renaissance princes built regular theatres for tragedy, but in the meantime, Western Europe produced its own kind of exalted religious drama.

CHRISTIAN DRAMA OF THE MIDDLE AGES

Four to five centuries after forcing the ancient theatres to close, the Church itself gave theatre a new start around 925. The beginning was very simple: three lines of dialogue (called a "trope") inserted into an Easter mass. The three Marys come

Roman theatre. Although it developed from the Greek theatre, the Roman theatre differed in that a raised stage and a very high scenic wall continued the structure of the large auditorium. It was used more for clowns, mimes, and spectacular dance shows than for plays. Drawn by Ethelyn Pauley.

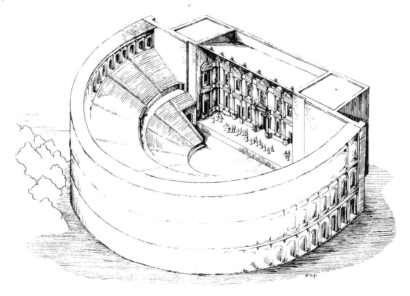

Eight different episodes staged simultaneously in sequence on the long platform at Valenciennes. Drawn by Martha Sutherland.

to the tomb to embalm the body of Jesus and are met by angels asking whom they seek. "Jesus of Nazareth, the crucified," they reply. Whereupon the angels show them the empty tomb and tell them to announce to the world that Christ is risen. The short drama was probably chanted by monks or priests; yet the impact of this most exalted of Christian messages, suddenly brought to life in the noble Latin of the church and followed by an exultant anthem of praise, must have been impressive. For before long, similar tropes were added to the Christmas and Palm Sunday festivals, and by the end of the tenth century this new *liturgical drama* had spread across Europe. A few churches even produced long plays for special occasions, and for five hundred years the joyful news of the Nativity, the Resurrection, and the triumphs of prophets and saints sang out in splendid chant. Modern-day productions and recordings by such groups as the New York Pro Musica have shown some of these plays to have astonishing power in their blend of sacred music and text, creating a whole new twentieth-century audience.

Much more spectacular in bringing the exalted stories of the Bible to medieval audiences were the outdoor *religious cycle dramas,* associated with the Feast of Corpus Christi in the fast-growing cities of the High Gothic period (roughly 1350 to 1550). This feast, held on the Thursday following Pentecost, emphasized the mystery of the bread and wine as the redeeming body and blood of Christ, in

A pageant wagon showing the play of the Nativity in a medieval street. As each wagon moved to the next playing place, another wagon brought the next episode, until the entire sacred history was presented. Drawn by Ethelyn Pauley.

a vital union of the human and the divine. While the liturgical drama in the churches remained formal, sung in Latin by priests well trained in music, the cycle dramas took on a vastly different tone, probably the most striking blend of the divine and the vulgar that Western culture has to offer. To make the meaning of Christ clear in the lives of the people, anywhere from twenty-five to fifty separate plays grew into a cosmic drama covering the whole story of the fall and redemption of man, from the creation and the fall of Adam, through the passion of Christ to the Last Judgment, with each episode requiring its own scenic unit, called a *mansion*. The plays were financed by the merchant guilds, who also used the event to open the midsummer trade fairs, and were performed in lively, everyday language by hundreds of local amateurs.

Often each guild was responsible for a single episode, assigned appropriately for the guild's special qualifications (shipwrights for the story of Noah and the flood, bakers for the Last Supper), and would build the mansion, train the actors, and provide costumes, props, and special effects. In some cities all the mansions were spread down a long platform in what we call *simultaneous staging*, as shown on page 91. In other places the mansions were placed in a large circle surrounding the audience, in a medieval variant of theatre-in-the-round. The most picturesque method was to put each mansion on wheels, or *pageant wagons* (page 92), spreading the cycle as a long procession through the streets, each wagon stopping to perform its play at a dozen or more places. In York, England, some forty-eight plays took up one long and exhausting day, while in Chester the episodes were combined into half as many plays spread over three days. The audience stood in the street, with special bleachers or raised pavilions for dignitaries and the wealthy.

Perhaps most significant for the average audience members was the way the plays expressed their own lives through local references and contemporary costumes and sets, giving an immediacy to the Bibilical events. Spectacular effects, also called *secrets*, often created by hired professionals, delighted the imagination and inspired the spectator with both the fearful power of the devil and the awesome presence of the divine in working out God's plan for mankind. Devils came out of the smoking hell-mouth amidst the beating of pots and pans. God, from his high Mandala amidst the choiring angels, sent Gabriel down for the Annunciation to Mary. While country shepherds with broad dialects offered their caps,

Everyman trying to escape the call of death. The medieval morality play, acted by a choral group of seven actor-dancers who play many roles without any change of the uniform, conventionalized dance costumes. The Guthrie Theatre, produced and directed by Robert Benedetti.

toys, and old horn spoons to the Christ child, a noisy King Herod carried his rage against this upstart, child "king of kings" right out among the audience. "To out-Herod Herod" was Shakespeare's way of describing such unrestrained "ham" acting.

The late Middle Ages and the early Renaissance developed two forms of exalted entertainment that provided a transition to the Elizabethan theatre. The first was the *street show* honoring a royal visitor to the city or town. Along the entry way, triumphal arches and elaborately decorated structures were erected, where actors, portraying famous kings and heroes, formed silent tableaux or honored the visitor with noble speeches as he passed in great procession. From these shows Elizabethan stage architects learned to combine several scenic symbols into one large structure.

The second form was the *morality play*, from which playwrights developed the art of long plots with sustained conflict and variety of detail. *Everyman* (c. 1475) is the most impressive of the morality plays. In a single strong plot, God sends Death to summon Everyman, but Everyman is not ready to present a reckoning of his life and is terrified of the journey. His earthly friends, represented by such allegorical characters as Fellowship, Kindred, and Worldy Goods, abandon him at the start, while the more sympathetic characters of Beauty, Strength, and Five Wits fall by the wayside. The theme of the play reaches its climax when only Good Deeds can accompany Everyman to the grave. Though *Everyman* is serious throughout, many sixteenth-century morality plays included scenes that laughingly satirized fashions, social life, and politics. One central character would undergo a series of tests as the Virtues contended with the Vices for his soul. Some morality plays included kings and princes as historical examples and, for all their serious moral concern, showed a great deal of humanistic tolerance for fun and revelry. From the morality form, Shakespeare learned to portray the part played by historical forces, moral duties, and private pleasures in the shaping of a prince, in such plays as *Henry IV* and *Henry V*.

TRAGEDY IN SIXTEENTH-CENTURY ENGLAND

The beginning of the sixteenth century also saw the beginning of two new approaches to exalted theatre. The first was a refined form that grew out of attempts by Italian poets and architects to attain to a classical ideal. The poets imitated what they took to be the perfection of Greek and Roman tragedy and comedy, and the architects refined the Greek and Roman theatre structures and *skene* with the newly discovered principles of perspective scenery—scenery constructed and painted to give the illusion of the third dimension and framed behind a formal archway called the *proscenium*. The second approach created a looser form and is of more immediate interest because its sensational methods filled the popular commercial theatres in London, Paris, and Madrid. This popular exalted theatre grew out of the sprawling religious plays of Medieval

Europe, out of the romantic stories about the adventures of King Arthur's followers and other knights, and out of the histories of kings and princes that had so impressed the populace in the street shows or tableaux. From the diverse materials of these several sources, the popular theatres kept the multiple plots, the comic clowns and servants, as well as the regal princes, the crowd scenes, the battles, sieges, processions, weddings, and coronations. They kept this vivid pageant moving across a platform stage through scene after scene with scarcely an intermission, by bringing on thrones, beds, or tables when needed, by using permanent doors, windows, and balconies, and by disclosing arranged tableaux behind curtains.

Romantic Tragedy of the Heroic Individual

Out of this popular drama, as sensational in its own way as a Broadway musical or a modern movie, a few English poets in the late sixteenth century, the age of Elizabeth I and Shakespeare, created a tragedy about romantic individualistic heroes. The great heroes of history walked onto the Elizabethan platform, defied the limits of medieval society, endured terrible suffering, expanded the bounds of the human spirit, and met their deaths still fighting and striving. The medieval world had taught that unreasoning fortune might raise man to the heights and then, like an ever-turning wheel, carry him on to his fall. Only by turning away from this world and seeking heaven, such as in the play *Everyman*, could human beings find true meaning. But the Elizabethan hero would accept no such human limitation. The hero of Christopher Marlowe's *Tamburlaine* (c. 1587), a shepherd who conquers the world, defies every limitation, even death itself. By his determination to control his own fate, he persuades even his enemies to join him. The play was so popular that, as with the modern adventures of James Bond and Luke Skywalker, Marlowe went on to create a sequel, *The Bloody Conquests of Mighty Tamburlaine*, but this time has his hero die at the end.

Mental aspiration and power to do good have more enduring appeal than worldly power for its own sake. For this reason, Marlowe's next play, *Doctor Faustus* (c. 1588), is more admired and produced today than *Tamburlaine*. In one sense, *Doctor Faustus* is a highly developed medieval morality play, with its emphasis on worldly versus heavenly values, but its real action, its conflict, is in the mind. By selling his soul to the devil in exchange for the removal of all human limitations for twenty-four years, Faustus can explore all experience and search after infinite knowledge. He calls up the image of Helen of Troy, the dream of immortal beauty, and sings his paean of praise:

> Was this the face that launch'd a thousand ships,
> And burnt the topless towers of Ilium?
> Sweet Helen, make me immortal with a kiss.

At the end the devil exacts the penalty, possession of his soul, and Faustus utters his curses and his remorse as passionately as he had proclaimed his pride and determination to explore all knowledge. Though he cannot exceed God's limits, the final impression is not of death and defeat but of the magnificent individual who dared.

This is one of the great patterns of Elizabethan tragedy: the daring assertion that expands the limits of the human spirit even as it is defeated. The impact of the deaths of Romeo and Juliet is heightened because they have snatched their moments of ecstasy from the hostility of the old feudal world. Antony and Cleopatra, Shakespeare's Roman commander and Egyptian queen, throw away countries and continents, but who would prefer their rival, the practical, successful, calculating Octavius Caesar? Macbeth, appalled, yet irresistibly drawn to the bloody deed of regicide, finally dares damnation itself in contempt for his own human weakness: "Lay on, Macduff, and damned be him that first cries 'Hold, enough!' " Throughout the best of the Elizabethan tragedies there is this generosity of spirit, this willingness to live and love, even in the face of almost certain defeat.

Players in an Elizabethan inn yard. The inn yard probably suggested some aspects of the Elizabethan stage. A drawing from C. Walter Hodges, *The Globe Restored.*

Shakespeare and the Majesty of Elizabethan Tragedy

It was in his history plays that Shakespeare first worked out his subtle and complex approach to tragedy. During the patriotic years following the defeat of the Spanish Armada in 1588, when plays about English history became popular, Shakespeare wrote eight plays presenting a panorama of the Wars of the Roses, England's century of struggle to curb the fighting barons and establish a strong central government. Splendid as this pageant of national history was, Shakespeare used it to explore the ironies and tragic undertones of the rulers and rebels whose private ambitions and guilts so strongly affected their public careers. The plays explored every phase of kingship, from the weak poetic voice of Richard II, who learned to be kingly only after he lost the crown and was on his way to the block to lose his head; through Prince Hal, who studies the art of kingship in the taverns and on the battlefield before assuming the throne as Henry V; to Richard III, the arch-villain who cunningly uses everyone in his bloody rise to power, leaving behind a trail of executed brothers, wives, nephews, and friends to satisfy his royal hunger. The triumphant end of the historical epic was the accession of Henry VII, the first of the Tudor family and grandfather of Elizabeth I. But it was in the great tragedies of his later years, especially in *Hamlet* and *King Lear*, that Shakespeare's tragic view reached its supreme expression. *Hamlet* will be discussed in Chapter 12, while *King Lear* will be discussed below, following a brief description of the Elizabethan stage.

The Elizabethan Stage

To the supreme examples of tragedy created by the Elizabethans, the modern theatre owes an incalculable debt, but it owes almost as much to the stage on which these dramas were played. Though not a single completely dependable picture of an Elizabethan stage remains, and though the living tradition was lost in three hundred years of picture-frame scenery, enough is known for it to stand as a beacon. Playwrights, designers, and directors, groping for some escape from the everyday detail of realism, have learned from the Elizabethan stage even more than from the Greek.

To return to the Elizabethan stage from a realistic age is to enter another theatre world. There was no front curtain and no proscenium frame, no painted scenery, no pretense of creating an actual place. The action unfolded in the midst of the audience, on a platform that was open to the sky and to the three rows of galleries that almost completely encircled both the stage and the space for standing spectators or "groundlings." The actor enjoyed direct contact with the audience instead of turning away in the strange pretense that it was not there. A splendid facade of two or more stories at the back of the open platform presented at least six openings, either for entrances and exits or for small scenes to be disclosed in doorways or behind small curtains. What happened to the characters was more important than where it happened, but when the audience needed

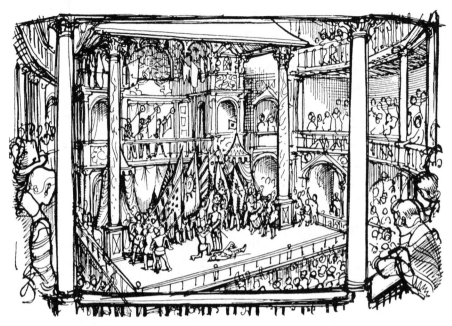

The Elizabethan public theatre, open to the sky. The final scene of Shakespeare's *Richard III* as seen from one of the galleries. The crowd of characters, the tents and banners on the forestage, and the trumpeters on the upper stage create an elaborate spectacle. A drawing from C. Walter Hodges, *Shakespeare and the Players*.

to know an exact place, the playwright had some character say, "This is the forest of Arden," or "What country, friends, is this?—This is Illyria, Lady." This arrangement invited the audience to use its nimble imagination as it followed many scenes across time and space without interruption or scene changes. Yet both clarity and variety were provided through exciting combinations of levels and playing areas. As a small curtain closed a scene on an inner stage, another group of actors might already be entering on the upper level or on the forestage.

Though the main acting space was this bare platform, contemporary sources refer to much splendor in the vivid colors of the facade and the columns painted like marble. Costumes, too, were elaborate and often as costly as the garments of princes. Many articles (or *props*) could also be brought on: thrones, tables, beds, altars, tombs, tents, trees. Add to these the many banners, pennants, and flags, and there is colorful pageantry indeed. Musicians played flourishes for the processions, accompaniment for the many songs and dances, and appropriate background music for the solemn scenes as well as for scenes of terror. That plain platform and facade could present a splendid pageant of romantic drama.

With the rediscovery of this flexible stage, Shakespeare's plays can be put on today with the sequence and rhythm of the original productions, without pauses, without cutting, and without the distraction of a different painted setting for each scene. The single formal facade, apparently derived originally from the throne pavilion and arches of the street shows, is often used as a backing for an "authentic" platform stage in modern productions of Shakespeare, just as it was in his own time. The platform is a place for actors to play out the action, and when it needs to be more specific, the audience's imagination, inspired by the words and actions of the characters, turns that platform and facade into field, forest, cave, mountain, private chamber, castle, or city gate. Many designers today prefer to start afresh and make a structure of steps, platforms, shapes, towers, and arches to suit the action of each particular play. With the help of modern selective lighting, they can give a playing area the atmosphere of a corridor, bower, throne, or altar and, when the action moves elsewhere, let that area retire into shadows. Thus the best possibilities of modern, medieval, and Elizabethan staging are combined. The play progresses without interruption, as small changes take place in view of the audience. Such a background creates

The Elizabethan "private" or indoor theatre used during the winter by the professional companies. A reconstruction based on recently discovered evidence. Drawn for this book by C. Walter Hodges.

more atmosphere than the standard "authentic" Elizabethan stage, and the flexible arrangement of many levels allows more interesting grouping and movement and more effective use of modern lighting.

Tragic Patterns in *King Lear*

King Lear was written at a time of bitter disillusionment in the European soul. Renaissance hopes were exhausted, the hopes that had buoyed up so many Italians a century before and so many Englishmen scarcely a decade before: hopes of reconciling Christianity and classic culture, of creating a liberated aristocracy and an enlightened state through humanistic education, and of reviving art, literature, and drama for the modern world on classic models. The liberated individual, no longer closely ruled by his trade guild or his parish priest, was free to make money and to lose it, free to rise rapidly in court or market or to fall to loneliness and disaster. The feudal order was breaking up and the old religious certainties were gone, resulting in frequent and widespread wars. Individualism, encouraged by humanistic education, ran riot in ruthless murders and court

A permanent setting for Shakespeare's *King Lear*, suggested by the primitive forms of Stonehenge. A design by Norman Bel Geddes.

intrigue. Even the heavens lost their old order through the new astronomy, as first Copernicus banished the earth from the center of the universe, then Kepler traced the earth's course around the sun not as a circle with one center but as an ellipse with two centers, and finally Galileo caught glimpses of other planets with their own moons. The feeling of this time of change was expressed in one of John Donne's poems as "all coherence gone."

The complex dramatic form that Marlowe and his contemporaries had shaped out of medieval traditions served Shakespeare well. The multiple-plot scheme, especially, emphasizes disruption and disorder in *King Lear*, with each plot developing intrigues of its own, while the waves that each stirs up reverberate through the other plots in so complex a fashion as to create a sense of cosmic disorder. The Elizabethan platform stage was backed by a solid facade, richly representing the earthly order of the throne, endorsed by the symbols of heavenly order above. But King Lear, having given his crown away, is out on the open platform, dispossessed, abandoned, while his thankless daughters possess the throne, and the heavens above resound with thunder to emphasize the dislocation of the natural order. If the action of Elizabethan tragic heroes is to dare, no hero of the age dares more than Lear. An eighty-year-old king with absolute power over his subjects, Lear dares the unthinkable—to give up all his kingly power, the very source of his identity, and place himself at the disposal of his daughters. Lear assumes that the power he wields over them is a natural power, innate within him, and that dividing his kingdom among his daughters will not change the love and respect they bear him. But Lear has much to learn and suffer before he reaches a true perception of who he is, and his rash action sets off an unparalleled chain of upheavals in every corner of his kingdom, extending even to the heavens.

The plot of *King Lear* begins quite simply. Lear calls his three daughters before him to divide his kingdom among them, so that he "unburdened" may "crawl toward death." He requires only one thing, that each daughter affirm her unconditional love for him. The elder daughters, Goneril and Regan, like master politicians, tell him what he wants to hear, but when he turns to the youngest— his favorite, Cordelia—she has nothing to say. "Nothing will come of nothing. Speak again," he commands, but Cordelia, too honest for her own good, tells him that her love extends as far as is appropriate, "no more, no less." "Why have my sisters husbands if they say they love you all?" This response so enrages the old man that he disowns Cordelia on the spot. "We have no such daughter," he pronounces, as though his word were sufficient in itself to erase the natural bond. Lear's friend, the Earl of Kent, tries to dissuade him from such rash behavior and is banished from the kingdom for his pains, under threat of death. Lear then divides the kingdom between his elder daughters, reserving for himself only a hundred knights, while he divides his time, one month each, between their two abodes. In several recent productions, including Lord Olivier's 1984 television version, Lear's arrogant sense of his own power is admirably revealed

King Lear curses his daughter, Cordelia, and disowns her as she kneels on a map of his kingdom. The Guthrie Theatre, 1974, directed by Michael Langham.

by spreading a huge map of England across the stage floor, where, like a towering god, Lear steps out the division of the land.

Lear barely takes up residence with his eldest daughter before the dire effects of his action begin. Goneril's servants know him not as king, but as "my lady's father," and, on her orders, neglect his needs. Only his Fool, a sadly comic court jester, reminds Lear that he himself played the fool, when "thou mad'st thy daughters thy mothers . . . when thou gav'st them the rod and put'st down thine own breeches." When Lear protests to Goneril, she takes away half his knights, diminishing his retinue to fifty. In a rage, he leaves her with his curse, to find comfort from his second daughter, Regan. But Regan is even more severe. She cuts his retinue to twenty-five, and has his personal servant (actually his old friend, the Earl of Kent, serving him in disguise) placed in the stocks. Then

Goneril and Regan together take all his knights away. Hurt beyond his powers to cope, Lear, with only his Fool for company, rages out into the stormy night on the lonely heath, while his daughters lock the doors against him.

> You think I'll weep.
> No, I'll not weep.
> I have full cause of weeping, but this heart
> Shall break into a hundred thousand flaws
> Or ere I'll weep. O fool, I shall go mad!

There follows one of the most awesome scenes in all of drama. Lear begins his monumental passion amidst a violent thunderstorm, stands shouting to the storm on the open platform, bereft of crown, of property, and now of his wits. A pathetic old man with no power left him in the world, he tries to command the erupting heavens—not to stop, but to match his daughters' evil by letting fall their thunderbolts on his white old head:

> Blow, winds, and crack your cheeks! Rage! blow!
> You cataracts and hurricanoes, spout
> Till you have drenched our steeples, drowned the cocks.
>
> · · ·
>
> Rumble thy bellyful! Spit, fire! Spout, rain!
>
> · · ·
>
> I never gave you kingdom, called you children;
> You owe me no subscription. Then let fall
> Your horrible pleasure. Here I stand your slave.

The storm in Lear's mind and the storm in nature merge into one unified expression of universal chaos.

The chaos of the play doesn't stop with Lear. Shakespeare parallels the Lear plot in a second parent-child conflict—the old Earl of Gloucester and his two sons, Edgar and Edmund. When Lear disowns his favorite daughter, Cordelia, Gloucester takes this as a sign, along with recent eclipses of the sun and moon, that all nature is falling into "ruinous disorder." Edmund, his villainous bastard-son, takes advantage of Gloucester's mood and tricks him into believing that his favorite son, Edgar, is plotting to have him killed. Edgar escapes his father's anger with his life, dresses himself in weeds, and hides in a hovel out on the heath disguised as "Tom o' Bedlam," a mad fool. Then when Gloucester learns that Cordelia, now the Queen of France, has landed an army at Dover to save King Lear from her sisters, he confides to Edmund a plan to join the insurgents. But Edmund immediately betrays his father, and Regan's evil husband, the Duke of Cornwall, punishes Gloucester by gouging out his eyes with the spurs on his boots and sends him out onto the heath, a crawling, bleeding, blind old man: "Let him smell his way to Dover."

No other scenes in all dramatic literature can match the passion Shakespeare evokes on that barren heath, where, in a raging storm, a Fool, a noble youth reduced to weeds and pretended madness, and two old men, one mad, the other blind and suicidal, try to understand their destiny. Step by painful step, Lear learns compassion for the weak now that he is too weak himself to be of any help, first for the Fool, then for the animals and birds, then for Edgar in his Tom o' Bedlam role: "Unaccommodated man is nothing more but such a poor, bare, forked animal as thou art. . . . Come, unbutton here," and he begins to change his own clothes for weeds in sympathy with this demented "natural."

The chaos that Lear's initial action had set off has hardly begun, however. While Lear endures his passion on the heath, unknown to him, Cordelia has taken up his cause against her sisters. Father and daughter are eventually, but briefly, reunited in a delicate scene of mutual love, as Lear, now clad in a simple robe of white, kneels to his angelic daughter, Cordelia, and each begs forgiveness of the other for the pain they've caused. Their bliss is short-lived, for they are soon captured by Edmund, who has joined forces with Goneril and Regan and their husbands to defeat Cordelia's invasion, but Lear's suffering has brought him to a new perception of freedom, and he happily goes to prison with his loving daughter.

King Lear (Morris Carnovsky) reunited with his faithful daughter Cordelia (Ruby Dee). Festival Theatre, Stratford, Connecticut.

> We two alone will sing like birds i' th' cage.
> When thou dost ask me blessing, I'll kneel down
> And ask of thee forgiveness. So we'll live,
> And pray, and sing, and tell old tales, and laugh
> At gilded butterflies.

While an enlightened Lear is on the rise, the villains of the play are working their own destruction. Goneril and Regan both fall passionately in love with Edmund. When Regan's husband is slain by his own servant for putting out Gloucester's eyes, Goneril becomes so jealous that she poisons Regan and, when her treachery is exposed to her husband, the Duke of Albany, she kills herself. Meanwhile, a mysterious knight comes to challenge Edmund for his treachery, and keeps his face concealed while he wounds him mortally in single combat. Only then does he reveal that he is Edgar, lately come from seeing his father, Gloucester, die: "His flawed heart . . . / 'Twixt two extremes of passion, joy and grief, / Burst smilingly," Edgar tells the assembly. Hearing this about his father, Edmund decides to do one act of good before he dies, and sends to rescue Lear and Cordelia, who are under his death sentence. So all the evil characters are dead, while all the good still live, except for Gloucester.

But Shakespeare does not let his characters get off so lightly. Just as hope seems finally possible, Lear comes in bearing the corpse of his beloved Cordelia, the final rack of his suffering. Albany offers him his kingdom back, but Lear doesn't even notice. Nothing remains of value to him now except one small thing—Cordelia's breath of life. The others stand by helpless as he tries to find a trace of life:

> no, no, no life?
> Why should a dog, a horse, a rat, have life,
> And thou no breath at all? Thou'lt come no more,
> Never, never, never, never, never.
>
> . . .
>
> Do you see this? Look on her! Look, her lips,
> Look there, look there—

With that, Lear dies—of a broken heart. Albany, trying to resurrect some sense from this dark and deadly time, offers the crown to Kent, Lear's faithful friend, but Kent declines. He must follow his master in death, leaving only Edgar and Albany amidst the devastation to take up the sad task of rebuilding.

No play so magnificently captures a sense of chaos and despair, a vision that has made it especially meaningful to the absurdists of our own nuclear age. Yet Lear's gradual discovery of love and compassion and the love and care that he receives from the band of outcasts—the Fool, the blind Gloucester, the exile Kent, the mad beggar Edgar, and the steadfast and pure Cordelia—also give the play great warmth. And so, like the dying Gloucester, the audience must feel the intensities " 'twixt two extremes," an exalted sense of joy at the spirit of love and care that endured the pain and nurtured Lear through his passion to a true understanding of love, and a horrific sense of grief at the enormous waste of human potential, the price paid for the perception. "The oldest hath borne most," Edgar says as the dead march plays. "We that are young shall never see so much, nor live so long." Like Edgar, we as audience may not quite understand what we have just witnessed; but in a good production we will feel its awesome power, and, in the true spirit of tragedy, "speak what we feel, not what we ought to say."

NEOCLASSIC TRAGEDY

The Elizabethan dramatists achieved great vitality in a sprawling, complex form that owed much to the medieval theatre. Half a century later, French dramatists went to the opposite extreme and created a neoclassic tragedy that surpassed that of ancient Greece in compactness, austerity, and polish. The new classicism, in public life as well as in art, was a triumph of simplicity and order over complexity and turbulence. The expansive energies of the Renaissance had led to conflicts and tensions that set Catholics against Protestants and barons against kings. But in the seventeenth century people were tired of religious wars and political conflict, and gradually Cardinal Richelieu brought the turbulent forces of France under the tight control of a central power. Paris was ready for an age of reason and order and for a heroic drama in which the violent personal forces and conflicting values were brought into controlled harmony.

At the beginning of the seventeenth century, Paris, like the London of Shakespeare, had a vigorous popular drama that mixed comedy and tragedy, kings and clowns, poetry and pageantry, blood and thunder. The populace might continue to be entertained with street clowns and acrobats, royal processions and public executions, but people of taste gathered in small theatres to watch tragedies of man's solitary struggle with the moral dilemmas of the day in carefully balanced plots that adhered to the neoclassic unities of time, place, and action and to strict patterns of heroic verse.

When neoclassic tragedy was codified with Pierre Corneille's *The Cid* in 1637, it was a classic distillation of the popular drama. Corneille took an earlier sprawling Spanish play, *The Youth of the Cid,* and cut it down to a few key scenes of the final episode, eliminated the giants, shepherds, princes, soldiers, and supernatural encounters, and shifted the emphasis from adventure to psychological dilemma. The Cid is called upon to fight a duel with the father of his love, Chimene. When he kills her father in the duel, her anger is so strong that he rushes off to battle, hoping to be killed himself. But he returns a national hero, intensifying Chimene's psychological conflict, and she chooses another champion to fight him. Though the Cid again hopes for death, he wins. At the end, his

The neoclassic stage of Paris in the middle of the seventeenth century. The characters in their "antique" costumes are copied exactly from an early edition of the play. The setting is a free reconstruction from several sources. Racine's *Andromaque*. Drawn by Martha Sutherland.

triumphs have almost conquered Chimene's distress, and the king suggests that she wait a year and then accept the Cid as husband. Leaving all battle scenes offstage, Corneille concentrated on scenes between two contending characters and scenes where a character analyzes choices. Every motive and every possible decision are carefully debated, and violent emotions are examined with utmost clarity. The Age of Reason produced not a cold debate without passion, but a passionate debate of reason. The Cid's choice is between love—a private good—and his duty to king and father—higher, public loyalties. Many a nobleman and merchant in the audience had experienced such conflict of personal desires and public obligations in the tightening rules of Louis XIII's absolute monarchy, and to reconcile private and public good made a triumphal ending.

While Corneille's plays stressed the triumph of human will, Jean Racine showed the appalling failure of the will. His heroines—for he specialized in the feminine—fall helplessly into evil, finding torturous justifications and rationalizations until time and their deeds bring destruction. *Phèdre* (1677), which has provided the foremost acting role in classic French theatre, is a terrifying study of tragic destruction. Phèdre, in love with her stepson, Hippolytus, is scorned by him. In revenge, she tells her husband, Theseus, that Hippolytus has defiled her. Theseus calls on the god Neptune, who sends a sea monster to destroy Hippolytus. In clear and passionate debate, Phèdre analyzes her own emotions. Loathing herself for her degrading lust, and, seeing herself caught in the fatal net, she turns her frustration into destruction. Yet even in her dying she remains a public figure, a queen of dignity and grandeur. The final effect is one of majestic sadness, for the violent passions and twists of her mind are all expressed in the most polished poetry, the most carefully selected impersonal diction, and the most perfectly proportioned and balanced episodes.

Scenery and costume took the audience back to a conventionalized world, far from the Baroque architecture and the lace, satin, and velvets, the petticoat breeches and wigs of seventeenth-century France. The setting was a simplification of the stage setting framed by a proscenium that was introduced in Italy in 1507, more than a century before. Two or three *wings* at the sides, painted as dignified columns of a private room in a palace, led to the *back shutter*. By modern standards, the costumes, with elaborate embroidery, capes, plumes, and wigs, may seem far from simple, but compared to the elaborate fashions of the audience, they were simple enough to seem "classic."

It is helpful to consider how very different *King Lear* would be if written in neoclassic form. There would be no comedy, of course, none of the Fool's bitter jests, no subplots, no songs, no thunderstorms, no onstage killings or blindings. The action would be concentrated on a few characters—Lear, Cordelia, Goneril, and Regan—who would be drained of individuality and whose richly vivid diction would be reduced to a uniform, stately verse. Lear would still have Kent to talk to—there would be no soliloquies—and the other minor characters would be abstracted into a few confidants. Lear's three daughters could be given a love interest that would be in conflict with their duty to their father. Goneril and Regan, both still in love with Edmund, would be torn by lust and jealousy to reject the king and eventually destroy each other. Cordelia could be in love with Edgar and together they could reveal the virtue of their love by helping to save Lear from the hypocrisy of the other sisters and come once again into the grace of Lear's affection. The division of the kingdom and the hypocritical vows, Lear's curses against his daughters, Edgar's challenge to his brother (not showing the actual fight), Lear's reconciliation with Cordelia, could all be retained, but always with a confidant present for each character—the play would have to be impersonal even in intimate scenes. No throne would be visible, for not the public but the private decision would be important. Though no such play was ever written, in 1681 Nahum Tate, an English neoclassicist, tamed Shakespeare's play in the directions set forth by the French. The poetry was refined, the Fool eliminated, and the love interests introduced. Most of all, the end of Tate's *History of King Lear* was a monument to decorum and good taste. The evil were all punished, while the divine Cordelia and the noble Edgar were rewarded with the crown by a grateful Lear, while Lear retired to "enjoy the present hour, nor fear the last." The play ended with Edgar glorifying Cordelia: "Thy bright example shall convince the world / That truth and virtue shall at last succeed." Tate's version of *Lear*, not Shakespeare's, was the one that played on English stages for the next hundred and fifty years.

Nineteenth-century romantics despised neoclassic tragedy as cold and over-refined and compared it to the dead-white plaster casts made from ancient sculpture. But the twentieth century turns back to it with great respect for its ethical concern, its self-examination, its debates on moral issues, and its direct scenes of personal conflict. From Henrik Ibsen's tight realistic plays of the late nineteenth century, set in one Victorian living room, to Jean-Paul Sartre's *No Exit* (1944), about three people confined in one room in hell, to Athol Fugard's two- and three-person dramas of apartheid South Africa in the 1970s and 1980s, modern drama has made frequent use of the compact neoclassic form to express the passion of personal choice and conflict. Far more than the Greeks, who used the elaborate effects of the chorus, the neoclassicists proved that an austere presentation of characters in a climactic action, with all preliminary episodes, all physical action, and all public events left offstage, can be very powerful.

MODERN TRAGEDY

It seems easy to see the magnitude of tragedy in other periods—Greek, Elizabethan, and neoclassic—but can tragic exaltation exist in the twentieth century? Many critics say no, among them George Steiner, who wrote a book called *The Death of Tragedy*. If tragedy is a heroic vision of humanity celebrating the triumph of spiritual nobility over physical defeat and death, how can it exist in an age that finds no heroism, but only conformity? How can a hero who dies for his or her ideals be admired by people who believe there is nothing worth dying for? How can plays deal with choice and free will when behaviorist psychology tells us that all action is determined by social forces? How can great misfortune inspire pity and fear in a society that insulates itself from unexpected disasters through social welfare, insurance policies, union contracts, and tax shelters? How can questions of human responsibility command attention when the mood of our culture is to abrogate responsibility, where even the most appalling individual deeds of destruction are met with a plea of innocence by reason of insanity, mistrial, or social and economic alienation? When things go wrong, it is not ourselves but the system we blame. Conversely, in a pragmatic age that emphasizes scientific study of the facts and the practical solving of problems, where is there room for tragedy? What is tragedy but a record and glorification of the unsolved problems of the past? Instead of brooding about the terrifying gap between the vision and the reality, practical people will get on with the immediate goal of making the world better and let the infinite—if it exists at all—take care of itself.

Still, whatever brashness or indifference we may assume, the need for tragedy to help us cope with our thwarted ideals remains, perhaps more in our age than ever before. For if we have chosen to avoid responsibility, we have done so partly because no other age has made people so fully responsible for their own destiny. In earlier societies, where social and economic position, lifetime occupation, place of residence, and life mate were determined by birth, average people could only perceive tragedy as happening to those above them. But where society assigns each of us the freedom to develop our own talents, select our own niche, and even pick our own value system, the opportunities for disastrous mistakes are multiplied, with only ourselves to blame. No wonder that society tries to protect itself against its own mistakes with every conceivable kind of insurance and government regulation. No wonder that every mail delivery brings new appeals from yet another organization to protect our rights, insure our security, and satisfy our longing for greatness. Increasingly, the gap between our dreams for greatness and the ever-present threat of failure finds its panacea in alcohol and drug addiction, in the divorce courts, and in the proliferation of religious sects. Even the most successful person, with public respect and a solid portfolio, can be confronted with cosmic loneliness. Disappointment, defeat, old age, and death are inescapably present, with all their pain and terror, as surely as they were present for Sophocles and Shakespeare. The reality can never equal the vision. Truly scientific people will seek some new equation that will help them face the discrepancy between their hopes and their reality. They will turn to tragedy.

Three Kinds of Tragic Characters

Three kinds of tragic characters have been celebrated in the Western struggle to control the human environment, and all three have led their authors beyond simple scientific materialism: heroes who are ahead of their time, ordinary people who become heroic to salvage a modicum of respect, and frustrated rebels who turn destructive.

Tragedy was not congenial to social reformers of our great-grandparents' time. They felt that in the long run science and reason could build an environment fit to live in, while tragedy would only encourage defeatist attitudes. Still, the appalling slums of the new industrial cities forced them to realize that the job of rebuilding could take generations and that, in the meantime, individuals would be defeated in such an environment no matter how hard they struggled. So they found modern tragic heroes—not helpless victims but individuals who see what is wrong in society and give their lives in the effort to change it. There is no reconciliation or justice in the defeat of such heroes, as in classic tragedy, but instead the audience takes on the guilt of the injustice and the responsibility for rectifying it. While radical thinkers have disapproved of classic tragedy, they have accepted the concept of heroes who are ahead of their time.

The greatest of such heroes is the Joan of George Bernard Shaw's *Saint Joan,*

In Shaw's play, Saint Joan discovers that even her friends must abandon her to the lonely pursuit of her cause. Seattle Repertory Theatre, 1979.

written in 1923, soon after Joan of Arc was declared a saint and nearly five hundred years after she was burned at the stake for heresy. Shaw presents her as the focus of great historical forces that were about to shatter the rigid feudal system and to usher in the national state and the Reformation. Joan is crushed by the powerful institutions she had threatened, but Shaw gives her tragic grandeur as she refuses to recant and faces the fire. The audience sees her suffer, knowing that what she stood for won out and that the church finally canonized her, but Shaw adds on an epilogue to show that the ghosts of her enemies who come to congratulate her would be horrified if she performed a miracle and came back to life. He believed in the power of the institutionalized environment, but also in the power of the creative individual mind that would be as much of a threat to modern institutions as to those of Joan's own time.

Far more deeply tragic, however, are plays that assume that progress does not solve all problems and that people must struggle to define their own individuality, even in the midst of unsettled and contradictory forces. Not Promethean defiance of the ruler of the universe but rather a very modest insistence on choice gives the twentieth-century individual heroic stature.

Tragedy of the little man. This setting for Miller's *Death of a Salesman* takes its multiple playing areas and its open platform from the Elizabethan stage, New York, 1949.

Arthur Miller's *Death of a Salesman* (1949) heads the list of plays that achieve tragedy on this modest modern scale by finding dignity in the struggle of an ordinary person. Miller treats Willy Loman, the salesman, with respect. Willy's wife, Linda says,

> I don't say he's a great man. Willy Loman never made a lot of money. His name was never in the paper. He's not the finest character that ever lived. But he's a human being, and a terrible thing is happening to him. So attention must be paid. He's not to be allowed to fall into his grave like an old dog. Attention, attention must be finally paid to such a person.

As disaster threatens, Willy fights back. He demands some explanation for his failure. He goes over the past to ask whether he was wrong in bringing up his sons to aim for the top, to be "well liked." He talks repeatedly to the image of his long-lost brother Ben, who made a fortune in diamonds, and wonders whether he himself was right to build his life on sales slips, appointments, and appearances. Willy does more than follow the crowd, and when he fails he is truly tragic.

Most critical discussion has centered on Willy's decision to kill himself in order to make his son Biff "magnificent" with the insurance money, emphasizing the importance to tragedy of the hero's arriving at a perception. But Miller thought it more important to show Willy steadfast, ironically happy in his death, than to show him realizing that his whole life had been a mistake. Mistaken or not, he is committed to his dream and dies for it. The other characters gain the perception and clarify the issues. In the Requiem at the end, each one has his say. Biff, at last sure of his own identity, declares, "He had the wrong dreams. All, all wrong. He never knew who he was." Curiously enough, Charley, the friend next door who had no patience with Willy's worship of success, is the one who defends Willy's dream: "Nobody dast blame this man. A salesman is got to dream, boy. It comes with the territory." The wife has the final word, and it is a question: "Why?" That question can never be answered because the life of a human being is always a mystery.

In some ways Blanche DuBois in Tennessee Williams' *A Streetcar Named*

Stanley's smoldering resentment of Blanche leads to rape. Rosemary Harris and James Farentino in Williams' *A Streetcar Named Desire*.

Desire (1947) is a restless victim of a difficult environment. She is already badly damaged, a wanderer from the old plantation system. She finds refuge briefly in the slums of New Orleans, where her sister has adjusted to life with an animal-like husband, Stanley Kowalski. But Blanche has visions of finer things and she tries to rescue her sister and herself. For a moment Blanche hopes to marry Mitch, the gentlest of Stanley's rough friends, and find herself a secure corner. But her past finds her out and destroys that dream. Refusing her chance for a merely sexual relationship with Mitch, Blanche fights to the last for a dream of something finer, choosing to remain herself and to be carried to the insane asylum rather than to submit like her sister. Stanley Kowalski also has a touch of the tragic. He sees his home threatened by a difficult and insulting intruder. When he rapes and destroys Blanche, his wife's sister, he knows he risks breaking up his own marriage, but he has his own kind of integrity to defend. The intensity of the conflict, with important values on both sides, gives the play considerable stature as tragedy. It involves struggle, questioning, suffering, and most of all, for Blanche, it involves choice. Trapped as she is like an animal in a cave with no choices left, she demands to choose, and leaves at the end with the doctor who is going to institutionalize her as though he were her gentleman escort.

Heroes who demand the right to choose and those who are ahead of their time affirm humanity's struggle toward greatness. A great many modern tragedies, however, center on a hero who is destructive. Henrik Ibsen's *Hedda Gabler* (1890) is an early example of such a hero. Hedda's Victorian society offers women no outlet for intelligence and energy, only complete submission to the desires of men and a smothering motherhood. Even interfering in the life of a young genius who loves her turns into a sordid shooting in a brothel, not the magnificent suicide she had expected. By the end of the play she is completely in the power of the very "respectable" Judge Brack, but she can still say no. She kills herself. The fascination of the play is in the power of destruction.

That love itself could be destructive fascinated the American playwright, Eugene O'Neill. In an early play, *Desire under the Elms* (1924), a melodrama of seething greed and lust, he has a young wife kill her own baby to prove that she loves its father, her elderly husband's son, and that she did not just use him to father her child to get possession of the family farm. Her outraged lover sends for the sheriff. Yet at the end he returns to share her punishment—an assertion of love and reconciliation with destiny that has much in common with classic tragedy.

In quite a different vein, the indigent family members of Sam Shepard's *Curse of the Starving Class* (1976) seem obsessed with finding ways to better themselves. Yet each creative effort that any family member makes—be it a 4-H project, a repaired gate, a long-awaited stock of groceries—another comes along and destroys. When they are not destroying each other directly, they play into the hands of outsiders who simply use them for their own greedy purposes. The image of mutual destruction is highlighted at the end by a story of an eagle that swoops down from the sky and picks up a cat in its talons:

> They fight like crazy in the middle of the sky. The cat's tearing his chest out, and the eagle's trying to drop him, but the cat won't let go because he knows if he falls he'll die . . . . And they come crashing down to the earth. Both of them come crashing down. Like one whole thing.

Jealousy is what motivates the court composer, Salieri, in *Amadeus* (1979), Peter Shaffer's treatment of the Mozart story. Jealous of the audacious prodigy, Wolfgang Amadeus Mozart, Salieri secretly plots to undermine his talent and reputation. Mozart dies young, but the work of the youthful genius overshadows that of Salieri, destroying him emotionally and socially in his old age. When he fails in an attempt on his own life, he is left an impotent invalid, suffering the fruits of his own destructive action.

The vision of destruction indicates a radical change from the attitude of those late nineteenth- and early twentieth-century thinkers who assumed that reality is good and believed in the great myth of progress. But what if the hope of

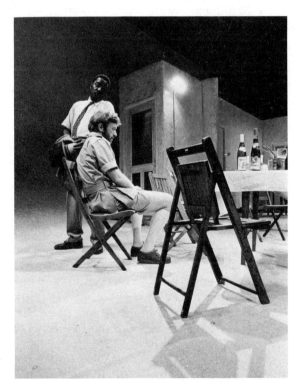

Guilt creates confrontation among friends. Athol Fugard's *A Lesson from Aloes* at the Baltimore Center Stage, 1981.

progress is itself a romantic delusion? What if nature is man's enemy and the scientific pursuit of reality is bound to destroy the old faith in human nature?

If this is the case, if truth is inhuman and things of the imagination are lies, then one answer is "Long live the lies!" Several dramatists began to talk about life-lies and to defend the illusions even if they were delusions with no relation to the real world. Ibsen explored both sides of the question. In *Ghosts* (1881) and *An Enemy of the People* (1882), he portrayed stupid, venal people trying to conceal the truth; but in *The Wild Duck* (1884) he showed that a misguided truth-seeker can be equally stupid and destructive when he insists on telling a happy husband that his wife has been the mistress of her employer and that their daughter is not his own.

The contemporary South African playwright Athol Fugard explores the yearning for illusion in several plays. In *A Lesson from Aloes* (1980), an Afrikaaner farmer and his English wife are visited by a colored friend, just recently released from prison. The family of the friend had also been expected to visit but doesn't show up. After some initial camaraderie, covering the family's absence, the friend finally asks the farmer point-blank if he had been the informer who had sent him to prison. The question is never answered, leaving the audience in the same position as the characters, wanting to believe in the beauty of this interracial friendship rising above the world of apartheid that surrounds it, yet knowing that the question itself is a betrayal. It hangs over the play like a poisoned cloud, exposing how little these two closest of friends really know or understand each other. Though the pretense of friendship remains, the thorns and bitterness of the aloes herb that the farmer raises is a symbol of the reality which the illusion tries to hide.

Poetry in Modern Tragedy

Until modern times, much of tragedy's exalted feeling was supported by the intensified language and rhythms of poetic verse, but the modern theatre's emphasis on realism changed that. Contemporary everyday people in the realistic kitchens and living rooms of their middle-class homes would sound strangely out of place if they spoke in poetry. Occasionally, however, poets created a new kind of poetry out of the vivid language and the folklore of the peasants to build exciting tragic scenes. Most notable is the work of the Irish writer John Millington Synge. Early in this century, he produced a somber, classically structured one-act tragedy, *Riders to the Sea* (1904), which is still cherished for its sustained mood and for a rhythmic prose that captures both the language patterns of the Irish peasant and the rhythm of the sea to which these Aran Island fisherfolk owed their lives and their deaths.

It remained for the short-lived twentieth-century religious drama movement to combine aspects of the medieval religious plays with the suffering and exaltation of Greek tragedy in a modern poetic idiom. The most striking example is T.

S. Eliot's *Murder in the Cathedral*, written for the 1935 festival at Canterbury
Cathedral in England. It dramatizes the martyrdom in 1170 of Thomas à Becket,
Archbishop of Canterbury. From the Greek theatre Eliot took the pattern of a
divine or saintly hero set against a chanting chorus of women whose spiritual
problems are involved with his. For the soliloquies and confrontations of Becket,
he used the sharp stanzaic and rhetorical forms of medieval and Shakespearean
verse. To the chorus of Canterbury women drawn to witness the martyrdom, he
gives his most vivid free-form verse. They feel the significance of the martyrdom
as a ritual sacrifice of the seasons:

> Winter shall come bringing death from the sea,
>
> . . .
>
> And the world must be cleaned in the winter, or we shall have only
> A sour spring, a parched summer, an empty harvest.

What is expressed in abstract rhetoric by the main characters is physically sensed
by these fearful women:

A Greek-like tragic chorus in a
twentieth-century play. The
women of Canterbury surround
their soon-to-be-martyred archbishop, Thomas à Becket, in
Eliot's *Murder in the Cathedral.*
Northwestern University Drama
Festival, 1965.

> I have smelt them, the death-bringers, senses are quickened
> By subtle forebodings . . .
>
>   .   .   .
>
> What is woven on the loom of fate
> What is woven in the councils of princes
> Is woven also in our veins, our brains,
> Is woven like a pattern of living worms
> In the guts of the women of Canterbury.

Though hailed as a poetic tragedy for the modern age, this new religious-drama movement subsided within a decade, with a few sporadic but notable new plays into the 1950s.

EXALTATION IN THE MOVIES AND ON TELEVISION

Movies and television have not shown many tragedies, even if we apply the term loosely to any serious play that ends in disaster or death for its principal character. Most good films of this kind have been adapted from stage plays, and in some of them the ending has been altered to leave a more cheerful impression. Still, more and more often in the last three decades, a complex dramatic situation has been allowed to reach a natural solution, whether favorable or unfavorable to the protagonist.

The youth rebellion of the sixties and seventies stimulated serious treatment of disillusioned youth. The first notable film about rebellious youth was *Rebel Without a Cause* (1955), in which James Dean began his brief career and catapulted to stardom as the ideal image of his restless generation. The phrase "rebel without a cause" fitted perfectly their unfocused kind of rebellion, and the film made a touching plea for compassion. Youth rebellion in the early sixties often had a hopeful coloring, in life and on the screen, with love-ins, rock music, and flower power. But as the Vietnam war became more hopelessly entangled and the military-industrial complex appeared more threatening, the motorcycling, leather-jacketed, pot-smoking heroes and heroines of the films took on an aura of desperation and doom. The establishment was against them, yet they had to assert themselves, search for their authentic selves by living in their own way; they had to find fresh innocence even in a world of violence.

A tragic fate for rebels soon became a trend. The four survivors of *The Wild Bunch* (1969) set out to kill a few enemies, but when the whole Mexican bandit army is thrown at them, they are seen as victims by the movie audience, not murderers. The naive youth trying to rob a bank in *Dog Day Afternoon* (1975) is not a criminal but a confused rebel, bargaining with an army of police to see both his male lover and his wife before making his last run. *Easy Rider* (1969) has historic overtones as a reversal of the old American dream of adventurers taking to the open road, looking for space and freedom in the West. Its long-haired rebels take to the open road on motorcycles, riding eastward from California to the New Orleans Mardi Gras. The open space and the beautiful mountains and high plains are still there, but small-town America has an irrational fear of the freedom and life-style of long-haired youth. In one town the wanderers are beaten by the rednecks, and after a disappointing glimpse of the Mardi Gras, they are killed by "respectable" citizens. They were doomed from the first. In a world of drawn-out war, of proliferating weapons, of ruthless competition and overkill, there is no room for the relatively innocent. The film has tragic implications not only for rebellious youth but for America, the traditional land of freedom, open space, and variety.

In *Rumble Fish* (1983), Motorcycle Boy, a seventeen-year-old former street-gang leader, returns to his old territory, having dropped out for a few weeks to see California. Motorcycle Boy's style is passive gentleness—not because he objects to violence, but because initiating action of any kind just seems pointless.

In *Rumble Fish* (1983), the Motorcycle Boy (Mickey Rourke) parallels his own life to that of the tiny Siamese fighting fish that try to annihilate each other when confined to pet-store tanks. In a film that is otherwise all black and white, the rumble fish suddenly appear in vivid color.

His gentle passivity carries with it a sense of doom that borders on tragedy. The audience watches him through his kid brother, Rusty James, who idolizes him and dreams of glory in a renewed unity of the gang. Though Rusty James seems blindly optimistic, his despair builds as he sees his hero move toward his inevitably violent death. The film is all in black and white, its colorless tones suggesting Motorcycle Boy's own sense of despair. He is also color blind, though he does remember seeing colors when very young. Then one bit of color emerges. Motorcycle Boy, as if by compulsion, is drawn to a petshop to watch the rumble fish, kept in separate tanks so as not to kill each other. Though everything else remains black and white, the fish are in brilliant reds and blues, symbols of some spirit that cries for escape—into a larger river that will free them from violent self-destruction. It is in freeing the fish from the tanks, as he might have wished to free his kid brother from the stagnation of street life, that the play's antihero dies.

These are not great heroic figures, and their lawlessness and violence are often childish. But they are searching for some kind of integrity and fresh innocence in an extremely difficult world. They are trying to find meaning in life. Knowing that, we can accept their failure and destruction.

Film, whether in movies or on television, is a medium of swift-moving action and does not lend itself well to the sustained exploration of a character passionately struggling with the kind of internal dilemmas we associate with tragedy. Rebellious victims can inspire the kind of action that film demands, but internal struggles are more often left to the stage. Film and television have instead strived to inspire exaltation not with internal struggles but with epic proportions. From the earliest days of film, artists like D. W. Griffith tried to capture the feeling of a whole era in such films as *Birth of a Nation* (1915), while *Gone with the Wind* (1938) takes in the whole period of the American Civil War. Both will be discussed as romantic films in Chapter 6. In the 1950s and 1960s, Biblical epics such as *The Ten Commandments, The Robe,* and *Ben Hur* sought to capture the scope of Biblical times as well as inspire audiences with religious ideas. But the excitement was in their scope, not in the inspiration, and what people talked about in *Ben Hur* was the thrilling chariot race, not its watered-down theology. Nevertheless, film has the potential for epic exaltation as no other form has, and when used to trace the generations of Alex Haley's family from an African village through slavery and reconstruction up to modern times in the TV series *Roots* (1976), or when it captures the life of an inspiring historical hero, as in *Gandhi* (1982), it achieves an almost breathtaking sweep and power.

The past two decades have fostered several exciting attempts to create a theatre of exaltation for our time. Jerzy Grotowski with his Polish Laboratory Theatre, Peter Brook at the International Centre for Theatre Research in Paris, Joseph Chaikin at The Open Theatre in New York, and Peter Schumann with his

Bread and Puppet Theatre in Vermont have all experimented with new forms of exalted communication. They have used combinations of mime, expressive sound, incantation, dance, symbolic gesture, music, sculptured puppets of heroic size, and masks or mask-like uses of the face to transcend language in their search for a new theatre of exaltation that might celebrate communal humanity in a society of alienation. These artists will be dealt with in more depth in later chapters along with other recent developments in theatre. Now we turn to comedy, to show how the theatre has provided compensation for the painful truth that is the substance of tragedy.

THE THEATRE OF LAUGHTER: FARCE AND HIGH COMEDY

5

High comedy teaches its characters how to maneuver in the intricate patterns of society. In Moliere's *The School for Wives* it is the husband who learns the hardest lessons. University of Masschusetts production.

Comedy is far more complex than tragedy and harder to define. In some ways it is closer to us than tragedy, for as tragedy imitates people striving toward their noblest and highest potential, comedy imitates them as they are, in all their clumsiness, pretentiousness, and folly. We see ourselves reflected in comic characters, we come to like them, and then paradoxically, we rejoice to see them beaten. We project ourselves onto the stage and yet at the same time remain detached, watching from a superior distance. Yet the word "comedy" is used for many different kinds of plays and for a wide range of attitudes they evoke: delight in the broad slapstick of farce, sophisticated enjoyment of high comedy, ambiguous satisfaction in stinging satire, and even enthralled absorption in romantic plays that stir no laughter at all. In some ages, all plays, whether serious or laugh-provoking, were simply called comedies. After all, the word "play" itself implies something that is done for sheer pleasure.

THE WAYS OF COMEDY

Laughter, that uproarious noise, that convulsive explosion of air and sound so like—and yet so different from—the barking of a dog, has never been fully explained. It brings sudden relaxation and deep pleasure. It seems involuntary and private; yet it most often occurs in social groups. It results when people suddenly recognize something left over, something that does not fit their usual expectations, something "funny." For incongruity is at the heart of comedy. Henri Bergson, in his essay *Laughter*, tells how we laugh at the conflict between living and the rules we try to impose on life. Whenever the mechanical becomes encrusted on the living, it is thrown off in laughter.

From very early times, festivals and holidays have been special occasions for breaking society's pattern and returning to a tradition of disorder, freedom, and license. A temporary ruler is crowned in mock pomp to preside over the revels, and at the end of the festival his throne is torn down in wild, destructive glee. According to one myth, the New Year holiday was a time for returning to an earlier age when a trickster god ruled the world, before the later, more serious gods invented hard work and strict rules. In Rome the Saturnalia in December was the reign of the early god Saturn and a time of release from all duties and expectations. Men dressed as women, and servants ordered their masters about. Another myth gave the New Year festival an even more ancient tie by recognizing an incongruity in the very nature of the creation, since the lunar calendar can be fitted into the solar calendar only if some four days—the holidays—are left over. Some mythologies held that creation gave form only to a finite island floating in the waters of chaos. During the new-year gap of four days, more of the surrounding primeval waters of chaos flowed into the circle of the year, renewing health and vitality. As people put on outlandish disguises to run,

Razullo.   *Cucurucu.*

The spirit of comic acting. The masked actors of the *commedia dell'arte* depended as much on their singing, dancing, acrobatics, and slapstick as on the words that they improvised around an agreed-upon story. Note the platform stage in the background. Engraving by Callot.

jump, race, dance, and act the holiday roles of revelry, they partook of that vital renewal. In singing satiric songs, in beating and cheating a scapegoat, in crowning and deposing a mock king, and in erecting and destroying festive buildings, the revelers found an outlet for the spirit of disorder that can never be eradicated from human nature.

For civilized people, comedy is the symbolic expression of that renewed vitality that can never be completely predicted or controlled. It expresses the vitality of spring, the bursting of winter's bonds, the rejection of rigid patterns of behavior, the breaking of limitations. Comedy attacks all rules and systems, but it is a controlled rebellion. It may point the way to improvement or, more often, it shows a way to accept the world as it is, a way to live at once with order and disorder, rule and rebellion. The audience stands, if not with the gods, at least with Puck in *A Midsummer Night's Dream*, and looks down with both amazement and delight at the foolishness of men and women.

> Shall we their fond pageant see?
> Lord, what fools these mortals be!

But Puck knows that in this human comedy all delusions of the night can be corrected in time.

Jack shall have Jill;
Naught shall go ill;
The man shall have his mare again, and all shall be well.

COMIC TRADITIONS OF THE PAST

Different periods have fostered particular kinds of comedy to suit their own needs. In ancient Greece, Aristophanes found a ready-made festival of spring fertility processions, with songs, dances, and competitions, installation of a ruler of the festival, ridicule and expulsion of intruders and obstructors, and a final ritual wedding and feast. Through this time-honored medium, his comic satires bitterly exposed the way Athens had allowed dictators of the war party to take over its democracy and had let irresponsible leaders of cults and fads corrupt its education, law courts, philosophy, and literature. The spring festival was a privileged time and free speech was treasured by Athenians, so even the war party could not censor the drama nor silence Aristophanes when he wrote some of the sharpest and most fantastic satires the world has ever known. In *The Knights* he

A sex strike leaves the men helpless in Aristophanes' *Lysistrata*. Phoenix Theatre, 1959, directed by Jean Gascon.

even lampooned the current dictator, Cleon, as an amateur sausage-peddlar selling baloney to the public. In *Lysistrata* one woman puts an end to the war by persuading the women on both sides to enforce a sex strike until their husbands make peace. *The Clouds* deals hilariously and caustically with intellectuals who have such lofty ideas they can dwell nowhere but in the clouds. Although Aristophanes' plays laugh at the struggles of simple people faced with difficult public problems, they also carry the assurance that simple people can do something about them.

After Athens was overrun by Alexander the Great and then by the Romans, the citizens were no longer free to take an interest in important public questions. The topical satire of Aristophanes gave way to the situation comedies and domestic farces of Menander, where the rebellion is not citizen against officialdom, but servants and sons against masters and fathers. This vigorous farcical form, perfected in Rome in the third century B.C. by Plautus and Terence, has been the model for popular entertainment comedy ever since, right down to the weekly television sit-coms of our own day.

Medieval Europe developed its own little farces, about clever lawyers caught in their own trickery, vice-ridden priests, domineering wives, and cheated husbands. But most significant is the way these robust tales intruded even into the great religious cycles. Like sculpture in the cathedrals, which included grotesque gargoyles and homely scenes of everyday life, the religious plays included both low and high characters and frequent bits of comedy. Medieval art and drama contributed greatly to the comic tradition, showing Shakespeare not only how to use comedy in serious plays but how to enrich both serious and comic plays with the grim, the grotesque, and the demonic.

The Renanissance saw three great achievements in comedy. The first was a popular comic theatre, the *commedia dell'arte,* in which masked servants like Harlequin and Pulcinella bamboozled rigid fathers, fanatic businessmen, jealous husbands, and pretentious scholars with broad slapstick, acrobatic acting, and outrageous disrespect for pomposity and authority. Working from scenarios of action rather than from plotted scripts, these Italian actors toured Europe for decades with their stock characters, their improvised plots, and an infinite array of well-rehearsed gags, called *lazzi,* which they adapted to whatever the current audience craved, much in the way of a vaudeville performer or a stand-up comedian. In this way they taught all of Europe, court and town, how to laugh at confusion. Their stock characters and visual gags became a rich source for generations of actors and playwrights, and their ability to relate directly to whatever situation or audience they encountered has inspired theatre directors to the present day.

The second comic achievement of the Renaissance was the romantic type of comedy most obvious in plays such as Shakespeare's *Much Ado About Nothing* or *As You Like It*. In such plays, idealized young ladies and knights, engaged in the loves and intrigues of an aristocratic court, are surrounded by a variety of col-

A print showing Harlequin shooting Pantalone with a water gun in a *commedia dell'arte* performance.

orful comic characters. The appreciation of comic characters as enjoyable and even lovable was a result of the new humanistic respect for individuality, explicitly taught at the beginning of the sixteenth century in Erasmus's *In Praise of Folly*. Without that attitude Shakespeare's humorous characters, from jesters, clowns, and bumbling rustics on up to the wise, playful, fat knight, Sir John Falstaff, would never have been conceived. To this day some overserious moralists cannot love them or indulge them in their foolishness. The third Renaissance achievement in comedy was a realistic satire made popular by Shakespeare's young friend Ben Jonson. In his *comedy of "humours,"* Jonson savagely attacked people's obsessions and took delight in exposing their greed and other vices as well as their gullibility and stupidity. In *Volpone* (1606), his greatest achievement, Volpone (the Fox), pretending to be on his deathbed, tricks a set of characters whose Italian names mean crow, raven, and vulture into giving him enormous gifts so that they will be heir to his fortune. There is no deed too outrageous for their greed, not even disowning their sons and prostituting their wives. In Jonson's plays, poetic justice finally prevails, for as each character lets his humour or obsession control his behavior, he constructs the very trap that will finally catch and punish him.

The latter part of the seventeenth century (the Restoration period in England) perfected what we now think of as high comedy, borrowing some of the best aspects of Renaissance comedy. England's Restoration playwrights borrowed the scathing, disillusioned view of reality from Jonson's comedy of humours and the charming, cultivated young lovers and the amiable fools from the romantic comedy, while Moliere in France borrowed the romping antics and stock characters of the commedia dell'arte as well. Before examining this highly developed social comedy, however, we must consider the basic, more universal type—farce.

FARCE, OR "LOW" COMEDY

What this world needs is a good laugh. After a wearing day, busy people yearn for a bit of horseplay to relax them, so they go to the movies or the theatre or they switch on the TV to watch the hectic problems of daily life reduced to mirth and nonsense. The Romans on their holidays went by the thousands to see a clown-

Corvino (the crow of Ben Jonson's *Volpone*) forcing his wife into adultery to satisfy his own greed. Organic Theatre Company, Chicago, directed by Stuart Gordon.

ish servant in a red wig and a wide-mouthed mask chased all over the enormous stage and beaten vigorously. Yet he would always be ready with a clever remark and a new scheme for getting the money or the girl. The commedia dell'arte clown, Harlequin, made his sword into a "slapstick" of two strips of wood, which gave a maximum of sound with a minimum of damage to the rump. For three centuries children and adults alike screamed with delight at Punch, a blithefully irresponsible puppet who turns on his nagging wife, Judy, on the whining cat, and finally on the devil himself, and gives them such a fast, noisy beating that it seems that the puppet heads will splinter.

Curiously, our loudest laughs are at someone else's pain. A good farce is exquisitely painful and excruciatingly funny. It turns the difficulties, restrictions, frustrations, and embarrassments of life into laughter. It relaxes the audience by first tying it into new knots of tension, then explodes the tension into guffaws and roars of delight.

The Elements of Farce

Farce is based on a threefold compact between the audience, the play, and the production. One term of that compact is the realism; the audience must recognize themselves in farce, whether the actor is Woody Allen, a circus clown in fantastic costume, or Mr. Magoo in a cartoon. The second element is the built-in irony of a false situation as the playwright carefully lets the audience know that it is all a mistake or a lie. He shows the putting on of the disguise, the concocting of the lie, or the beginning of the mistaken identity. In actuality, it is painful to see a husband deny his wife and upbraid her, but not in Plautus's *Menaechmi* or Shakespeare's version of the same play, *The Comedy of Errors*, because the audience knows it is not really the husband but his long-lost twin brother. Suicide is no laughing matter, but in the funniest scene in Alan Ayckbourn's *Absurd Person Singular* (1974), a woman doggedly sets about to kill herself. The audience knows that she has no very good reason for suicide and that she will not succeed, so it is hilariously funny to see her try while other characters in the play help her out, completely unaware of her intent.

The third element is the comic treatment created by the director, the designer, and the actor. The actor may contribute a squeaky or reedy nasal tone, a peculiar inflection or some odd movement pattern to reinforce the comic quality of a character. In broad farce, actors do not hesitate to use lisping, stuttering, limping, and tics. Woody Allen's hesitant nasality, Inspector Clouseau's clipped phony accent with its idiosyncratic mispronunciations, and Carol Burnett's facial contortions and ear-tingling squeals of excitement have created some of the most memorable farcical moments of recent film and television. A floppy hat, an old-fashioned plaid, or a garment too large or too short may give just the needed incongruity. Or notice the hilarity of an incongruous disguise in the 1890 farce, *Charley's Aunt*, where the young man, impersonating his own aunt, repeatedly forgets and shows his trousers or smokes a cigar, rousing screams of terror in the audience as he almost gets caught by the girls. Moments of undress or threats of exposure cause violent laughter because they come close to breaking our strong taboos. Bright-colored underclothes heighten the effect while preventing any actual exposure.

Even more important in the comic treatment are the intensities of the performance. Speed is the most obvious farcical intensity. Play anything fast enough and, as long as the audience can stay with it, it will be funny. Charlie Chaplin's Monsieur Verdoux counting money at superhuman speed can never be forgotten. Chase scenes, whether of couples running around restaurant tables in Thornton Wilder's *The Matchmaker* or of automobile thieves fleeing over curb and cliff in the silent movies, are high points of delight. Beatings, fights, struggles, pratfalls—all create enormous energy. To speed, farce usually adds the intensity of sound—startling noises, crashes, collisions, explosions. At the end of the first act of *The Matchmaker* two young men are jumping with delight because at last they can take a day off from the store. Thornton Wilder adds a whole battery of sounds as the tomato cans in the store below explode and cans and debris fly up through the trap door. Emotions in a farce are also exaggerated

Charley forgetting to pretend to be his own aunt. *Charley's Aunt*, Academy Festival Theatre, Lake Forest, Illinois. Directed by Christopher Hewett.

Farce with romantic charm—hiding, listening, deceiving. Wilder's *The Matchmaker*. Barter Theatre production, Abingdon, Virginia, 1977.

to the fullest intensity. In a serious play sorrow and pain are suppressed and indicated subtly as subtext, but not in farce. A farcical character in distress will cry, will bawl, will wail, will squall, till all audience empathy is released in uproarious laughter. And the audience will laugh even harder when the cause for the crying is untrue, as in Moliere's *The Imaginary Invalid*, when the daughter cries over her dead father, who, very much alive, is listening to the whole thing. If he also starts crying in sympathy, as some productions have him do, the audience lets out all stops. The various intensities—speed, energy, noise, physical action, and exaggerated expression of emotion—all illustrate a basic truth of low comedy. Characters must be convincing, yet played with such single-minded, demoniacal obsessiveness that the audience's empathy spills over into laughter.

Farce also makes use of many mechanical patterns: duplications, repetitions, sequences, reversals, delays, surprises, interruptions, and sudden breaks in pattern. Identical twins dressed alike, or two people who find themselves in the same predicament, can be a source of endless amusement as they move in unison, in opposition, or in sequence. Duplication of movement is so funny that in serious plays directors take great care to see that two actors do not by chance sit, turn, or step in unison. Duplication with variety depends on incongruity, as when a short and a tall person are made to look or act alike. Sometimes the sequence of repetition is continued with several examples. To see a dozen Keystone Cops tumble out of a car too small to hold them and scramble after a suspect, all falling over the same obstacles, rolling downhill and piling up in a ditch, was one of the delights of movie-going in the "Golden Age" of film comedy. To see a neurotic couple bumble their marital discord through a sequence of friends', ex-spouses', and parents' bedrooms, oblivious to the shambles they leave behind at every turn, is one of the delights of Alan Ayckbourn's technique in *Bedroom Farce* (1975).

The Popularity of Farce

In spite of its enemies, farce has been the most popular of all theatre forms for more than two thousand years. Literary critics have attacked it as trivial and vulgar, and highbrows of all periods have despised it simply because it *is* funny, a turning away from important things. Being dead serious is supposed to be more profound. Yet year after year, night after night, the broad laugh has been as indispensable a part of the lives of millions of people as their food and sleep. On the movie screen, Peter Sellers' Pink Panther can strike again and again, with ingenious variations on a few ludicrous situations, with dire catastrophe and hilarious recovery, and an untiring public welcomes even the posthumous films created from outtakes of his earlier movies. On the television screen Monty Python and the endless variations of "Laugh-In" or "Saturday Night Live" have survived for years on their special variety of imaginative foolishness.

There are at least three reasons why farce continues across the centuries to delight its audience. In the first place, it is a release of pent-up dormant life, like the arrival of spring. The two boys in *The Matchmaker* break away from the store in Yonkers. They go downtown to the big city; they kiss some girls, take them out to a restaurant, and almost get arrested. Their crabby boss himself gets into unexpected adventure and brings home a wife and a much more tolerant disposition. It is as important to thaw out his tyranny and stinginess as it is to thaw the frozen ground before new things can grow.

A second source of pleasure in farce is the reassurance it brings—the reassurance all great clowns have brought—that a person can take it. The clown takes his beating and survives; by his wisecrack and his comeback he proves his spiritual superiority to his fate. The clown has always been the butt, the victim, the fall guy, the little fellow that something always happens to. He is all of us, unlucky, put upon, mistreated. But he never admits defeat. He can always show his indifference to pain, and sometimes, just sometimes, he has a chance to snatch his own unexpected victory.

It is that superb aplomb in the midst of disaster that makes the best moments of the great clowns so memorable. At one moment in the film *A Night at the Opera*, the Marx brothers are frantically fleeing along the galleries high up in the backstage rigging in the opera house. The next moment they are serenely sailing through the air on the tie ropes as the scenery flies up and down around the performers. Who can forget the quiet assertion of Charlie Chaplin in an early short film, *A Night Out,* when as he is being dragged away by the collar, he picks a daisy and smells it? It is very painful to keep a bit of individuality in a regimented world, but the clown does it. We also may remember Chaplin's unquestioning absorption in his job on a swaying ladder as he cleans the street sign each time the ladder brings him by. In *The Kid* he is a proud society man refusing to bow down to poverty and rags, twirling his cane, taking off his fingerless gloves with elegance, reaching for his cigarette case (a sardine can), and carefully tapping his choice of the butts he has picked up. In the midst of hostile surroundings Chaplin blithely follows the life and logic of his own mind in complete disregard of his enemies. While he sweeps a pawnshop, a rope on the floor suddenly becomes in his mind a circus tightrope, and he an expert tightrope performer beloved and applauded by the crowd. While fleeing through an enormous house, he suddenly stops before a vast birthday cake to play pool and golf with bits of the frosting, making every shot count. In farce, the world may be reeling and humanity hostile, but the clowns possess what has been called the "incalculable strength of the weak."

Farce delights in the reverse of the noble virtues. Instead of the heroic defiance and courage we find in romantic heroes, instead of the ability to overcome any obstacle, the comic hero is totally inept in practical matters. Farce shows the youth leaving home to go out and kill the dragon and rescue the enchanted maiden but running back into the house before the dragon quite gets him. Farce emphasizes the realistic details that the truly romantic story omits. As the dragon charges with breath of flame, your sword sticks in the scabbard. As you mount the stairs to the princess's tower, you bump your head on a beam. As you slowly move in to kiss her, you are interrupted by a sneeze. In true romance, your clothes always fit. You never have to worry about money or weather or the law. But in farce your friend with the money is late, the rain shrinks your clothes, and the policeman puts you in handcuffs. No one believes you or understands you, least of all when you speak the plain truth. Romance can soar with poetry into celestial clarity, but farce has to stumble along on the clumsiness of prose. Yet with unconscious ingenuity the hero of farce wins in the end. In Woody Allen's film *Love and Death* (1975), in part a parody of Tolstoy's *War and Peace,* the simple little man, trying to live up to the part of a military hero, is repeatedly put down but never conquered. Even when he is dead, his ghost dances off through the trees to some clowns' paradise.

In the outrageous spoofs of Mel Brooks, farce moves over into parody. His audiences laugh not only at the antics of the characters but at the irreverent treatment of noble and serious subjects—at race relations and epic Westerns in his 1972 classic, *Blazing Saddles,* or at our serious history lessons in *History of the World, Part II* (1981), where everyone from a Roman emperor to a Renaissance pope to Adolf Hitler is reduced to an incompetent, maniacal fool.

Besides giving us strength to free the spirit and to hold the chin up, farce has a third function. It makes an important philosophical synthesis. It is a device for accepting the basic incongruity of everyday living, for spanning the ideal and the real without denying either. Farce accepts the discrepancy between the finite and the infinite; it affirms the infinite as it laughs at us for being bogged down in the finite. In particular, it accepts both the pattern of conformity and the impulse to break the pattern. Ultimately, farce does not demand revolutionary change. Students who revel in the spring at the beaches of Fort Lauderdale and Malibu or who let down their hair at a Friday night bash in a downtown bar have no intention of denying the disciplined regimen of classes, papers, and exams. Similarly, farce has no wish to abolish the rules, the policemen, the parents, the husbands, the wives, the jobs—the conformity that gives structure to our daily lives. But it does expect to bend the rules, to get around the officer, to vary the conformity. It reaffirms order in the universe as a whole, but it suggests that on the lower levels there may be considerable incongruity. In the very successful farcical movie *M*A*S*H* (1970), and in the long-running television serial based on it, the frantic, overworked doctors in a field hospital are completely conscientious. Not for a second would they neglect their constantly arriving, wounded patients. But when a brash young woman administrator arrives, determined to enforce strict rules, they must undermine her authority. After they hide a microphone under her bed and broadcast the sounds of her lovemaking over the whole camp, they are allowed to leave the camp for a brief rest, and they also get permission to bend the rules and do their work in their own way. It is not surprising that many famous comic figures have come in contrasting pairs—Don Quixote and Sancho Panza, the clever slave and the stupid slave of Roman comedy, Pierrot and Harlequin, Mutt and Jeff, George Burns and Gracie Allen, Laurel and Hardy. These are symbols not only of the affinity of different social classes but also of the companionship of incongruous temperaments.

In the world of farce, society itself is a conglomeration of selfish individuals, clumsy institutions, and foolish customs. In youth we are hemmed in by parents and policemen, but half the time they are busy or stupid, and we can get around them. When we grow up, our work, our families, and the causes we are committed to would absorb every last minute of our lives if we let them. But we can escape into the relaxation of farcical laughter, for without laughter human beings would long ago have torn themselves and their neighbors apart.

HIGH COMEDY

Whereas the low comedy of farce is one of defiance, relaxation, and survival, the high comedy of wit and manners is a comedy of correction, a civilizing force for humanity. Truly civilized society exists, of course, only where women freely participate as equals of men, adding warmth to intellectual discussion and permitting both men and women the impersonal appreciation of the opposite sex. Likewise high comedy, the most civilized of comic forms, did not develop until women became important as characters, until Moliere and Shakespeare brought them in to confront, to outwit, and to stand up to men, with pride and assurance. Ever since William Congreve's women, in the 1690s, set a classic precedent in laying down the law to their men, playwrights have put a proud, independent woman at the center of nearly every comedy.

The civil world of high comedy creates a vision of fashionable and sophisticated people matching wits and exploring human relations. In its drawing rooms, corporate offices, and political cloakrooms, business deals are made, political intrigues are sketched, plots foiled, secret scandals revealed, and marriages and affairs arranged through the clever conversations and wily maneuvers of urbane, charming people who enjoy the social games to the fullest. In its dialogue, unlike the dull and disconnected trivia of most real-life conversation, every line sparkles as it hits the mark precisely in a constant interplay of retort and repartee. In its plots, experienced adults pick their way skillfully and confidently among the pitfalls of a complex social world, maintaining their individuality while outwardly conforming to the expectations of the group.

One of the greatest ambitions for many people—often the reason they work so hard for money or fame—is to be accepted in society, to "arrive," to know the language and manners of the in-group. After adolescents have freed themselves from their parents (the subject of countless farces) and have established at least a minimum of financial and professional independence, they are ready to find their role in the gatherings of the social group. There they will hear both casual gossip and public comment on everything from current fashion and human behavior to the latest trends in institutions and ideas. Much high comedy is concerned with the social education of both old and young, through their own and others' mistakes, learning even to laugh at themselves. It is no wonder that several high comedies have been called "schools"—*The School for Husbands, The School for Wives, The School for Scandal.*

To be fully accepted into the social group, one must first be attractive to the group, and in society, a good part of that attractiveness comes from one's manners, behaving in the manner of the group. Everyone who has tried to establish a place among new acquaintances has experienced this delicate process of orientation, of getting to know the fashions, becoming fluent in the vocabulary, discovering the right gathering places, the acceptable work routines and recreation, whether on a new job, in a new community, or at a new school. But every college student has also amusedly and sometimes painfully watched the green freshman who never sees beyond this superficial level, who has to flaunt the latest fashion, the "in" jargon, the right places to be seen, and whatever behavior is expected of Jane or Joe College, sacrificing independence to the need for acceptance. Every high comedy has its share of fops and faddish fools who think themselves in fashion when they merely reflect the surface manners of the tyrant

Cecily and Gwendolyn comparing diaries in New York's Circle in the Square production of Wilde's *The Importance of Being Earnest*, with Kathleen Widdoes and Patricia Conolly. Directed by Stephen Porter.

group. English high comedy of the seventeenth and eighteenth centuries delighted in labeling such characters with appropriately laughable names: Sir Novelty Fashion, Lady Would-Be, Sir Fopling Flutter, and Mrs. Betty Modish.

But the real test of success in society comes at the next level, where one balances the attractive and good manners with independence, with one's own individuality, requiring a high skill in the social game. The mannered fops of high comedy often form only a background to the true wits who suffer the fools gracefully, who know that society will always have its fools. They skillfully maintain their distance with the best of manners, without bitterness or peevishness, knowing that, at worst, the fools will only expose their own folly and, at best, through good example, they may improve.

To keep one's independence in the game may require, at times, a disguise, a protective mask that disarms hostility with a smile. When Cecily and Gwendolyn in Oscar Wilde's *The Importance of Being Earnest* think that they are engaged to the same man, they slug it out verbally with more devastating blows than any prizefighter's, but they never lose the smile that keeps communication open or the elaborate phrase that just keeps the attack from becoming personal. Cecily concludes one of their most caustic rounds with a cool invitation to her guest: "May I offer you some tea, Miss Fairfax?"

But the protective disguise is the negative side of high comedy. High comedy also offers positive joys for its characters to experience and its audiences to share. One of these is to tease the fools, to draw them out, to help them expose their follies and, just perhaps, correct them. George Bernard Shaw delights in this method in the famous "Don Juan in Hell" section of his *Man and Superman* (1903). Doña Ana, an aristocratic lady, is outraged after her death to find herself, a faithful daughter of the church, in hell. "But I have sincerely repented," she insists; "I have confessed . . . I loved confession." But Don Juan assures her that she is indeed in hell. "Oh!" Doña Ana exclaims indignantly, "and I might have been so much wickeder! All my good deeds wasted! It is unjust." George Meredith believed that by such exposure, comedy corrects the faults of humanity, through gentle laughter, without the "pain of satiric heat" or the "bitter craving to strike heavy blows." In *An Essay on Comedy*, he wrote of this Comic Spirit as a "sunlight of the mind."

A second joy in high comedy is to laugh at oneself, a very hard thing to do, but satisfying when one manages it. Such acceptance requires the self-knowledge of maturity, the confidence of being an individual able to play one's role. When Beatrice and Benedick in Shakespeare's *Much Ado About Nothing* are about to destroy a fragile relationship because they are so determined to be witty, their friends bring out sonnets each has written declaring their mutual love. Benedick, caught in the tangle of his own wit, confesses, "A miracle! here's our own hands against our hearts. Come, I will have thee." Yet he cannot resist one last crack: "but, by this light, I take thee for pity."

Still another delight of comedy depends on disillusionment, a full awareness of human limitations. As Louis Kronenberger says in *The Thread of Laughter*,

> Comedy is always jarring us with the evidence that we are no better than other people, and always comforting us with the knowledge that other people are no better than we. It makes us more critical but it leaves us more tolerant.

Thus, high comedy brings a triumph of balance, spanning the inner and the outer, the self and the other, independence and interaction, self-respect and friendship or love.

High Comedy in the Seventeenth Century

Though there were glimpses of it in both ancient and Elizabethan drama, high comedy was the achievement of the seventeenth century, the first great age to produce a leisure class with the inclination to devote itself to human relations and to the forms and manners that make a society possible. For more than a century, the increasing complexity of the perceived world, with several religions in conflict, many suns in the sky, and new continents across the seas, had fostered a fanaticism in religion, ideologies, national politics, and economics which had caused devastating wars to ravage England, Germany, and France. At the same time, a century of humanistic education, with its emphasis on the social graces of good manners, eloquence, and wit had nurtured an educated class whose members were weary of fanaticism and ready for detached sophistication, ready to salvage from an era of shattering disillusion a sane stability through tolerance and a comic detachment towards life.

It is no accident that modern science and the new comedy were both born in this era, since both require such detachment, a separation of man as objective observer from man as a subjective holder of values, beliefs, and feelings. In Paris and London, cultivated men and women gathered in the salons, at the royal court, at the coffeehouses of the town, and in the walkways of the parks, and there they set about exploring urbane, subtle, complex, and civilized patterns of human behavior. Out of this new and self-conscious sense of what it was to be a lady or gentleman grew this new kind of comedy.

The Achievement of Moliere

The foremost comic writer of France in this era was Moliere (pseudonym of Jean-Baptiste Poquelin). After training in the popular touring companies of the provinces, he came to the Parisian court in 1658 and became the favorite of Louis

Farce, formality, and fantasy—Moliere's *The Imaginary Invalid.* Eastern Illinois University production, directed by Gerald Sullivan.

XIV. Like Ben Jonson, whose play *Volpone* was referred to earlier in this chapter, Moliere often chose characters with monstrous obsessions, but whereas Jonson cynically has his characters finally destroyed by the fruits of their obsessions, Moliere is more gentle and urbane. He always balances his obsessed fanatics with good-natured though irresponsible young people and one or two characters of mature reason and benevolence, who inject rationality and compassion and who often take impish pleasure in shaking some sense into the fools.

In his last play, *The Imaginary Invalid* (1673), a healthy man is convinced that all that's keeping him alive is the constant medication from his doctor and his druggist, who stuff him with enough pills and purge him with enough enemas to kill a man of lesser constitution. Driven by his obsession, he determines to marry his daughter off to a quack doctor, so as to get free medical advice. Though already in love, she cannot bring herself to go against her father's wishes. The plot is complicated by a fortune-seeking wife who can't wait for him to die so that she can collect on his will. Fortunately, a sensible brother and a wise and witty housekeeper contrive an elaborate indulgence of his obsession that finally exposes all the parasites, and they arrange a romping mock ceremony to initiate the invalid as a doctor, so that he can prescribe for himself. Their ironic teasing of the fool wins freedom for both him and the young couple by freeing him from his foolish dependence on doctors. In other plays, Moliere uses similar witty but compassionate methods to humanize a whole range of misers, affected ladies, would-be gentlemen, and chauvinistic husbands. Unlike the Roman playwright Plautus, from whom he drew many of his plots, Moliere always has at the center of his plays women of wit and sense to provide variety, complexity, and a light touch of teasing that moves the play toward the civility of high comedy.

Seven years earlier, Moliere briefly moved all the way into high comedy in *The Misanthrope*, not bothering to include the low-comedy scenes on which his other plays depend for so much of their fun. Here an adult couple, free from all restrictions, explore their social relationships with other free adults. Celimene keeps herself at the center of a circle of adoring beaux through caustic wit and malicious character sketches of all her friends. With triumphant, smiling wit, she outdoes her rival in double-edged attack. The overly frank Alceste, the misanthrope of the play, falls in love with her, but objects violently to her befriending people with whom she finds so much fault and to her obvious enjoyment of the social group. He despises flattery and even politeness, but fails to recognize that his own obsession with sincerity is a fault. So when Celimene is finally trapped in her own hypocritical wit, he cannot understand why she, a girl of twenty, refuses to abandon society and go off to a deserted island with him. They separate forever, unable to achieve a workable relationship.

In a comedy of Moliere, the audience senses, and the characters sometimes do also, that each person must have absolute trust and respect for the other as an independent being or there can be no real human relations, only lies and deception. A century before Jefferson, Moliere was defining the basic equality of all human beings and the independence of the individual. His plays constitute a social declaration of independence, though his deep skepticism made him realize that full respect for independence is rarely achieved.

The Golden Age of High Comedy

Moliere was a pioneer in the intricate maneuvers of high comedy, but a full achievement of high comedy in the uniting of two proud and independent individuals remained for a few aristocratic playwrights and a small audience of London sophisticates in the years following the restoration of the English monarchy in 1660. In their plays, the comic crudeness of unsophisticated characters and the comic wiliness of the fops and giddy women are mere foils for the maturity of one central couple, who learn to play the roles of free, well-adjusted adults, discarding their masks of hostility and caution for the joys of love and partnership.

The characters in Restoration comedy begin where most of Moliere's couples end, free from family restraints. Free as well from serious political and economic affairs, they are ready to devote their wit and leisure to the game of human relations. That game includes gossip, intrigue, flirtation, discussion of social behavior, and a good deal of sexual promiscuity. Many people have objected to the downright wickedness of the characters, but their defenders point out that the best Restoration plays take sex for granted as an easy relationship and concern themselves with the more difficult relations that involve pride and self-respect.

The first fully developed hero of Restoration comedy, Dorimant in Sir George Etherege's *The Man of Mode* (1676), samples casual sexual relations, insisting on freedom and variety only because he is determined eventually to find someone who is not so casual. One mistress tries to hold him by his vows of love, but he casts her off with indignant irony: "Constancy, at my years! . . . Youth has a long journey to go, madam: should I have set up my rest at the first inn I lodged at I should never have arrived at the happiness I now enjoy." Dorimant's female counterpart is to be found in many Restoration comedies but is perhaps expressed best in Millamant, William Congreve's heroine in *The Way of the World* (1700): "Why, one makes lovers as fast as one pleases, and they live as long as one pleases, and they die as soon as one pleases: and then, if one pleases, one makes more." Such women—rich, independent, proud, sophisticated, but unspoiled by the shallowness around them—were quite capable of taming their men, even while they reveled in the joy of the game.

Love between such characters is bound to be difficult, and many of the best comic scenes between lovers, from Shakespeare's Katherine and Petruchio and Beatrice and Benedick to the couples in such modern musicals as *The King and I* and *My Fair Lady*, are built on antagonism that is both exasperating and enjoyable. The antagonism has a most delicious resolution for Millamant. When she finally agrees to marry Mirabell, in their famous proviso scene that substitutes for a romantic proposal, she sets up a curious but agreeable marital independence: "Let us never visit together, not go to a play together; but let us be very strange and well-bred. Let us be as strange as if we had been married a great while, and as well-bred as if we were not married at all."

High Comedy in *The School for Scandal*

The most famous stage duelists in love are Sir Peter and Lady Teazle in Richard Brinsley Sheridan's *The School for Scandal* (1777), created more than a century after the Restoration. Lady Teazle is an attractive young woman from the country newly married to Sir Peter, a gruff old London gentleman: the ingredients for one of the most popular plot complications of high comedy. As is common in old husband/young wife plots, the old man cautiously chose a woman from the country, expecting naive simplicity and gratitude. But Sir Peter's caution was wasted:

> 'Tis now six months since Lady Teazle made me the happiest of men—and I have been the miserablest dog ever since that ever committed wedlock! . . . Now she plays her part in all the extravagant fopperies and fashions of the town as if she had never seen a bush or grassplat.

Likewise, the young wife chose the old husband to escape the boredom of country living, where her "daily occupation [was] to inspect the dairy, superintend the poultry, make extracts from the family receipt-book, and comb my aunt Deborah's lap dog." Her situation, Lady Teazle frankly tells Sir Peter, was "a very disagreeable one, or I should never have married *you*." Yet for all his anger, Sir Peter will remain a comic victim of his teasing wife: "Though I can't make her love me, there is a great satisfaction in quarreling with her; and I think she never appears to such advantage as when she's doing everything in her power to plague me."

What Lady Teazle does to plague Sir Peter is try to be like the other fashionable ladies of the town, by dressing fancy, by idling away her time with her scandalmongering friends, and, most important, by having a flirtation with another man, which brings us to the second plot of the play. Two young brothers, Charles and Joseph Surface, are both attracted to Sir Peter's young ward, Maria. Sir Peter steers her away from Charles, a good-hearted rogue, for he knows him to be a dissipated spendthrift and even fears that Charles may be after his own wife. The elder brother, Joseph, is really in love only with Maria's fortune, but has persuaded Sir Peter that he is a serious young man of high moral character, just the person for the beautiful young heiress. Maria cannot abide Joseph's hypocritical moralizing, however, so Joseph warms up to Lady Teazle to get her support. When Lady Teazle mistakes Joseph's intentions, thinking herself the object of his interest, she gets the fashionable flirtation she wanted, and he gets entangled in his lust for her even more than in his fortune hunting.

Charles Surface selling off the family portraits to his own disguised uncle. Sheridan's *The School for Scandal*, Stratford Festival of Canada, 1970, directed by Michael Langham.

"I begin to wish I had never made such a point of gaining so *very good* a character," Joseph confesses in an aside, "for it has led me into so many cursed rogueries that I doubt I shall be exposed at last."

Joseph and Charles are involved in yet one more plot. Both hope to inherit the fortune of their uncle and Sir Peter's close friend, Sir Oliver Surface, who has just returned to London after living many years in the East Indies. Sir Oliver, not trusting Sir Peter's evaluation of his nephews, decides to put them to the test himself. Learning that Charles is in desperate need of funds, he visits Charles at the family home disguised as a money-lender. There he finds Charles partying with some drunken friends in the barren rooms, stripped of all their treasures by Charles's profligacy. All that remain are the portraits of the family ancestors. Charles promptly starts to sell these off to his disguised and horrified uncle, selling "judges and generals by the foot—and maiden aunts as cheap as broken china." But the old man is given to his own whims, and Charles does one thing to win his heart. He refuses to sell one portrait, that of Uncle Oliver in his youth. "The rogue's my nephew after all!" Sir Oliver exclaims. "I forgive him everything! . . . A dear extravagant rogue!" As a second test, Sir Oliver pretends to be a poor cousin in desperate financial straits. From Joseph he gets noble sentiments and a brush-off, but no cash, while Charles generously gives some of his new wealth from the sale of the portraits—before it all goes to pay his debts.

Sheridan intricately weaves these several plots into a series of skirmishes of wit and ironic delight. We watch Sir Peter drive his wife toward infidelity by trying to hold on to her too tightly. We watch Lady Teazle getting caught in her own attempts to be fashionable. We see Charles almost destroy his chance for the inheritance and then unknowingly recover it by a whim. We see Joseph leaping from one hypocritical stance to another, angering his uncle when he is trying to appear most moral. We see Sir Oliver using his disguises to find out the truth and finding more truth than he bargained for, so that finally he ignores what he doesn't want to see and makes his judgment on a personal whim—"He wouldn't sell my picture!"

At last the whole entanglement comes to a head in one of the most famous scenes of comic irony in all of theatre: the screen scene. Lady Teazle has innocently gone to Joseph's apartment to "see his library," but finds that his designs on her are not so innocent. Too late! Sir Peter arrives. She quickly hides behind a screen and overhears Sir Peter tell Joseph about a love letter to her from Charles (a forged letter that Joseph had himself arranged) but that he loves her so much he will willingly give her her independence. Just then Charles arrives, and now it is Sir Peter's turn to hide. He heads for the screen, but is intercepted by Joseph who confesses that he has a little French milliner hidden there already. Sir Peter, delighted to find his moral friend has a human weakness, hides in a closet instead.

Now two characters are hidden on the stage, both from each other and from Charles. The audience in delight watches Joseph trying to keep both his guests and his intentions concealed, while Charles, with his usual bluntness, clears his own reputation and very nearly incriminates Joseph to the hidden listeners. Before the scene ends, Joseph is forced to bring Sir Peter into the open, lest he overhear too much, and Charles, hearing about the French milliner behind the screen, completes the joke on his moralizing brother and pulls the screen down. There stands Lady Teazle—confronted by an amazed Charles, a horrified Sir Peter, and a mortified Joseph.

In the next act, the scandalmongers of the town descend in full force on Sir Peter, teasing him unmercifully till he drives them from his home in a rage. But when his friend Sir Oliver laughs at him as well, Sir Peter begins to laugh at his own predicament, if grimly. He forgives Lady Teazle for her indiscretion, but with a newly found respect for her independent nature, and she, having learned her lesson well, resigns from the school for scandal and returns the diploma they had given her. The good characters, thus, have learned how to maneuver in this social world, so as not to be victims of their own foolish desires and biases, nor victims of the world's hypocrisies and lies. At first trapped in the scandal, they are finally schooled by the scandal to a happier and more civil way of life.

High Comedy in the Modern Theatre

After Sheridan, English high comedy was largely superseded by sentimental comedy. With the pragmatism of nineteenth-century scientific and industrial growth and the rise of the middle class, it seemed destined to disappear altogether. In the 1890s, Oscar Wilde, reacting against pragmatism and scientific determinism, briefly popularized a high comedy which explored characters trying to live life as though it were art. The crowning achievement of his "art for art's sake" drama is *The Importance of Being Earnest* (1895). A young country gentleman, Jack Worthing, escapes his duties and the responsibilities of raising a young ward by inventing a callow younger brother, named Earnest, whose irresponsible escapades regularly demand his attention in town. In London, Jack becomes Earnest and even courts a young heiress under the assumed character and name of the invented brother. His best friend in town, then, decides to go down to the country as the invented Earnest, to court Jack's attractive young ward. For the characters in Wilde's play, lying becomes an art. Not only do the young men invent fictional persons for their own convenience, the young women fall in love with the invented persons because their names are Earnest, and they invent elaborate love relationships with them which they record faithfully in their diaries and in the love letters they write to themselves. But the topsy-turvy world that these characters create out of the fictional presentations of themselves turns out to be more true than the reality they so delightfully color over. In a scene that rivals the most improbable discovery scenes of melodrama, Jack learns that he is the long-lost cousin of the girl he wants to marry, that the best friend who has shared his escapades is really his younger brother, and, most ironically, that his name actually is Earnest. He confesses to his intended: "It is a terrible thing for a man to find out suddenly that all his life he has been speaking nothing but the truth. Can you forgive me?"

But Wilde's was an eccentric view of a changing world and had no important followers. Much more in tune with the needs of a pragmatic and industrial society was George Bernard Shaw's special blending of high comedy with the social-problem play. He widened its scope beyond the personal relationships of lovers, parents, and friends, to show characters involved in social, political, and philosophical problems. In play after play his idealistic and romantic characters learn good manners and independence, but more important, they learn how to be practical and, above all, useful. Even a secondary character like Violet, in *Man and Superman*, won't let her young man defy her wealthy father by acknowledging her as his wife: "We can't afford it," she says. "You can be as romantic as you please about love, Hector, but you mustn t be romantic about money."

Eliza Doolittle, the curbstone flower girl of *Pygmalion,* acquires good speech and good manners as a way out of a degrading life of poverty and premature old age. Then she learns one thing more: independence—independence from both the tyranny of poverty and the tyranny of class. She acquires a skill that makes her useful, and with the independence that skill provides, she can take her place as part of Shaw's creative life force. (For a detailed treatment of *Pygmalion,* see Chapter 13.) Shaw's *Major Barbara* starts as a drawing-room comedy of family relationships, but moves out of the drawing room to a Salvation Army shelter to show Barbara's work in offering food and salvation to the poor, then to her father's factory as she decides that it is more useful to offer jobs to the poor and a life purpose to the workers who now are no longer poor. In his witty discussion of poverty, wealth, power, and religion, Shaw anticipated by half a century the social legislation that would try to use power and money to abolish poverty and free individuals to find a higher spiritual life.

Though the techniques of social maneuvering and witty repartee have not altogether disappeared from modern comedy, they appear more often as adjuncts to popular situation comedies that laugh at pretentious and naive people trying to live by the latest fads and trying to lead other people to believe that they are "with it." Each generation produces its share of such folly, whether it's the middle-class small-towners of Kaufmann and Hart's *The Man Who Came to Dinner* (1939), trying to share the "good life," when a famous guest breaks his leg on their doorstep and is stranded with them for several weeks, or whether it is a whole array of Neil Simon's middle-class incompetents trying to fantasize themselves out of the tedium of urban and suburban normality in plays like *Plaza Suite, The Last of the Red Hot Lovers,* and *Barefoot in the Park.* Such situation comedies tend to laugh at the social maneuverings as resulting from neurotic insecurity (which will finally be resolved by returning to the stability of conventional morality) rather than as a process of rising to the creative independence that characterized high comedy at its best. In *Chapter Two* (1979), Simon moves closer to true high comedy. A marriage between a widower and a divorcee is threatened when each tries to make the partner into his and her image of the perfect marriage. Even after marriage, their two apartments appear side by side on stage as visual reminders of their separateness. At last they learn to respect each other's independence and plan to get a new apartment free from memories of the past, where they can begin what one critic has referred to as their "chapter three."

THE DEVELOPMENT OF TRAGICOMEDY

Comedy has taken one other major direction in twentieth-century theatre: the devastating form of *tragicomedy.* Its characters, who display the comic spirit of survival, are nevertheless made to suffer and are often destroyed with all the horror of tragedy. Both medieval cycle drama and Elizabethan tragedy had included comic elements, and Renaissance playwrights often mixed comic and tragic plots in the same play, but the term tragicomedy has taken on new meanings since its Renaissance beginnings.

In *The Thread of Laughter,* Louis Kronenberger points out that "comedy is not just a happy as opposed to an unhappy ending, but a way of surveying life so that happy endings must prevail." Traditional comedy always reassures us that everything will turn out all right in the end, that the misunderstandings will be cleared up, the couples reunited, and the parents reconciled to their children, for comedy traditionally ends with all the central characters on stage to celebrate the resolved conflict and the impending wedding of the embattled couples. Tragicomedy gives no such reassurance, though its characters often act as if it does. They seem to view life as a comedy, though they are, in fact, engaged in tragedy. At the same time, tragicomedy lacks tragedy's sense of exaltation. For all its horror, tragedy retains a kind of optimism in the perception and reconciliation of the tragic hero and in the restoration of order. Not so tragicomedy. Its heroes are much more the victims of wanton destruction or stupidity and are often destroyed without understanding why. Instead of restoring order at the end, tragicomedy often shocks us with a kind of numbing desolation. The playwrights of this new genre will be treated in detail in Chapters 7 through 10, but a few examples here will illustrate the power and range of this new use of comedy.

The Russian playwright Anton Chekhov created such characters out of the dying aristocracy of tsarist Russia around the turn of the century. *The Three Sisters* (1901) would seem to be high comedy. Three fashionable daughters of a famous general are stuck in a rural village, surrounded by pretentious schoolmasters, stuffy officials, and an array of snobbish, temperamental, and fawning officers of the regiment, and a hopelessly unfashionable local girl who has eyes for their scholarly brother. The young ladies are at the center of this social circle, though their dream is to return to Moscow, where really cultivated people will occupy them with sparkling conversation and sophisticated ideas. But the ladies seem to assume that the dream will occur on its own, that all they need do is bide their time until glorious opportunity saves them from their stifling provincialism. By the end of Act IV, however, not only have they not returned to Moscow, the regiment has left them stranded. They have been squeezed out of their fashionable drawing room by the local girl who is now married to their brother and is raising a set of very unfashionable children. All their hopes for a better life have gradually been drained away. Their ending is perhaps more comically pathetic than tragic (Chekhov did call his plays comedies), but their lonely uselessness captured the spirit of a whole class of their Russian contemporaries, living on the dreams of past glory and failing to find a way back to a world that no longer existed or a way to take hold of their own futures.

Even more devastating is the tragi-comic vision of Sean O'Casey in his plays of the Dublin slums during the Irish wars for independence from 1916 to 1923. Here would seem to be the opportunity for heroic patriotism, but O'Casey created clowns instead, low comedy characters who feed their egos by puffing themselves up into tin-horn soldiers and revolutionaries, cynical critics who scorn the patriotic fools, and self-indulgent hangers-on who get their laughs, their glory, or their pint of stout by feeding on the egos of others, so long as they don't have to work or pay for it. The second of these plays, *Juno and the Paycock* (1926), is a domestic farce, with Captain Boyle, an irresponsible, out-of-work husband who has terrible pains in his legs whenever honest work threatens, his nagging wife, Juno, and his parasite companion, Joxer. A windfall inheritance suddenly has the whole family putting on airs of respectability, buying on credit, and, most shockingly, throwing a celebration party during the funeral of a neighbor boy who was shot in a raid on a revolutionary hideout.

But the inheritance disappears in lawyers' fees, the furniture is repossessed, the daughter, now pregnant, is abandoned by the young lawyer who mismanaged the inheritance, and, finally, their son is shot by the revolutionists as an informer. Though the characters act as if they live in a world where happy end-

The ghost of a slain comrade has come to haunt Juno's and Captain Boyle's son in the Guthrie Theatre production of O'Casey's *Juno and the Paycock*, 1973. Directed and designed by Tomas MacAnna.

ings must prevail, the terror of the revolution forms a constant background to their action until it finally extends its devastating reach to them. In a touching lament for her slain son, Juno cries in anguish: "These things have nothin' to do with the Will o' God. Ah, what can God do agen the stupidity o' men!" But the play ends with Captain Boyle and Joxer in an outrageous and pathetic bit of drunken, philosophical farce, exclaiming, "th' whole worl's . . . in a terr . . . ible state o' chassis!"

Among the bitterest mixtures of the comic and serious is The Theatre Workshop's show, *Oh, What a Lovely War!* (1957), under the direction of the English director Joan Littlewood. Inspired by their research into World War I, the group improvised scenes of high comedy about Europe's political and social leaders in the salons and industrial cartels of Paris, Berlin, and London, planning a glorious war, and scenes of low comedy about the common people dancing and singing their boys off to heroic patriotism. By contrast, scenes on the battlefields showed the emotional side of the war, the foot soldiers trapped in the lonely trenches, while slide projections and flashing news lights above the stage announced the facts and figures of the battle casualties recorded in the newspapers and official war records of the time, and revealed the magnitude and horror of the gruesome slaughter that this comedy had created. A musical review structure combined with a "living newspaper" background created a devastating anti-war play for our time.

The serious drama of the twentieth century has found some of its most striking expression, not in tragedy or comedy, but in plays that mix the comic and tragic, showing the seeds of tragic waste in the comic exposure of human folly. Nevertheless, comedy in its more traditional forms remains the favorite in the theatre. Farce is the staple of what the English director Peter Brook admiringly calls the "Rough Theatre," the truly popular theatre, while the spirited independence, zest, and wit of high comedy ensure that form's lasting appeal to audiences who know "the way of the world."

THE THEATRE OF THE ROMANTIC

6

The fairy spirit Ariel serves his master Prospero in *The Tempest*. But the magic staff of
power is here treated ambiguously. Who is really in control? Prospero's quest for the ideal
is as elusive as all romantic quests. Ellis Rabb
and Tom DeMastric in *The Tempest* at the
Old Globe Theatre, 1975. Directed by Ellis
Rabb.

P eople may go to the theatre for an exalting experience or for a good laugh, but among the most common attractions of the theatre is romance. People want exotic settings, stirring music, colorful dances, and a heart-throbbing story of long ago or far away. They want to escape the dull pettiness of everyday living to experience the infinite variety life has to offer. They want to identify with romantic heroes who take great risks, who embark on adventure-filled journeys or quests. Though our ordinary lives may be frittered away in frustrated impulses, tentative efforts, and delays, we like to relate to the romantic heroes and heroines living life to the fullest. They make no compromises, apologize to no one. Every choice is crucial, every issue clear, and when they are defeated, they go down fighting, sure that the very rightness of their cause justifies their actions and that even their defeat will help others along the path of honor and justice that they chose.

It is an axiom of the romantic theatre that no one is tongue-tied or clumsy. Romeo pours forth his soul to Juliet in Shakespeare's inspired verse or in Gounod's operatic song. Gravity is ignored as skaters swing around curves and leap over obstacles with complete power over space. Ballet dancers rise into the air and land again without a suggestion of weight or muscle, for the romantic theatre, whether of drama, opera, or dance, takes us beyond the limitations of the material world into a world with laws and ideals of its own.

THE BIRTH OF THE ROMANTIC IDEALS

The two great ideals of romance, the ideals of the knight-champion and of the knight-lover, developed during the Middle Ages and still influence our concept of what people should be. Feudalism first created the ideal of the knight-champion, loyal to his lord and always ready to fight in his defense. The Crusades developed that champion into the knight-errant, ready to wrest the Holy Land from the infidel or to go about rescuing innocent maidens in distress. In a sacred ceremony, he dedicated his sword to his lord and himself to protecting the poor and persecuted and to the endless fight against evil.

The ideal of the knight-lover, which only the feminist movement in our own time has seriously challenged, was created by the troubadour poets under the influence of Eleanor of Aquitaine, who was, at different times, Queen of France and Queen of England. It is no exaggeration to say that the idea of passionate, dedicated, transforming love was the invention of these poets of the twelfth and thirteenth centuries. Until that time, male-female relationships were youthful adventures or family partnerships. Love was not associated with marriage, for the strict doctrine of the medieval church declared all passion, even in marriage, a sin; marriage was an alliance of convenience, not of personal attraction. In fact, it would be three hundred years before the rising middle class and its new ideals would make it possible to unite love with marriage. Shakespeare's *Romeo and*

Juliet, written about 1594, was the first great poetic drama to celebrate that union.

But romantic love was invented outside of marriage. It was, in fact, assumed that the lady was already married to someone else, so the attachment was secret. The adoration of woman became a new religion, with the woman on a pedestal and the man at her feet, an abject slave. This "Court of Love" game, which gives us the words *courting* and *courtship* as well as *courtesy,* was one of the major attempts made to shift the emphasis in the relation between the sexes from the physical to the spiritual. Courtly love requires the woman to be very difficult and distant. The young man gets one glimpse of her beauty and is transformed forever, showing a long list of medical symptoms—he can't eat or sleep, he grows pale, he wanders in melancholy groves by moonlight. He may write poems for his lady or serenade her, but he actually sees little of her, while she sets him difficult tasks that may take years to perform. Sometimes his adoration is so extreme that he deems it a sacrilege to win or touch her, preferring to yearn unhappily for the ideal than to desecrate it by turning it into reality. That dilemma has greatly complicated the psychology of love to the present day, but it has been a great inspiration to romantic art.

The knight, whether champion or lover, was a solitary figure, dedicated to his lord or lady by vows and sustained in those vows by his own sense of honor. This solitariness contributed two other elements to the romantic ideal—an assertion of individualism and an uncompromising belief in freedom. Together these ideals provided for a myriad of rebellions, journeys, trysts, duels, and adventures to fill the stages and to excite the appetites of adventure-seeking audiences for centuries to come.

Dedication to love and adventure made Shakespeare's plays the first great romantic dramas. Starting in his history plays, with their wars and rebellions, their songs and their clowns, their intimate family meetings, and their processions and coronations, Shakespeare presented his audiences with the whole range of human experience in magnificent costume and pageantry. Richard III, a scheming villain, wicked enough for a child's tale of adventure, is finally killed by a righteous young champion. King Henry IV, though he establishes England's security in a troubled age, does so by dishonorably supplanting the poetic young Richard II. When his own power is challenged, his idealist son, Prince Hal, leaves his tavern revelry to rescue him and then goes on to become the successful warrior king, Henry V, conquering France and returning with the French princess as his bride. Shakespeare added characterizations and ironies that transcend the basic plots, filling the plays with the infinite variety and the eternal themes of romance.

Even more than the histories, Shakespeare's comedies breathe romance. Set in moonlit woods, in fabulous gardens, and on far-off seacoasts, they enchant their audiences with a range of characters and adventures to rival the most lavish spectacle of modern filmdom. *A Midsummer Night's Dream,* set at the court of the mythical King Theseus of Athens, is a prime example. Here amid plans to celebrate Theseus's wedding to the Queen of the Amazons, love and courtship are alternately explored at four separate levels. First comes the formal courtship of the king and his bride, with public vows and courtly promises to faithful supporters of the crown. Then a quartet of mismatched young lovers display every possible manner of jealousy, fidelity, hopeless pursuit, undying devotion, and broken vows, as they escape the tyranny of parental orders into the midnight forest. Lost in the darkness, they fall under the spell of the mischievous fairy, Puck, who abruptly reverses the directions of their loves, causes them to hate where they had loved with total devotion, and to love where they had once hated.

At a third level of love, the fairy king and queen work out a mature couple's problems of a love gone stagnant, as they plot for power and independence, yet crave a relationship that permits mutual access and respect. Finally, all these loves are parodied in a play-within-the-play prepared by local rustics to entertain at the wedding feast. The tragic story of two lovers who choose to die rather than live without each other is rendered into a comic burlesque by the inept performers. Fearing their play will offend or frighten the ladies of the court, they keep

The moonlit woods of romance. Shakespeare's *A Midsummer Night's Dream* at Indiana University, directed by Howard Jensen.

reminding everyone that the lion is not a real lion, that the heroine who dies is really a local boy who is very much alive, and that nothing about the play—its characters, its incidents, or its emotions—is, in fact, real. This world of Shakespeare's comic romances is a world of accident, chance, evil, and delusion, where everything is transitory, and where beauty and virtue pass too quickly. But it is also a world of faith, love, and hope, of noble purpose and high adventure, and a world where characters like the impish fairy, Puck, can cause endless confusion, but can also finally save the misguided lovers from the irreversible disasters of their own romantic inclinations.

ROMANCE IN THE MODERN THEATRE

After the American and French Revolutions new romantic ideas gave fresh impetus to the old formulas. Following Rousseau's exaltation of the free human being, heroes became rebels against corrupt society, either stirring up wars of liberation or seeking out the isolation of some remote spot to search for ultimate meaning. To the new romantics, all of nature was there to be explored, as they strove to grasp all experience, to catch glimpses of ultimate truth, and to bring their own existence into harmony with the universe. For such a mission, their own physical existence was both a curse and a blessing. Cursed by the restrictions of bodily needs and physical laws, they could not soar unencumbered to the heights, could never rise completely above the human demands of mere survival, and they might even be corrupted into accepting the comforts of the flesh and the ease of society as life's most important goals. On the other hand, a weak or deformed body and social rejection might bless them with constant reminders of the limitations of a mere physical existence, causing them to look beyond the flesh for true fulfillment. Romantic plays of the nineteenth century are filled with grotesque heroes in Gothic settings—hunchbacks, consumptives, blind beggars, and amputees, not to mention starving artists and students in attic rooms—all suffering with a passion that helps them to appreciate the full intensities of all experience.

The romantic rebel, hemmed in by restrictive society or torn by self-doubt, might embark on great adventures far from home. Before the theme of the Crusades had faded, the discovery of America opened up to Europeans an even greater adventure to the west. Ever since, the advancing frontier of the New World and its westward movement have provided endless opportunity for adventure, for open space, for rugged individualism, and for the freedom of a life in harmony with unspoiled nature. As explorers of the wilderness of a strange land, as settlers starting a new and better society, as pioneers possessing a new continent, Americans especially have seen themselves in the romantic sweep of history, a sweep that continues into the excitement of moon landings and space explorations and the popularity of science fiction. The frontier can just as easily be a creative challenge—a new scientific discovery, a cure for a disease,

Romantic melodrama in Russia. The nobleman abducts a girl from the poor man's house. The State Dramatic Theatre production, Leningrad, 1832. From Derjavine's *A Century of the State Theatre.*

a triumphant performance, or a heroic athletic accomplishment. The romantic movement has glamorized the intense dedication to which artists, teachers, scientists, and professionals of all sorts devote themselves in preparing for the unseen triumph that may never be known or measured. Out of our anguished frustrations we dream of a free, intense, romantic deed, and a good-looking actor or actress taking on the quest becomes the incarnation of our romantic dreams.

Structure of the Romantic Play

The essence of romance is freedom. Where realism is bound by fact and classicism by logic, the romantic play is bound by neither. On the contrary, the romantic hero gains freedom by triumphing over the everyday world of fact, and the romantic play gains freedom by disregarding the strict logic of the classical form. The compact classic play, whether ancient or neoclassic tragedy, is tightly organized by logic and by the strongest chains of causality, while its individual hero is summed up in the one great decision he or she makes.

The romantic structure stands in sharp contrast to the classic. It is usually very loose, with many characters involved in many different episodes and treated in a variety of comic and serious moods. On first impression, the romantic play may seem to have no unity at all. The story is told from the beginning with the kind of wandering narrative children love. Spectacle is lavishly exploited, seemingly for the sheer love of color and movement. The romantic hero goes from one big scene to another, taking part in impressive social, religious, or political ceremonies that have no apparent connection with one another.

This free structure expresses the romantic view of the universe as complex, infinitely varied, paradoxical, and mysterious. Since it is an open universe, unfinished and unmeasured, no one act or crisis is all-important. The characters must all try many things, their individuality developing gradually as a result of

Early perspective setting of solid two-faced or angle wings. Two rows of wings on a sloping floor lead up to a painted cloth drop to give the illusion of a long street. The Tragic Scene from Sebastiano Serlio's *Architecture*, Book II, Paris, 1545.

wide experience. Not one conscious decision, but many decisions, made in the heat of action in many situations, are what shape the romantic character, who in turn gives unity to the play.

This structure can be explained aesthetically as well as philosophically. Where classic art emphasizes unity, romantic art revels in variety in order to represent the broad scope of human experience. To the romantic nothing could be more insipid than the classic play with its one even, noble tone. Romantic artists feel such zest for experience that they want to include everything in the story, especially what is picturesque and intense. But the variety they present is not without order or meaning. They combine comedy with tragedy, prose with poetry, clowns with kings, crowd revelry with individual distress, and the grotesque with the charming in order to increase the intensity of each experience by contrast with another.

A Picture Stage for Romance

Romantic enthusiasm for all manner of experience in the drama gave rise to production methods to provide the broadest kinds of sensory experience as well. The picture-frame stage, first developed as a solid three-dimensional architectur-

Climax of a seventeenth-century opera. Jupiter and his celestial court are let down in a cloud machine. Flat wings on perspective lines lead to the backdrop. Drawn from Italian sources by Martha Sutherland.

The effect of a horserace is created with treadmills and a moving panorama. From *L'Illustration*, March 14, 1891.

al setting for the courts of Renaissance Italy, had already evolved into a complex wing-and-backdrop system for spectacular court masques and operas in the seventeenth century, when scenery that could be visibly changed on stage became all the rage. Two rows of painted *wings* along each side of the setting led back to a painted canvas *backdrop* at the rear. At a signal from the prompter, a hidden stagehand at each wing would slide it offstage, revealing another wing just behind it, and at the same time other stagehands would pull up the backdrop by hidden ropes, revealing another backdrop behind it. Thus the change could be made in a few seconds without having to drop a front curtain.

The romantic dramas began to call for three-dimensional effects to be added to the painted scenery—mountains to climb, stairways to descend, lakes (with real water) to drown in, burning buildings, and moving ships. The changing of steps, platforms, and solid structures was done behind a closed curtain, and nineteenth- and twentieth-century engineers devised elaborate and expensive machinery—pulleys and ropes for flying heavy scenery, wagon stages, turntables, and even elevator stages—to speed up the changes. But it still took so long to get a beautiful picture ready to disclose to the audience that opera composers sometimes wrote an intermezzo to fill the time and maintain continuity.

During the nineteenth century the picture stage reached a peak of painted illusion, especially in the popular melodramas, with as many as thirty tableau effects used in a single play. *Ben Hur* started its great career in 1899 with as much emphasis on pictorial effects as there was in its later movie versions. The first act alone had fourteen changes, each setting designed by a different painter. The chariot race was run by real horses and chariots on a treadmill, as a panorama painted on cloth and attached to huge rollers moved across the back of the stage. The galley scenes that filled the stage with rows of oarsmen faded into a scene of the tempestuous sea, with a boat that sank out of sight through the stage floor, leaving Ben Hur and his captain tossing on a raft.

Similar painted settings were expected for Shakespeare, giving *Othello* a real Venice, complete with gondolas, and *As You Like It* a Forest of Arden with real woodland animals scampering about, despite the long set changes that broke up Shakespeare's cinematic rhythm of continuous action through many short scenes. It is no wonder that modern producers have returned to the simplicity of Elizabethan stage forms and let the splendor of Shakespeare appear in the costumes, the processions, and the words themselves.

Cyrano de Bergerac: A Romantic Play

Though it comes well after the romantic movement had passed its height, no play captures the spirit of romanticism more pleasingly than Edmond Rostand's *Cyrano de Bergerac* (1897). Cyrano is a brave French soldier from the time of Richelieu and the Three Musketeers. His one defect is a nose so enormous that he claims it "marches on before [him] by a quarter of an hour." Endowed with astonishing strength, prowess, and wit, he compensates for his defect by feats of swordplay and equally cutting wordplay, constantly exposing himself to challenges that test the limits of his aspiring soul. He begins his action by ordering a popular but incompetent actor off the stage, paying from his own threadbare pockets for the returned admission fees of the disappointed audience and for his own vindicated sense of beauty. When challenged by a foppish favorite of the Count, he fights a duel while composing a ballad in honor of the occasion, never missing a step or a rhyme, concluding both duel and ballad, in perfect harmony of mind and body, with the triumphant line, "and then as I end the refrain, thrust home!"

Cyrano the knight-champion, who preserves beauty, defends friends from hired ruffians, goes into battle for king and country, yet maintains his personal integrity against a corrupt and fawning society, excites an audience's admiration; but it is as knight-lover that he elicits our sympathy. For Cyrano is in love, with Roxane, the most beautiful woman in Paris, and like a true knight-lover he worships her from afar, because he is terrified that his grotesque nose will make her laugh at any suggestion of love between them. When he learns that she is

Cyrano (Walter Hampden) fights his duel in rhyme in a revival at Hampden's Theatre, New York, 1926.

already enamored of Christian, a handsome but tongue-tied new cadet in his company, he devotes himself to her happiness by concealing his own feelings and helping Christian find a poetic manner of wooing that is worthy of Roxane. Concealed in the darkness under her balcony, he even speaks the words of love himself until Christian climbs up to claim the well-earned kiss. From the war zone, Cyrano writes daily letters whose eloquence finally wins the heart of Roxane to love the soul of their composer instead of merely his handsome face. But before Cyrano has the chance to reveal himself as author of the letters and the object of her love, Christian is killed in battle. While Roxane mourns, Cyrano sustains her delusion, and only years later, as he is dying, does she learn that it was Cyrano's soul she loved. But Cyrano dies without regret; inspired by Roxane's beauty and grace, he has managed to live his life without one stain on his romantic quest to be "in every way admirable." (For a more thorough treatment of *Cyrano de Bergerac*, see Chapter 11 on the art of the playwright.)

MELODRAMA: ROMANCE SIMPLIFIED

Melodrama, the most popular romantic form, has often been called the poor man's romantic play. It simplified the complex romantic rebel of the early nineteenth century, who had sought full exposure to all types of experience, by dividing him into two characters—a spotless hero and a deep-dyed villain. As its name implies, melodrama used music, not just songs but background music to underscore and intensify the emotional scenes or to set off each movement, gesture, or speech. Often long sequences were performed in pantomime, and when a climax was reached the tableau might be held still for several seconds while the drum rolled. Anyone who has watched old silent movies with a good musical background will recognize the device. The most exciting sequence was the chase, as the heroine fled the villain—out windows, over roofs, off bridges, through fires and earthquakes, floods and trainwrecks. To complete the thrill for the spectator, the scenery had to keep moving and make room for all kinds of platforms, steps, towers, trapdoors, and trick effects.

The scripts for the popular nineteenth-century melodramas may seem "hokey" when we read them today, and some theatre groups have made fun of them in burlesque revivals for audiences who like to laugh at the exaggerated trite sentiments and overblown patterned gestures of a bygone era. But the dialogue was written to be played against a strong musical background and orchestrated by spectacular stage effects to astonish, amaze, and, above all, speak directly to the feelings of the audience. To the romantic, truth comes from the feelings, not from the intellect. The highly successful revival of *Dracula* in the 1977–78 Broadway season shows how the old formulas have not lost their power when put in the hands of skilled technicians and talented performers, such as Frank Langella, who play the roles seriously.

New old-fashioned melodrama can be equally successful, as England's Royal Shakespeare Company proved when it staged Charles Dickens' *Nicholas Nickleby* to packed houses in its 1980 season. David Edgar's adaptation of the novel not only played up the pure hero Nickleby against the villainy of his money-grubbing uncle, it carried delighted audiences through nine and a half hours of melodramatic suspense and pleasure while following the ups and downs of the hero's fortunes through all manner of situations: from sweatshop employment to tavern brawls to travels with a provincial acting company. While courting disaster for himself, the hero saves a pathetic mentally retarded boy from the whippings of an evil schoolmaster, saves his sister from the seductions of a villainous lord, and saves his intended from a forced marriage to an old man. In 1981–82, the show played to sell-out crowds in New York at the record price of $100 per seat, and then, in 1983, was adapted for American television where its success was repeated in 1984.

ROMANCE IN THE MOVIES

The melodrama of the nineteenth century built one of the widest popular audiences in history, and when movies developed in the early twentieth century they followed the same path as the stage to romance and melodrama. Hollywood for more than three decades was truly the "city of dreams."

Film captures the epic sweep of the American Civil War in *Gone with the Wind*, with Clark Gable and Vivien Leigh.

Movies have excelled in three areas of romance. First, they are able to show history with an epic sweep, already discussed as film's special brand of exaltation. American history has been a romantic favorite of Hollywood from the beginning: colonial and frontier history, the history of the West, and best of all, the Old South and the War between the States. Starting with *The Birth of a Nation* (1915) and its epic view of the years of war and reconstruction, Hollywood presented the Old South on a grand scale, with armies in battle, wild rides of the Ku Klux Klan, pure women and brave men of North and South, tender meetings and farewells, and encounters with villainous carpetbaggers. With this movie, D. W. Griffith established the importance of film as an art. *Gone with the Wind* exalts with its epic sweep, but it is also one of the most impressive romantic spectacles ever filmed, and when it returns, as it has done every few years since 1939, it shows us the Civil War all over again: plantation scenes, battle scenes, the wounded lined up on rows of stretchers, the burning of Atlanta. But beyond this it shows us the people, treated in depth and perfectly acted, with Clark Gable as Rhett Butler, the English actor Leslie Howard as the gentlemanly Confederate officer, and sharply contrasted characterizations by Vivien Leigh as the calculating, ruthless, anti-heroine Scarlett O'Hara and Olivia de Haviland as the sweet, compliant wife—all romantic characters set in changing tensions and conflicts.

A second area in which film excels is in creating the mysterious and supernatural atmosphere of the sacred quest. Though most such attempts have not risen above melodrama, the 1980 film of the Arthurian legend, *Excalibur*, lifted its audiences into a medieval world of dark purposes, noble strivings, miraculous events, and demonic vengeance to fulfill the most romantic urge. Not only does it show the complex motives of the noble King Arthur, building his ideal of Camelot out of a gloomy, strife-ridden land, it also shows the shining purity of Sir Lancelot overcome by his desire for Arthur's queen, Guinevere. When he takes on a self-imposed exile to preserve his own and the nation's purity, he infects the land with corruption again. It shows the cynical magician, Merlin, using his powers to help Arthur, but powerless against the hidden evils that erupt from inside. It shows Arthur's nephew Mordred, a living symbol of the nation's repressed perversion, bent on overthrowing this citadel of the ideal. Finally, through effects which only the camera can achieve, it exposes its audiences to the Gothic horror and splendor of mysterious chambers, celestial halls, living skeletons, magic swords, eerie swamps, and the submerged beauty of the Lady of the Lake.

Finally, the movies excel in sheer melodrama, which today has the same appeal in movies and on television that it had on the nineteenth-century stage. By setting a good hero against a wicked villain, melodrama captures the most elemental sympathies. Whether the villain is a cattle rustler, a city gangster, an international terrorist, or an intergalactic power monger, we know that the hero must come quickly to the rescue. Moreover, film technology thrives on immersing its audiences in spectacular effects: plunging them into the holocaust of the terror-disaster films of the 1970s—*Earthquake, The Towering Inferno, Jaws;* taking them aloft to share the feats of *Superman;* and transporting them to the farthest galaxies—the *Star Wars* series—or into the new dimension of the computer—*Tron,* where they come face to face with exotic enemies and weapons, supernatural powers, and machines with personalities. But still the spotless hero combats the deep-dyed villain, against a background of electronic music and special effects, which are there to surprise and thrill the audience and to build a tension, pathos, and excitement that the thin stories, flat characterizations, and shallow dialogue were never meant to accomplish on their own.

GRAND OPERA AND ROMANTIC DANCE

Romantic theatre reached its highest perfection in opera and ballet. Both opera and dance, of course, have a rich history of their own, a broad musical literature, and a discipline of performance training, in most respects quite different from those of the dramatic theatre. Moreover, the sympathetic and ironic appeals that are major attractions in the dramatic theatre are rarely more than a secondary interest in opera, and often do not exist in dance at all. Instead these forms appeal more to the sensory and aesthetic experiences, to the pleasure derived from the beauty of music and movement, communicating directly with the audience's own sense of rhythm, harmonics, and tonalities.

Performances of nineteenth-century grand opera and ballet are the most highly perfected forms of romantic theatre one can see today. Most spectacular of all are the grand operas, which have many appeals—their large effects, their romantic moods, their dramatic melodies, and their glamorized show of the long ago and far away. Some people are attracted chiefly by the spectacular scenes in which music underscores the surge of the crowd. Festivals with dances and choruses; public ceremonies, with the pomp of guards, rulers, and courtiers, and the color of mixed groups of townspeople or peasants; special church services, rendezvous of gypsies or supernatural beings—these create the sense of events in which the audience can take part, and no grand opera is complete without them. The nineteenth-century German composer Richard Wagner supposed he had spectacle enough in *Tannhäuser,* with a scene in Venus's cave, processions of pilgrims, and a royal song contest, but he could not get a production in Paris until he added a ballet to the Venus scene of the first act, and then some members of the audience were furious: They had arrived late and missed the ballet, when everybody knew the ballet of an opera was supposed to be in the third act. For them spectacle was all.

Mozart and Italian Opera

Both opera and ballet began in the aristocratic European courts of the sixteenth and seventeenth centuries. Opera began as an experiment in reviving the spirit of Greek tragedy, with a stylized, intoned speech called *recitative*. In the seventeenth century the spoken recitative came to be used for dialogue, while the characters' emotions were expressed in solo *arias*, duets, and larger ensembles. When dances were added and scene designers learned how to make spectacular scene changes, grand opera became the most impressive of all Baroque entertainment.

By the end of the seventeenth century when Mozart began composing, middle-class audiences had come to demand less grandiose music, heroes with whom they could identify, and scenes both of farce and sentimentality. Mozart was able to combine all forms, new and old, comic and sentimental, and still tell a dramatic story while enabling highly skilled singers to show off their voices in a wide range of vocal forms. He raised opera to an expressive power it had never before known. In *Don Giovanni*, which many music lovers consider one of the high points of all music, Mozart takes the old Don Juan story about seduction,

Grand opera. A spectacular setting that spans the old Roman sports amphitheatre in Verona. The triumphal scene in Verdi's *Aida*, 1971.

murder, and damnation; he builds it to a climactic scene when the statue of the murdered father comes to life, the music rises to a swelling power, and hell opens up to engulf the Don. Mozart lets a comic servant dominate much of the opera, and his Don keeps a brash cynicism almost to the end; yet the whole range of comic and serious feelings is expressed in the most charming and graceful music. Most impressive is the way in which he perfected the group scenes involving three or more characters. Each singer expresses a different, often changing, reaction, yet all are in harmony as the music builds to a climax. Near the beginning of Act II, Donna Elvira comes onto the balcony at night, angry at her faithless seducer, Don Giovanni, yet still fascinated by him. From below, he hears her, disguises his servant in his cloak, and begins a serenade in order to get her out of the way so that he may pursue her maid. At first he is pretending love, the servant is laughing, and Donna Elvira is protesting, until gradually all are caught in the spell. There is action, change, development, yet all are united in beautiful melody and harmony. If opera-goers are at first more interested in the straightforward solo arias, with more experience they begin to respond to the passages that express many complex and changing emotions.

For most opera fans, romantic theatre means the Italian opera of the nineteenth and early twentieth centuries, especially the works of Giuseppe Verdi—*Rigoletto, La Traviata,* and, most impressive of all, *Aida,* written for the opening of the Suez Canal and first performed in 1871. He used conventional forms that audiences were familiar with, but his extremely dramatic arias create character, express inner emotions, change dynamically from one part of the song to another, and drive the drama forward from beginning to end. *Aida* is a tragic story about a conquering hero who is loved by both an Egyptian princess and an Ethiopian slave girl. The triumphant entry march that greets the hero when he returns victorious from a great battle is one of the most famous of all marches and a great temptation to enthusiastic producers. There are legends of outdoor productions with dozens of chariots, with elephants, camels, and horses by the hundreds prancing round and round the stadium as several bands play the march strains over and over. Added to the royal and military pomp is an almost equal array of ceremonial marches of priests and priestesses, with chants, prayers, and dances. Yet both the military and the priestly elements contribute to the story. It is the war that brings the slave girl's royal father as a captive, tempting her to find out the hero's battle plan, and it is the inflexible priests, guardians of respectability, who condemn the hero to death for inadvertently revealing his plan.

By contrast, one act of *Aida* takes place at night on the banks of the Nile, with the music evoking a lush atmosphere of moonlight in a strange continent. The priests lead the princess to the temple for a vigil before her marriage to the hero while he has a farewell tryst with the slave girl, Aida. This tangle of love, jealousy, and betrayal is immersed in the rich blue atmosphere of the exotic night, created by lighting, setting, and music.

Wagnerian Opera

The German operatic tradition, created by Richard Wagner in the mid-nineteenth century, has directly influenced twentieth-century theatre. Wagner disliked the "set songs" of traditional opera, with their definite beginnings and endings; they were too much like concert pieces. His ideal for his romantic, superhuman stories was a *Gesamtkunstwerk*—a composite work of all the arts—which moved through an entire act with no place for a pause or applause. The result was a continuous symphonic poem with voices. He enlarged and enriched the orchestra and wrote the vocal parts as single strands woven with the instruments of the orchestra into a complex web. Instead of separate arias, the music developed through short, bold melodies, called *leitmotifs*, or leading motifs. Each motif is associated with a particular character or idea—an ingenious way to make the music carry the story and even the inner drama. A character's motif is heard not only when he or she is speaking but also when someone else is speaking or thinking of that character, as a kind of musical rendition of *subtext*.

Wagner's most impressive operatic accomplishment is *The Ring of the Nibelungs*, a series of four long operas tracing a legendary story of northern gods contending with men and dwarfs for a magic hoard of gold deep in the waters of the Rhine. It includes the story of Siegfried, who kills the dragon and wakes the princess who has been sleeping within a wall of magic fire. With the rippling waters of the Rhine, the murmuring of the forest, the magic fire, the birds and rainbows, the mists around Valhalla, the mountain castle of the gods, there is enough descriptive music to hold an audience for hours. Yet there are also joys and sorrow and the strong-willed conflict of superhuman beings. For even the gods are swept along by passions greater than themselves. At the end Valhalla sinks, carrying the old gods down in flame and water to make way for a new world. In celebration of the Wagner centennial, the 1983 season saw a spectacular production of the entire ring cycle televised from Wagner's own Festspielhaus (Festival Theatre) in Bayreuth, Germany.

Both Wagner's theoretical writings and his example have had great influence on the modern theatre, not only for particular reforms, such as darkening the auditorium so that audiences could more completely lose themselves in the drama, but for the concept of an inner life of the drama. This inner life is not the words or even the plot, but a dynamic sequence, constantly surging in rhythmic waves from beginning to end. Anticipating the techniques of modern acting, the performer must follow the inner sequence, and his words, tones, and movements, as well as the accompanying music and sound effects, must follow and express that surging rhythm. A Swiss designer, Adolphe Appia, followed the lead of Wagner and showed how, through the plasticity of changing lights, all visual elements could follow the same inner life.

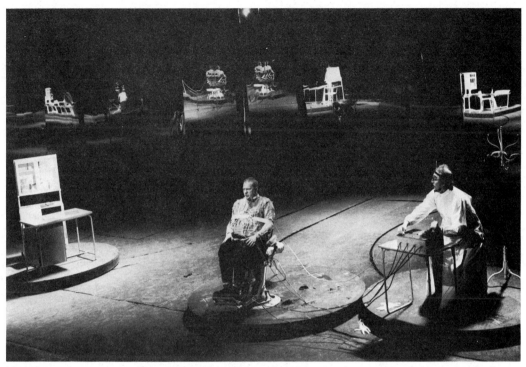

Modern emotions in opera. The helpless little man protests being treated as an object by a cruel, unfeeling world. Berg's *Wozzeck*. Teatro La Scala, Milan, 1971.

Romantic Dance

An even purer form of romance than opera is preserved in the ballet. No other form of art so directly expresses our simplest, most frequent daydreams. Nowhere else is reality so refined and idealized. Nowhere is the human body more charmingly displayed. The tights and the tutu, the precise movement so perfectly keyed to the music, and the soft lighting transform the erotic into romantic yearning. All is seen behind the veil of the imagination.

Ballet movements are abstracted from movements of real life—stepping, leaping, landing, kicking, turning—but they are selected and simplified. In this ideal of beauty, charm, and dignity, the back is held rigid, the head high, the toes are turned out, and the feet and hands are limited to a few precise positions. Every movement begins and ends in a set pose. Only occasionally in the solo character parts does personality or emotion or even facial expression find a place. One of the pleasures of a good ballet is the exact duplication as a line of balleri-

The exquisite grace of body form will always be one of the special pleasures of ballet. Bonnie Moore of the Washington Ballet Company. Photo © James E. Strickland.

nas, dressed alike, make exactly the same movements in unison, sequence, or opposition, lifting the audience into an exotic world of total harmony and rhythm.

The Development of Ballet

With a tradition of more than four centuries, ballet has gone through three major stages of development: The Renaissance courts gave it pattern and stateliness, the classic academies of the seventeenth and eighteenth centuries formulated its technique, and the romantic theatre of the nineteenth century gave it soul and drama. During the Renaissance it was practiced by the aristocrats themselves, who liked to dress up and act the parts of shepherds and nymphs or Greek gods and goddesses. During the seventeenth and eighteenth centuries ballet became more strictly disciplined, calling for systematic training in the five basic positions of the feet and the neat and elegant positions of the head, arms, and hands. The

Romantic drama in ballet. The prince captures the Queen of the Swans. Martine van Hamel and Vladimir Gelvan in *Swan Lake*. Restaged by David Blair for the American Ballet Theatre, 1976.

skirt was shortened to show the elaborate foot movements, and both men and women wore a stiff bodice or tunic.

But it was the nineteenth century that made ballet the perfect expression of romance, first by having the women dance on their toes, completing the denial of human weight and gravity, and second by its development of romantic themes in story ballets. The main theme of romantic ballet is the irresistible lure of the ideal, which draws human beings away from the real, often to their destruction. In the first great romantic ballet, *La Sylphide* (1832), James, a young Scotsman, sits by the fire on his wedding day dreaming of an ethereal creature, a *sylphide*, who dances with him but always eludes him. At his wedding she snatches the ring and lures him out to dance on the moors. When he tries to catch her with a witch's scarf, she dies, leaving him to discover that his earthly bride has married another man. In *Swan Lake* (1877), for which Tchaikovsky wrote such seductive music, the hero falls in love with the Queen of the Swans, maidens who are under the spell of a wicked magician. The two lovers finally plunge into the lake,

Extreme intensities in modern dance. Martha Graham and Merce Cunningham in *Letter to the World*, a dance interpretation of the life of Emily Dickinson, including some of her poems.

thereby breaking the spell, and are seen in an enchanted bark, united forever in the world of the ideal. These and other romantic stories gave opportunities for both idealized folk and classical dance, with formal lines of dancers, solos, duets (*pas de deux*), and both small groups and large, creating an ideal world of graceful bodies in perfect discipline and control. As sylphs or swans or other exotic creatures, ballerinas can glide or even float like wisps of cloud, appearing weightless *en point* (on their toes) or in the effortless lifts of their male partners. To this day a new ballet dancer has not really arrived until winning acclaim in a star role of one of the great romantic ballets of the last century.

A RIVAL: MODERN DANCE

Early in the twentieth century another form of dance appeared to challenge the supremacy of ballet. The way to "modern dance" was opened by Isadora Duncan, an Irish-American girl from San Francisco, who for the first three decades of the century had the artistic world of Europe at her feet—her bare feet. As a symbol of freedom and rebellion, she threw off the slippers, tight bodices, and fixed positions of ballet and openly defied conventional morality in her personal life. On both continents she stimulated great public interest in "aesthetic dancing," and "interpretive dancers" in loose robes and veils floated about while a piano or small orchestra played light classical music.

Ruth St. Denis and Ted Shawn, in the 1910s and 1920s, trouped the country with a company of young dancers in carefully prepared numbers based on local color, many with Oriental or American Indian themes. Three of those young dancers, Martha Graham, Doris Humphrey, and Charles Weidman, set up their own schools and performing companies in the late 1920s, where they worked out new techniques for achieving their new form of theatre. They became the founders of modern dance. They used regular theatres for their major performances, but broke away from the scenic patterns of Broadway as disdainfully as they broke away from the techniques of classical ballet. They abandoned pretty costumes and flaunted their stark leotards. Instead of picture scenery, they used drapes, blocks, and abstract shapes; instead of soft string orchestras and waltz tunes, they called for percussion and harsh dissonance; instead of lightness, daintiness, and delicate poses, they offered weight, struggle, and tension. At first their performances seemed as abstract as cubist paintings, as wild and ecstatic as primitive rituals, as heavy and straining as wrestling matches. They explored the natural relation of movement to breathing, to tension and relaxation, to work and play, and especially to gravity—that natural force which ballet hides or denies.

Martha Graham was the most distinctive figure. Graham embodied the tight nervousness of modern life, expressing its inner tensions with her rigid lips, stiff hands, stark costumes, and percussive movements characterized by sudden jerks, sharp accents, and short, broken gestures. She did falls, she stamped her feet and clapped her hands, she walked on her knees, she crouched, she sprang, she suddenly pulled her head between her knees. In one of her most distinguished works, *Appalachian Spring* (1944), she depicts the inner conflict of a young bride, facing both the joys and the uncompromising demands of hard work and a strict behavior code in a stark rural setting. A group of young girls in soft, flowing cotton dresses and bonnets, moving in graceful, easy, circular movements, express the ease of youthful freedom she is relinquishing for marriage. They are teasingly contrasted against a stiffly formal and puritanical preacher, while the staunch and humorless groom waits for her to assume her new, mature role of wife.

Once the audiences got used to the new approach to movement, they realized that the modern dancers had much to say—about modern life, but most of all about modern feelings, about revolt and independence, sympathy for the struggling masses, the vital sweep of America, religious idealism, the half-hidden fears in the depths of the soul. By the 1960s modern dance had become as much a part of the dance world as ballet, with most dancers being trained in both forms and often dancing in both styles. Ballet influenced modern dance and modern dance influenced ballet, and blends of the two were common. The result has been an almost explosive excitement in new forms and new choreographic styles, so that in 1975 the *New York Times* featured an article that acclaimed dance as America's "most vital art form." In Chapter 10 we will see how both forms have enriched the contemporary theatre.

THE MUSICAL

For more than half a century, in the American theatre romance has meant a musical. Though usually referred to as musical comedy, it often carries such deep emotion, such rich characterizations, and even so much serious thought, that "comedy" is misleading. The American musical has come to be admired by audiences around the world and recognized as America's most distinctive theatrical contribution. Borrowing from the sentimental Viennese operetta, from the

"The rain in Spain" scene from the Broadway production of *My Fair Lady*. Eliza Doolittle breaks into a tango with her tutors.

satirical Parisian comic opera, even from the English Christmas pantomime, and using ideas from vaudeville, music hall, and burlesque, Americans have created a form that catches the energy and dash, the combination of skepticism and faith, of sophistication and sentimentality that is the active image of America. For years serious critics held the musical in disdain but at last have come to recognize that when story, characters, music, dance, and spectacle are integrated in a musical, it is one of the highest achievements of the modern theatre.

Song and Dance in the Musical

Obviously audiences go to musicals expecting lots of songs and dances: intimate love songs, comic specialty numbers, big production numbers—the more the better. But a musical is not just a revue that moves from one song to the next; it is a dramatic story, usually centered on two sets of romantically attached characters surrounded by several secondary characters with dramatic problems which often parallel those of the hero and heroine. The story carries them through the ups and downs of their relationship until their conflicts are resolved—usually happily—just as one might expect from any drama. But unlike just any drama, the ups and downs find their expression in songs and dances. The characters express musically the depths of sorrow and the ecstasies of joy that mere words could never contain. When Eliza in Lerner and Loewe's *My Fair Lady* (1956) at last begins to pronounce her vowels correctly, she turns her practice sentence about "the rain in Spain" into a tango, and she and her two teachers celebrate their triumph in a wild release that is one of the high points of the show. As no musical is complete without its love song, Eliza later expresses her love in a waltz, "I Could Have Danced All Night!" Likewise, Tony, after meeting his Puerto Rican love in Leonard Berstein and Stephen Sondheim's *West Side Story* (1957), is overcome and cherishes musically the very sound of her name:

> Maria!
> I've just met a girl named Maria,
>   And suddenly that name
>   Will never be the same
> To me.

The characters are so consumed by their feelings that nothing will do but to release them in lyrical rhythm and passion.

Song can express frustration as well, as Nellie Forbush finds in Rodgers and Hammerstein's *South Pacific* (1951) when she thinks she is jilted and angrily starts doing the only thing left for a military nurse on a remote island: "I'm gonna wash that man right outa my hair, and send him on his way!" As is so often true in the happy world of musicals, she is joined by a whole bevy of nurses who share her frustration, turning even the unhappy moments into a group experience that draws the audience in with its rhythms and catchy melodies. In *My Fair Lady*, Henry Higgins works out a personal conflict between his insufferable pride and his real love for Eliza in his final song after she has walked out on him. He alternates between vehement determination—"But I shall never take her back, if she were crawling on her knees"—and plaintive recognition of his desire to have her back: "I've grown accustomed to her face!"

The song lyrics often carry important ideas in the musical as well. Oscar Hammerstein's frequent concern with racial prejudice is expressed forcefully in the *South Pacific* song, "You've got to be taught to hate and fear, . . . you've got to be carefully taught!" when Lieutenant Cable realizes too late that prejudice is keeping him from his Polynesian sweetheart.

Even more striking as a musical plot device is the *reprise,* the repetition of or variation on a song made familiar early in the show. The song usually occurs first in a lighthearted, even joyful situation. Its reprise is often late in the show, in the midst of crisis, expressing the character's need to come to a major decision, to confront and deal with his or her changed circumstances. The reprise is one of the most intense ironic techniques of the musical, reminding the audience both of an earlier state of joy and of all the conflicts that have intervened up to the present crisis. In the pre-war Berlin of *Cabaret* (book by Joe Masteroff, music by John Kander, and lyrics by Fred Ebb—1966), the Jewish fruit seller, Herr Schultz, and the lonely spinster, Fräulein Schneider, celebrate their planned wedding with a duet, "Married," which then turns into an exciting dance, with all their friends sharing their joy. But before the curtain closes on the scene, swastika armbands fill the stage with the impending threat that awaits them. Later, after Fräulein Schneider breaks off the match, intimidated by Nazi pressure, Herr Schultz does a sad reprise of the song, retreating once again into his acquiescent shell. In quite a different vein, *Cabaret* opens in the decadent atmosphere of the Kit Kat Klub, where the Emcee welcomes the audience to the cabaret with the song "Wilkommen," and invites them to share the reckless, live-for-the-moment world of Berlin's night life. When Sally Field, a young English girl, arrives in Berlin, it is to immerse herself in this world of irresponsibility. At the end of the show, having gone through a failed love affair, the broken relationships of her friends, as well as an abortion, she rejects the invitation of her American friend to break from the corruption of a society gone insane. While the Emcee does a reprise of "Wilkommen," Sally flings herself into a wild acceptance of this welcome with her own lyrical appeal: "Come to the Cabaret." Though the song expresses Sally's denial of reality and responsibility, it is for the audience a shocking revelation of how real people can be sucked into such evils as Nazism.

The reprise may come after a crisis, as it does with the title song of Michael Stewart and Jerry Herman's *Hello, Dolly!* (1964), and express the joy of everything being resolved. The familiar tune and beat announce the happy resolution, while characters and audience share the pleasure of the entire company joining in a final celebration—the eleven o'clock song—that will send the audience from the theatre humming the tunes and tapping their feet to the happy rhythm.

This brings us to yet another element of song and dance, the group ensemble. With few exceptions, musicals include crowds of singers and dancers in big production numbers of colorful costumes, picturesque formations, and boundless energy, spaced through the show. The spectacle is a great pleasure in itself, but, like the chorus of Greek tragedy or the crowds of Shakespeare, the singers and dancers in a musical often extend the dimension of the show, so that the central characters exist as part of a larger world—not always a happy world, but a world that sets off and reflects the inner conflicts and emotions of the principals. So the wedding in Harnick and Bock's *Fiddler on the Roof* (1964) brings together families and friends and the entire Jewish community of the Russian village, who share not only the joys of the celebration, but also the oppression of totalitarian officialdom that surrounds them and the eroding faith of a younger generation. The basket social in Rodgers and Hammerstein's *Oklahoma!* (1943) brings together merchants, cowboys, and farmers, all trying to bring the Oklahoma territory to statehood, while competing with each other both for the ladies and the land. The freedom-seeking young people in Ragni, Rado, and MacDermott's *Hair* (1967) draw in flower children, draft protesters, and liberal intellec-

A musical about dancers that is mostly dance. Bennett's *A Chorus Line*.

tuals, as well as the middle class and middle aged, and finally they even invite the audience onto the stage to join in the final celebration of "doing your own thing."

Not only large crowds, but multiple groups of secondary characters parallel, complement, and contrast with the central characters, creating a sense of community and building a social and geographical background. In *South Pacific* when they are all put together—"There Is Nothing Like a Dame" for the lusty American Seabees, "Bloody Mary" for the Madame, "Bali Hai" for the exotic native girls, and *"Dites-Moi"* for the French planter's children—we have the whole background for Lieutenant Cable's sad love and Nellie Forbush's more hopeful love.

Dance, while adding to the color and energy of any musical in the big production and specialty numbers, may also express the character's inner emotions, as Eliza's tango does in *My Fair Lady*. The landmark breakthrough for this use of dance was Agnes de Mille's choreography for *Oklahoma!* in 1943. The show startled the theatre world by replacing the conventional opening dance of singing, kicking chorus girls with a quiet scene of the hero, Curly, singing "Oh, What a Beautiful Morning!" to the aunt of his girlfriend, Laurie. But it was in the "Dream Ballet," where dance expressed inner emotion, that De Mille set a new trend. Laurie, fearing that she has been too high-handed with Curly and become too involved with the dangerous Jud, dreams her fears in a ballet that leaves Curly beaten and herself trapped by the lust of a demonic villain. Then she wakes to face the reality of having to go to the basket social with the odious farmhand. (The even more revolutionary realistic use of ballet that Jerome Robbins introduced in *West Side Story* will be discussed as a theatrical blend in Chapter 9.)

Recently, entire shows have been given over to dance, such as *Dancin'* (1978), literally a showcase for the choreography of Bob Fosse. Dancing is both the subject and the form in *A Chorus Line* (1975), Broadway's longest-running hit and a 1984 movie. The simple story has a dance director for a new musical auditioning young people for the chorus line. Only two characters are given much story—a lonely young male gay and the ex-wife of the director, out of a job, and hoping to make a comeback by starting again in a chorus line. But as each dancer performs and speaks briefly about him- or herself, we are given a cross section of youthful hopes and ambitions.

The Musical Celebration of America

Above all, the American musical celebrates America, its history, its traditions, and even its temperament. Jerome Kern's *Show Boat* (1927) pictures the mid-America of the nineteenth century, with all its color, its gambling spirit and quick success, its restless changes and disrupted family life—a picture made sharper

Local color in a folk opera. The main action is reinforced by the acting and singing of the chorus. In this picturesque setting every window is an acting area. Heyward and Gershwin's *Porgy and Bess*. New York, 1935.

by its background of black workers and mulatto girls. One of the brightest shows of the 1930s was George and Ira Gershwin's *Of Thee I Sing*, which opened in 1931 and continued through the Roosevelt–Hoover campaign of 1932. A sharp but good-natured thrust at American elections, George S. Kaufman's satirical book for the show is distinctively American. It points up imperfections with the utmost clarity, yet with that amused indulgence which makes fanatical reformers despair of America's ever reaching perfection. To show a presidential election being run as a beauty contest, campaign oratory spiced up with wrestling, and nine Supreme Court justices hopping into a football huddle to pronounce on the sex of the President's child, is to remind Americans, as Aristophanes reminded the ancient Athenians, that a pompous politician can be as self-serving as anyone else.

In 1935 the great Negro folk "opera" *Porgy and Bess*, brought togther a number of traditions. Dorothy and DuBose Heyward created the story of a gentle cripple, Porgy, who wins the trollop Bess from the strong man only to have her lured away by Sportin' Life, the high-stepping dope peddler from Harlem. At the end Porgy leaves home with only his goat cart to search the world for his woman. George Gershwin studied the group rhythms and melodies of the Gullah Negroes and produced the first operatic music that seemed authentically American. His songs express the tenderness of love, a cheerful defiance in "I Got Plenty o' Nuttin'," a humorous reflection on Biblical stories in "It Ain't Necessarily So," and, most powerfully of all, the fears, amusements, laments, and prayers of the crowd. *Porgy and Bess* is a celebration of American regionalism, but, like any classic, it has lasting power. Its revivals as a movie in the 1960s, as a grand opera in 1976, and as Radio City Music Hall's winter spectacular in 1983, were all popular successes.

The top musicals of the forties—the decade of giants like *Oklahoma!, Carousel, Annie Get Your Gun, Finian's Rainbow,* and *South Pacific*—included the sorrows of separation and death, but even when they were set in picturesque, faraway places, they celebrated American strength and faith, that great "willingness of the heart" that has always seemed so peculiarly American. In the 1950s, Meredith Willson's *The Music Man* (1957), old-fashioned and brassy, continued the tradition of the big energetic productions set in the romantic America of the past, while Irving Berlin's *Call Me Madam* (1950) gave Ethel Merman one of her great roles as a female ambassador carrying the American spirit into post-war Europe, and George Abbot's *Damn Yankees* (1955) turned the great American sport, baseball, into a middle-aged man's dream, when he sells his soul to a sinister but comical devil to help his favorite team win the pennant.

America as the dream of the immigrant was dramatized in *Flower Drum Song* (1958), *Fiorello!* (1959), and *Fiddler on the Roof* (1964). *Flower Drum Song*, set in San Francisco's Chinatown, treats the conflicts created by second-generation assimilation to the new world. *Fiorello!* is set in a New York City ridden by graft and corruption, where minority groups struggle to find their places. They are led by that great little hero, Fiorello LaGuardia, the half-Jewish, half-Italian champion of the people, who went to Congress and then served for years as mayor of New York. *Fiddler on the Roof*, taken from the Yiddish stories of Sholem Aleichem, projects the immigrant back to the narrow but colorful ghetto communities of central Europe. The old father, Tevye, struggling to keep a balance between the traditions of his people and the new ideas of his children, is finally driven out of his old-world home and moves to America. Early in this century such old-world backgrounds were the subject of broad comedy and ridicule, but by the mid-1960s audiences could look with both amusement and affection at the minorities who brought their local traditions and their high hopes to America.

Even the bitter and sometimes bloody conflicts of America's labor unions have been set forth in the musical theatre. It was a great day in 1937—the heart of the Depression, the New Deal, and labor–industry unrest—when a musical revue called *Pins and Needles,* produced and acted by the International Ladies Garment Workers Union, showed a sense of humor. Its love songs took such forms as "One Big Union for Two," and "Sing me a song with social signifi-

Modern street violence danced to music. Bernstein's *West Side Story*. New York, 1957. Choreographed by Jerome Robbins.

cance—nothing else will do. It must be packed with social fact, or I won't love you.''

Though *West Side Story* seems to be the most strikingly original and one of the most harmonious of all American musicals, it is yet a summary and perfection of the whole line, giving the audience almost everything it had learned to expect. There are dances and songs of group unity for the juvenile gang, songs of love and of dreams of the future, a tongue-in-cheek celebration, ''America,'' sung by girls recently arrived from Puerto Rico, and a sardonic-comic song, ''Gee, Officer Krupke,'' mocking the police and social workers. There are satire, violence, gang warfare, and murder, yet such an obvious love of New York, such a strong assertion of the hope that love can win over hatred, that this musical must be described as a celebration of America. In 1972 *Grease* was already making fun of the early rock and roll fads of the 1950s, but its continued popularity proves it to be as much nostalgia as mockery. More recently *Barnum* (1980) has brought audiences back to the spectacle of the big top and to the irrepressible

"The oldest established permanent floating crap game in New York." *Guys and Dolls*, University of California at Northridge.

initiative of that great flim-flam artist of the nineteenth century, P. T. Barnum, while *Annie* (1977) has taken us back to the idealism of the Roosevelt era, where a ragamuffin orphan could join forces with an industrial magnate to triumph over all manner of evil.

In the last several decades the musical has been modified in directions that move it far from the romantic glamour of the early musical comedies. The first direction, as in shows like *Evita* and *Sweeney Todd*, was toward bitter, sardonic moods that seem more akin to a realistic than to a romantic theatre. The second new direction, epitomized by *Hair*, has been toward the more open flowing forms, the mass-group choruses, and the rock-music rhythms of rebellious and aspiring youth. These two groups of musicals will be discussed in Chapter 9 and 10. Despite these new directions, one of the most successful musicals of the 1983–84 season was a brand new old-fashioned musical, Harvey Fierstein and Jerry Herman's *La Cage aux Folles*. Its subject matter—the domestic life of two middle-aged homosexual men, one a transvestite, and the "straight" son of one of the men, who wants them to go back in the closet to avoid embarrassing his fiancee and her narrow-minded parents, suggests the liberation that infused the theatre with new material in the 1970s. But its form is as traditional as a 1940s Rodgers and Hammerstein show, and Fierstein's book and lyrics extol all the values of home and family, of honor and faithfulness, that were the hallmark of the joyous musicals of an earlier era.

Guys and Dolls: A Romantic Musical

Among the many high points in American musical theatre, few are higher or more American than *Guys and Dolls*. Abe Burrows and Jo Swerling based the book on a well-known Damon Runyon short story, while Frank Loesser wrote songs and lyrics to match the lovable and cynical night-life hustlers of Runyon's beloved Broadway. Running three years on Broadway after its original opening, it was later made into a successful movie and in 1983 was the first American musical to be staged at the Tyrone Guthrie Theatre in Minneapolis, twenty years after Guthrie had paved the way for America's regional theatre movement.

As with most musicals, two couples form the central love interests. The first couple is an unlikely pair—Sky Masterson, a high-rolling gambler (the basis for his nickname, Sky), and Sister Sarah Brown, a beautiful and virtuous Salvation Army girl—who come together to their mutual surprise through a wager. Both resist the inevitable attraction but recognize their mutual feelings in a duet, "I've Never Been in Love Before." The second couple—Nathan Detroit, who runs "the oldest established permanent floating crap game in New York," and Miss Adelaide, a singer at the Hot Box—have been engaged for fourteen years, though Adelaide has fed her mother a story about a happy marriage to a husband who works at the A & P and the arrival of five children. Frustrated at Nathan's prolonged evasion of setting a date for the wedding, she has developed psychosomatic symptoms:

> In other words, just from waiting around
> For that plain little band of gold,
> A person . . . can develop a cold.

This love quartet is surrounded by an array of gamblers, pickpockets, hookers, bookies, chorus girls, and an oompah mission band. The heat is on for Nathan: from the cops, who want to close down his crap game; from his gambling clients, especially Big Jule, a threatening thug visiting from East Cicero, Illinois, who *will* have their game; and from Adelaide, who is going to break off their engagement if Nathan continues running his crap game. He needs $1,000 to get a new spot, so he bets Sky Masterson that Sky can't get the girl he names to go to Havana, Cuba with him. Just then Sister Sarah Brown appears and Nathan, sure of his ground, selects her for Sky's challenge. Sarah is having her own trouble. If she doesn't have a successful prayer meeting, the mission will be closed, so Sky promises her a dozen genuine sinners at her next meeting if she will have dinner with him at his favorite restaurant. When she learns that the restaurant is in Havana she demures, but the pressure is on from the General, giving the audience a chance to enjoy an exotic scene in the Caribbean.

The array of characters, together with the dramatic conflicts Burrows has structured into *Guys and Dolls,* gives Frank Loesser and the choreographer, Michael Kidd, ample opportunity to present the audience with all the variety that a romanticist could hope for: the bookies picking their horses in "Fugue for Tinhorns" set against the mission hymn, "Follow the Fold"; a joyful and inebriated Sarah finding the joys of love in "If I Were a Bell," while Adelaide laments the result of *her* love, a cold; the gamblers shooting craps to a ballet in the sewers and praying a gambler's prayer, "Luck Be a Lady," before ending up at a mission prayer meeting with "Sit Down You're Rockin' the Boat." Adelaide's Hot Box provides showgirl songs that range from a country ditty, "A Bushel and a Peck," to the high-class "Take Back Your Mink." All are set off by the theme song, "Guys and Dolls":

> When you meet a gent paying all kinds of rent
> For a flat that would flatten the Taj Mahal,
> Call it sad, call it funny, but it's better than even money
> That the guy's only doing it for some doll.

This song provides the "eleven o'clock" reprise that ends the show in a grand finale to send audiences out of the theatre refreshed and humming, as only a musical can do.

ROMANCE AS PSYCHOLOGICAL STRUCTURE

Romance was under strong attack in the early twentieth century. Over-literal minds were impatient with fantasy and dismissed romance as a child's daydream of old fairy tales and legends. Over-serious reformers, especially the revolutionary Marxists, attacked it as bourgeois, as another opiate of the people that, like conventional religion, distracts workers from their duty to the state and wastes their time and emotions. Realists are skeptical of romance because they think its impossible ideals make people unwilling to face the world as it is.

The objection that romance is escape is no longer convincing. A fantastic parable may be the best way to understand a real situation. Since Freud, psychologists have recognized that the great romantic stories fascinate both children and adults because, like dreams, they express the search for identity and destiny in the half-hidden depths of the mind. Audiences seeing a romantic play may momentarily forget the immediate problems and burdensome complexities of their lives. But they wake from their dream with their egos strengthened and a new perspective on the patterns of human aspiration and desire.

Like the romantic playwright of earlier times, dramatists of today want to deal with a complex, baffling universe that is mystical and surreal rather than real, that is illogical and disconnected rather than clear. To a considerable degree they follow the structure of the romantic drama. But before we arrive at an analysis of the work of recent playwrights, we must examine the development of the drama of realism, which dominated the stage for more than fifty years.

THE THEATRE
OF REALISM

7

Documentary realism. The Federal Theater
Project production of *One Third of a Nation*,
1938, shows a montage of poverty in a burning tenement.

R ealists a hundred years ago turned away from what they believed was the romantic's outmoded and hopeless striving for unreachable ideals and set out to create an "illusion of reality" on the stage. Settings, properties, costumes, speech, and movement were to correspond so exactly to the world outside that audiences would forget they were in the theatre, supposing instead that they were looking into a real room with one wall removed, the "convention of the fourth wall." The picture frame of the proscenium arch became a kind of picture window through which audiences saw ordinary people engaged in a "slice of life." Not the far away and long ago but the here and now, not exotic heroes and villains but ordinary problems, not dreams and fantasies but a scientific study of actual life, based on careful observation of real people in real places—these were to be the subjects of this new experiment in theatre. Truth was the byword.

The scientific spirit of the century indeed transformed the theatre. It taught writers to be objective observers, carefully studying the complex influence of environment on real people with basic human drives. From the beginning of the nineteenth century, increasing interest was shown in biology. The climax of biological study came in 1859 with the publication of Charles Darwin's *Origin of Species*, which offered the theory that all animals, including people, evolve from lower forms and that, by "natural selection" or "survival of the fittest," only those animals that are suited to their environment will survive.

Another powerful influence on nineteenth-century thought was materialism, an almost inevitable companion to the science, technology, and industrial growth of the era. Materialism, coupled with the spirit of the scientific age that gave realism its birth, infused realism with a belief in progress. Theatre, by carefully and truthfully examining people in their material and social environment, could expose their problems, reveal the causes, and thus serve the noble end of social evolution.

The most visible effect of these new attitudes in the theatre was the absorbing interest in detailed stage properties and little pantomimed business on the stage. Objects became as important as actors. They not only documented for the audience the authentic qualities of the environment but also gave the actors a sense of reality as they interacted with the environment. Anton Chekhov, the great Russian dramatist of the period, created characters out of their little daily actions. One director who worked with him wrote,

> He represented human beings only as he observed them in life, and he could not dissociate them from their surroundings: from the rosy morning or the blue twilight, from sounds, odours, rain, trembling shutters, the lamp, the stove, the samovar, the piano, the harmonica, tobacco, the sisters, the in-laws, neighbors, song, drink, from everyday existence, from the million trifles that give warmth to life.

That last phrase—"the million trifles that give warmth to life"—might be the motto of the whole realistic movement.

NATURALISM

Realism refers to any play that tries to create the illusion of a real place on stage where ordinary people live their everyday lives. In the 1880s a deeper wave of realism, called *naturalism,* went much further than the exploration of daily life by probing into the violent forces that lie beneath the surface. The naturalistic realists set about making people face the basic facts of hunger, greed, and sex—drives that it would be dangerous to ignore. Sigmund Freud, a Viennese physician, was soon to insist that if the basic drives are not given normal outlets, they may emerge indirectly in distorted and destructive ways, and that our emotional health depends on making the conscious mind aware of the hatreds and drives we have suppressed for fear they are not respectable. Naturalism was also based on an explicit philosophy of *determinism*—the belief that there is no freedom of will or choice but that all is "determined" by heredity and environment—a philosophy that grew directly out of Darwin's ideas on natural selection and evolution.

In 1881, the French novelist and playwright Emile Zola described the kind of dramatic characters appropriate to naturalism: "I am waiting for someone to put a man of flesh and bones on the stage, taken from reality, scientifically analyzed, and described without one lie. . . . I am waiting for environment to determine the characters and the characters to act according to the logic of facts combined with the logic of their disposition." Zola and his fellow naturalists objected to nineteenth-century melodramas and farces because they never faced a real problem. After several acts of suspense, the missing papers were recovered, the accused hero was proven innocent, the long-lost child was found, or lightning struck the villain. No one had to face a major loss or adjust to people who had both good and bad qualities. Audiences who were shocked at plays that actually faced real problems sanctimoniously pronounced, "Keep your eyes on the stars," but the naturalist answered, "And fall into a ditch!"

Zola wrote several naturalistic plays, but the Norwegian playwright Henrik Ibsen, with *A Doll's House* (1879) and *Ghosts* (1881), was already becoming the European champion of naturalistic truth versus conventional hypocrisy. In *A Doll's House*, Torvald, a stuffy businessman, is horrified to learn that his charming wife, Nora, has innocently forged her father's name to borrow money. Though she did it to save her husband, he fears that her exposure will disgrace him, and he turns on her in bitter anger. When someone offers to cover up the scandal, Torvald forgives her, preparing the audience for the traditional, all-is-forgiven reconciliation. Nora, however, has now seen his selfishness and hypocrisy and realizes that he has never treated her as an adult. She walks out of the house to make her own life with a slam of the door that was heard all over the Western world. *Ghosts* made an even sharper attack on convention by bringing the subject of venereal disease to the stage and by indicating that the leading character, Mrs. Alving, should have ignored the moral judgment of her pastor and walked out on her debauched husband. In the end she must face the horrible dilemma of either giving poison to their son, whose mind has been destroyed by the inherited disease, or of caring for him as an idiot. But the play does not tell us her decision; it leaves her staring at him in horror, "her hands twisted in her hair." Naturalistic characters must make painful choices, not merely toy with the picturesque problems of romantic heroes, and Ibsen leaves his naturalistic audiences caught on the final question. They must decide for themselves where the characters' action will lead after the curtain falls.

For the serious treatment of the problems of "real" people, Ibsen perfected a form already popular, called the "well-made play," a very compact play of few characters, with careful exposition, logical progression, great suspense, and strong conflict, all leading up to surprising climaxes and impressive curtains with all the problems resolved. Because the "well-made play" was already familiar to

Nora shying away from Torvald's attempt at reconciliation. Claire Bloom and Donald Madden in Ibsen's *A Doll's House*. The Playhouse, New York, directed by Patrick Garland, 1971.

Realism or naturalism showing the influence of environment on character. The grouping is complex and varied, clear but not obviously designed. Kingsley's *Dead End*. New York, 1935. Directed and designed by Norman Bel Geddes.

audiences of popular melodramas, Ibsen could use it to show men and women rebelling against the basic attitudes of nineteenth-century society and then startle audiences with endings that challenged their expectations.

Much realistic and naturalistic literature displayed a zealous determination to tear off the mask of respectability and show human nature in its brute vitality, to face facts, to expose corruption and hypocrisy. "To make man better," Chekhov said, "you must first show him what he is." After a century of industrial revolution, European cities were a mass of slums, but the Victorian middle class enjoyed its idealized stereotypes in sentimental literature and refused to look at the poverty and misery that abounded. George Bernard Shaw made respectable people look at some of the unpleasant facts of economic life. In *Major Barbara*, for instance, he showed that slum properties from which church-going landlords collected their rents bred disease and crime, and that society would do better to build a decent world for the workers than to depend on such charities as the Salvation Army to keep the workers from rebelling.

Both the radicals of the time, who looked for a revolution of the workers, and the liberals, who put their hope in new laws, labor unions, education, and slum clearance, welcomed the new realistic art. It would show people the actual conditions, expose the problems, and make the public aware that even slum dwellers had human feelings. Since that first enthusiasm, realistic art has helped to bring about so vast a transformation of human environment in all the industrialized nations of the world that artists in emerging nations everywhere continue to regard "social realism" as the most important form of art.

In America, interest in realism began to grow after World War I, especially in the decade of the Depression, from 1929 to 1939. Sidney Kingsley's *Dead End* (1935) reinforced the hopes of the New Deal of the Franklin D. Roosevelt era and exploded the myth that the poor can help themselves. It brought together on the stage a slum alley and the courtyard of a luxury apartment house and studied the effects of these entirely different environments on each other. The play shows in detail how alley boys learn to be gangsters. An alumnus of the slums, now a famous killer returning home for the last time, teaches the boys how to follow in his footsteps, thus goading a young architect to work toward improving the housing of his slum neighbors instead of dreaming of escape with the rich. But the main impact on the audience comes not from the story of the architect or the gangster but from a succession of moods, blending together many small conflicts and discords of characters drifting, struggling, suffering, and dreaming of impossible escapes.

IMPRESSIONISM: A METHOD OF DEPICTING REALISM

Such an emphasis on moods occurs frequently in realistic and naturalistic plays. Most, in fact, use techniques both in writing and production that correspond to the techniques of impressionism in painting and music. While we don't usually apply the term *impressionism* to realism, we can understand realism far better if we notice that painting, music, and drama responded in much the same way to the same historical developments of the late nineteenth century and that the aesthetics of impressionism in painting and music are much the same as those of realism and naturalism in the theatre. Hence we may speak of realistic plays in which strong conflicts are kept muted as impressionist.

Impressionism was developed in the second half of the nineteenth century in reaction to the strident intensities of romanticism. Instead of choosing heroic subjects for large canvases, painters became interested in the passing moods of the local landscape, the atmosphere of various times of day, and the special qualities of such objects as jugs, tables, and fabrics. Claude Monet wanted to catch in his paintings the impression of a cathedral half lost in the haze of early morning or a Japanese garden in the varying atmospheres of the changing seasons. The French composer Claude Debussy was fascinated by sea, clouds, mist, and rain, by the thought of a cathedral with its chimes deep under the sea or by the local color of a Spanish town at festival time. In the 1890s he was working out a music of new harmonies, weaving many little themes into rich textures of mood and avoiding most of the conventional harmonies and expected progressions.

Now, nearly a century after impressionism reached its first flowering, the basic attitude toward life that produced it is clearer to us. The techniques of impressionism—in painting, the tiny dots of color, the bold brush strokes, the blurred lines that blend gardens, bridges, trees, and people into soft-focus images that almost disappear into the background; in music, the overlapping sequences, the massed chords, the exotic harmonies that blend the fragments of melodies into muted discords; in the theatre, the details of setting and properties, the overlapping bits of dialogue and background sounds, the tentative gestures and movements that blend the characters and the locality into rich moods—express the belief, explicit in the plays and implicit in painting and

Realism and impressionism—a mood of nostalgia and indecision. The scene is indoors, but no visible wall divides it from the cherry orchard, a symbol that dominates the lives of the characters. Andrei Serban's production of Chekhov's *The Cherry Orchard*, Lincoln Center, 1977.

music, that human beings have no freedom from the environment of which they are both product and helpless victims. This belief, as we have seen, is basic to naturalism. Foreground disappears into background, melody into accompaniment, and individual decisions into unconscious natural and social forces. People may try to escape the environment or struggle against it, but they are themselves threads in a complex web. In impressionist plays, as in impressionist music, there is never a decisive beginning or end, never a clear-cut climax or turn, because no one is expected to make a major decision. Violence may smolder beneath the surface and even erupt offstage, but the main characters are bewildered victims who do not understand their own feelings. In presenting such passive people, the playwright weaves a complex pattern from suggestions of mood, hints of half-formed desires and impulses, and fragments of abortive action, which can be more expressive than the strong plot of a typical nineteenth-century play.

Theatrical Impressionism: *The Three Sisters* and *Trifles*

Anton Chekhov's *The Three Sisters,* already discussed as a tragicomedy in Chapter 5, shows how impressionistic patterns were worked out in the theatre. The sisters fret at the dullness of their provincial town and dream for four acts of escaping to Moscow, but they are trapped by their own attitudes and habits, while Moscow slips further and further into the maze of unfulfilled hopes. Masha had married a local schoolmaster at age eighteen, thinking him the cleverest of men. Now, seven years later, she finds him a boring pedant, while she dreams of going "home" to Moscow where her brother, Andrey, will become a professor. Olga, the eldest, nobly entered the teaching profession, but the boring work gives her constant headaches, and she dreams of returning to Moscow and of marrying, not seeming to notice how marriage has only added to Masha's boredom. Irene, the youngest, just turned twenty, lies in bed mornings dreaming of Moscow and of getting a job to fill her days with satisfying work, not seeming to notice how work bores Olga. Andrey's professorship seems to be their main hope for getting to Moscow, but he has fallen for a vulgar local girl whom they despise.

The play opens on a bright day in early summer. Irene's birthday is the occasion for everyone gathering—friends, family, and officers from the local regiment—but the birthday itself never comes into focus. Each character may for a moment show excitement over a gift, an offer of congratulations, or a birthday cake, reminding the audience repeatedly of the celebration. But the enthusiasm is always diffused by some petty concern, by the inappropriateness of the gift (Masha's husband gives the same book each year), or by a sarcastic remark. In addition, the characters never all focus on the same thing at once. Instead, they are dispersed around the room in separate groupings, carrying on separate conversations, constantly frustrating the audience's desire for unity. The conversations also counterpoint each other ironically. While Olga tells her sisters how she

Each grouping has its own focus in this impressionistic treatment of Chekhov's *The Three Sisters*. Intiman Theatre Company, Seattle. Directed by Margaret Booker.

woke up this morning "happy," and "felt such a longing to get back to Moscow," two men, deep in their own conversation, enter and quite unconsciously comment on Olga's feelings: "The devil you have!" the first one says to his friend, to which the second replies, "It's nonsense, I agree."

By the end of Act I, two hopes for the future dominate: The sisters expect to go to Moscow at the end of summer, and Andrey hopes to marry the local girl, Natasha. When Act II opens, we quickly learn that it is now mid-winter. The date for going to Moscow has passed unnoticed, and they are now counting the months till they will go to Moscow in June. Andrey's hoped-for marriage has already taken place, and Natasha is fully established in the household with a new baby, ready to take over Olga's room for a nursery, while Andrey, apparently having forgotten his great love, only speaks of the boredom and confinement of marriage. Irene now works at the post office, but gets no satisfaction from the work and wants to change jobs or get married. Olga wants out of her teaching job and would still like to get married, but will finally be pushed out of her room and end up living at the school as headmistress. Thus, the characters drift through the play, constantly reminding us of their hopes and dreams, trying to find some meaning in their lives, but uncontrollably distracted from taking decisive actions. The audience is made to sympathize with their deep-felt desire for something beautiful and meaningful in their lives, yet must look with tolerant amusement at the way they simply drift, allowing meaningful events to pass by unnoticed.

Some of the moods and techniques of impressionism appeared in America as early as 1916 in Susan Glaspell's one-act play, *Trifles*, where everything occurs by indirection and suggestion. The main character, a farm woman suspected of her husband's murder, never comes on stage. On stage we see the sheriff clumping around looking for a sensational motive, while his wife and a neighbor woman look over the little things about the house—the "trifles." Gradually, through the women's idle chatter, we are able to reconstruct the lonely life the woman led, with nothing but a morose husband and a songbird for company. When the women discover the stiffened body of the tiny bird, its neck wrung, lying in the folds of a sewing basket, we come to know how the woman's lonely desperation, smoldering for years beneath the surface, finally erupted and drove her to kill her husband.

Impressionism accepted the idea of human helplessness in a baffling world, but sought for understanding and compassion. If it could not trace any clear purpose or larger meaning in the absurd contradictions of life, it could at least discover a rich, vibrant texture in the relation of the characters to the environment. Not all realistic plays are impressionistic, of course, but even those that involve decisive characters and melodramatic action will require acting and directing methods that call attention to complex motivations and the subtle effects of environment on the characters.

NEW THEATRES AND A NEW ACTING METHOD

Impressionist plays—indeed, all the new plays of realism and naturalism—demanded not only a new kind of playwriting but a new kind of theatre and new acting styles. No realistic play had a chance in a huge nineteenth-century theatre with its tiers of balconies built to accommodate up to four thousand people. The large stage, intended for spectacular romantic scenes and operatic choruses, was a vast open space with scenery consisting of painted flats and backdrops. The actors were expected to act close to the footlights, where their large gestures could be seen and their oratorical voices heard clearly throughout the house.

The movement for a more intimate theatre started with a few bold, enterprising groups late in the nineteenth century and was so successful that by the 1920s practically all the new theatres of Western Europe and America had, at the most, a thousand to fifteen hundred seats. The idea of intimate theatre has won out, and today, most new college theatres seat no more than three or four hundred.

The first great step toward both realism and intimacy in the theatre was taken in London in 1865 when Squire Bancroft and his wife refurbished a small neglected theatre and found a new director and playwright, T. W. Robertson. Robertson put his actors in the midst of real furniture, and real doors, ceilings, and windows, and used the upstage as well as the downstage areas. He achieved a more subtle and more realistic ensemble acting than had been known before, making his sentimental scenes and everyday people convincing through an intimate, everyday kind of delivery and everyday kinds of activity. His critics made fun of his "teacup and saucer" realism, however, and soon it came to seem mild and superficial.

A stronger impetus was given by the Norwegian rebel Henrik Ibsen. He founded no theatre, but his plays were the inspiration for new theatres throughout the world. The first of these new "free" theatres—free, that is, from commercial control and state censorship—was the Théâtre Libre in Paris, founded in 1887 by André Antoine, who earned his living as a gas clerk. In a tiny hall, using real furniture, some of which Antoine carted through the streets from his mother's dining room, he and a group of amateur actors soon attracted a sizable audience. Within ten years, similar free theatres had sprung up in Berlin, London, and Dublin, where they inspired such new playwrights of realism as Gerhart Hauptmann, George Bernard Shaw, an admirer of Ibsen, and John Millington Synge, respectively. Most important of the new theatres, however, was the Moscow Art Theatre, founded in 1897 by Constantin Stanislavsky and Vladimir Nemirovich-Danchenko. Anton Chekhov was the new playwright who ensured its success. It established itself as a lasting institution and is still the principal theatre in Moscow.

In America the intimate theatre came a little later. From 1916 to 1920, on Cape Cod, the Provincetown Players introduced the naturalistic one-act plays of their gifted playwright, Eugene O'Neill. The Provincetown Playhouse, which they established in 1919 in a converted stable on MacDougal Street in New York, was even smaller than the realistic theatres of Europe, but it made an enormous impression. Soon the Theatre Guild, and even the commercial producers, adopted its ideals of honesty and realistic acting. Like the Off Broadway theatres of recent decades, the "free" theatres started on a small scale, with ideals of acting, directing, and playwriting quite different from those of the big commercial theatres. Though short-lived, they pointed the way for others and proved that a new audience was ready.

In the intimate theatres the proscenium arch as a decorative element was simplified, leaving only a functional opening for viewing the "slice of life." Footlights, with their distasteful associations with glaring, romantic spectacle and ham acting, gave way to overhead spotlights that simulated the normal directions of natural lighting. The *box set* is the basic setting in realism, using three walls and a ceiling, with the illusion that the fourth wall has been removed.

A cellar is the lodging place of Gorki's derelicts in the Moscow Art Theatre production of *The Lower Depths*, 1902.

Though actors have occasionally supposed a fireplace and even windows in the missing wall, most groups soon found it better to ignore that wall and to keep the actors facing in toward the properties and action on the stage.

Directing and Acting in the Realistic Theatre

With changes in theatres and plays came new principles of directing: keep the actors focused on some center of interest on the stage; make full use of many different playing areas, especially the upstage areas; enrich the action with frequent use of properties and bodily reactions. The visit of the Moscow Art Theatre company to New York in 1923 left a lasting impression as the ultimate in "art that hid all art." Nothing was obviously arranged, yet everything was meticulously clear. The actors seemed to have their backs to the audience constantly and to be absorbed in the other actors or in something behind the furniture; no one ever moved out into a clear open space; no one ever seemed to turn toward the audience. Yet behind the casualness was such careful planning that for every important line the speaker just happened to have his face visible. Despite what appeared to be informal composition and random movement, the attention of the audience was always carried straight to the important person or action. Though each character seemed completely independent of the others, so strong was the basic rhythm that they all became part of one compelling action. There was no star, no predominant character, but rather a perfect ensemble. The foreground and background were one, and costumes, doors, lamps, window curtains, and lights—no less than the actors—performed their parts.

Beginning in 1897 at the Moscow Art Theatre, Stanislavsky gradually worked out a systematic "method" for training actors to play the new realistic drama, a method that was to become the basis for most actor training in Russia, Western Europe, and America—everywhere that realism gained importance. It was not enough to fill the stage with real furniture and properties and to pull the actors back from the footlights for more quiet, intimate acting. It was not enough to give them small properties to handle. In order to give life to such complex characters as those in *The Three Sisters,* baffled or overwhelmed by the environment and their own motivations, the actors needed to find the inner life of the characters, a life beyond, between, and sometimes in contradiction to the words. They had to find the "inner text," the subtext, to add a complex richness to the actions, voice tones, and words.

The main reason for the success of the Stanislavsky method is the precision with which it expresses the materialistic vision of human beings trapped by

Realism. Diagonal lines and dynamic variations of level create a total sense of environment in this University of Texas production of *Who's Afraid of Virginia Woolf?*, directed by James Moll.

heredity and environment, victims of their baser drives, their wills thwarted, unable to express their feelings even when deeply moved. Mute violence stirs through the inner being, coloring daily movements and breaking into the ordinary voice tones. Without deliberately raising the voice or asserting a gesture, the method actor can move an audience deeply by suggesting a dark, inarticulate tragedy that is held in. We will examine that method in more detail in Chapter 13.

FACTUAL REALISM ON SCREEN AND STAGE

The drama, like the novel, has always relied heavily on factual material as a source. But it was the movies that first realized the possibilities of using factual material directly for informative entertainment, without "plot," with real people in real-life situations as actors, and with minimal arrangement of the filmed scenes.

The Film Documentary

While Hollywood was producing Cecil B. DeMille's colossal spectacles, superromantic films with Rudolph Valentino, and equally unreal pictures about the social games of wealthy people, Robert Flaherty created the documentary, a type of film that had enormous influence not only on movies but on television, epic theatre, and other forms of stage drama. In 1922 he filmed *Nanook of the North*, showing the daily life and trials of a real Eskimo family, and in 1934, *Man of Aran*, showing life on an isolated island off the coast of Ireland. Flaherty's photography and editing made these studies of real life as absorbing as any fictional film.

The 1930s saw the development of documentaries which challenged public policy in studies of such problems as misuse of land and water and the decay of cities. By the 1970s documentary movies were treating a wide range of political and social problems, everything from the evils in mental hospitals and nursing homes to racial injustice and corruption in business and politics. A striking film made in Japan in 1970, which received wide circulation in America through the anti-nuke movement of the early 1980s, was *Hiroshima: A Documentary of the Atomic Bombing*. Using clips of film taken before and following the bombing of the city on August 6, 1945, it showed the horrors found in the remains of the city, as well as the often futile attempts to help the survivors, and it traced the effects that were still emerging thirty-five years later. The movie ends with the devastating effects from test blasts of the much more powerful H-bomb, which would be the weapon of any future nuclear conflict.

A documentary that captures human motivation as well as human suffering is *Harlan County, U.S.A.* (1976), made by Barbara Kepple over a four-year period in a coal-mining community in Harlan County, Kentucky. It deals with a strike in 1973, but it shows the poor homes and hard daily routines of the miners and their

Simplified realism for the strong tensions of several groups of Americans in a shabby hotel in Mexico. Williams' *The Night of the Iguana*. Indiana University production, directed and designed by Richard L. Scammon.

families as well as the confrontations with spokesmen of the company, armed strike-breakers, and police. The director's sympathy is with the miners, but she gives an honest, unsensational view. She is especially successful in filming the women, individually and in groups, showing the grim, worn faces as the women carry out their own plans for opposing the common enemy. Contrasting scenes, after the strike is won by the miners, show the return to normal living, with close-ups of relaxed or smiling faces, some of the miners singing. The picture carries implications about all communities of hard-working, impoverished people leading dangerous lives, with little defense from the thoughtless or callous decisions of employers.

Documentary realism is a staple of television. Every important political event is the subject of a "special report" that provides background material and a summary and analysis of the event itself. Extensive accounts of interesting geographical areas, scientific discoveries, space flights, celebrities, significant historical events are brought visually into the home. The viewer is bombarded with factual material, much of it with suspense, confrontation, and other dramatic elements, even if it does not tell the story of a fictional character. Among television's more successful attempts to document human behavior have been some of the "Odyssey" documentaries of the early 1980s. In one episode, "N!ai: The Story of a Kung Woman," a young woman is followed over a twenty-seven-year period, from childhood and marriage in the free Namibian bush country through the relocation of her people by South African whites, with all the social and economic disorientation that followed. Here, instead of the intimate exposure of an isolated family, the details from N!ai's life come to stand for traumatic change in a whole culture.

Theatre of Fact

A stage equivalent of the film documentary, sometimes called *theatre of fact*, differs from the documentary in using professional actors, but it adheres closely to the factual material on which it is based. Instead of pictures and flashbacks, it uses only words, often the exact words spoken as testimony as in a trial. The playwright's control comes in selecting which facts and words to include and which to omit, and therein lie the strengths of this form—and its dangers.

Many artists prefer to avoid the controversy that comes from representing real events and real people in the theatre by changing the names and consistently keeping the details slightly different from actuality. Then the play is clearly a metaphor, a semblance, a work of art with carefully controlled aesthetic distance. Since the theatre is more immediate, more public, than the other arts, people cry out, "That's not the way it was!" when things get too close to their own knowledge and experience.

An even larger artistic problem occurs when a sentimental array of external facts is substituted for a deeper, more probing realism, which, in the words of Ralph Waldo Emerson, "dare[s] to uncover those simple and terrible laws which, seen or unseen, pervade and govern." Such is the weakness of the movie *All the President's Men* (1976). For all its treatment of the facts in the story of two reporters who sought the truth about the Watergate break-in and cover-up during Richard Nixon's campaign for reelection, it remains essentially a melodrama, with spotless reporter heroes and deep-dyed bureaucratic villains who try to cover their own tracks.

The Trial of the Catonsville Nine, staged in a church in 1971 by the Phoenix Theatre, uses actual court records to probe into America's court system. Daniel Berrigan, one of the nine defendants who had broken into a selective service office in Catonsville, Maryland in May 1968, willfully removed and burned draft records and then waited peaceably for the authorities to arrive, recreated the trial in which all the defendants were convicted for their act of civil disobedience. To the audience, the professional actors seemed to be the defendants themselves on trial. Using the actual words of the trial, they openly professed their illegal act, but pleaded their defense on moral justification and on the personal backgrounds that brought each of them to that draft board office. But more than the pleas of the defendants, the deeper reality that confronted the audience was that the court system had no room for recognizing the higher law to which the defendants were appealing. This was disturbingly accented by the judge's final instructions to the jury, that it was not to judge the case "on the basis of conscience." Reaction to the play was strong. Nevertheless, it won praise mainly from those who already agreed with its attempt to discredit the American judicial system.

The responses aroused by plays and films dealing with the Nazi extermination camps have revealed special problems. The extermination of more than six million people is too shocking ever to be forgotten, and emotions run strong. In what perspective can we think about it? How can we relate it to other human deeds—the bombing of Coventry, Dresden, Hiroshima, the Jonestown mass suicides, the massacre of Palestinian refugees in Lebanon? Who is responsible? In the 1960s a powerful play by Peter Weiss, *The Investigation* (1965), showed not the extermination camps, but only the witnesses and survivors as they testified at the trial, with selections of actual testimony. In Germany the play aroused controversy, though it appeared to be a simple documentary, an example of theatre of fact.

Even more disturbing was the story-like treatment in Rolf Hochhuth's play *The Deputy* (1963). It asks why important people, Pope Pius XII, for instance, did not do something to stop the wholesale killing of the Jews. In story form, Hochhuth depicted the Pope, afraid of disturbing his already difficult relations with the Axis regimes in Italy and Germany, failing his opportunity. The play brought angry denials that the Pope could have been expected to do more than he did. The same idea expressed in an editorial or a speech might have been disturbing, but it would not have had nearly so strong an impact as the play. The stage gives the solid appearance of objective reality; what is said and done there seems much more than the subjective opinion of an author.

Whatever the artistic approach, the emotions surrounding recent historical material are bound to raise controversy. The 1978 television series "Holocaust" was a fictional reconstruction of the Nazi attempt to exterminate the Jews, incorporating appropriate historical people, places, and events. In ten episodes it moved relentlessly through the entire period, showing the human factor by dramatizing many different types of people caught up in the horror: those who planned it, those who went along with it, those who turned blind eyes as though it weren't happening, as well as those who tried in small and big ways to resist it—bureaucrats, family members, professionals, shopkeepers. No one escaped the searching eye of this monumental and painful study of human motivation under duress. Many could not bring themselves to watch it because of its intense horror. The whole series was played in West Germany where a new generation, born after the war, watched in shock the cascading events of their own history, while those who had lived through it tried to account for the unaccountable.

Since "Holocaust," several television specials have focused on specific personalities of those years of the Third Reich. A 1982 special, "Playing for Time" (1982), focused on one of the victims, a young entertainer and her degrading methods of surviving the concentration camps. This special was attacked for its controversial casting of Vanessa Redgrave (an avowed supporter of the PLO) in the role of the entertainer.

American Realism of the 1950s: *A Raisin in the Sun*

Realism was what American theatre audiences expected in the 1950s, so it was the obvious style for Lorraine Hansberry to choose for *A Raisin in the Sun* (1958), the story of a black family's struggle to rise out of the Chicago slums and out of the ghetto mind-set that threatened them even more than their slum surroundings. But realism was also a sound choice artistically; its style admirably expressed the action and themes inherent in Hansberry's subject.

The Younger family lives cramped together in a tiny South Side Chicago apartment: Walter Lee and Ruth Younger, their ten-year-old son, Travis, Walter Lee's sister, Beneatha, and their "Mama," Lena Younger. Life is a struggle for

Walter Lee and Beneatha enacting a dream of their African heritage in *A Raisin in the Sun*. Eastern Illinois University, directed by E. G. Gabbard.

the Younger family from the moment the curtain rises. A single room with one window is both living room and kitchen, and as an alarm goes off and Ruth comes in to shake Travis awake on the couch, we see that it is also the boy's bedroom. Races to get to the bathroom down the hall before the neighbors do punctuate this early morning scene, interspersed with making beds, getting breakfast, ironing clothes, and a pattern of family squabbles while everyone hurries to get off to school or to work. Money is a struggle. When Ruth doesn't have fifty cents for Travis to take to school, Walter Lee magnanimously produces it, plus an extra fifty cents for a treat, but later has to get from Ruth his own streetcar fare. Deep family love is obvious at every level, but the crowded, dingy apartment, the need to stretch too little money, and the drudgery of laboring in other people's kitchens and chauffeuring other people's cars put a heavy toll on the family.

Mama enters from her room only after this morning hullabaloo. She dominates by her very presence, strong of body and of character and protective of her family. She goes straight to the window, opens it, and brings in a "feeble little plant," which she nourishes with tender care. One short speech by Mama joins plant and family in parallel struggles against their environment: "My children and they tempers. Lord, if this little old plant don't get more sun than it's been getting it ain't never going to see spring again."

But the struggle is not aimless. The characters dream, and their dreams inspire their action. Beneatha has dreamed since childhood of becoming a doctor, since she saw a badly injured boy healed by medical skill. Walter Lee dreams of rising above his demeaning role as chauffeur, driving his own car, being looked up to, being someone his son can be proud of. Mama and Ruth dream of escaping from the slums to a real house, with a yard where Travis can play, a garden where Mama can grow things, and, most of all, air and space to nurture family unity and growth. As preface to the playscript, Hansberry quotes a Langston Hughes poem that underscores the characters' dreams and also gives the play its title:

What happens to a dream deferred?
Does it dry up
Like a raisin in the sun?
Or fester like a sore—
And then run?
Does it stink like rotten meat?
Or crust and sugar over—
Like a syrupy sweet?

Maybe it just sags
Like a heavy load.

Or does it explode?

All their dreams have been deferred, Mama's for many years. With her husband, Big Walter, she had taken this apartment as a young bride only until they could afford the real house they dreamed of. That was almost forty years ago. Walter Lee has to play at being the generous father until he can get his riches and his respect. Beneatha's dream is so remote that she tries one form of self-expression after another, with no apparent satisfaction—African folk dance, guitar, photography. Ruth's dream for a happy family life seems equally remote, and when she learns she's pregnant, she is so afraid of the added burden to their lives that she considers an abortion.

The dreams might have festered for years, but the legacy of Big Walter's dream for his family—a $10,000 life insurance policy—hangs over them as both a hope and a cloud. Ruth insists that Mama use the money on herself, while Beneatha clearly expects it to provide for her education. But Walter Lee is most insistent; he wants to invest in a liquor store to make them all rich and looked up to. When Mama sees the dreams tearing her family apart, she uses $3,500 of the money as down payment on a house in the suburbs. In a passionate appeal, Mama tries to make her son understand:

> I—I just seen my family falling apart today . . . just falling to pieces in front of my eyes . . . We was going backwards 'stead of forwards—talking 'bout killing babies and wishing each other was dead . . . When it gets like that in life—you just got to do something different, push on out and do something bigger . . . *(She waits)* I wish you say something, son . . . I wish you'd say how deep inside you you think I done the right thing—

But Walter Lee is shattered by her lack of trust in him:

> What you need me to say you done right for? *You* the head of this family. You run our lives like you want to. . . . So you butchered up a dream of mine—you—who always talking 'bout your children's dreams . . .

As an act of faith, Mama finally gives him the remaining money—$3,000 to put in an account for Beneatha's schooling, the rest for himself. Walter Lee's dream has so distorted his judgment that he gives all the money to one of his cronies to invest in the liquor store. Sure that he is now on his way to great wealth, he describes to Travis the "good life" ahead, with gardeners and convertibles and college catalogues from

> all the great schools in the world. . . . Just tell me where you want to go to school and you'll *go*. Just tell me, what it is you want to be—Yessir! *(He holds his arms open for* TRAVIS*)* You just name it, son . . . *(*TRAVIS *leaps into them)* and I hand you the world!

But the dreams are about to explode. Mama's dream goes first when Mr. Lindner, representing the all-white neighborhood where she's bought the house, offers them a profit not to move. The tension is electric, but it unites the family in their determination to follow Mama's dream. They order Lindner from their home, Mama gets her plant ready for the move, and the family showers her with moving gifts, gardening tools—and from Travis, a sun bonnet. Reality in another form explodes the remaining dreams. Walter Lee's friend has absconded with the money—his investment, Beneatha's education, and with them the hopes of escape from the slums—all vanished.

Mama, only by determined strength of character, rises above her initial fury. But Walter Lee, aimlessly trying to grasp some shred of sense, opens up new chasms. He decides to play the world's game—to take the money that the whites have offered. When Lindner returns, Walter Lee promises to put on a show: "Maybe I'll just get down on my black knees. . . . Yasssssuh! Great White Father, just gi' ussen de money, fo' God's sake, and we's ain't gwine come out deh and dirty up yo' white folks neighborhood." Mama cries in anguish, "Son—I come from five generations of people who was slaves and sharecroppers—but ain't nobody in my family never let nobody pay 'em no money that was a way of telling us we wasn't fit to walk the earth. We ain't never been that poor. . . . We ain't never been that dead inside." She mourns the level to which her son has sunk, but he is still her son, and when Beneatha denies him as a brother, with nothing left in him to love, Mama rises to her full motherly eloquence:

> Child, when do you think is the time to love somebody the most; when they done good and made things easy for everybody? Well then, you ain't through learning—because that ain't the time at all. It's when he's at his lowest and can't believe in hisself 'cause the world done whipped him so. When you starts measuring somebody, measure him right, child, measure him right. Make sure you done taken into account what hills and valleys he come through before he got to wherever he is.

When Lindner arrives, Walter Lee sends Travis out, but Mama intervenes. Walter Lee must make his son understand what he is doing. Here, in front of his son, things finally come clear for Walter Lee. He begins quietly, simply, describing his family as plain people, chauffeurs, domestic workers, "and—uh—well, my father, well, he was a laborer most of his life." But the image of his father raises from his memories a new vision—"My father almost beat a man to death once because this man called him a bad name or something, you know what I mean?" Lindner doesn't know, and suddenly Walter Lee is portraying his family not as plain, but as proud.

> That's my sister over there and she's going to be a doctor—and we are very proud. . . . What I am telling you is that we called you over here to tell you that we are very proud and that this is—this is my son, who makes the sixth generation of our family in this country, and that we have all thought about your offer and we have decided to move into our house because my father— my father—he earned it. . . . We don't want your money.

Following the patterns of earlier realistic plays, Lorraine Hansberry has shown the destructive effects of environment on the Younger family: the years of

Walter Lee Younger (Ossie Davis) stands protectively with son Travis, while Mama (Claudia McNeil) stolidly resists the white man's bribe to give up her house. *A Raisin in the Sun* on Broadway.

poverty and struggle in a confining slum and the tensions of broken dreams that slowly drain the vitality from life. But she also shows how the generations of pride that have been the Younger heritage, handed down by Big Walter's legacy and Mama's strength of character, finally bear fruit. They no longer have the money, but Mama has found her dream, and Walter Lee has claimed his manhood in the reality of his family, not in some illusive pipedream. As in earlier realistic plays, Hansberry also accents the reality that still lies ahead at the end of the play. The family leaves the apartment for the last time and, as the lights dim, the door opens and Mama comes back in—to get her plant. The environment will be new, the house and yard and open space will provide a fresh beginning, but like the plant, the family must still be nurtured through the turmoil that the new neighborhood will bring. For realistic characters, life goes on after the final curtain, and Mama's plant is a closing reminder of the past from which the characters have come and the future toward which they are going.

(For a detailed view of another realistic play, see Chapter 13, where George Bernard Shaw's play *Pygmalion* is used to highlight the work of the actor in the theatre.)

FILM REALISM AFTER WORLD WAR II

New Realism in Italian Films

While Hollywood, at the end of World War II, was still caught up in formulistic romantic stories, big studio monopolies, and a "code of decency" that forbade such things as explicit sex, profane language, venereal disease, childbirth, and even a double bed in a married couple's house, Italian filmmakers rediscovered the harsh reality of direct realism. Roberto Rossellini finished *Open City* in 1945 as the Germans were leaving, presenting actual street scenes and using harsh black

Realism in Italian film-making. A bricklayer who caught the eye of director Vittorio DeSica as the star in *The Bicycle Thief*. The vacant market, the huddled crowd under the awning, and the forlorn boy protecting himself from the rain show the use of environment to reflect the condition of the characters.

and white film because he could not afford better. But the sun-drenched Roman streets, the sharp shadows, the tenement rooms, and the fresh, nonprofessional performers made a very exciting, unsentimental picture of violence and terror at the end of the war. Vittorio DeSica filmed *Shoeshine* in 1946 with street urchins as actors, and when a bricklayer's face caught his fancy, a man who had never acted before became the star of *Bicycle Thief* (1949). American audiences especially were fascinated by the real people, real streets, real economic problems, and real political passions, and the Italian film quickly became one of the strongest influences on Western cinema.

The masterpiece of Italian realism was Federico Fellini's *La Strada* (1954), a touching story of tramp carnival performers. A coarse wandering entertainer, Zampano, played by Anthony Quinn, picks up a young, retarded girl, Gelsomina. He buys her, in fact, from her impoverished mother. She learns to play a trumpet, to dance, and to do her part in making their living, accepting Zampano's rough treatment and infidelities. They join a troupe of carnival people, and an acrobat befriends her. When Zampano kills the acrobat and he and Gelsomina are outcasts on the road, Zampano is unable to cope with her grief, and he abandons her. Obsessed with the memory of the girl, he eventually finds the village where she had wandered, only to learn that she is dead. In the last sequence he throws himself to the ground on the shore of the gray sea, overcome by grief and despair. Here, with excellent naturalistic acting and directing, are the basic elements of nineteenth-century naturalism—inarticulate characters driven and destroyed by crude natural forces, in harsh but rich-textured surroundings, invoking not our moral judgment but our compassion and objective understanding.

Belated Realism in American Movies

Through the 1950s and into the 1960s, Italian, British, Swedish, and Indian filmmakers provided a continuous supply of the new realistic movies to American "art-film" theatres, but American filmmakers could not get far with realism until there were major changes in public attitudes and in the film business itself. The movies were the entertainment of the masses. Following a notorious Hollywood scandal in 1922 that brought threats of national censorship, self-appointed guardians of morality and an industry-imposed "code of decency" saw to it that nothing was shown that might shock a conventional American family. Neither the subjects dealt with nor the manner of presenting those subjects must soil the respectability of small-town America. Overt violence and oblique references to sex were acceptable, but no serious treatment of human psychology. Not until *Gone with the Wind* in 1939 was the word "damn" heard from the American screen.

After World War II important changes paved the way for stronger realism in American movies. For one thing, the power of Hollywood studios was broken, partly by legal action which separated production from distribution, partly by independent producers working in foreign countries and using new material. But the biggest blow to Hollywood was television. By the 1950s television had become America's mass entertainment. As thousands of movie houses closed, the movies became an art for the minority. When the movies and radio in the 1920s had taken the mass audience away from the stage, the legitimate theatre had lost its wide support, but as a minority art it greatly improved. It no longer had to conform to the lowest common denominator of taste or the most conventional ideas of what is proper. In the same way the moviemaker had greater freedom as a worker in a minority art. Moreover, censorship had become less stringent through a series of legal decisions, and in 1953 the Supreme Court ruled that the screen shares with the press the protection of free speech guaranteed by the First and Fourteenth Amendments to the Constitution. In its earlier days Hollywood had neglected or greatly modified the naturalistic plays of Eugene O'Neill, but in the 1950s and 1960s the even more shocking plays of Tennessee Williams were put on the screen without flinching from the themes of cannibalism, castration, and homosexuality.

By the mid-seventies taboos in subject matter and language had almost ceased. Frank, sometimes crude, treatment of unconventional sexual behavior, emotional instability, and the use of drugs became commonplace. Dialogue was liberally sprinkled with profanity, and the introduction of nudity brought the occasional erotic scene. But it was extreme violence that became most fashionable, often for the sheer excitement of it, with no attempt to suggest that it was natural or inevitable.

We remember that Aeschylus dealt with violence offstage in ancient Greek tragedy, and even then showed how the chain of violence, ever provoking more violence, could be broken by a shift from private vengeance to public justice, a change that required religious and psychological reconditioning. Aeschylus had a hopeful view that violence belonged to an early, primitive age and could be replaced by higher concepts of order. In *A Clockwork Orange* (1971), violent cruelty is considered a mental aberration that might be altered by psychological reconditioning. But the film shows that the reconditioning does not prevent the patient from being beaten up by his former pals. Many conservative people condoned the violent and shocking scenes of *The Godfather* (1972) and *The Exorcist* (1973) on grounds that the films made an appeal to moral or religious principles. Yet they turned around and condemned the frank sexual scenes of *Last Tango in Paris* (1972), though the film had both a strong psychological interest and a superb sense of style. Our Victorian heritage of a puritanical attitude toward sex persists; but we lack any comparable deterrent to excesses of violence.

The harsh ruthlessness of modern life was seriously explored in the violence of several movies of the late 1960s and 1970s. *Midnight Cowboy, Easy Rider,* and *The Wild Bunch* in 1969, *Mean Streets* (1973), and *The Deerhunter* (1978) all delved deeply into characters who were both the perpetrators and victims of extreme violence or victims of the insurmountable perplexities of modern life that drove them to commit violence. The director Martin Scorsese in *Taxi Driver* (1975) sent his psychotic character through the strange night lights of city streets, encountering ugly violence and immoral behavior, until he starts on a killing spree himself, killing anyone he disapproves of. At the end he is driving his taxi again, as if nothing had happened, leaving the audience puzzled. Should they consider him a hero, or is the ending an ironic comment on indifference to the law? One demented youth so confused the movie with reality that he fantasized an affair with its leading actress and finally attempted to assassinate President Reagan to get her attention.

In a world of assassination, wars, lawless heads of state, business bribes, and street crimes that may or may not be punished, it is no wonder that writers and movie-makers see "reality" in harsh and bloody terms, frankly shown without evasion or cover-up. Nevertheless, by the 1980s film violence had become so common that serious movie-makers were turning their attention to other methods of film realism, while extreme violence was left to the commercial exploitation of such movies as *Halloween* and *Friday the Thirteenth,* where it was purely a box-office attraction for mass entertainment.

The special quality film brings to realism is the illusion that the camera is actually recording events as they occur, making audiences feel as though they are experiencing them firsthand. When this quality is given its full power, its ability to serve realism seems to be unmatched. Two films of 1981 made important artistic use of this aspect of film realism. Warren Beatty's movie, *Reds,* was for the most part a romantic adventure story about the radical young American journalist, John Reed, who became embroiled in the Bolshevik cause around the time of the 1917 Russian revolution, with his lover, Louise Bryant, and died in his efforts to aid the revolution firsthand. The movie takes us to such realistic events as a Cape Cod rehearsal of an early Eugene O'Neill play for the newly formed Provincetown Players, with O'Neill present, and to the spectacle of the storming of the Winter Palace in Petrograd. But the unique device that the film offers to create the most striking sense of authenticity is a series of statements, interspersed throughout the movie, by more than two dozen real-life witnesses. The film cuts to a close-up of the aged faces of such famous witnesses as Will Durant, Henry Miller, George Jessel, and Rebecca West, who then briefly reminisce about John and Louise in memories that range from gossip to fact to one rather whimsical rendition of a song in a cracked voice.

A very different type of realism is created by the Polish director, Andrzej Wajda, in *Man of Iron.* The movie follows a fictional TV journalist whom the government sends to infiltrate a workers' rebellion in Gdansk and to smear one of its leaders. Instead he himself gets caught up in the movement. Though the character is fictional, the events are real, and the film ends with the 1980 fall of the government and official recognition of the Polish workers' organization, Solidarity. It incorporates authentic footage of tanks in the streets and police beatings, many cast members who were real characters, still participating in the events at the time the film was being shown to the public, and Lech Walesa, the leader of Solidarity, playing himself in the film, both as a public and private person. For those who saw the movie at the 1981 New York Film Festival, its sense of authenticity was heightened by daily headlines in the newspapers—that Lech Walesa was in danger of being arrested, that Solidarity was being outlawed, and that a new government was imposing martial law, under the fear of Soviet intervention.

Many people have argued that, since the camera can far surpass the stage in showing reality, live theatre should give up realism and try to put on stage only the fantastic, the artificial, and the truly theatrical. Yet film, by so easily using its textures of reality to validate fantasies, sentimental stories, conventional characters, and shopworn ideas, still caters largely to the idle daydreams of the masses. Only the determined script-writers, directors, and moviegoers—ardent fighters with the spirit of Zola and Ibsen—can forget easy entertainment and deal with real life.

REALISM ON THE TELEVISION SCREEN

Broadcast drama grew up through radio to television as a distinct form, and its relation to the audience is different from that of the movie or stage play. The viewers are not out for a special occasion but are sitting at home, alone or with family or friends. Every week or every day, amidst countless commercials, they are expecting the same familiar news broadcasts, variety shows, comic or dramatic series, and soap operas in neat thirty- or sixty-minute programs. Such a relaxed audience does not encourage the development of serious drama. Nevertheless, the late 1940s and 1950s saw a remarkable growth of live television drama—new plays brought to the screen several times a week and a new school of playwrights who explored the documentary realism and quiet intimacy of radio drama to develop a form that was especially suited to television. The miniature masterpiece of this "Golden Age" of television drama was Paddy Chayevsky's *Marty* (1954, aired again in 1982 and 1984), about a worker in a butcher shop who finds relief from loneliness in the big city by marriage to an unglamorous girl as lonely as he. This and other plays of the period penetrated gently but insightfully into realistic conflicts between mothers and sons, frustration and anger in crowded apartments, and conflicts between the values of the big city and the small town or old city neighborhoods. But realistic insights were not enough to save this form of drama from the simultaneous expansion of the national economy and of the television audience in the late 1950s and 1960s. The wider, more affluent audience was not interested in little plays about little people or in themes of frustration and the acceptance of limitations—the themes of intimate realism since Chekhov.

The staple of sixties realism was the rescue hero, descended from the romantic rescue heroes of radio in the 1930s and 1940s. But now, instead of an adventurer like the Lone Ranger or Sergeant Preston of the Yukon, he or she was usually a doctor (*Dr. Kildare*), a lawyer (*Judd for the Defense*), or teacher (*Mr. Novak*) who gave mature professional advice and undertook to face complex, often personal, problems that could not easily be solved. By the seventies, a generation raised on television began to demand a realism related directly to the fears and frustrations of modern living. *All in the Family* was one of several series that brought social and political problems into the home in a mild way. The father, Archie Bunker, was laughed at for his bigotry again and again, but the emphasis was on the amusing eccentricity of his wife and that time-honored element of domestic drama, the ingenuity of wife, husband, and children in getting the better of one another or in cooperating for some good end. *Lou Grant* explored the responsibilities a metropolitan newspaper has in confronting public problems and the effects the reporting itself has on those who are the news. Meanwhile, the "soaps" became a national phenomenon, as millions of people stopped in the middle of their busy days to immerse themselves in the day-to-day traumas of their favorite soap characters, who encountered every imaginable crisis of modern life in hospitals, on the jobs, in their social lives, and in the intimacy of their homes.

A much deeper kind of serialized realism found a home on American TV when public television introduced from England the BBC series *Upstairs, Downstairs* in the early 1970s. Taking as its subject the romantic period of stately homes and live-in servants of Victorian and Edwardian England, it authentically reproduced all the most detailed social and physical aspects of the time. It followed both the upper-class family and an array of upstairs and downstairs servants through decades of daily living, squabbling, and adjusting to the changes that entered their lives through personal crises, the death of monarchs, a world war, and new social and economic conditions. This series was among the early Masterpiece Theatre offerings, which have specialized in realistic dramatization of historical novels and short stories.

Soon American producers caught the spirit of the trend. *Roots,* Alex Haley's attempt to follow the history of his ancestors from Africa through slavery and Reconstruction up to his own generation, was the major breakthrough. Though the material was often romanticized, it caught the American audience's desire to know the truth about black history from the inside, and it won the largest viewing audience in television drama history. This miniseries was followed by *Holocaust, Franklin and Eleanor, Playing for Time,* and a variety of others, so that by the early 1980s, television's persistent fare of trivial entertainment was regularly interspersed with penetrating, realistic treatments of great works of literature, historical events and movements, and important figures in history. At least one weekly series, *Hill Street Blues,* has demonstrated that there is an audience for authentic treatment of internal, day-to-day problems in a San Francisco precinct house, and that genuine drama need not depend on the spectacular chases, rescues, and violence that have usually characterized police shows.

An interesting attempt to create a fictional documentary was ABC Television's *The Day After* (1983). Pre-show publicity and warnings of potential psychological trauma in small children from the show's graphic depicting of the aftermath of nuclear war drew an estimated viewing audience of one hundred million. The attempt to document what would happen to the people of a small university city in Kansas who lived on the edge of a nuclear attack turned out to be a rather standard melodramatic disaster film. But the two-hour panel discussion by an all-star group of statesmen, humanists, and political commentators which followed the film was one of the most penetrating treatments of all sides of the arms race question that had yet been seen by a mass audience. The outlook for television as a realistic medium is promising and becomes more so with the pay television networks expanding through the use of cable.

Just as realism never replaced all earlier styles, so realism has not been replaced by the new developments of the twentieth century. It remains the most familiar norm, the approach expected by the general public in the theatre and on movie and television screens. That does not mean that realism has shown no change since it was first established a century ago. Many new offshoots have appeared, and in Chapter 9 we will look at some of the more important of them. But first we will look at some of the twentieth-century reactions against realism.

THE THEATRE OF DISRUPTION

8

Beckett's tramps test a rope to see whether it
is stout enough to hang them in *Waiting for
Godot*. Bert Lahr and E. G. Marshall in the
original New York production.

*P*eople have always recognized disruptive elements in their world, but only in the twentieth century have they become so fascinated by lack of order that much of their art is devoted to demonstrating it. Tragedy has traditionally looked at humanity's attempts to direct us back from disorder toward reconciliation, while comedy has dealt with limited anarchy and controlled chaos, then created laughter out of surprise and incongruity. Mythologies, religion, and philosophy have always tried to account for some kind of balance between order and chaos. In very early times, the spirit of holiday took over the five days of disorder at the new year, when the surrounding waters of chaos flowed back into the floating island of creation. The five-day break in the 360-day cycle of the year was the time for all to revel, to defy normal rules, and when the festival was over, normal ways were resumed. In Hindu mythology, the four-armed dancing god Shiva had one hand to destroy the world and one to create it all over again. Early Christians looked for a Second Coming when the world would be destroyed by fire, never to be needed again, as it would be replaced by the perfection of a new heaven and a new earth.

The spirit of realism, however, with its scientific discoveries, its technology, its social reforms, and its almost unwavering belief in progress, embued the modern world with the conviction that this world itself was evolving toward a state of perfection. Education, experimentation, hard work, and knowledge of the laws by which nature, society, and the human mind work would solve all human problems, if not immediately, at least in generations to come. World War I was hailed as the "war to end all wars"; the League of Nations and later the United Nations were to bring about harmony among nations; technology could eradicate hunger, disease, and drudgery from life; and as late as the 1960s Lyndon Johnson's "War on Poverty" became the next logical step in humanity's march toward the Great Society. Realism in the arts, with its eye toward understanding everyday people and exposing the nature of their day-to-day problems, has always sought to serve this noble goal.

The war to end all wars, however, has been followed ever since by an almost constant state of war in one part of the globe or another; technology has placed the earth under threat of extinction, if not from nuclear weapons, then from environmental pollution and the depletion of earth's natural resources; poverty has increased even in the most affluent nations, and in some parts of the globe famine is so widespread as to appear insoluble. Assassination, international terrorism, street violence, and threats of unemployment or an impoverished old age leave almost no one untouched by the unpredictable dangers of living in the modern world.

Over the ages art has been primarily concerned with order, with tracing possible paths through areas of apparent disorder. But many twentieth-century artists are so dubious of the old paths that they are more inclined to prepare the traveler for a rough journey than to trace new paths out of the disorder. Yet there are new paths and some fragmentary maps pointing toward possible reconstruction of order.

Plays about disruption, understandably enough, are not easy to classify, but theatre people have been able to discuss most of them under five or six key headings. For the works of the early twentieth century, *symbolism* and *expressionism* and, in the plays of Strindberg, *dream* are the important terms. For drama since 1940, *existentialism* and *theatre of the absurd* are the key terms.

SYMBOLISM AND THE INNER DRAMA

No sooner was naturalism getting under way in the nineteenth century, when a number of poets set themselves against its scientific, rational view. They felt that objective, materialistic art ignored important aspects of the mind and spirit. Such poets as Arthur Rimbaud and Stéphane Mallarmé rejected both nature and reason; instead, they attempted to evoke the eternal beyond the visible by creating suggestive symbols. Like painters of the time, they were fascinated by symbols of humanity's alienation—masks and harlequin tramps and clowns. They cultivated free association of words and images, inducing abnormal states of mind—hallucinations, hysteria, and madness—through the use of drugs and alcohol and through frantic sensuality. To them, love was a demonic force linked with death.

The symbolist poets had considerable influence on the theatre. Ibsen used much symbolism in his later work, even in plays that seemed realistic—white horses seen before a death in *Rosmersholm*, a tower that was the architect's fatal challenge in *The Master Builder*. The symbols suggested irrational forces driving men and women—sometimes to fulfillment but more often to destruction. But the chief importance of symbols was as images of the mind in dream plays and expressionistic plays.

Explorations of the Mind: Strindberg and Pirandello

The first great explorer of the new geography was the Swedish playwright August Strindberg. For some years after the breakup of his second marriage, Strindberg was on the verge of insanity and put himself into a private hospital for the insane. He wrote several autobiographical novels analyzing his torment and developing his mystical idea that God sends pain to men and lures them into hateful relationships in order to purify them. But a more important result of those "inferno" years was a new dramaturgy, a series of plays that used many details from his private life but set them on the stage with revolutionary techniques. To express man's inner suffering and guilt, he invented phantoms and dream images that could appear out of nowhere, dissolve, and change. Eugene O'Neill called him the "precursor of all modernity in our present theatre."

The student and the Hyacinth Girl
perform a dance of life in front of
a seated Buddha. Strindberg's
The Ghost Sonata at the Yale
Repertory Theatre, directed by
Andrei Serban.

The Ghost Sonata (1907) is one of Strindberg's plays that strongly influenced later theatre of disruption. Its details are presented as real, but fantastic things happen: Dead people come out of a closet to speak and phantoms of the past come back as in the mind. One of the play's most memorable images is that of the Cook, a grotesque ogre of a woman who appears only briefly, but who sucks all the nourishment from the food before serving the family, a symbol of the guilt and self-hatred that saps all their strength and motivation. Strindberg sets into opposition the dream fantasies of a hopeful young Student and a bitter Old Man, Hummel. Old Hummel attempts to strip the masks and hypocrisies from others, to expose their guilt and hatreds. But when they also strip him of his pretenses, he rushes out to destroy himself. The Student escapes from the room of old guilts to seek a young Girl in a beautiful "Hyacinth Room," where they try to relate to beautiful blossoms rising toward heaven, like Christ, out of the hell of this earth.

But the Girl dies and the Student cries out passionately to heaven for mercy and innocence.

The other great germinal figure in the exploration of the mind was the Italian playwright Luigi Pirandello. As steeped in pain as Strindberg (he spent years looking after his insane wife), Pirandello created a more metaphysical terror in his plays. Perhaps all living is acting before a mirror, he seems to say, a mirror that distorts or gives several different reflections. Must each person keep on acting, since the only reality is the fleeting reflection? Where writers of high comedy find zest and entertainment in the idea that life is acting a role, Pirandello found only pain.

Pirandello's plays made a worldwide impression and were probably more influential than Strindberg's dream plays in causing a profound change in the theatre's treatment of reality. Though his plays are often realistic enough on the

Photographer's impression of a Pirandello play. The characters are caught in the shifting planes of reality. Pirandello's *Six Characters in Search of an Author*. University of Texas production, directed by Francis Hodge.

surface, they challenge our very sense of what is real. In *Henry IV* (1922), modern characters suddenly appear in a medieval court. We then learn that servants and relatives of a nobleman have for years kept up a pretense of living in the period of the German Emperor Henry IV because, as the result of an accident while masquerading as Henry IV, the nobleman thinks he really is Henry IV. When the relatives, accompanied by a psychiatrist, stage a shocking surprise in the hope of curing him, he confesses that he has long since regained his sanity, but has chosen to remain Henry IV rather than be subjected to the illusive uncertainties of his own life. He chose to live in the past because history, like art, is settled and fixed. But in a fit of anger he kills a cynical friend. Now, though he is not really Henry IV, he realizes that he must forever live as though he is, trapped in a reality that he himself invented. In *Six Characters in Search of an Author* (1921), six people interrupt a rehearsal in a theatre and insist that the director write a play about them. They show him painful scenes from their story, disagreeing violently with each other and with the actors over the real relations between the father, mother, stepdaughter, and rejected son. The suicide of a younger son provides a sudden interruption both of the unfinished story of the characters and of the contention between the director, the real actors, and the real-unreal characters, who are now never to be fixed in art and never to agree on what the characters' reality was or is.

Acting, as an image, has proved to be an even more fruitful metaphor of humanity's uncertain condition than Strindberg's dream images. Pirandello went further than Strindberg: he implied that experience is not merely the disarrangement of reality in the dream-like twilight zones of the mind, but that there *is* no systematic reality in the world—that the world of thought, undependable and multiple as it may be, is prior to, and basic to, any knowledge of the "facts" of reality.

EXPRESSIONISM

Strindberg's and Pirandello's disturbing explorations of the mind and of the nature of reality soon gave way to *expressionism,* a more positively disruptive movement that was already a major force in Germany while Pirandello was writing in Italy. The realists and naturalists had rebelled against the cheerful sentimentality of Victorian life, but the new theatre forms, beginning with expressionism, have been rebellions against realism. Realism seemed too dull and quiet, with its understated dialogue, restrained acting, and commonplace surroundings. Where naturalism showed a helpless victim controlled or overwhelmed by the environment, expressionism showed an angry little man spitting back at a machine-made, fragmented world. Expressionism reveled in sounds, colors, rhythms, and movement, all presented directly to the audience—a style labeled *presentationalism,* as distinct from the *representationalism* of the realistic style.

Expressionism in the movies. Setting, costumes, and movement are treated as seen in the nightmare of a distorted mind. *The Cabinet of Dr. Caligari*, 1919. Directed by Robert Wiene.

Expressionism in drama was in keeping with what was happening in the other arts at the end of World War I. Painters like Picasso and Georges Braque were smearing raw colors on their canvases, using cubistic angles and planes, paying little attention to the surface appearance of reality. Musicians such as Schoenberg and Mahler were breaking away from the muted moods of impressionism, the controlled discords of Debussy and Ravel, to explore polytonality, atonality, the twelve-tone scale, and the interruptions, sharp contrasts, complex rhythms, and violent climaxes of postimpressionism. Isadora Duncan and other dancers had broken from the formalized steps of the ballet to open the way for a freer use of body movement in dance. Why should the theatre disregard the excitement of vivid colors, strange shapes, loud sounds, and machine rhythms, at once fascinating and terrifying?

The spirit of revolt rejected the bourgeois-imperialist-military dominance in Europe. Already during the war, in 1917, a group of disillusioned artists in Zurich, led by Tristan Tzara, started the Dada movement, which deliberately destroyed patterns and made nonsense of the conventional. It was a negative, partly satiric impulse, but it discovered possibilities of excitement as well as of shock in the juxtaposition of incongruous fragments. Its fur-lined teacups and pasted collages of scraps and objects suggested new ways of using texture even as they defied conventional thinking. If the war was the result of bourgeois conventionality, the Dadaists said, then let's destroy the whole tradition—in fact, all tradition, political, cultural, and artistic. Dramatize the insanity of a military-commercial machine age. Explode firecrackers. Disfigure the Old Masters; paint a beard and mustache on the Mona Lisa. Destroy the institutions and habits that have enslaved and misled mankind. Open the way for a new world through the spiritual brotherhood of man.

Out of this postwar spirit of revolt in the 1920s expressionism was born. Following the experiments of Strindberg, expressionism was, first, a revolt against an objective view of the world in order to show the subective view of the inner mind, especially in its tortured and distorted states. Second, it was a reaction to the mechanization and dehumanization of mankind. Thus the dream and the machine were the two poles of postwar expressionism.

The Techniques of Expressionism

In this time of artistic ferment, almost everything that could be called "experimental" was tried on the stage. Some attempts were silly and ineffective, yet a number of important theatrical techniques were invented or adapted from older forms. We can classify these techniques into four groups: first, techniques for dramatizing the inner life; second, the use of sounds, movements, and color to build to a climax; third, the use of stylized (that is, rhythmic and sustained) voice and movement patterns and stylized decor to suggest the unreality of a dream or the monotony of a machine; and fourth, generalized, as opposed to individualized, characterization.

The simplest way to dramatize the inner life was to revive the soliloquy and the aside, letting characters put into words their private thoughts, or "stream of consciousness." For soliloquies the spotlight became very useful, allowing one character to speak his or her thoughts while the background and other characters sank into shadow. The opening scene of Elmer Rice's *The Adding Machine* (1922) is a long stream-of-consciousness monologue by Mrs. Zero as she is going to bed; she reveals the resentment she feels at the empty life she has led in twenty-five years of marriage to the little bookkeeper Mr. Zero. The most famous use of asides is in O'Neill's nine-act psychological drama *Strange Interlude* (1928). It is a realistic play at one level, but the action is suspended repeatedly, and the dialogue is interrupted while one character at a time utters his or her subtext aloud for only the audience to hear.

A dream fantasy that actually shows the inner thought is often more powerful than words. Though used in several earlier plays of the expressionist period, the most famous and perhaps most powerful example of this technique is Laurie's "dream ballet" in the musical *Oklahoma!*, as described in Chapter 6. Laurie dreams that her wedding to Curly turns into a nightmare at the altar, with Curly becoming the hated Jud and the bridesmaids turning into barroom molls who force her into the arms of Curly's demonic rival.

The second technique of expressionism is the building of a climax by means other than speech. Something more powerful than the soliloquy of a single actor is needed to show an inner crisis, especially since audiences have come to expect very restrained acting. The Greeks, Shakespeare, and Racine wrote long speeches, expecting the actor to use a wide range of voice and movement to build with appropriate crescendos to a climax. But a machine-age theatre has other resources. When Rice's Mr. Zero is fired, to be replaced by an adding machine, an external crescendo of effects builds to the climax in which Mr. Zero stabs his boss. First the soft music of a distant merry-go-round is heard, and slowly that part of the floor with the desk and stool starts to revolve. As the boss goes on

O'Neill's image of the elms brooding over the house in *Desire Under the Elms*. From the Provincetown Playbill.

with his impersonal spiel—"Sorry to lose an employee who's been with me for so many years. . . . I'm sorry—no other alternative—greatly regret—old employee—efficiency—economy—business—business—*business*—BUSINESS"—the platform revolves faster and faster, and the sound rises to a thunderous climax—then a flash of red, followed by total blackness.

Stylization, the third technique of expressionism, is a deliberate break with realistic decor, speech, and movement. Stylization in stage design immediately indicates unreality by omitting some details and distorting others. Since the emphasis in expressionistic plays is on the insane or abnormal state of the modern world, the distortion directly expresses the abnormal view of the subjective mind. Walls lean, posts curve, roofs hang without support, the right angles of normal life become acute angles and sharp points. Objects menace with hands, eyes, pointing fingers. In Georg Kaiser's *From Morn to Midnight* (1916), a tree takes on the appearance of a skeleton. Scenery moves before the eyes, falls, leans in, swings around, taking an active part in creating the nightmare. Even in Eugene O'Neill's naturalistic tragedy *Desire Under the Elms*, two huge elms "brood oppressively over the house . . . like exhausted women resting their sagging breasts and hands and hair on its roof, and when it rains their tears trickle down monotonously and rot on the shingles."

Intensified rhythm is the most conspicuous performance aspect of expres-

Actors, performing in the mechanical patterns of robots, demand to be taught how to reproduce, in *R.U.R.* Theatre Guild production, designed by Lee Simonson.

sionistic stylization. The rhythm of a realistic play is always subordinated to the atmosphere of the place, but in the dehumanized megalopolis of the expressionist, rhythm becomes insistent, often dominant. It is usually based on endless repetition of the same movement and sound, such as the monotonous flow of an assembly line or the marching ranks of troops of soldiers.

The fourth technique of expressionism generalizes the characters. The central character must represent Everyman, almost as in the medieval morality play. Whether the stupid eternal slave Mr. Zero, or just The Young Man or The Poet, the central character is the dream figure for audience identification, the truth-seeker. That generalized personality moves in a phantom world of even more impersonal characters. Our name for such a machine person, robot, comes from a 1921 play by Karel Capek called *R.U.R.* (Rossum's Universal Robots), in which a few people still trying to be human contend with mobs of mechanized robots. The Cashier—the hero of *From Morn to Midnight* (1916), who steals money and abandons his dull family so that he can try all the vices that money can buy— finds at the races a chorus of identical attendants, and then, at a cabaret, nameless guests and nameless girls in masks. The Salvation Army Lass leads him to a Salvation Army hall, where nameless penitents make their confessions against a chorus of derisive scoffers. One group of actors, with quick changes of costume, serves for all the nameless mobs in such a play, because they are all part of the same dehumanized nightmare of modern life.

The Influence of Expressionism

As a movement, expressionism declined rapidly, lasting only from 1910 to 1925, partly due to its weaknesses: It was too hysterical and rhapsodic, and its lack of real characters made it too mechanical. But the swift loss of interest in it resulted even more, perhaps, from a changing attitude toward the machine. Where the old heavy machines were noisy and required the monotonous motions of many workers, later machines were quieter and more nearly automatic. Generations of people growing up with machines have learned to use them as inconspicuous servants in the background of their lives. The nightmare has lost most of its terror.

Nevertheless, expressionism has left an unmistakable mark on the conventions of modern theatre. Arthur Miller used expressionistic techniques ingeniously to show Willy Loman's inner mind in *Death of a Salesman,* as he had his character's mind lapse from present reality into staged scenes of his memories. Willy himself is a kind of Everyman, the essence of the salesman, with himself as the only visible product he is selling. Even the terror of the noisy machine can still be felt when Willy is fired. As Willy begs for human consideration, his young boss is caught up in his latest mechanical gadget, a wire recorder, on which he has just recorded his young son reciting, in order, the capitals of all the states. After Willy is left alone, he beats his fists on the desk, accidentally turning on the

As Willy Loman plays cards with his neighbor Charley, the dream-image of his older brother Ben appears (lower left). The isolated spotlight makes him appear as a figment of Willy's imagination. Miller's *Death of a Salesman*. The University of Michigan.

recorder with its mechanical repetition of a meaningless list. There is a naturalistic explanation for this machine, but the inhuman noise with its terrifying effect on a helpless Willy is a vivid moment of expressionism.

A similar moment of obsessive terror makes the inner life of Blanche DuBois clear to the audience in *A Streetcar Named Desire*. Any new moment of panic makes her relive in memory her young husband's suicide. The audience hears dance music growing louder and louder—and then the pistol shot. Yet no one thinks of *Streetcar* as anything but a completely realistic play. Realistic theatre and film have so completely absorbed the incidental expressionistic techniques of presenting a subjective experience that no one takes special notice. The dream character Uncle Ben moves in and out of *Death of a Salesman*, visible to some characters and invisible to others, without disturbing the sense of reality. It is not even necessary to give him artificial or dream-like rhythms and movements.

Expressionism is a frequent element in plays of the free forms that became popular in the sixties and seventies. In David Rabe's *Sticks and Bones* (1971), a Vietnamese girl whom the returned American soldier had abandoned moves about his family home, visible to the soldier and the audience, though not to his family. In Arthur Kopit's *Wings* (1978), the audience is made to experience Emily Stilson's stroke entirely through visual and sound effects. She sits quietly in an armchair reading a book, when quite suddenly the clock beside her begins to tick loudly, skips a beat, then stops as her reading light goes out. We see her face for one terrified moment before a blackout, when the stage explodes in a clamor of metallic noise, wind, babbling voices, and a droning airplane; then, in flashes of light, we see her wandering aimlessly through insanely revolving screens, as white-coated figures dart in and out. In the early stages of her recuperation, her doctors and therapists speak to her, but we hear their speech only as unintelligible gibberish, or the colors of a fresh bouquet of flowers and the hum of a floor polisher are intensified by lighting effects and sound amplification to a level beyond what her senses can endure. Without the techniques invented by expressionists, many of the most powerful moments of the modern theatre would never have been created.

EXISTENTIALISM IN THE THEATRE

Existentialism, the philosophy that came to dominate much of the thinking of the 1940s and 1950s, especially that of the playwrights, grew out of the disillusionment that followed World War II, just as expressionism grew out of World War I. Thoughtful men and women, despairing of the traditional values formerly found in nature, science, politics, and history, turned inward in the hope of rediscovering a genuine identity, an authentic life of the self. The sense of disruption was far greater than that felt after World War I. Not only was there a more drastic break with the past, with old buildings destroyed, old institutions discredited, and old patterns of life broken; now a radically new element had appeared—the nuclear bomb. The holocaust at Hiroshima in 1945 seemed to put an end to all that had gone before. If the result of three centuries of science was to be the annihilation of every living thing on the globe, what was to be gained by studying science? Even if destruction could be avoided, the new age of political and economic power to follow the release of nuclear energy would be so radically different that all traditional values would seem irrelevant.

A Philosophy of Disillusionment

Many people were disillusioned with political action. The methods of liberalism seemed too slow, its piecemeal gains inadequate. In 1917 the Russians had turned to communism, and in the twenties and thirties the Italians and Germans had turned to fascism and Nazism, but it soon became clear that none of these regimes permitted individuality. Yet even in France, England, and America, where liberal institutions survived, the individual felt lost in the masses, a nameless object in a crowd. The impersonality of the city and the constant stream of commercial advertising and political propaganda, a stream that increased with the spread of television after 1946, deprived people of a sense of authentic life; all experiences were secondhand.

In this depressing spiritual climate, existentialism became the support of many intellectuals. Its great appeal was its rediscovery of the self, a complete entity with an authentic inner life, free to choose, free to create values, whether the universe supports them or not. By facing death and nothingness, individuals find the courage to be; by accepting isolation and loneliness, they find strength in freedom. Their fear and uncertainty mark the authenticity of their experience. Just as their death will be their own and not a statistical abstraction, their choice is their own and they create themselves in making it.

After a century of scientific objectivity, of exact measurement, of facts and statistics, existentialists were ready for the opposite extreme—subjectivity. If scientists insisted on defining reality, nature, and history apart from human values, then there was no reason to pay attention to science or history. Many existentialists wrote as though science and history did not exist and ignored nature as though they had never been outdoors in their lives.

The existentialist mood appeared first in France during the long trauma of the German occupation. From 1940 to 1944 each moment seemed one of critical decision—whether and to what extent to collaborate, or whether to say no and face the consequences. Character seemed purely a matter of individual decision, not the result of social forces or natural environment. As thinkers developed their point of view, they discovered that a similar philosophy had been outlined a hundred years earlier by the Danish religious philosopher Søren Kierkegaard, who emphasized a person's isolation, uncertainty, and anguish in making choices "in fear and trembling." His ideas were simultaneously reawakened by German theologians imprisoned for their ethical stands against Nazism.

Some Existentialist Playwrights

The existentialist movement after World War II was developed most of all in the plays, novels, and essays of two Frenchmen, Albert Camus and Jean-Paul Sartre. Camus' novels made a much stronger impression than his plays, though *Caligula* (1945) interested many people because of its startling hero, who follows the logic of his idea of absolute freedom to the point of killing his friends. Sartre's essays are probably more important than his plays, particularly two published at the end of the war: *Existentialism Is a Humanism*, probably the most widely read definition of existentialism, and *Forgers of Myths*, which made a radical redefinition of theatre, repudiating the tenets of naturalism. To Sartre, individual differences of human beings, the qualities due to heredity and environment, were unimportant. Following the tenet that existence precedes essence, a person or a character in a play achieved identity only as he or she made a decision. By choosing, individuals define themselves and are individually responsible for that choice, even if it is simply to say "no." A large number of plays since the war have been designed to say "no."

As if to illustrate Sartre's ideas, Jean Anouilh in 1943 wrote his version of Sophocles' *Antigone* and actually got permission for a Paris production from the German occupation authorities. It is a political play in which a girl defies a dictator, but Anouilh presented both sides of the dilemma in a way that made his play acceptable even to Nazis. Sophocles' Antigone believes that the laws of the gods are more important than the commands of men; the Chorus and the prophet, Tiresias, support her, and finally Creon, the dictator, admits he was wrong and she was right. Anouilh, on the other hand, completely isolates his Antigone, allowing her no support outside herself. She has no real belief in God, and she cannot validate her sacrifice from external facts. Still, by saying "no" to Creon's world she creates values for herself. At the end, her weak sister Ismene makes the same decision. Choice is contagious; other individuals may be influenced by example.

Jean Anouilh's modern version of *Antigone* as staged at the University of Missouri uses dance to show Antigone's isolation. Directed by Pamela Bongas.

Anouilh changed the character of Creon from Sophocles' conception even more than that of Antigone. In the Greek play, Creon is a tragic figure whose pride is humbled, but the modern Creon remains set in his cold, impersonal view to the very end. He compares the state to a storm-tossed ship that he has taken over because somebody has to issue orders. The mob must be led, and anyone who disobeys orders must be shot. He cannot believe that Antigone—or any human being—would go against the herd instinct. "*No* is one of your man-made words. Can you imagine a world in which trees say *no* to the sap? In which beasts say *no* to hunger or to propagation?" But existentialism, as Sartre pointed out, is a humanism. Individual decision raises man above the animals—or locks him in to what his decision has made of him. After Antigone is dead and Creon's son and wife have killed themselves, Creon is trapped in the official role he has laid out for himself, and nothing remains for him but to go to his cabinet meeting at five o'clock.

THE THEATRE OF THE ABSURD

Existentialists derived values, not from the group, but from themselves as they made decisions. From this they derived a strong sense of commitment, enabling them to work actively with organized groups when they approved of their aims. By contrast, the theatre of the absurd, the avant-garde theatre of the 1950s and 1960s, discovered no values worthy of commitment. The absurdists even celebrated the breakdown of language and communication and deliberately baffled their audiences. If confusion and chaos are the human condition, then the form of the play itself must present its audience with interruption, discontinuity, incongruity, and senseless logic and repetition. Eugene Ionesco called his first play (*The Bald Soprano*—1950) an "antiplay." Some absurdists went so far as to write no play at all, but to arrange a set of directions for both actors and audience in a "happening." While existentialists like Anouilh, Sartre, and Camus wrote carefully constructed plays to show how the world has no dependable order, the absurdists expressed disorder in the very form of their writing.

It is significant that three of the most important absurdist playwrights chose lives of exile, living in Paris and writing in a language other than their native tongue—Samuel Beckett, an Irishman; Eugene Ionesco, a Rumanian; and Arthur Adamov, an Armenian-Russian. A fourth, the Frenchman Jean Genet, set himself apart from humanity as a criminal and pervert, glorying in his defiance of law and normalcy. These men chose to emphasize in their lives the alienation that Camus described in a much-quoted paragraph in his classic essay *The Myth of Sisyphus:*

> [I]n a universe that is suddenly deprived of illusions and light, man feels a stranger. His is an irremediable exile, because he is deprived of memories of a lost homeland as much as he lacks the hope of a promised land to come. This

divorce between man and his life, the actor and his setting, truly constitutes the feeling of Absurdity.

The breakdown of conventional language—the use of empty phrases that obscure communication and destroy all sense of identity—was the subject of Ionesco's *The Bald Soprano*. He got the idea from the numerous meaningless phrases in an English phrase book written for foreigners. During a social evening, the Smiths and the Martins courteously and charmingly repeat statements that are completely inane and also contradictory. The Smiths exhaust all processes of logic in debating whether a ring of the doorbell always or never means there is someone there. The Martins reach the amazing conclusion that since they arrived in London in the same compartment of the same train and live in the same room, they must, by coincidence, be husband and wife. But after a theatrical climax, the Martins take the place of the Smiths and start the evening over again. While expressionist heroes contended with a depersonalized, nameless crowd, in search of their own identity, here all is inanity. The characters have no hunger, no conscious desires, no identity. They are interchangeable, and everything ends where it started.

In America Edward Albee used absurdist techniques to satirize the clichés of family living in *The Sandbox* (1959), as well as in *The American Dream* (1960). Mommy and Daddy, characters in both plays, never rise above infantile baby talk as they try to dispose appropriately of Grandma. In *The American Dream* she is to be taken away by the "van man," and in *The Sandbox,* with the end near, they dump her in a sandbox with a toy shovel for her to bury herself. A hired flute player stands by and a young muscle man, who has not yet been given a name by the "studio," does calisthenics in the background. An "off-stage rumble" at last announces Grandma's death, and "brave Mommy" and "brave Daddy" leave, while the young man comforts the rejected, senile Grandma in the role of the angel of death.

Things, objects that give meaning and rich texture in naturalistic plays, become in absurdist plays of the 1950s and 1960s the grotesque symbols of human emptiness and terror. In *The Dumbwaiter* (1960), the English playwright Harold Pinter shows two hit men awaiting orders for their next assignment in a basement flat. A noisy dumbwaiter suddenly clanks down from some undefined room above. Inside are notes commanding that various gourmet foods be sent up. These men have built their lives out of following commands sent through clandestine messages. But now the dumbwaiter's messages, demanding impossible results, pose a terrifying threat, and the men scrounge desperately among their own snacks for something to satisfy the greedy machine. The younger of the two, who has already been asking too many questions about their job, defies the machine and its unreasonable orders and almost lures his older partner into his defiance. Just in time, the older man reverts to his role of unquestioning obedience and prepares to obey a note slipped under the door—commanding him to shoot the next person who enters through the outside door. The door begins to open and he points his gun, ready to fire. His partner enters—for a moment the two freeze; then the curtain closes.

Role-playing

Jean Anouilh's Antigone and Creon had defined themselves by assuming roles in the crisis of decision-making, but Jean Genet takes role-playing much further. The compulsion to act a role, a role that becomes more real than reality, is a major theme of his drama, where play-acting scenes conjure up more grotesque images than Pirandello ever created. Genet follows some of the principles set forth by the French dramatic theorist Antonin Artaud in his influential work *The Theatre and Its Double,* which advocates that theatre return to the intensity of primitive rituals, of cruelty, incantation, and dream. Genet's plays in various ways act out rites, whether the social rites of servants pretending to be their mistress in *The Maids* (1947) or the ritual violation and murder of a white woman in *The Blacks* (1959). All Genet's plays include observers watching a performance, recognizing with mixed feelings the Freudian images of their own suppressed desires.

The brothel in which Genet's *The Balcony* (1957) is set is more than an ordinary brothel; it furnishes not only mirrors but costumes, settings, and actors so that the clients may act out their secret desires—to be a bishop hearing the lurid confessions of a young woman, a judge ordering a half-naked executioner to whip a beautiful young woman, or a triumphant general riding a horse, played by an almost nude woman wearing a tail. Outside, a revolution is taking place in the town; the chief of police eventually puts it down by presenting the madam as the new queen and getting her clients to act as a real bishop, judge, and general. The chief gets his own fulfillment, the achievement of an image, when finally a client comes to the brothel and wants to play "chief of police." Everything returns to normal and the madam gets ready for her next clients. The indecent rites of role-playing go on in both the brothel and the real world. As in Pirandello's *Henry IV,* the play-acting becomes more real than the reality outside.

Desolation and Despair: Beckett's *Waiting for Godot*

Samuel Beckett seemed haunted by images of confinement, with the conscious mind as prison. In *Endgame* (1957) the two main characters are shut up in a bare room with two eye-like windows that can only be reached by a ladder and look out onto nothingness. Their greatest fear is that some new life will appear on the horizon and offer the delusion of hope. Winnie in *Happy Days* (1961) is buried to her waist, and later up to her neck, in a pile of dirt. She cheerfully goes through daily activities of praying, brushing her teeth, telling her story, singing her song. She worries that she won't get everything done before the day ends and fears lest she finish too soon, leaving nothing to occupy her in the silence, yet always

Theatre of illusion—Genet's *The Balcony*. Identity is achieved by playacting in a brothel. One of the clients plays the role of a general with a girl as his horse. The University of Michigan.

consoling herself that "this will have been another happy day! *(Pause.)* After all. *(Pause.)* So far."

Beckett's *Waiting for Godot* (1950) is the masterpiece of the theatre of the absurd; of all the plays it is the most perfect in its form, the most complete in its desolation, the most comic in its anguish. Two lonely tramps are waiting for Godot, who sends word every day that he will not meet them today but surely tomorrow. The place where they wait is a desolate road, empty save for a stick of a tree not sturdy enough to hang oneself on. But the tramps are also theatrical clowns, using comic routines of vaudeville days, putting on and off their hats, boots, shirts, and coats, arguing, interrupting, telling jokes, munching carrots or turnips, paying mock deference to each other, stumbling and falling, alternating groans with sudden squeals or grimaces. Even the most painful moments are exploded into laughter by their clownish antics; the characters will do anything to avoid the terror of silence. After one interminable silence, Vladimir suggests a distraction:

VLADIMIR: What about trying them.
ESTRAGON: I've tried everything.
VLADIMIR: No, I mean the boots.
ESTRAGON: Would that be a good thing?
VLADIMIR: It'd pass the time. *(Estragon hesitates.)* I assure you, it'd be an occupation.
ESTRAGON: A relaxation.
VLADIMIR: A recreation.
ESTRAGON: A relaxation.
VLADIMIR: Try.
ESTRAGON: You'll help me?
VLADIMIR: I will of course.
ESTRAGON: We don't manage too badly, eh Didi, between the two of us?
VLADIMIR: Yes yes. Come on, we'll try the left first.
ESTRAGON: We always find something, eh Didi, to give us the impression we exist?
VLADIMIR: *(impatiently).* Yes yes, we're magicians.

Vladimir and Estragon (John Kani, left, and Winston Ntshona) listen intently for the tick of a gold watch lost by the officious Pozzo (Bill Flynn) in a scene from *Waiting for Godot* at Long Wharf Theater, New Haven, Connecticut. Directed by Donald Howarth.

To the existentialist, freedom is a challenge; to Beckett's tramps, freedom is hell. They have no inner resources, no friends, no memories, and no orientation to place or time; they don't know where they were last night or, indeed, if this is the Saturday they were told—they think—to wait for Godot; and a little boy who comes to announce each day that Mr. Godot will surely come tomorrow never remembers having seen them before. If the eternal waiting of the two tramps seems pointless, equally so is the endless movement of the two remaining characters: a fat master, Pozzo, driving his slave, Lucky, by a rope around his neck, pausing to lunch and amuse himself before going on. When the two reappear in Act II, Lucky's rope now leads a blind Pozzo until he stops from exhaustion and they collide in a helpless heap on the ground. So they will continue: going blindly forward until they collapse, lying there until they can get up, then forward again without end—tied to each other by their mutual need, with no destination and no purpose except "On!"—a hideous but comic image of all masters and slaves, all employers and employees.

The play has a remarkably strict form, expressive of its meaning. The form of each act is a series of moments. Each moment starts with an assertion, a plan, or a hope, then quickly dissipates it. Discontinuity is both the theme and the form, deflation the theme and the comic method. The second act's repeating the first-act pattern, with only slight development, has a formal perfection that is like mathematics, logic, or music.

Toward the end of the play, Vladimir has one moment of total consciousness while his friend Estragon sleeps, but he quickly represses the unbearable thoughts.

> Was I sleeping, while the others suffered? Am I sleeping now? To-morrow, when I wake, or think I do, what shall I say of to-day? That with Estragon my friend, at this place, until the fall of night, I waited for Godot? That Pozzo passed, with his carrier, and that he spoke to us? Probably. But in all that what truth will there be? . . . Astride of a grave and a difficult birth. Down in the hole, lingeringly, the grave-digger puts on the forceps. We have time to grow old. The air is full of our cries. *(He listens.)* But habit is a great deadener. *(He looks . . . at Estragon.)* At me too someone is looking, of me too someone is saying, He is sleeping, he knows nothing, let him sleep on. *(Pause.)* I can't go on! *(Pause.)* What have I said?

Though, at the end, the two tramps consider hanging themselves from the feeble tree with a bit of rope that Estragon uses for a belt, the rope breaks when they test its strength and Estragon's pants, unnoticed, fall down about his ankles. Then, as at the end of Act I, one character asks, "Well? Shall we go?" and the other replies, "Yes, let's go." And just as at the end of Act I, "They do not move."

Waiting for Godot does not point to any known source of values, yet it is a passionate cry for some new faith and, in that sense, is a very religious play. No economic improvement, no psychological adjustment, no doctor's pill, but only a new definition of mankind, a new relation to the universe will serve these forlorn creatures. In its exploration of the last possibility of emptiness, the play may be considered a turning point. Anyone with such passionate need for the spiritual plane will either renew old definitions of God or find new ones.

Intrusion and Menace: Pinter and Shepard

The most popular writer in English to follow the absurdists is Harold Pinter, though on the surface his plays seem like realistic plays about ordinary people. Pinter's characters, like those of Ionesco, are caught up in obsessive talk, issuing cascades of clichés, volleys of irrelevant chatter, or rapid-fire, terse phrases punctuating the pauses—Pinter's famous pauses—which may as in Beckett hide a terrifying silence. But Pinter's is not an empty universe; it is full of undefined menace. It is a world of insiders versus outsiders, stirring one of our most primitive fears, that of an invader breaking in and driving us from our homes. The threat is made all the more terrifying by the ambiguity of relationships. Often the insider invites the intruder in, welcomes him and finds they have much in common. In *No Man's Land* (1975), the insider is a rich literary epicure, guarded by two attendants, while his guest, a tramp, is a cultivated poet who never made it. In a sustained, bristling battle the adventurer-tramp is defeated. To make sure that their host never seeks such an encounter again, the two attendants put him through a ritual committing him to forgo any change, any existentialist uncertainty. He is now in "no man's land," "which never moves, which never changes, which never grows older, but which remains forever, icy and silent." Like Pirandello's Emperor Henry IV, he is fixed forever.

The simplest melodrama of undefined menace is Pinter's *The Birthday Party* (1958). Its hero, Stanley, thinks he has found a secure boarding-house refuge in an obscure off-season resort, but two strange bullies arrive from some mysterious organization, terrify him until he is speechless, and take him away. His simple-minded landlady does not even notice that anything is wrong.

Dominance and the unsettling fear of its loss form the theme of Pinter's *The Homecoming* (1965). Max, a seventy-year-old father, dominates his household by means of fear, even beating up his prizefighter son, Joey, with a surprise power punch to the stomach and a stick laid across the head. A second son, Lenny, however, is gradually usurping Max's power. When a third son, Teddy, returns home from America for a visit, all three men turn their aggression on him and set out to take his wife, Ruth, for their own sexual needs and to set her up as a commercial prostitute on the side. Instead of resisting, it is she who lays down all the conditions, including a personal maid and a complete wardrobe, while her husband watches submissively, spellbound by the power struggles he seems incapable of joining. Whenever any of the family tries to control Ruth through shock or intimidation, she simply picks up their threats on her own terms and outdoes them. On their first meeting, Lenny tries to take a glass of water away

Stanley forced to play a game by his tormentors, while one of them threatens to break his glasses in Pinter's *The Birthday Party*. Karamu production at the Boston Winter Arts Festival, 1966.

from her. She calmly replies, "If you take the glass . . . I'll take you." He backs off, nonplussed by her response, but she continues on the offensive, inviting him onto her lap to have a sip; then she drains off the glass with a laugh and calmly goes upstairs.

Where Beckett's silences are filled with a fearful nothingness, Pinter's silences and pauses are menacing. Max is finally brought to submission at the end through the silence of the other characters, experienced by the audience through his own pauses. Ruth sits relaxed, with Joey kneeling at her feet, and Lenny stands watching, while Max tries to reestablish his dominance:

> Listen. You think you're just going to get that big slag all the time? You think you're just going to have him . . . you're going to just have him all the time? You're going to have to work! You'll have to take them on, you understand?

Pause.

Does she realize that?

Pause.

Lenny, do you think she understands . . .

He begins to stammer.

What . . . what . . . what . . . we're getting at? What . . . we've got in mind? Do you think she's got it clear?

Pause.

I don't think she's got it clear.

Pause.

You understand what I mean? Listen, I've got a funny idea she'll do the dirty on us, you want to bet? She'll use us, she'll make use of us, I can tell you! I can smell it! You want to bet?

Pause.

She won't . . . be adaptable!

He falls to his knees, whimpers, begins to moan and sob. He stops sobbing, crawls . . . round her chair, to the other side of her.

I'm not an old man.

He looks up at her.

Ruth aggressively offers Lenny a sip of water in Pinter's *The Homecoming*. Michael Miller and Kathe Argo in the Old Globe Theatre production, San Diego.

The swordplay of two combatants is expanded into the feeling of full-scale war through special lighting effects and towering background pillars. Shakespeare's *Henry V* at San Diego's Old Globe Theatre.

A new old-fashioned musical with all the glamour of Follies chorines, played by men in drag. *La Cage aux Folles* on Broadway swept the 1984 Tony Awards.

The dynamics of modern dance, with sharp contrasts of light and shadow, posture, groupings and isolation. *Blues Suite,* choreographed by Alvin Ailey. Alvin Ailey American Dance Theatre.

The art of makeup. Reed Jones prepares to go onstage for his role in the Broadway musical *Cats.*

Sixteen-foot puppets convey the stoic earthiness and gentleness of peasants, dwarfing the ineffectual busywork of the humans below. Bread and Puppet Theatre, Glover, Vermont.

A modern reconstruction of an Elizabethan-style theatre makes an ideal setting for Shakespeare. Utah Shakespeare Festival Theatre.

Modern realism in Ibsen's *Ghosts*. The sunlight penetrating the dark room and the dark lives of its inhabitants is both a symbol of hope for renewed life and an ironic expression of the "joy of life" the characters have thrown away. San Diego State University.

A set composed of actual photographs for Broadway's *The Tap Dance Kid*. More than 200 movable light boxes make up the walls of the set; new scenes are created by illuminating different combinations of boxes or by pivoting the boxes. Using Kodak's Duratran display film, the images even wrap around corners to form a giant sculpture. Set designed by Paul de Pass and Michael Hotopp.

A giant minstrel mask is a sardonic reminder of these black performers' bitter heritage, which continues to haunt them into the present. Ntozake Shange's *Spell #7* at the University of Michigan.

Operetta on the high seas. Kevin Kline as the Pirate King in the New York Shakespeare Festival production of Gilbert and Sullivan's *The Pirates of Penzance* in Central Park.

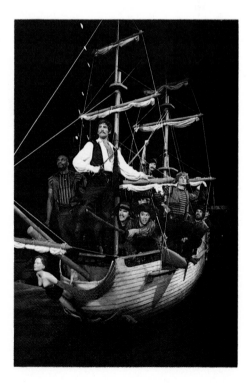

A surrealist setting creates an impishly fragmented world for a modernistic opera. Metropolitan Opera Guild production of Francis Poulenc's *Les Mamelles de Tirésias*.

Detailed fragments of a realistic decor set against a dark background spotlight the comic world of Wilde's *The Importance of Being Earnest*. University of North Carolina at Wilmington. Set designed by Dennis J. Sporre.

Romantic love that leads to tragedy. The balcony scene from *Romeo and Juliet* at the Utah Shakespeare Festival.

The 1960s urge for liberation is expressed in the sets, costumes, and staging of this Living Theatre production of *Yellow Methuselah*. Imprisoned in their net costumes, the actors perform more as a chorus than as individuals, giving a sense of the powerlessness of the person.

A two-level skeletal set on a revolving stage against a lighted cyclorama makes a "machine for action" for a production of *Macbeth*. State University College at Oneonta, N.Y., designed by Junius Hamblin.

Bright colors and fussy details tell the audience immediately that they are viewing comedy. Sheridan's *The School for Scandal* at the University of Missouri.

Do you hear me?
He raises his face to her.
Kiss me.
She continues to touch JOEY's *head, lightly.* LENNY *stands, watching.*

The language, as in all Pinter plays, is simple, vivid, and direct, yet set off as it is by the insistent stillness of the pauses, it shows Max being driven to intense dramatic change.

In the American theatre, the California playwright Sam Shepard has frequently created a similar sense of menace through surrealistic methods. Every moment is treated by the characters as completely real; yet the conditions of reality keep changing. In an early one-act play, *Cowboys #2* (1968), two young men, Chet and Stu, on a stage bare except for a sawhorse with a blinking caution light, suddenly become Mel and Clem, two old prospectors on the desert of the Old West. As if on command from whistles heard offstage, they shift in and out of their alternate characters. At first they seem to have some control over the shifts in roles, but as old men, they are attacked by Indians and the desert heat, and as young men they spew out their hatred for the moral pollution of sprawling suburbia and freeways until they lose all control. Stu apparently dies from the imaginary arrow he took in the side as Clem. Chet tries in vain to rouse him, but fails both as Mel and as Chet, while the sounds of horses and Indians and car horns mingle and build in intensity offstage. Then two men who had been whistling the offstage commands enter and begin reading in a monotone, line by line, from the beginning of the play. Here is role-playing to match Pirandello, external menace to match Pinter, and a no-man's land outside time and space—a theatre stage in fact—reminiscent of Beckett; but the effect on the characters is intensely real.

In *Buried Child*, a slightly more conventional play for which Shepard won the Pulitzer Prize in 1979, a young man, Vincent, stops in a rainstorm at the Illinois farm of his grandparents after an absence of six years, and finds reality already changed. In the bizarre world he enters, no one recognizes him: neither his grandfather who lies sick on the couch, pouring out invectives and pleading for whiskey; nor his father, who has reverted to a child-like mentality, obsessed with the idea of a child buried in the backyard; nor his uncle, a spiteful and lecherous amputee who assaults Vincent's girlfriend. The grandmother is not present, being out on an all-night caper with her minister. Meanwhile, the backyard garden, which has not been seeded for thirty years, is suddenly bursting with bumper crops, which Vincent's father keeps harvesting, filling the stage with carrots and ears of corn. On the pretext of going out for whiskey, Vincent escapes from this nightmare to an all-night drive across Illinois and Iowa. He returns drunk, smashes sacks full of empty whiskey bottles against the porch wall; then he comes in to assert his identity and take over the farm. As his grandfather dies, his uncle disappears out the door, and his grandmother goes up the stairs to her room, he claims his identity and his inheritance, ignoring the mud-covered figure of his father, who reenters with the rotten corpse of a small child in his arms.

Unlike Pinter's characters, Vincent is able to separate himself from the menace of past evil, able to claim the identity no one will give to him, able to rise out of the uncertainty to a conviction about himself as the heir to the family. He freely accepts both the evil of its skeletons and the rich bounty of its crops.

PROMISE OF RECONSTRUCTION

Sam Shepard's is only one of the voices that have begun to provide antidotes to despair and menace. Human beings are not necessarily helpless in the grip of natural or irrational forces; they have the power of the creative mind to sustain and rescue them. The primacy of the creative power of the mind is shown in *Rosencrantz and Guildenstern Are Dead* (1967) by the English playwright Tom Stoppard. Most of the play is an absurdist drama about Rosencrantz and Guildenstern, the two nonentitiies who are called to the Court of Elsinore to solve the mystery of Hamlet's strange behavior but who wander helplessly, finding out only that they are to be sent to England to be killed without explanation or reason. Unable to find any purpose in the orders they are given, they are very much like the two tramps of *Waiting for Godot*. But this play is not merely another absurdist play. In the first place, their Elsinore is not quite the empty universe of the Beckett play. There seems to be something going on within the court, though they are left at the edge, unable to understand. However, it is the presence of The Players (the actors who visited Hamlet's court) that indicates in the play a new age that has gone beyond the absurd. The Players know they are facing the same death as Rosencrantz and Guildenstern, but they are creative artists, not miserable victims of that elementary knowledge. They have learned all there is to know about death by acting it in its multitudinous forms. As creative artists they also know about life, and hence they are free. They know who they are and what they have to do with their lives.

American existentialists have never been quite so despairing as the Europeans. The world we Americans picture, even at our loneliest, has never been so empty as that of Beckett's tramps. Somewhere, we believe, religion, history, and human purpose are to be found, even if we have to create new definitions and hunt out new paths. Memories of our heroic leaders of the past and the heroes of our poetry, novels, and popular myths are there to cheer us in our desolate night.

One such mythical figure is Kilroy, the popular image of the nameless, wandering American soldier of World War II. In Tennessee Williams' surrealist and absurdist fantasy *Camino Real* (1953), Kilroy staggers out of the desert into a walled Latin American village where fugitives from history as well as fiction are trying to escape. He is beaten, made to dress like a clown, cheated by a gypsy's daughter, and dissected by an anatomy teacher while two laughing street clean-

The absurd world of Rosencrantz and Guildenstern (above) on the fringe of events that lead them to their pointless deaths in this University of Massachusetts production is balanced (below) by the creative joy of the Players in a Cleveland Playhouse production of *Rosencrantz and Guildenstern Are Dead.*

ers with a white can wait for his body. No image is spared of seediness, deception, exhaustion, and cruelty. Yet there are echoes of the past to remind us of the triumphs of the human spirit. Camille, the legendary courtesan who made the mistake of falling in love, and Casanova, now King of the Cuckolds, find companionship and solace in each other. Lord Byron departs to sail back to Athens, to contemplate the Acropolis with its reminders of an earlier dream of purity and freedom. At the end, Kilroy and Don Quixote go out the high gate to cross the "terra incognita" toward the mountains. It is not a futile life-lie but an indomitable courage we see in the hearts of Williams' characters. The walled town is not the whole universe but a temporary prison from which people may escape if they have imagination and faith.

The need to find faith, to survive one's own and humanity's cruelty, is what motivates Quentin, the central character of Arthur Miller's *After the Fall* (1964). The guilt in his hell paralyzes creative action. Quentin, as the central consciousness of the play, faces an unseen Visitor in a kind of confessional, and he relives whole segments of his life in brief memory flashes which are played in pools of light on many-leveled platforms. He watches people innocently build intimate relationships, only to see them cruelly destroyed by the unreasonable demands they make on each other: his mother viciously emasculating his father with insults when he lost everything in the stock market crash of 1929; the suicide of a close friend, abandoned by everyone, including Quentin, out of fear of association with his Communist activities in the 1950s; and the breakdown of two marriages when they demanded his total loyalty without giving back the support he himself needed. All these memories are played out with the tower from a Nazi death camp rising behind them, a monument to human cruelty and guilt—the cruelty of the perpetrators and the guilt of the survivors who live, haunted by the fear that to have survived such cruelty somehow makes them guilty too. Into the play comes one survivor, Holga, a new relationship for Quentin—if he can somehow overcome his fears of entering on new paths of destruction. The play's answer is finally for Quentin to accept his own humanity, to learn to live with his imperfection, and most of all to forgive.

> To know, and even happily, that we meet unblessed; not in some garden of wax fruit and painted trees, that lie of Eden, but after, after the Fall, after many, many deaths. Is the knowing all? And the wish to kill is never killed, but with some gift of courage one may look into its face when it appears, and with a stroke of love—as to an idiot in the house—forgive it; again and again . . . forever?

In the same year as *After the Fall*, Lorraine Hansberry found a different answer to absurdity in *The Sign in Sidney Brustein's Window*. Sidney, a radical writer for an underground newspaper, moving in a circle of friends at the forefront of liberal causes, has sunk into lethargy and alcohol as he watches the ideals that had moved the group in the past disintegrate. Backbiting, deal-making, hypocrisy, and unthinking cruelty have taken over, all so that the newspaper, which stood against such things, can survive. When sanctimonious intolerance from former friends causes his sister-in-law's suicide, he finally stands alone to take up his pen and fight the "seething madness" of the world. He declares himself

> a fool who believes that death is waste and love is sweet and that the earth turns and men change every day and that rivers run and that people wanna be better than they are and that flowers smell good and that I hurt terribly today, and that hurt is desperation and desperation is—energy and energy can *move* things.

The despairing view held by the absurdists could not last long among playwrights. The nature of theatre art is to give shape to the bewildering complexities of human action and experience, and once audiences had come to grasp the absurdities, the irrational forces, and the menacing insanity that threatened from inside as well as from the universe itself, the nature of art demanded the search for new paths through the disorder. Besides dramatizing the experience of disorder, however, the theatre artists of disruption had also challenged most of the traditional conventions of dramatic plotting and theatrical staging, so that those who followed them to search for new paths were among the most liberated theatre artists in history. This newly won freedom inspired an extraordinary variety of experimentation in the 1960s and 1970s, which will be the subject of Chapter 10. But over the cries of despair, the more positive voices of realism and its many offshoots still dominated Western theatre through the first half of the twentieth century. We will look at some of the more important offshoots and transformations that occurred in realism in the next chapter.

REALISM
TRANSFORMED

9

Real objects and rough textures in a kind of junk sculpture reveal all the seams in this multiple setting for epic theatre. The gods descend in a rickety elevator in Brecht's *The Good Woman of Setzuan*. University of Texas production.

*I*n the hundred years since realism began to dominate the theatre, various transformations have occurred, not from efforts to abandon realism, as we saw in Chapter 8, but to find more effective ways of presenting reality. Among these transformations are selected realism, Oriental realism, stylized realism, and, most important of all, epic realism. Before looking at these transformations, however, we should look at certain blends that mix realism with other kinds of theatre, not so much from conscious effort to create new styles as from the simple mixing of familiar theatrical elements by playwrights, directors, and actors.

THEATRICAL BLENDS

In Chapters 6 and 7 we considered romance and realism as separate genres; indeed, in their beginnings they reflected quite different attitudes toward life. As time passed, each tended to encroach on the territory of the other until, by mid-twentieth century, new plays were more often blends of the two than clear examples of either. Similarly realism, which its early proponents took with deadly seriousness, is now found commonly in high comedy and even in farce.

Realism and Romance

Such romantic forms as the musical, opera, and dance have been influenced by realism and have been adapted to show complex characters interacting with grubby environments, or even the strange obsessions of the inner mind. One would hardly recognize the roots of the musical *West Side Story* (1957) in the Viennese operettas of the late nineteenth century, where all was glamor and charm, where a handsome prince and a beautiful woman in disguise might experience sorrow and joy and even heartrending disappointment, but only if it were very remote and picturesque. Indeed *West Side Story* stretched our view of the romantic musical to the breaking point. It was an adaptation of that most romantic of plots—the story of Romeo and Juliet, lovers who defy the medieval world of feuds and hatreds and give their lives to bury their parents' strife. But the treatment was very different from the conventional one. The opening was not a show number, with singing and kicking, but a scene of a gang suddenly arriving in a slum street of New York, moving tensely in dance rhythm as they looked around quickly, first in one direction, then another, for a possible enemy. The movement was patterned, exact, unmistakably dance, yet also the simplest, most direct expression of the gang's realistic intent to claim its territory. That scene and others in the play could be described as realism.

We need a new term for this blend of realism and romance that had, by the middle of the twentieth century, defined a distinctly new attitude toward life. If art is a celebration of life, why not celebrate in song the less glamorous moments as well as the joyous and ecstatic ones? Starting with *Pal Joey* (1940) the American musical has done just that, using hardened city types, sardonic moods, and destructive and antisocial aspects of human character. *Pal Joey's* hero, a conniving hoofer who shows the unsavory side of the American success story, repelled much of the regular musical audience of its time, despite a superb Rodgers and Hart score and Gene Kelly as the star; but two successful Broadway revivals, first in the 1950s and again in 1976, show that its style was to catch on. One of the elements that has kept the small-cast musical *The Fantasticks* (1960) running for twenty-five years—the longest running show in musical history—is its cynical twist on a romantic story. Two fathers bring their love-struck children together by building a wall to keep them apart. But the live-happily-ever-after ending falls apart when the children find out they have been tricked. In Act II, the disillusioned young hero runs off to find excitement elsewhere, only to be led on a whirlwind confrontation with the evil of the world by a sardonic master of tricks, El Gallo. At last he returns to his father and his bride, ready to appreciate life without romance at every turn.

In the 1970s, Stephen Sondheim's musicals began to explore new realms between realism and romance. *Company* (1970) seemed the complete opposite of romance, with its abstract setting of pipe frames and elevators and its lonely bachelor hero watching his friends' marriages at their worst, but its wit and lively music caught the wry mood of the New York audience. In *A Little Night Music* (1973) Sondheim moved nearer the charming and sad moods of romance, but here is no brassy, romantic joy, only tenuous, delicate moods, almost as casual and impressionistic as Chekhov, much of the music sung by a chorus of women no longer young.

Nowhere is Sondheim's blend more complex than in *Sweeney Todd, the Demon Barber of Fleet Street* (1979). He combines a Gothic horror story of vengeance in a panorama of nineteenth-century London's industrial poverty with a melodramatic love story and an almost operatic score. The songs range from lyrical love ballads to a wild chorus of escaped lunatics careering through the London slums announcing disaster. In one delightful duet of comic grotesquery, Sweeney lays out a plan to use his barbershop as a slaughterhouse of vengeance, while his landlady, Mrs. Lovett, decides to use his victims in the meat pies she sells in her shop. Together they wittily and musically savor the flavor of pies spiced with priests and clerks, lawyers, grocers, and bankers: "We'll serve anyone . . . / And to anyone / At all." Slashed throats, trap doors, fiery ovens, belching chimneys, a ranting, insane beggar woman, evil officials, and a trick barber chair (it catapults Sweeney's victims down a chute from the barbershop to the bakery shop below) contrast with a heroic young sailor and the barber's beautiful long-lost daughter, who rise to romantic heights out of the corruption and social injustice, but not without doing some murder of their own. On the one hand, the barber, who had become a demonic avenger because of evils

Mrs. Lovett (Angela Lansbury) and Sweeney Todd (Len Cariou) celebrate a practical way to dispose of Todd's victims in the New York production of *Sweeney Todd*, 1979. Directed by Harold Prince.

society did to him in an environment where his once youthful naiveté could not survive, is given a romantic twist through the use of song and dance and the audience's love for the underdog. On the other hand, the romantic maiden in distress, saved by the spotless hero, is given a naturalistic twist when she shows herself to be the true daughter of her father by shooting the man her hero could not bring himself to kill.

Even opera has felt the impact of naturalistic determinism, though only a small group of people go to hear modern opera. Alban Berg has attracted some devoted followers through the dense, tortured music of *Wozzek* and the more cheerful music of *Lulu*. Kurt Weill, who composed for both popular musicals and serious opera, set to music Elmer Rice's *Street Scene*, one of the strongest studies of people defeated by their environment.

Realism and Comedy

The popular theatre has softened realism even more often through comedy. What we might call "comic realism" has enough details of environment and daily living to make it seem realistic, while it borrows from romance a story of love or defiant individualism and a leading man and woman who, if not heroic, show a touch of idealism. It may have such moods of impressionism as a blending of many small frustrations with local color, but the conflict usually reaches a definite climax of success or defeat. Thus it captures some of the excitement of melodrama. This is the easiest kind of play to act, and the set design usually requires only the skill of an interior decorator to reassure the audience with the familiarity of its middle-class homes. Most television sitcoms and much of the light entertainment of community, dinner, and resort theatres could be called comic realism, or comic romance.

A more sophisticated example of the popular mixed genre is Albert Innaurato's *Gemini* (1978). Set in an Italian working-class neighborhood in Philadelphia, it follows the identity problem of an overweight young man who fears he has a homosexual attraction for the younger brother of his WASP, Ivy League girlfriend. Every attempt to confront the problem directly, when the two pop in to visit him during a summer vacation, is diverted by a never-ending flow of interruptions. The play takes on the frenetic pace of farce, as one eccentric "local" after another pops in and out. But the central problem is never out of focus for long, and Innaurato's colorful characters, precise dialogue, and details of daily living lend it the sharp truthfulness of naturalism.

In a very different way, Brian Clark's *Whose Life Is It Anyway?* (1978) deals with a former art teacher who has been completely paralyzed from the neck down and now faces a lifetime in institutions. He fights occupational therapists, the courts, and the medical bias for preserving life, insisting that all support systems be removed so that he may die with dignity. Though the subject provokes serious thought about one of modern medicine's most important moral questions, the central character's wit and his satiric thrusts at conventional biases bring it close to high comedy. Brian Clark, a former drama teacher in England, had written the play partially to prove that he could use the principles he had been teaching in the classroom to form a successful play. *Whose Life Is It Anyway?* proved him correct by following the traditional climactic structure of melodrama. In 1980, because of this formulistic structure, it took only slight revision to turn the protagonist successfully into a woman, played on Broadway by Mary Tyler Moore.

A far deeper use of comedy for naturalism was presented by several Irish

Christy Mahon (David Birney) lionized as a hero (above) and attacked by Pegeen (Martha Henry) (below) in Synge's *The Playboy of the Western World,* 1971. Lincoln Center Repertory Theatre, directed by John Hirsch.

playwrights many years ago, though Irish audiences were not always willing to see either humor or truth in the picture of themselves on the stage. J. M. Synge's *The Playboy of the Western World* (1907) caused riots in Dublin and America by seeming to slander Irish womanhood. We see the play as a serious study of the effects of heredity and environment on personality development. A group of peasant girls, longing for romance and excitement in their remote village, glorify the brave deed of a lonely young man, Christy Mahon, who thinks he has killed his father. Spurred on by their enthusiasm, he becomes the hero they want him to be, until the father appears—wounded, not dead—and the most entranced of the young girls viciously attacks Christy, having discovered a vast distance between a romantic story and a "dirty deed." But Christy has tasted enough glory to know what he really is capable of doing, and he and his father, in the true spirit of comedy, leave the "fools" of County Mayo behind to romp gaily across the western world.

Sean O'Casey's brawling mixture of comedy and harsh reality amid the derelicts of war-torn Dublin in the 1920s has already been discussed as tragicomedy in Chapter 5. In the 1950s, Brendan Behan followed in the footsteps of his countrymen with a new mixture of reality as comedy. *The Quare Fellow* (1954) shows a variety of inmates in a Dublin prison, joking, conniving, posturing, dreaming of freedom, and playing tricks on each other and on the guards in the outrageous and audacious manner of farce. But all this is set against the background of the "quare fellow" (someone under sentence of death) waiting on death row for the inevitable execution, which occurs at the end of the play. Though he is never on stage, the other characters never forget the quare fellow and his fate, and they frequently become violent or morbid in their concern. But they are survivors; they must live in the face of death, and they turn the prison into a microcosm of society, with all its pathos, all its absurdity, and all its humor.

SELECTED REALISM

Before such hybrids as we have been describing appeared—in fact, shortly after the realistic movement began—a modified realism, a form we may call *selected realism*, became the major pattern for realistic plays. Its artists still believed in the cause-and-effect interplay between characters and their heredity and environment, but unlike the naturalists, their work does not follow the philosophy of determinism—that people are helpless to control their world and their actions. The selective realist sees people struggling with choices, selecting actions within the possibilities that their heredity and environment allow. Such struggles may lead to at least partial triumph. Escape is not just a futile dream as it seems in Chekhov's naturalistic plays. Many people have escaped the slums or other cramping environments.

Some plays, like Shaw's *Man and Superman* (1903), suggest that defeat is not actually a bad outcome. The tone of Shaw's play is that of a vigorous high-comedy quarrel between a man and a woman, but the theme is the same naturalistic attempt to escape. Jack Tanner, feeling that marriage would be the end of his intellectual independence, struggles to escape the wiles and powerful appeal of Ann Whitefield, who seems the essence of blind nature. She will use him and destroy him just to propagate the race, with no regard for his human, intelligent purposes. Yet when he does capitulate there is no defeat. He has had a dream of a great debate that his predecessor Don Juan holds in hell, a dream that ends with Don Juan and Doña Ana leaving the comfortable world of hell to tackle the difficult job of creating a higher, more intellectual man—a superman. When Jack realizes that woman, whom he has seen as the blind force of nature, may also will the intelligent, as Doña Ana did, he willingly gives in to nature by marrying. Shaw's *Pygmalion*, described in detail in Chapter 13, is a good example of selected realism.

The characters of selected realism have selective power within their "real" worlds; a few bold ones even assert their will with sharp, sometimes comic actions. So too, the scripts and settings are selective, not presenting the overwhelming "slice of life" detail of the naturalists, but only enough detail for the action or for local color. When plays give their characters some control over their destinies, it is fitting that the setting reflect similar artistic control in line, form, proportion, rhythm, color, and even a fair amount of symmetry—elements that would be neglected or hidden in a slice-of-life play. Designers feel much more challenge in creating in the style of selected realism.

STYLIZED REALISM

Both naturalism and selected realism kept an objective view of one actual place at a time. But that objective view was not enough when the naturalistic character felt menaced by the machine age and when irrational fears burst into the conscious mind. It was not so much the naturalistic environment that was terrifying, as it was isolated images that the subjective mind responded to in that environment: rhythmic, mechanized sounds, dehumanized groups of people, fragments of many past experiences. This explosive conflict called not for selected realism but for *stylized realism*, which kept the central character intact but presented the violence of the conflict by breaking the environment into fragments through abstraction and distortion, much in the manner of the expressionists discussed in Chapter 8.

Eugene O'Neill's *The Hairy Ape* (1922) is a prime example of stylized realism. Yank, a ship's stoker, is a typical naturalistic character who makes a blind attack on his environment, ignorant of how to improve that environment, but acutely aware of his spiritual anguish in not belonging to it. He has identified himself with the steel, the coal, the power and speed of his time, but he finds that the

Stylized realism. Yank, realistically portrayed, out of place in the mechanistic formality of Fifth Avenue society. O'Neill's *The Hairy Ape* in a 1922 production by the Provincetown Players.

machine age needs only his muscle. He has become a dehumanized brute. When the daughter of the shipowner calls him a hairy ape, he leaves the ship in a rage, throwing himself against the rich people coming out of a Fifth Avenue church. But they are like store-window mannequins. Without looking to right or left, they walk along in rows, repeating in stylized, mechanical rhythms the phrases of their inane chatter. In some productions they wear masks. The street and the people are shown subjectively, stylized and distorted as they would appear to Yank's bewildered mind. It is only his surroundings that appear unreal, however; Yank remains a naturalistic victim, but one who refuses to accept his fate and explodes in violence.

The expressionistic distortion in *The Hairy Ape* is only incidental, intended to show the mental state of the main character. The more extended and systematic stylization of the environment makes O'Neill's *The Emperor Jones* (1920) an expressionistic play. Yet in this play, too, the main character is a naturalistic victim in explosive conflict with the environment. A clever black Pullman porter, Brutus Jones, exploiting the ignorant natives of an island in the Caribbean, has made himself Emperor. When his subjects become restless he tries to escape, but in the terrors of the jungle night he loses his veneer of civilization and is destroyed, not so much by the natives as by his own fears. The environment is stylized by the use of a regular drumbeat (timed to the speed of the human heartbeat)—one of the most famous theatrical devices of early twentieth-century theatre. It starts early in the play and continues without interruption through the brief scene-breaks, gradually accelerating to the end. The environment is stylized also in the phantoms that appear to Jones each time he pauses in his flight. Each hallucination goes further into his past, peeling off another level of his consciousness. First there are just vague shapes, then the crap games, fights, court trials, and chain gangs of his own past, and finally the crocodile gods of his primitive ancestors—all stylized in mechanical, terrifying rhythmic movement. By using an abstract and symbolic form, O'Neill makes his play suggest the violence of colonial peoples, ready to turn on their exploiters and destroy them even when, as here, both exploiter and exploited are black.

Stylization is now a common tool of stage and screen. It is the main way by which Bernard Pomerance helps the audience to see simultaneously the inner beauty and the outward deformities of John Merrick in *The Elephant Man*, as

Stylized realism and expressionism. Jones in his fantasy sees the enormous crocodile god. O'Neill's *The Emperor Jones* in a Yale University production, designed by Donald Oenslager.

described in Chapter 2. In addition, by staging the dream of Dr. Treves, Pomerance has used a basic device of the expressionists to reveal the inner turmoil going on in the doctor's mind.

ORIENTAL INFLUENCES ON REALISM

One important transformation of Western realism has resulted from contact with Oriental theatre, especially that of China. On first contact, Chinese theatre would appear to be anything but realistic. The first play in the Chinese manner put on in the West caused gales of laughter at its childlike conventions—a property man shaking bits of paper snow from a box as the actor cries, "How cold it is!" or putting a row of cushions on the floor for the actor's death scene. But it was the Chinese theatre that suggested to Thornton Wilder his new approach to realism in *Our Town* (1938), the most beloved treatment of the everyday lives of everyday people in small-town America that our theatre has produced. Wilder had spent part of his boyhood in China where his father was an American consul, and he was fascinated by the free, highly imaginative methods of its theatre. From the Chinese theatre he learned that even the events of everyday life can be presented by actors on an open platform, reacting not to a realistic setting but to the private thoughts and personal relations of the character. After the success of *Our Town*, the West began to see Oriental theatre not just as ceremony or playful fantasy but as a fundamental way of treating reality. We will discuss Wilder's play in detail later in connection with epic realism.

Symbolic painting of a sacred pine tree in background. Oriental thrust stage for actor, chorus, and musicians. Japanese Noh theatre on the estate of a feudal lord. Drawn by Bobbie Okerbloom.

Still a living art, Chinese theatre uses conventions established more than a thousand years ago. The stage has no front curtain, scenery, or realistic properties. A temple canopy sometimes held up by two lacquered columns decorates the acting area, and the back of the stage is a decorated screen or beautiful embroidered cloth that carries the imagination into romantic realms of fancy but tells nothing about the individual scenes. Both the orchestra and the property man are on stage and visible at all times. Each actor, a man (or a man impersonating a woman), enters by one of the conventional doorways in the back cloth, mimes the opening of sliding doors, and comes down to tell the audience exactly who the character is and what he plans to do.

The few scenic effects are highly conventionalized. To indicate mountain country, small panels painted with the traditional mountain-and-stream pattern are brought out and leaned against a chair or table. A painted cloth held up on a pole by attendants represents a city gate. Simple chairs and tables serve any need for levels—hills, walls, river banks. But such devices are subterfuge: It is the actors who create the reality—marching, riding, shouting, brandishing weapons, fighting furious duels with all the rage of battle but rarely coming close enough even to touch weapons with the opponent. The property man provides chairs or other properties for the actors as they are needed, making no attempt to

Scenic spectacle combined with make-believe for the Japanese popular theatre. Eighteenth-century Japanese Kabuki theatre. Drawn by Bobbie Okerbloom.

A colorful imitation of the Chinese stage, with the property man at one side and the orchestra at the other. *The Circle of Chalk*, University of Iowa production, directed by Harold Crain.

hide his actions. He sets chairs on a table and the performer climbs a high mountain pass. To indicate a journey by chariot, the actor crouches and trots between two flags on which wheels are painted. Using only a whip to indicate that he is riding a horse, the actor shows great skill in suggesting the essence of a person getting on or off a horse.

The characters also sing many songs—indeed the Western name for the drama is "Peking Opera"—and there are formal dances and stylized movements. The orchestra reinforces the melody and rhythm of the songs and uses numerous instruments to mark each step and gesture: flutes, violins, gongs, drums, bells, cymbals, and blocks of wood. Occasional adaptations of Chinese plays have met with success in Europe and America, especially among college theatre groups, but the highly specialized skills of voice, mime, gesture, and dance that true Chinese theatre requires are not within the range of Western actor training. Rather our appreciation has come from recurring visits of Chinese performers and of the Peking Opera and from a widely distributed short film, *A Night at the Peking Opera*, which showcases the wide range of styles found in Chinese theatre.

Though the West attempts few Oriental plays, it has moved enthusiastically toward the freedom and imagination of the Oriental style. When Edmond Rostand wrote *Cyrano de Bergerac* in 1898, he had Cyrano protect a friend by fighting one hundred hired ruffians. In keeping with Western theatre's realistic bias, Rostand made this fantastic fight occur offstage between acts. Staging such a fight would have strained both the theatre's resources and the audience's credulity. But the Peking Opera showed how a simple Monkey King could single handedly rout a whole army of gods and demigods on stage and never raise the question of credibility. He simply used the stylized dance-like movements of the martial arts. Taking their cues from the Chinese, playwrights today feel free to have scenery changed before the eyes of the audience; the use of masks, symbolic properties, and fragments of settings is acceptable, even expected by today's theatregoers.

The English playwright, Peter Shaffer, was impressed by a short comic episode of the Peking Opera in which an innkeeper sneaks into the room of a guest whom he mistakes for a highwayman. He steals his sword in the dark and prepares to kill him. Meanwhile, the guest, a young knight, awakens, senses his

Chinese influence in Western theatre. The technical effects are fully visible to the audience, and actors play horses in *Equus*. National Theatre Company, London. Directed by John Dexter.

danger, and, in a wild tour de force of dance, comic mugging, and martial art skills (with whisker-breadth escapes from the sharp swords), he manages to disarm his attacker in the dark. All of this occurs, of course, under full stage light, allowing the audience to enjoy the comic irony and the performance skills. Shaffer capitalized on this idea for his domestic farce *Black Comedy* (1965), in which the audience has no trouble supposing the visible actors to be in a conventional living room, totally darkened by a blown fuse. Shaffer went even further with Chinese theatre techniques in his hit drama *Equus* (1973). Here on a bare stage, surrounded only by those actors not in the scene, an emotionally disturbed boy undergoes psychiatric therapy for having blinded five horses. Space and time are completely fluid. As the psychiatrist probes the boy's memories, the actors playing characters from those memories move into the playing area—bringing their benches with them to watch a pornographic movie, or in other cases transforming the empty space into a horse stable, an open field, or a bedroom, by means of their acting alone. Most memorable are the horses, played by men wearing skeletal frames of horses' heads and hooves, crowding into the stable to be curried and fed, or prancing and galloping around an open field. In one instance, a booted rider appears and by himself plays both horse and rider, even taking the boy up on his own shoulders to ride double. This Oriental fashion for portraying animals has been used in several modern plays of widely different styles. In the musical *Camelot*, the serious drama *Becket*, and the epic drama *Indians*, some of the leading characters came prancing on, wearing the frames of hobbyhorses around their waists.

Although Japanese theatre has not exerted as strong an influence on Western drama as the Chinese, it too has fascinated some theatre artists. The Irish poet William Butler Yeats attempted some dance dramas in the spirit of the mystical Noh drama of Japan more than fifty years ago. The 1951 Kurosawa film, *Rashomon*, challenges our ability to know reality by telling about the rape of a woman and the murder of her husband from four different points of view: that of the woman, that of the bandit who committed the crime, that of the dead husband (through a medium), and that of a witness who never came forward to help or to testify at the trial. A powerful stage adaptation of *Rashomon* has had great popularity in college theatres. In 1975, Stephen Sondheim turned to the Japanese Kabuki theatre for the principal effects in his musical *Pacific Overtures*. Japan had been used as settings for the Gilbert and Sullivan operetta *The Mikado* and for Puccini's opera *Madame Butterfly* more than half a century earlier. But Sondheim's borrowing was in a more realistic spirit. The story deals with the opening up of Japan to Western influence after more than two centuries of isolation, through the exploratory visit of Commodore Perry. Sondheim not only blended into his songs some suggestions of Japanese music but used a Japanese orchestra, with musicians sitting crosslegged at the side of the stage, and presented many episodes with the conventions of the Kabuki stage. One number was the famous Kabuki Lion Dance, performed by Commodore Perry in appropriate costume. But the Japanese touches were, after all, rather superficial, and the final number was danced by a chorus of Americanized Japanese in Western dress with the exuberant style of any new Broadway musical.

EPIC REALISM

The most important transformation of realism is *epic realism*. It differs so greatly from the early naturalistic theatre that many people label it as a revolt against realism. Like stylized realism and expressionism, it breaks the world into separate fragments, but unlike them, it pieces all the fragments together into one meaningful picture of the real world. It does not break into dreams and fantasies, though it often simplifies the realistic scenic elements to the point of abstraction in order to show the wide sweep of an institution or an idea. The word "epic" comes from Aristotle, who made a sharp distinction between the dramatic form, which concentrates on one action in a limited time and space, and the epic form, which, like Homer's long narrative poems the *Iliad* and the *Odyssey* involves many people and covers many episodes in many times and places. Aristotle did not believe that theatre could handle the epic type of action, but twentieth-century theatre artists, as well as the Romantics and Elizabethans, have done just that time and again.

One of epic theatre's earliest proponents, the German director Erwin Piscator, argued in the 1920s that theatre should be a forum for ideas. What happens to the characters is less important than what happens to the audience as they weigh ideas, examine evidence, and consider not only what occurs but the alternatives that might have occurred if the characters had acted differently. As in the narrative form of the novel, what happens to the characters is in the past, told and demonstrated by the presentation. The future tense that we normally associate with drama is centered not in the characters but in the audience, who must make judgments and decisions. Thus, epic theatre develops a totally new relationship with its audiences, for it is a place where real things happen to them, inspired by the theatrical events they have witnessed or debated. The characters and what they do are part of a demonstration—typical examples to illustrate some idea or point of view.

Like the theatre of fact, epic realism is a form of documentary, but it has its own special methods. Where naturalism might show one realistic scene of people waiting in a breadline, an epic treatment of the economic problem might show briefly the farmer, the banker, the miller, the wheat failure in Siberia, the famines of East Africa, the operation of the stock market, and a congressional hearing—all part of the picture of scarcity, high prices, and hunger. As a technique, it dramatizes many episodes, connecting them by an idea rather than by the causal development of its characters; mobile scenery carries one from episode to episode, constantly reminding the audience of its theatricality. Those watch-

Odets' *Waiting for Lefty* at the Arkansas Repertory Theatre. In the background the union workers are shown by means of larger-than-life projections.

ing are then bombarded with all sorts of devices that help them to consider the larger significance of the episodes: moving pictures and projections, symbolic images, songs and ballads, actors who step out of character to address the audience directly as actors, and narrative and dialogue that view the episodes from a later time.

American Epic Theatre in the Thirties

In the Depression decade of the 1930s, such large problems as public health, housing, wages, and farm income often seemed more important than stories about individuals, and America developed its own form of epic theatre. The most memorable of the depression epics is Clifford Odets' *Waiting for Lefty*, produced in 1935 by a commune of young theatre radicals called The Group Theatre. It interrupts the strike meeting of a taxi drivers' union to cut in, on the forestage, short scenes of the desperate home lives of five drivers, while the whole circle of union members is dimly visible in the background—a reminder that individual frustration could be relieved only by union action. In its historic first production, the audience is reported to have joined in at the end in a rousing call for "Strike!"

For the theatre documentary called the Living Newspaper, New Deal journalists joined with theatre workers to present reports on national problems. When Roosevelt in his second inaugural address called attention to the plight of one-third of the nation—"ill-housed, ill-clothed, and ill-fed"—the Federal Theatre Project organized a Living Newspaper about housing, called *One-Third of a Nation*. In a large setting of a four-story tenement, a fire and a family tragedy led a little man, Mr. Buttonkooper, to ask police, politicians, and inspectors how conditions had gotten so bad, why property owners did so little to improve them, and what might be done by government-supported housing. Many demonstration scenes were brought onto the forestage. One of the most vivid showed the history of New York City in miniature, as land dealers set up a little plot of grass, with street signs a few feet apart, and sold off one lot after another to the crowds of immigrants who arrived and sat close together on the stage, each filling his plot of land.

More important, however, in shaping the ultimate form of epic theatre have been two plays of Thornton Wilder: *Our Town* (1938) and *The Skin of Our Teeth* (1942). These are not usually called epic because, instead of social, economic, and political problems, they deal with historical and mythical events and philosophical and religious ideas. In *Our Town* Wilder wanted to present an idealized picture of growing up, getting married, and dying in an American town before the complexities of large-city living had changed the meaning of family and town, and to present the human value and beauty of each moment in time. He did not agree with the naturalists' view of everyday life as restricted, petty, and degraded.

Wilder found the conventions of the Chinese stage perfectly suited to his purpose. He planned *Our Town* to be produced with no front curtain, no scenery, no romantic lighting, and no properties beyond a few chairs, two ladders, and some garden trellises pushed on at one point "for those who think they have to have scenery." He used a Stage Manager as demonstrator, combining the Chinese property man with a Prologue-Expositor, letting him comment directly to the audience, bring on scenes or interrupt them, and play small roles himself—a clerk at the soda fountain, for instance. The Stage Manager brings in testimony by a historian and a geologist to add a dimension of the past—the time of the settlement of European immigrants, the earlier times of Indian tribes, and the time of the stone formation of millions of years ago. By contrast, when certain characters appear on stage, he describes their futures—up to and even following their deaths.

The first act shows the daily life of the town, from preparations for breakfast and the morning rounds of the newsboy and milkman to the return from choir practice in the moonlight and the settling down for the night. In the second act, the daily kitchen and breakfast activity is aimed toward getting ready for the

Wilder's *The Skin of Our Teeth* produced as a theatrical fantasy in the tradition of American musicals. In a New Jersey living room, a mammoth and a dinosaur are family pets. San Diego Old Globe Theatre production, directed by Jack O'Brien.

wedding of Emily and George, but before the wedding scene itself, a flashback to a drugstore scene shows the first time the couple knew they were meant for each other. In the third act, Emily, now dead, arrives in the cemetery, where, in chairs set in rows to represent graves, the other dead sit and speak. Emily realizes that she can revisit the living and decides to look in on her twelfth birthday. Soon the pain of seeing people so immersed in daily living that they don't notice the details of life becomes too strong and she gladly returns to take her place on the hilltop. The act ends with the dead quietly talking about the stars and the millions of years it takes their light to reach the earth.

The Skin of Our Teeth may be considered an even better example of epic realism. From the framework of a present day New Jersey, it covers an even wider range of time than *Our Town*, juxtaposing first the Ice Age, then the flood, and then an unspecified modern war. Besides being a modern family, the main characters are also Adam and Eve and Cain. The play dramatizes the perennial need to pick up some threads of civilization and start over again after a catastrophe. The epic method includes the use of an expositor speaking over a loudspeaker, slides, allegorical figures, myths and parables, and a parade of actors quoting passages from Plato, Spinoza, and the Book of Genesis.

The Epic Realism of Bertolt Brecht

Most discussion of epic theatre centers on the plays and theories of Bertolt Brecht. He is appreciated as much for his unique characters, for his poetry, and for the anguished plight of his main figures as he is for the special techniques of writing and production that he gave to the modern theatre.

Brecht started writing in the chaotic disillusionment of 1920s Germany, when old ideas were being questioned and new forms were being tried in both politics and art. During World War I, he had been a medical orderly helping to patch wounded men up quickly so that they could go back into the trenches and be shot at again. After the war he saw in Germany the lines of unemployed, the abortive attempts of labor groups to gain control, the terrible inflation that wiped out all savings, and in the cities corruption, venality, and exploitation. Traditional theatre seemed to Brecht incapable of reacting to these problems. His idea of a more exciting theatre grew from the satiric songs of the cabaret, the rowdy give-and-take of the sports arena, and the frank theatricality of the circus. He was also impressed with two unusual Max Reinhardt productions: *The Circle of Chalk* in the Chinese style and the eighteenth-century comedy *A Servant of Two Masters* in the improvised style of a *commedia dell'arte* troupe.

Brecht's most sensational success came in 1928 with *The Three-Penny Opera,* a musical satire based on John Gay's *The Beggar's Opera,* which had been the sensation of London in the 1720s and had had a triumphant revival there in the 1920s. Brecht created his own grotesque picture of the world of beggars, thieves, and corrupt officials, of love, exploitation, and betrayal, with bitter comments on human depravity and forebodings of destruction. Yet the bitterness is lightened by irony and song. The young composer Kurt Weill, creating his own German version of American popular music, wrote songs for it that are still sung. The play has been popular with university drama groups and has had several professional revivals.

Whereas this early play showed a cynical, demonic individual—Macheath, or "Mack the Knife"—triumphing in a ruthless world, *Mother Courage and Her Children* (1941), like most of Brecht's later plays, shows a more sympathetic character trying to survive in a world that outrages all sense of what is human. Dragging her peddler's wagon across central Europe through the Thirty Years War in the seventeenth century, Mother Courage earns her living from the war, loses her sons to its corruption, and sees her daughter scarred, maimed, and finally shot for trying to help its victims. The many songs, instead of giving charm to the piece, increase our ironic awareness of the senselessness of the war.

Epic realism. Titles, projections, voices. Abstract, cut-down setting that, with slight changes, serves many separate episodes. Brecht's *The Private Life of the Master Race,* an indictment of the Nazis, written before World War II. Texas Tech University production, directed by Clifford Ashby.

One of Brecht's most widely produced plays, *The Good Woman of Setzuan* (1943), takes the form of a parable and borrows in method from the Chinese theatre. Three of the highest gods roam the earth in search of one good person, to prove the goodness of the moral system they have offered humanity. When the only kind-hearted person they can find is a prostitute, they set her up in a shop so that her goodness can have the respectability of an honest living. Her kind heart, however, finds no place in the world of trade. To save herself from complete ruin, she disguises herself as a male cousin who can deal ruthlessly with her parasitic kinsmen and her business associates. But she finds no way to reconcile the two ways of life and pleads to the gods for help. They only smile and tell her, "Be good!"—leaving the audience to conclude that perhaps they themselves should change the world of starving dependents and ruthless trade and not ask one young woman to try to lift the universe.

Many of Brecht's ideas developed as negative attacks on the established conventions of the realistic stage. He despised traditional audiences who looked for emotional thrills or drifted in pity and empathy for helpless heroes. Such audiences could not think or judge. Their emotions were stirred, then exhausted, and at the end they accepted the fate of the characters as inevitable. Worse yet, they accepted the imperfections of their own world. Brecht wanted to wake up his audiences, to make them think, question, consider alternatives, and, ultimately, change their own world. Hence he theorized a great deal about breaking the illusion, about devices to interrupt the audience's involvement, to keep emotions in check. He wanted on stage the objectivity of a scientific lecture, with important demonstrations. His is the first major theory of theatre to give primary importance to the audience's synthesizing experience, insisting that they could weigh the social implications far better by standing at a distance.

Brecht's term for achieving this distance, *alienation*, has caused much confusion; many people supposed that he wanted to give only a dull lecture. He invented the term to persuade actors (who were afraid of breaking the illusion) that there was a more stimulating kind of theatricality than illusion, one that could delight, amaze, shock, fascinate, and outrage the audience, and, most important, could cause them to carry the ideas of the play from the theatre into their own world. Today, when we so easily accept the methods of epic theatre, we realize that it is not cold acting but the interruption of the narration, the sharp contrasts of scenes, and the juxtaposition of multiple ironic devices that set the characters at a greater aesthetic distance—in *Our Town* as well as in the plays of Brecht.

Epic Techniques in the Theatre Since Brecht

Once audiences had become familiar with epic theatre techniques and once theatre artists saw their potential for a freer, more open style of production, they quickly adapted them to many subjects that could not be handled by the tradi-

History, fantasy, realism, symbolism, and dance combine with Oriental freedom in Kopit's *Indians,* an epic drama about race relations. A model for the set, designed by Oliver Smith.

tional theatre. Whether through film projections and the mixing of fictional scenes with factual information in the antiwar play, *Oh, What a Lovely War!* (1963), or through the simple story-telling method of the musical *Pippin* (1974), epic techniques became part of the accepted conventions of the modern theatre.

Arthur Kopit used epic form successfully throughout *Indians* (1969), a serious study of the misunderstandings between the white man and the Indian, and a parallel to the U.S. involvement in Vietnam. The hero is Buffalo Bill, friend of the Indians, friend of the President, creator of the popular image of the sharpshooting scout of the West. But, in *Indians,* he is prancing on a hobby horse. In his Wild West Show he presents Indians, real and fake, to white audiences all over the world, gradually breaking through the mask of the showman to realize what he, and all white people, had done to the confused Indians. Serious scenes of a congressional delegation are interwoven with buffalo-hunting scenes, Indian dances of self-torture, and scenes from Buffalo Bill's Wild West Show. Some of these are completely fake, but one is of an actual chief, who, using an authentic speech from history, is required to reenact at each performance his final, tragic appeal for help for his dying people before their surrender. The play opens and closes with a scene of glass museum cases showing wax figures of Buffalo Bill and the Indians, and at intervals in the play prehistoric masked gods of the plains are brought on. If the stage cannot, like a film, show a cineramic battle and the massacre of thousands, it can show a powerful dance-mime of a dozen Indians spreading a great sheet of snow, on which they lie down to be frozen in their final anguish. The stage can use realistic scenery when it needs to, but by using only symbols and fragmentary scenes, it can often focus directly on the meaning in ways that literal realism cannot.

Among the most surprising uses of epic theatre is the Andrew-Lloyd Weber and Tim Rice opera *Evita* (1978). It treats the life of Eva Peron, the power-hungry Argentine actress who rose from an illegitimate birth to become, via a series of bedrooms, the first lady of the land, revered by the masses. With epic proportion the opera follows her entire career, including the outrage of her enemies and the devotion of her *descamisados* (shirtless ones). The play begins with the announcement of her death and a magnificent funeral, with adoring crowds deifying Evita's memory in the "Salve Regina" they sing. Thus, from the beginning, the audience knows how Evita's story will end, so they are free to explore in fascination the story itself, her ruthless rise to power, her appeals to popular sentiment, to the public's need for her glamor. Even more important to epic alienation is the character of Che Guevera, Latin America's roving revolutionist. Though Che probably never knew Eva Peron in real life, he is a constant presence in the show, a kind of narrator/devil's advocate, interrupting the public spectacle as well as the most intimate scenes with cynical challenges to Evita's motives and to the public's glamorized image of her. Even at the beginning we hear his mocking voice rise over the pomp of the funeral: "O what a circus! O what a show." The mourners continue devotedly, but Che reminds the audience of Evita's motives and of the public's glamorized image of her.

> As soon as the smoke from the funeral clears
> We're all going to see—and how!—she did nothing for years!

Her husband's rise to power is staged as a game of musical chairs, reducing the image of his statesmanship to the level of winning a parlor game. When Evita goes abroad to win European support for her husband's government, a single song carries her through her "Rainbow Tour," while the Argentine crowds back home enthusiastically greet the reports of each of her triumphs on the tour, then gradually diminish and disperse as the triumphs lose their glow. At the end of

Film of goose-stepping soldiers gives an epic sweep to the "musical chairs" rise to power of Juan Peron in the New York production of *Evita*. Directed by Harold Prince.

the show, Evita's dying is treated in a "Montage"—reprises of the songs that highlighted various stages of her career, giving the audience one more chance to piece all the events together, to shape a whole picture of the woman and her effect on the people. Though Evita is the subject of the opera, the epic techniques constantly force the audience to look critically at her and, equally, at the society that made her possible.

REALISM: THE PERSISTENT VIEW OF OUR AGE

In spite of the ways in which realism has been expanded in this century, the basic impulses persist. Audiences have grown to expect that any play might confront them with the alienation devices of epic theatre or might break into the subjective point of view of stylized realism, but the conventions of selected realism in play-writing, scenery, and acting are what audiences still normally expect and what the modern theatre has usually provided. In fact, there have been frequent resurgences of extremely realistic plays in recent decades. This resurgence was particularly strong in England in the 1950s and 1960s on both stage and screen. It introduced new material, especially about life in the industrial cities, material that seemed fresh and robust to London audiences used to genteel plays about the upper class. It was John Osborne's *Look Back in Anger* that really started this new realism when it electrified its audiences in 1956. Jimmy Porter, the main character, is caught in an environment he hates, but he is not inarticulate. He spits back with a fiery anger that gave a name to a generation in Britain: the Angry Young Men. The welfare state is a boring fact that leaves him frustrated. The old establishment is intact, and he is still outside the regular social order. Jimmy does not fight for any social cause; his problem is spiritual, as shown in his relationship with his wife, Alison. He torments her and drives her out, and he can accept her only when she too is humiliated and crushed by intense suffering. Though *Look Back in Anger* lacks the wide scope of Sean O'Casey's and Eugene O'Neill's plays, its depth of suffering, its cry for compassion, its vividness of speech almost put it in the class of their best naturalistic plays.

The movement of angry young men was short-lived, but by the 1970s, a whole new generation of English playwrights was looking with rather hopeless compassion at middle- and working-class English men and women and immigrants from the former colonies who had lost their roots with the fading of the empire, people who were searching for some meaning in their drab lives or trying to pretend that the values they had been brought up to believe in still had meaning. David Storey, Pam Gems, David Mercer, Simon Gray, and David Hare are just a few of the playwrights who followed these disoriented characters into their London flats, their middle-class suburban houses, their athletic locker rooms, and their ghetto schoolrooms to examine the numbing effect on people afraid to look too closely at their own emptiness. David Storey's *The Changing Room* (1971) shows a football team of working men who play on weekends for extra money. They arrive in the locker room, put on their playing clothes, then after the tough game change back to street clothes and go home. When one of them is injured, the bravado of casual companionship weakens for a moment, and we get a glimpse of human concern—but only a glimpse. Personal feeling is dangerous.

The teachers' lounge in a third-rate English public school is the setting for Simon Gray's *Quartermaine's Terms*, produced by the Long Wharf Theatre in New Haven (1982) and in New York (1983). Amidst the general flurry of between-class and after-school activity, Quartermaine, the most sedentary teacher of the lot, commands our attention, our contempt, and finally our pity. He is without personality or imagination, without family or social life. A night out for him is to babysit in the homes of colleagues, which he does for free—to make himself needed. His teaching, probably mediocre even in his best days, has deteriorated to pathetic incompetence, recognized by students and colleagues alike. But he is congenial and unthreatening. He is, in short, a fixture. But when the old headmaster dies, a young dynamic man takes over, and Quartermaine is justifiably told not to return next term. We see him standing at the end, lost and alone. This teachers' lounge, which he can never enter again, was his sole basis for identity. The play passes no judgments either on those who covered for Quartermaine's many terms of incompetence or on those who finally eject him from the school. In the best tradition of naturalism, it shows us a character whose environment changes, leaving him with no resources to adapt—not a victim, not a tragic hero, but simply a pathetic human being rejected by the movement of social forces he did not foresee or understand.

Two lonely people try to break through their inhibitions to achieve a relationship. Robert Darnell and Monique Fowler in Lanford Wilson's *Tally's Folly*. San Diego's Old Globe Theatre production, directed by Andrew J. Traister.

Selected realism has persisted no less strongly on the American stage. Though experimentation with free and open styles was the rage during the 1960s, by the mid-seventies playwrights were concentrating largely on everyday kinds of people in realistic environments with problems rising from their social and hereditary backgrounds. David Rabe, whose antiwar plays *The Basic Training of Pavlo Hummel* and *Sticks and Bones* (both 1971) had been partly nonrealistic, wrote *Streamers* in 1976, where the agreeable relationship of three army trainees (one black man and two whites) is disrupted by a disgruntled friend of the black man and finally erupts in racial hatred and violence. Lanford Wilson, whose early plays had explored styles ranging from epic to absurdist, won the Pulitzer Prize in 1979 for *Talley's Folly*. Though it includes chatty direct address to the audience at the beginning and end of the play, its setting is a realistic boathouse, complete with crumbling floors and weak beams. There its two characters, a middle-aged Jewish refugee and a 31-year-old sterile spinster, crack their egg-like protective shells to reveal the secrets of their past, which have made them misfits in a small midwestern town, but which make them right for each other.

Beth Henley's *Crimes of the Heart* (1981), outrageously funny from start to

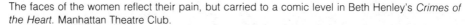

The faces of the women reflect their pain, but carried to a comic level in Beth Henley's *Crimes of the Heart.* Manhattan Theatre Club.

finish, looks closely at three small-town sisters from Mississippi trying to get through a bad day: Granddaddy is in the hospital with "blood vessels popping in his brain"; the youngest sister is out on bail for having shot her husband because she didn't like his looks; the eldest sister is facing her thirtieth birthday, with no marital prospects, singing happy birthday to herself over a one-candle cookie; and the middle sister is finally admitting that her Hollywood singing career is a "bust." Henley affectionately displays her characters in a small-town kitchen where they cannot deal with their feelings about the corpses of the present until they lay to rest the corpses of their past—a father who abandoned them and a mother who hanged herself along with her pet cat. The central values of selected realism are here: compassion, endurance, a desire to break through the illusions which, though they deny reality, may help you get through a bad day, and the belief that understanding a problem is the first step toward solving it.

ETHNIC THEATRE AND THE REALISTIC IMPULSE

One strikingly new theatrical impulse emerged with the development of realism: the conscious use of theatre by minority and ethnic groups to unite and liberate their people. Ethnic theatre is not a style in the sense that naturalism or epic theatre are styles, but it shares with realism the desire to present a true picture of the life of the ethnic group in its struggle for recognition and release from oppression, and it is rooted in realism's belief in progress.

The Irish Renaissance

The most visible among the ethnic theatres since its beginnings at the turn of the century has been the Irish. Ever since the 1500s, Ireland had tried to free itself from English domination, in Parliament and on the battlefield. The 1890s brought a new approach to independence—a cultural revolution, an attempt to reaffirm Ireland's rich native heritage by publishing and translating the ancient legends and by restoring the Irish language, which was all but forgotten in the major cities, though still spoken in rural areas of the West. Though Irish playwrights and actors had enriched the English theatre for centuries with their comic brilliance, there was no Irish theatre. With the new spirit of nationalism, a few writers began to try their hands at plays, and in 1898, two Irishmen, Edward Martyn and the poet William Butler Yeats, met with an Englishwoman, Lady Augusta Gregory, to form the Irish Literary Theatre. The manifesto that resulted from their meeting clearly set forth their ethnic goals: "to build up a Celtic and Irish school of dramatic literature, . . . to bring upon the stage the deeper thoughts and emotions of Ireland," and to show Ireland as the "home of an ancient idealism" instead of the "home of buffoonery and easy sentiment," as it had been depicted on the stages of England and America. After a couple of shaky productions, the group joined forces with William and Frank Fay, two actors trained in the realistic style, and Yeats persuaded a young poet, John Millington Synge, to return from Paris and start writing plays about his own people. Together this small group of amateurs founded the Abbey Theatre in 1904, which has gone on through a tempestuous history to become the National Theatre of Ireland.

Though Yeats preferred the poetic style of symbolism to express the deeper truths of mythic Ireland, it was the realistic production style of the Brothers Fay combined with Synge's naturalistic treatment of peasant life and his rendition of the images and rhythms of the Irish language into a rich and colorful dialect that were to make their mark on the new theatre. Synge's classic one-act tragedy, *Riders to the Sea* (discussed in Chapter 4), and his comedy *The Playboy of the Western World* (discussed earlier in this chapter) are among the most sensitive treatments of peasant life ever written. In the 1920s, it was to the Abbey Theatre that Sean O'Casey brought his tragicomedies of Dublin's war years, doing for Ireland's cities what Synge had done for rural Ireland, capturing the spirit and rich language of the Dublin slums. Though the theatre had been founded to help the Irish see themselves as they really were rather than through the stereotypes of the English theatre, the view was not always welcomed. Both *Playboy* and O'Casey's *The Plough and the Stars*, with its unheroic treatment of the 1916 Easter Rebellion, caused riots in the theatre.

Among Ireland's contemporary playwrights, Brian Friel stands out for his efforts to uphold the spirit of that 1898 manifesto, writing and producing plays to express the deeper thoughts and emotions of both modern and historic Ireland. In the 1980–1981 season, his play *Translations* played to packed audiences in every major city in Ireland and was hailed by critics as a kind of "national treasure." *Translations* is set in the 1820s when English soldiers went through the West of Ireland changing all the names of places from Irish into English equivalents. It is a tale of love and intrigue that uses both the English and Irish languages, but it is really about language itself as the true expression of the soul of a people. Its most remarkable effect comes in a love scene between an English soldier, who speaks only English, and a peasant girl, who speaks only Irish. After several fruitless attempts to communicate through words, they finally manage to express their feelings through nothing but a loving articulation of the Irish names for local places, the only words in Irish that the soldier knows.

Yiddish Theatre

A somewhat longer tradition belongs to the Yiddish theatre, with its roots in the Jewish communities of Eastern Europe. Jewish writers had always used the local national language for their work, since Yiddish was not for literature. Starting in the 1820s, a few began to write in this spoken language of the people both as a means of capturing untranslatable feelings and of reaching a wider audience. But it was in New York, beginning in the 1880s, when vast waves of immigration gave New York City the largest concentrated Jewish population in the world, that Yiddish theatre found its center. In his book *Unser Teater*, Jacob Mestel cites the goals of its leaders: "The Yiddish theatre must become the artistic home for contemporary Jewish life; it must use Jewish subject matter, emotions, and style which will bring the people into a feeling of being closer and at home." Such motives came as a direct response to a yearning that the young immigrants felt in this new land, as recalled by Solomon Adlheit:

> For us everything here appeared prosaic, at dawn to the shop, at night back from the shop. Young people confided to one another their lonesomeness, their need for their folkways, they came together with one hope, something to keep us together, a cultural center perhaps.

The most beloved of the Yiddish writers was Sholem Aleichem, often compared to Dickens for his rich treatment of life in the tenements and back alleys of the cities, and to Mark Twain for his penetrating humor. One of his most popular folk tales, *Tevye the Milkman*, is one of the stories that was many years later adapted into the hit musical *Fiddler on the Roof*. *The Dybbuk* (1914), by the Russian Jew S. Anskey, is perhaps the most important play of the Yiddish theatre. It is a mystical play in which a young student dies while experimenting with magic religious rites to try to win the love of a young woman. On her wedding day, he enters her body as a dybbuk (an evil spirit). To draw the dybbuk from her body, the religious community, led by the rabbi, go through an ecstatic and intoxicating ceremony, drawing out their own suppressed passions. They finally succeed, but not without revealing that the girl had been promised to the student. She hears his voice calling her and goes toward it to her death. *The Dybbuk* has been widely translated and produced, and was adapted by Paddy Chayevsky into a successful Broadway show in 1959, *The Tenth Man*. More than any other play, it changed the image of the Jewish character in the theatre, eliminating the comic stereotype and introducing the Jewish youth of pride, dignity, and intelligence.

Black Ethnic Theatre

In the United States, black theatre has become one of the most important theatre movements of modern times. Plays by black Americans had been written even in slavery (though probably not produced), but the treatment of blacks in mainstream American theatre paralleled the stereotypes of the Irish on the English stage—characters of buffoonery and easy sentiment. An early movement of black vaudeville-like theatre revues began before World War I at Harlem's Lafa-

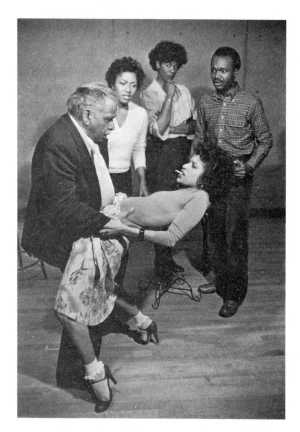

The domestic life of American blacks as shown in a 1940's play, *Anna Lucasta* by Philip Yordan. Revival by the New Federal Theatre, directed by Ernestine M. Johnston.

yette Theatre; a few white playwrights such as Eugene O'Neill with *All God's Chillun Got Wings* (1923) and Paul Green with *In Abraham's Bosom* (1924) made some attempts to deal realistically with American blacks; and Cleveland's Karamu Center began casting all plays without regard to color in the 1920s. A surge of new plays by black playwrights rose briefly in the government-sponsored Black Federal Theatre Project of the 1930s, and then disappeared almost without a trace when Congress abandoned the project in 1939, but only a smattering of serious plays by black playwrights ever reached the professional stage until Lorraine Hansberry's *A Raisin in the Sun* opened on Broadway in 1958 to become a smash hit and go on to win the New York Drama Critics Circle Award. Hansberry's play, discussed in detail in Chapter 7, is a moving and penetrating study of a modern black family in Chicago, but its characters are largely trying to adjust to a world of white values, while facing the problems of moving into an antagonistic white neighborhood. Lorraine Hansberry herself saw the play as an attempt to "help a lot of people to understand how we are just as complicated as they are—and just as mixed up—but above all we have among our miserable and downtrodden ranks—people who have the very essence of human dignity." With such an aim, *A Raisin in the Sun* seemed to be an answer to a call that Montgomery Gregory had issued in the early 1920s:

> Our ideal is a National Negro Theatre where the Negro playwright, musician, actor, dancer, and artist in concert shall fashion a drama that will merit the respect and admiration of America. Such an institution must come from the Negro himself, as he alone can truly express the soul of his people.

But many of Lorraine Hansberry's contemporaries were already looking for something more than the respect of America—especially white America, and they scorned *Raisin* as a play for whites. What they wanted was not Negro the-

Spanish-language theatre by La Compañia de Teatro Repertorio Español, in a production of *Los Soles Truncos* by Rene Margues, 1975.

atre, but black theatre, written and produced by, about, "and, most significantly, for black people." This new revolutionary attitude among blacks in the 1960s produced a dynamic theatre that would have a permanent impact both on the black community and on the American theatre. But this we will save for treatment in Chapter 10.

As in the black theatre movement, both Asian-Americans and Spanish-Americans began in the 1960s to express their ethnic problems through theatre. Spanish-language theatres sprang up in urban New York and among the farmworker populations of Southern California, trying to define their own culture within the larger population and protesting the way their workers were exploited. Chinese-Americans in cities like San Francisco were more likely to deal with the difficulties experienced by second- and third-generation young people trying to reconcile the cultural differences between the old world and the new. Both Hispanics and Orientals, like other ethnic groups, have come to see theatre as an artistic medium through which they can explore the problems of their people and work toward bettering their condition.

National Theatre of the Deaf

Though not strictly an ethnic theatre, the National Theatre of the Deaf, founded in 1967 by David Hayes at the Eugene O'Neill Memorial Theatre Center in Waterford, Connecticut, shares some of the impulses that have motivated ethnic theatres. Much of its work has been to present the standard repertoire of plays, using elements of speech, Ameslan, sign language of the deaf, pantomime, and dance in a unique theatrical style that makes the world's great drama accessible to deaf people. More important, however, has been the training of deaf theatre artists, who can now begin to use theatre to express the silent world in which they live, with all the problems, joys, and passions that it holds for them. It was on the urging of Robert Steinberg, one of the founders of the National Theatre of the Deaf, that Mark Medoff wrote *Children of a Lesser God* (1980), about the struggles of a deaf woman who marries her hearing speech teacher. Sarah Norman has been deaf from birth but is too proud to learn to speak. She knows that her inability to hear will make any sounds she utters grotesque, labeling her a freak. She is fluent at signing, however. One of the most remarkable elements of *Children of a Lesser God* is its constant use of signing. As in Brian Friel's *Translations*, two languages are going on simultaneously, and here the silent sign language dazzles the audience with its fluency and its amazing ability to communicate what we are sure we cannot understand. Phyllis Frelich, one of the leading actresses of the National Theatre of the Deaf, served Medoff as a consultant throughout the writing, then played Sarah in the New York production, going on to win the 1980 Tony Award as Broadway's best actress of the year, in a role that has only one spoken speech.

It seemed likely early in this century that realism would drive out all "artificial," "conventional" forms of theatre, or that expressionism or symbolism or some other *ism* would drive realism off the stage, to remain only in the documentary film. But neither displacement has occurred. Realism has been a strand in most of the newer forms, and realism itself, even in the extreme form of naturalism, will probably last as long as the practical problems of people themselves keep a large part of our attention. To show people in relation to their own environment is to "show it the way it is."

A LIBERATED THEATRE

10

Liberation in performance methods and in the
spirit of rebellious youth. The Broadway production of *Hair*.

*T*he decades of the 1960s and 1970s saw unprecedented liberation in the theatre. A new aesthetic was beginning to form, and in its early stages no idea seemed too outrageous, no method too unconventional not to get some kind of performance and a willing, if not always ecstatic, audience. This new impulse was fueled by a spirit of rebellion among youth and minority groups that swept the country, reaching a climax of anarchy in 1968, the year that several hundred thousand young people gathered to celebrate their music and their life-style in a rock festival at Woodstock, New York. More ominously, riots spread through Paris and Chicago, while protests and demonstrations closed down some American college campuses. Champions of youth liberation led the pack, but not far behind were workers for black liberation, women's liberation, gay liberation, Indian liberation, and others.

The youth rebellion was most visible because it spread through all classes. Young people the world over rejected the aggressive competition and sterile respectability of suburbia and developed a subculture of enclaves and communes with their own costume style and explored heightened states of consciousness through popular music, sexual freedom, drugs, and occult practices. When something as harmless as a fashion in hair length angered conventional older people, it convinced rebellious youth that everyone over thirty was hopelessly devoted to materialism, police power, and war. Long hair became a symbol of rebellion, joy, sexual freedom, peace, and brotherhood.

The psychology of the youth rebellion is made clear by the comparison the anthropologist Victor Turner makes with the initiation ceremonies of several traditional cultures in central Africa. In the middle part of the initiation—after the youths have broken from the daily patterns of society and before they are reborn and reintegrated as responsible adults with set roles—in that unstructured time, they feel the joy of freedom and a mystic sense of unity with one another, with all mankind, indeed with the universe. Turner calls this sense of cosmic identity "humanitas"—characteristic of the strong group loyalty among rebellious youth in the 1960s. Initiation often involved some humiliating gesture, as, for instance, putting on the clothes of humble people. To the initiates it was like a return to some primeval age before the differentiation of classes, or even of the sexes. Similarly, the "hippie" style borrowed the jeans of workmen, the ragged scraps of tramps and clowns, and the beads and headbands of Indians, and, to express contempt for traditional values, sported patches of the "stars and stripes" on faded blue jeans.

This joy in group solidarity, this *humanitas,* is glorified in the musical *Hair* (1967), performed as an "American tribal love-rock musical" by a cast of about twenty-five. Only a few characters emerged with names. One young man was expelled from school and another was drafted. The tribe celebrated the burning of a draft card (actually a library card), the glory of long hair, the defiance of rules and restraint, and the use of marijuana. The songs and dances wove together images of Hindu love gods, black and white companionship, love-ins, hopes of peace and freedom, with draft boards, the Vietnam War, the Indian wars, Shakespearean actors, Buddhist monks, and Catholic nuns. With an orchestra on one side of the bare stage, actors bringing on suggestive props and symbols as needed, and actors stepping in and out of roles, *Hair* used the happy, imaginative flexibility of the Oriental theatre and the mobility of epic realism to celebrate group joy and the hopes of rebellious youth.

BLACK LIBERATION

Black Liberation also reached its extreme in the late sixties. The more aggressive blacks took a militant turn, declaring that Black Consciousness must recognize implacable hostility between blacks and whites and work for complete separation. Some dreamed of a black state carved out of the nation. Others joined radical groups that hoped to destroy Western society. Many converted to Islam, hoping to find in the Third World a base for self-respect and identity that seemed unattainable under what appeared to them a hypocritical, racist Christianity.

LeRoi Jones set the revolutionary pattern in black theatre with such plays as *The Slave* and *Dutchman* in 1964. *Dutchman* dramatizes the danger black people face when they allow whites into their private world. The setting is a subway car hurtling through the bowels of the city. A young, middle-class black man, Clay, notices a white woman, Lula, smiling at him through the window, and he smiles back. The next thing he knows she is inside the car sitting down beside him. She promptly ignores him; then suddenly, as he reads a magazine, she accuses him of staring at her through the subway window. Now, with Clay on the defensive, she starts luring him with a "come-on," while casually eating an apple. He follows her lead, only to be cut off abruptly: "What do you think you're doing? . . . You think I want to pick you up, get you to take me somewhere and screw me, huh?"

The audience quickly becomes as confused as Clay by Lula's unpredictable behavior. She seems to know all about his past, his friends, his habits, and even about the party he's going to. Yet she continues to alternate her moods from intimate chatter to contemptuous attacks on his attitudes and beliefs, while a disoriented Clay tries to remain composed. But Lula seductively leads him on, getting him to confide his personal dreams to her and even invite her to the party. Then, in an outrageous public display, she gets up, starts improvising a vulgar blues song-and-dance in the aisle, and tries to get Clay to join in: "Come on, Clay. Let's rub bellies on the train. The nasty. The nasty. Do the gritty grind, like your ol' rag-head mammy. . . . OOOOweeee!" When he rejects her invitation, she gets more animated and vicious:

> Come on, Clay . . . You middle-class black bastard. Forget your social-working mother for a few seconds and let's knock stomachs. Clay, you liver-lipped white man. You would-be Christian. You ain't no nigger, you're just a dirty white man.

At last Clay breaks. He throws her down into a seat, slapping her hard across the mouth. Then he takes to the aisle, spewing out his contempt for her and her white world.

> I could murder you now. Such a tiny ugly throat. I could squeeze it flat, and watch you turn blue, on a humble. For dull kicks. And all these weak-faced ofays squatting around here, staring over their papers at me. Murder them too. . . . It takes no great effort. For what? To kill you soft idiots?

But Lula only replies, "You fool!" When at last he has vomited out all his hatred and reaches to grab his books, Lula plunges a small knife into his chest, then calmly orders the others in the car to get rid of the body. The car empties as Lula straightens herself out and jots something into a notebook as her next young black victim enters the car.

Dutchman is a numbing experience in the theatre, even shocking in its implications. It seems almost a warning to blacks not to expose their true feelings lest they be vulnerable to the white man's conscious effort to destroy them. It was no surprise when its creator abandoned his French and Anglo-Welsh names, LeRoi Jones, and took the African name Imamu Amiri Baraka.

Baraka's extreme call for separation had its followers. Charles Gordonne's *No Place to Be Somebody* (1969) explored the world of a fair-skinned black, Gabe Gabriel, trying to resolve his own racial identity by creating a play in which he, as writer, plays a leading role. His hope that nonviolence instead of revolution can solve his problems lies in his hero, a powerful man named Johnny who stands up to both black and white racists. But this character that Gabe has created has his own plans, to set up his own Black Mob—"We at war, Gabe. Black ag'inst white."—forcing Gabe into the violent act of shooting him to preserve nonviolence. Suddenly Machine Dog, a mysterious figure in shabby military garb, appears to accuse Gabe of slaying a true brother:

GABE: He made me kill him! He . . .

MACHINE DOG: Hush yo' lyin', trait'ious tongue! Ver'ly, ver'ly, I say unto you! You has kilt all them li'l innusunt cherbs'a the ghetto. . . .You has scortched an' scalded them black Moheekuns an' stuffed them in the very stoves they cooked on! Se la! An' ay-man!

The play ends with Machine Dog's bitter accusations. But Gabe returns for an Epilogue to confront the audience directly with the ever-changing role that he must play to provoke them constantly to attention. Dressed as a "Black Lady in Mourning" with "a black shawl draped over his head," he will go out among them to "mourn the death of a people dying. Of a people dying into that new life."

No Place to Be Somebody is a response to the complex dilemma of the black revolutionary movement. While it accepts violence as a means to liberation, it also foreshadows future voices that may pave the way toward "that new life." Of

Samm-Art Williams' *Home* at the Negro Ensemble Company, with Michelle Shay, Charles Brown, and L. Scott Caldwell.

the many black theatre companies that sprouted up across the nation in the 1960s, none has done more to foster those new voices of liberation than New York's Negro Ensemble Company, founded by Douglas Turner Ward. No play has more eloquently captured the yearning for liberation than that company's production of Samm-Art Williams' *Home* (1979). It traces the life of a Southern black, Cephus, from his farmboy youth, through escape to the big city, draft evasion and jail, joblessness and welfare, disease and despair, to his return to the honest labor and creative values on the farm. What makes *Home* more than a typical change-of-fortune melodrama are the poetic language and the conventions of its production format. Cephus is played by a single actor, but all the other roles—old, young, male, female, black, white—are played by two women who take on whatever role they wish by a simple costume addition—a bow in the hair, a shawl, an army helmet, a minister's stole, a boy's cap. Sometimes they are characters in Cephus's odyssey; other times they act as a chorus, helping the audience to collapse time and space and see the whole of Cephus's life from the larger viewpoint of American black history and culture. The action is staged on four neutral platforms, with place defined by the actors and the lines they speak.

The fact that the place itself never changes, though Cephus is constantly on the move, and the fact that the actors never change, though they play multitudes of different roles, suggest that "Home" is right there all the time, ready to be grasped once the inner yearning is acknowledged, ready to be offered once others are willing to help, to extend themselves, to choose roles of grace instead of confrontation.

RESIDENT NONPROFIT PROFESSIONAL THEATRE

The growth of black theatre companies from coast to coast in the 1960s was part of a much larger movement to decentralize the professional theatre in both the United States and Canada. Before 1920, most towns of any size could boast a "little theatre," but the coming of movies and radio, followed by the Great Depression and World War II, wiped out such theatres. Only the most hardy, like California's Pasadena Playhouse, Chicago's Goodman Theatre, Virginia's Barter Theatre, and The Cleveland Playhouse, were able to survive, and for decades live theatre to most Americans meant local amateur groups doing recent Broadway hits or road companies from New York playing only the large cities.

In the late 1940s two young Texas women with a pioneer spirit began to change all that. Margo Jones began a small arena theatre in Dallas, Theatre 47, where she not only brought live professional theatre to enthusiastic audiences but also encouraged the work of such bright new playwrights as Lillian Hellman and Tennessee Williams. A former schoolmate of Margo's, Nina Vance, founded Houston's Alley Theatre with the $2.14 she had in her pocket. She spent it on 214 penny postcards to invite everyone she could to an organizational and fund-raising meeting. Over thirty-five years later, the Alley Theatre is still thriving.

Canada made a more spectacular start in 1953 when the British director Sir Tyrone Guthrie helped to found a Shakespeare festival at Stratford, Ontario, which quickly became a Mecca of superior theatre for Canadians and U.S. citizens. Its touring company, The Canadian Players, went on the road each winter and brought the best of the classics to enthralled audiences on both sides of the border.

In the United States through the 1950s and early 1960s, a few venturesome spirits started companies in such far-flung spots as Honolulu, Milwaukee, Memphis, San Francisco, Seattle, Sarasota, Florida, and Williamstown, Massachusetts, but the theatre that marked the turning point from little regional theatres to a major movement of resident professional companies was the Tyrone Guthrie Theatre which opened in Minneapolis in 1963. Guthrie, sparked by his success at Stratford, decided that the United States was ready for a major repertory company that could produce the classics at a top professional level while encouraging the development of local audiences and theatre artists. The indifference he encountered among civic leaders is revealed by a story Sir Tyrone loved to tell about the mayor of one large city who met with him only because he thought Guthrie was representing a Scotch whiskey firm.

Success breeds success. Within twenty short years, almost three hundred nonprofit professional theatres from New Brunswick to Hawaii, from Alaska to Florida were challenging the commercial theatre for the right to be truly called the American theatre. This movement, sometimes referred to as the Regional Theatre movement, has liberated both audiences and theatre artists from the provincialism and conservatism of the commercial theatre, whose aim has always been to serve its investors, not the art of theatre. As a result, today, instead of looking to Broadway, most young theatre artists, whether playwrights, actors, designers, or directors, find resident professional companies a much richer place to establish roots. America's most powerful new playwrights not only got their start away from Broadway; they maintain close contact with the theatre where they got their start, and it is to these theatres that the commercial producers of Broadway must turn to find next season's hit and every season's innovations.

LIBERATION OF THEATRICAL FORM

This decentralizing has been the most visible change in American theatre in recent years. In the long run, however, the experiments many of the new groups made in theatrical forms could change future directions of theatre even more than the decentralizing. Turning their backs on tradition and on commercial success, small groups of enthusiastic young actors, usually guided by an imaginative director, began experimenting with new kinds of plays, new production techniques, and new relationships between actor, character, and audience.

The experiments took widely different directions, but they shared one common motive—liberation: personal liberation, psychic liberation, sexual liberation, political, economic, and social liberation, and, most significantly, artistic liberation. There was a common feeling that Western culture had become stultified, that traditional art forms concealed truth instead of revealing it, that Western value systems alienated people instead of creating a sense of community. Men and women were becoming imprisoned in a slick, materialistic, mass-produced value system imposed by an unwieldy social structure that had lost its direction and reason for being. Radical methods were needed, not just to reform but to challenge Western society at its very roots, to raise individual consciousness, to purge humanity of its sickness, and to find more direct methods of communicating among people. In the theatre, traditional methods were seen as merely soothing people into accepting their own decadence. The new theatre set out to change all that.

Many theatre people turned to Antonin Artaud, the French prophet of a new ritual approach to theatre. In 1938 Artaud had published *The Theatre and Its Double*, calling for a new theatre as drastic therapy for the sick soul of the modern world. In 1931, while watching the dancers of the Balinese theatre perform in Paris, Artaud found his vision. With no need to understand the language, he found that the sounds, gestures, and action transcended reality and put both performers and audience in direct contact with the unconscious, with the dark, mystic powers of the soul. This ritual art made popular entertainment seem trivial. To Artaud, it made modern Western theatre, merely repeating its standard "masterpieces," seem outworn, false, and barren. He dreamed of a new theatre that would stir up in both actor and audience the vitality of the primitive soul. Such a transformation might require a holocaust. The theatre would have to become a "theatre of cruelty," with every impulse carried to the utmost extreme, and, like the plague, drain the abscesses of a sick world.

> The theatre [Artaud wrote in *The Theatre and Its Double*] like the plague is a crisis which is resolved by death or cure, and the plague is a superior disease because it is a total crisis after which nothing remains except death or extreme purification. . . . [T]he action of theatre, like that of plague, is beneficial, for, impelling men to see themselves as they are, it causes the mask to fall, reveals the lie, the slackness, baseness, and hypocrisy of our world.

For Artaud, essential for the cure was to abandon theatre buildings in favor of a large room with the audience in the center and the action in the corners, to disregard the play and playwright and use words for their mood or percussive impact. He wanted to confront the modern lie with the truth and vitality of a primitive magic ritual, to reach his audiences, not through their minds, but through their skins.

Political activists found a clearer voice in the philosopher of the New Left, Herbert Marcuse, and his reinterpretations of Freud and Marx. Freud had maintained that people had to keep a tight reign on their desires (the pleasure principle) because of the practical demands of daily living (the reality principle). Marcuse argued that modern technology had enslaved people to the system and deprived them of pride in their work, while modern bourgeois entertainment was a mere opiate to help hold them in the bonds of this slavery. The pleasure principle could release them. In *The Aesthetic Dimension* (1977) he showed how art and theatre must reawaken the new proletariat by contradicting both the beliefs and attitudes that have enslaved them and by creating a new artistic language that embodies the very ideas to be expressed:

> The critical function of art, its contribution to the struggle for liberation, resides in the aesthetic form. A work of art is authentic or true, not by virtue of its content (i.e., the "correct" representation of social conditions), nor by its "pure" form, but by the content having become form.

While Artaud had called for theatre to assault its audience's senses, to speak to them "through the skin," so as to cleanse society collectively in the ritual of theatre, Marcuse calls for theatre to challenge and contradict the audience's beliefs about itself and society and lead them to a new language of the theatre and to a new reality through revolutionary means.

Neither of these radical perceptions about humanity can lay sole claim to theatre liberation; yet together they formed a climate that demanded experimentation in almost every area of theatre—its subject matter, its creative and performance methods, and its relation to its audiences.

The Theatre of Confrontation

Several of the experimental groups sought to break down the barriers between audience and performer, often confronting audience members with direct questions, challenging them to reorder their lives to the ideas of the group. The Living Theatre, under the direction of Julian Beck and Judith Malina, was the most controversial of these groups and the most persistent in its attack on the establishment. When unpaid back taxes closed it down in 1963, the Living Theatre found a responsive audience in Europe—until their 1968 production of *Paradise Now* ended in conflict with the police at the Avignon Festival, and they were ordered to leave town.

Back in America in the glow of defying the European establishment, the company produced a sensation with *Paradise Now* on a cross-country tour. Some

A moment of ritual exhaustion in The Living Theatre production of *Paradise Now*.

spectators were annoyed when the suffering, cooing, caressing actors and actresses came into contact with the audience. Others were outraged at the long scenes of writhing, almost naked scrawny bodies in a drama that seemed to get nowhere. But nothing before had so fully excited the rebellious spirit of youth.

Paradise Now was meant as a spiritual and political voyage for both actors and spectators. It took the audience through eight different stages, corresponding to rungs on an ascending ladder, to lead them to a state of freedom, open to permanent, nonviolent change. Each stage or rung consisted of a ritual or ceremony, a vision, and an action. The opening ritual began with thirty-seven long-haired, near-naked actors coming down the aisle, saying to each member of the audience, "We are not allowed to travel without a passport"; "I do not know how to stop war"; "I do not have the right to take off my clothes." Suddenly the audience was aware of the policemen at the doors and joined in the chant, voicing their sympathy with all rebels against authority. Each ritual was followed by a presentation of a Vision. The first of these was of Indians passing the peace pipe and then transforming themselves into human totem poles, only to be shot down by the murderous bullets of civilization. Later visions showed different kinds of violence transformed to love.

The culminating section of each rung was an Action step urged upon the audience. Frequently the actions applied directly to whatever city the company was playing in at the time, as in the following appeal from the Avignon Festival:

> There are 400 prisoners in the Avignon Jail in the shade of the Palais de Papes. Why are the prisoners there? Who will form a cell to free all men?
> Stop the fear.
> Stop the repression.
> Stop the punishment.
> Make it real.
> Do it now.
> Come up on stage.
> Begin.
> Who will form a cell to increase the underground press, to make newspapers, leaflets, posters, to tell the people of Avignon what's going on in the world?
> Make it real.
> Do it now.
> Come up on stage.
> Begin.

Pop mysticism with the hypnotic power of ancient ritual, images of sex, savagery, and salvation together enticed audiences to share the anarchic vision of revolution, or, by contrast, angered audiences who rejected the play's appeal. It is

Kattrin (Leeny Sack) in a 1974 production of Brecht's *Mother Courage.*
Scene 9, which is taking place both
inside the Performing Garage and
outside on Wooster Street in New
York City.

no surprise that out of such tactics violence erupted and that the French police closed the show.

Confrontation often sprang from the nature of the playing space in the work of The Performance Group, started in 1968 by Richard Schechner with a few students from New York University. The group performed in a garage reconstructed into an "environmental theatre," that is, a theatre with no formal stage, where space is arranged to fit each particular play, and where the audience sits and stands around or among the actors so as to become part of the action. Schechner wanted to integrate the actor, the art, and the spectator into one event that blended the immediacy of primitive ritual with the reality of the present. For his production of Brecht's *Mother Courage* (an epic drama that shows Germany's Thirty Years War as an all-consuming power that draws every resource and every person in by its insatiable hunger), a large door behind part of the playing area was opened up to show the street beyond, where unwitting passers-by would suddenly appear as part of the panorama of the play. They were sucked into the play as they might have been sucked into the war, though we could watch them escape down the alley, while the characters remained.

A Return to Theatre's Roots

Several groups that were to influence the new directions in theatre form did so by exploring the very roots of the theatrical impulse. They tried to bypass the complex conventions that centuries of tradition had encrusted on the theatre. They believed that society, by honoring the conventions instead of the theatrical impulse, had domesticated the theatre, tamed it to serve the commercial inter- ests of producers and to flatter and soothe its audiences. The reforming groups wanted to rediscover those elemental relationships that brought performer, spectator, and theatrical event together to express humanity's deepest needs.

We have already seen (page 6) how Jerzy Grotowski developed the idea of "poor theatre," a theatre that stripped away all nonessentials (settings, makeup, music and lighting effects, and even written texts) and, instead, brought togeth- er artists who shared similar needs—the only basis for true creativity, according to Grotowski. In his Polish Laboratory Theatre workshops, the artists created together out of their needs. They worked to remove whatever physical and emo- tional blocks interfered with their own self-awareness and self-expression and kept them from encountering other human beings at the elemental level. When a play was ready for the public, it was not so much a performance to be viewed as it was a sharing of the work. A small audience, only forty to a hundred specta- tors, would be brought into an environment that placed them at the heart of the action, where their own needs would be illuminated through experiencing the play. They watched the torture and martyrdom in *The Constant Prince* as if look- ing down the wall of a hospital operating room or a cock-fighting pit and they watched the hallucinations in *Kordian* as fellow inmates between the beds of an insane asylum—close but with no direct contact. When the Polish Laboratory Theatre played in the United States in 1969, only a very few could get tickets, but almost everyone connected with the theatre talked about it, and many tried to imitate its methods, whether they had seen them or not.

In Paris, the English director Peter Brook gathered actors, poets, directors, and musicians from all over the world at his International Centre for Theatre Research to try to discover collectively the basic theatrical communication that precludes language, or, rather, that partakes of all cultures and all languages. Like Artaud, Brook wanted a theatre rooted in ritual, and like Artaud, he accept- ed the theory that human nature, shaped by eons of primitive ritual, is basically violent and cruel.

Brook's career has been devoted to eradicating the "deadly theatre," a term he used in his 1968 book of theory *The Empty Space* to describe the conventional, commercial theatre that merely flatters its audiences with what they expect or bores them with what they think they are supposed to admire. He prefers what he calls "rough theatre," the lusty entertainment of common people, but best of all is "holy theatre," which he identifies with ritual and "the invisible."

Brook came to his experimental center from England's Royal Shakespeare Company where he had distinguished himself as one of the twentieth century's most important interpreters of Shakespeare, always challenging his audiences with new ways of looking at familiar plays. An absurdist approach to *King Lear* in 1962 was followed in 1968 by an environmental theatre approach to *The Tempest* and, most controversial of all, a harsh and bawdy gymnastic approach to *A Midsummer Night's Dream* in 1970. The King and Queen of the Fairies and the mischievous Puck swung on trapezes and spun silver plates on sticks in an intensely lighted setting that suggested a gymnasium with padded walls. Even the young human couples expressed the twists and turns of their mixed-up loves as acrobats, leaping and tumbling. The play was good robust fun, but hardly the usual "charming" love story in the moon-drenched magical forest of traditional productions. Nevertheless, all the poetry was there, clearly and beautifully spoken.

Titania makes love to the ass's head. A very unconventional production of *A Midsummer Night's Dream*—one with acrobatic actors. Royal Shakespeare Company, directed by Peter Brook.

In 1971 Brook formed his International Centre for Theatre Research to prepare a monumental mythic show for the Shiraz-Persepolis Festival of the Arts in Iran. The environment for the piece was an open space in front of the tomb of King Artaxerxes III, high on a mountain ledge overlooking the ruins of the ancient palace at Persepolis. Margaret Croyden, in a review, described how audiences arrived after an hour's bus ride through the Persian landscape and a twenty-minute climb up a winding mountain path from the palace ruins below. There the actors, from twelve different countries, sat in yoga positions, dressed in their native clothes: American jeans, African dashikis, Persian robes. Then, on the highest cliff above them, a spotlight caught a lone figure chained to a rock, Prometheus perhaps, punished by the gods for stealing fire for humanity. As if to confirm the image, a great ball of fire suddenly appeared, descending on a chain from a nearby mountain peak to the humans below, who caught it in a cauldron and from it lit a torch.

When the actors began to speak, it was in no familiar tongue, but rather a new ritual-like language called "Orghast," built out of pure sound, combined with Latin, Persian, Greek, Sanskrit, and Avesta, the ancient sacred language of the Zoroastrian religion. Audiences had to follow the sounds and inflections as they might listen to music rather than to ideas expressed through words. Starting with the Prometheus legend, the story combined myths from Greece, Spain, Persia, Africa, and Japan. The ambiguous power of light, starting with the theft of fire and the Titan's punishment, moves across the play, weaving into one myth after another. A captive Spanish prince, borrowed from Calderon's *Life Is a Dream*, is freed from the darkness of a cave, only to revert to primitive violence in the unaccustomed light. A Japanese tyrant-samurai wakes from a dream to find he has ceremonially killed his wife and child. When he seeks absolution for his crime, he is blinded by the purifying fire. An African carrying a small lamp confronts the blinded Samurai with his huge torch in a "ritual battle of fire" that transcends the cultural boundaries of two continents. Fire, the most ancient of man's conquests, has brought both wisdom and suffering, light and blindness.

In 1972, with another international company of actors and several landrovers, Brook ventured on a six-week trek across the deserts of Northern Africa, where he hoped to find villagers with no preconceptions about what theatre is. Since the audiences would share no common language with the actors, he wanted to present and improvise simple stories to find some primitive idiom of sounds and meanings that might transcend differences of language and race. Among their successes was what was called the "Shoe Show," improvised around an enormous pair of army boots worn by one of the American actors. When the boots were placed in the center of the circle of actors and audience, they became magic, able to transform a hag into a beautiful woman, an invalid into an acrobat. They might be traded for other shoes, temptingly offered by a sorceress, or, when acquired by an audience member who was unwilling to give them up, lured back by a shoe collector. No plot was needed, no words found in any dictionary, but simple direct actions, expressive sounds, and a unified focus on a simple object brought audience and actors together to share the delights of the creative imagination.

Since returning from the African adventure, Brook has continued his experiments with language and ritual, but he has also continued to do innovative productions of traditional theatre classics. Both Chekhov's *The Cherry Orchard* and the opera *Carmen* were sensations in the 1981 Paris theatrical season. Meanwhile, as *Carmen* was being brought to New York in 1983, Brook was already at work on plans for his next experiment which takes him to India and the Far East to stage *The Maharabatta*, a thirteen-volume Sanskrit epic.

In 1963, as a result of dissatisfaction with the established trends in the contemporary theatre, Joseph Chaikin led a group of actors and four writers to form the Open Theatre to conduct workshops in improvisation and voice and body expression. Over the next decade, their work led them away from the alienation which had characterized the Living Theatre, toward a communal art. Instead of focusing on conflicts as traditional theatre did or on social comments about oppression as epic theatre did, the Open Theatre sought to turn the actor's body

Grotesque image of mutual destruction. Two oversized cardboard puppet figures with actors inside destroy each other by removing strips of cardboard. Van Itallie's *America Hurrah*. New York, 1966.

Three actors form a chorus of one in *The Serpent*, as staged by E. C. Gabbard at Eastern Illinois University.

into a living testimony to liberation. *Contrast* replaced *conflict* generating "the possibility of choice." In the words of Karen Malpede, who has chronicled their work, "the Open Theatre arrived at a fragile freedom based on the proof that there are always two ways of being—the one we have been taught and the one we are learning. At any instant—but only with strict attention and highest energy—it is possible to move from one into the other." The Open Theatre through its disciplined exercises and its imaginative performances sought to open the passages for moving to this new way of being.

The early work of the Open Theatre included such protest plays as *Viet Rock* and *America Hurrah* (1966), but their true voice began to emerge in 1968 with *The Serpent*, a mixture of mime and incantation that explores stories and themes in the Book of Genesis. After some opening scenes that establish a modern context of the Kennedy and King assassinations, four women form a chorus that both narrates the mimed action of Biblical stories and provides ironic comments on the action. Their incantatory repetitions constantly remind us that we are no longer "in the beginning" when God created the heavens and the earth, but "in the middle . . . going toward the end," when we must, like the mimed characters before us, make choices based on where we have been. We watch the characters explore the most basic realms of choice and discovery: the first discovery of sex, with its pleasures (extended to the audience by the chorus passing out apples) and its guilt; the first murder, in which Cain deals with rejection and has to learn how to kill. We also see more modern characters, moving into old age with limits they have set upon themselves, blaming husbands, mothers, and the complexity of life for their limits, for their dying.

Until 1973 the Open Theatre continued to explore and refine the ways they were finding to move from the self to the other. In *Terminal* (1970), they explored the subject of death to open themselves and their audiences to a new sense of life. In *The Mutation Show* they took case histories of people who had been deprived of normal existence until they were grown (Kaspar Hauser, a boy who lived for sixteen years confined to a box and two youths who grew up with a wolf pack) and, using a carnival motif, explored the joys, the confusion, and the anger of characters discovering the outside world, civilization, and the processes of thought for the first time. It is no simple narrative that tells these stories, but emblematic presentations that express the essense of imprisonment and freedom. The carnival consisted of a Mutants Gallery, where the actors expressed contemporary psychological deformities: The Man Who Smiles, The Thinker, The Petrified Man. The actor playing Kaspar is pulled brutally from his box by his keeper and lifted to his shoulders, and the keeper begins to walk. On his journey, Kaspar begins to notice things, begins to see the world around him, and as he does, his body takes on a new will. He climbs higher on his keeper, stretches out to see in all directions, until his keeper, overburdened, throws him from his shoulders and leaves him screaming, separated, alone and terrified. The actions of the play are repeated with grotesque then comic variations, and the repetition itself reveals the possibilities for release, to free us from the imprisonment of our own mutations.

The Open Theatre disbanded in 1973, largely because they had accomplished what they had set out to do. It was now time to take their discoveries and the liberation they had found for themselves into new areas of the theatre.

Experimental Groups of the Eighties

Like comets, the Living Theatre, the Poor Theatre, and the Open Theatre quickly captured attention and then faded or dispersed. But in their wake came a galaxy of offbeat groups, equally dedicated to the search for a modern theatrical idiom. To do justice to all the varied efforts would take a book in itself, but several whose work has endured into the 1980s cannot be ignored. The modest work of

A series of images, actors, and sounds, in changing relationships, creates a logic of its own. Foreman's *Rhoda in Potatoland*. Ontological-Hysteric Theatre, New York, 1976.

the Mabou Mines Company, noted for their visual interpretations of the works of Samuel Beckett, for their narrative acting style, their mixed media productions, and their collaboration with musicians, sculptors, painters, filmmakers, and video artists, has achieved in small compass the visual excitement of the painter's art and the poetic and dramatic intensity of theatre. Richard Foreman has explored the nature of reality in his Ontological-Hysteric Theatre. His "Rhoda in Potatoland" (1976), where reality is totally undependable, and where Rhoda finds that people and things may move away suddenly, tilt over at odd angles, or speak her thoughts for her, seems almost a modern version of Alice's surprisingly disturbing Wonderland. In Foreman's 1983 offering, *Egyptology*, Kate Manheim, his perennial spokeswoman for external consciousness, crash-lands in the play's Egypt, a world still undependable and also violently, sometimes farcically sinister. Guns, razors, cartoon-like bombs and severed heads being tossed around, a menacing flock of ice-cream cones, a skeleton manning a keyboard, and Manheim inside a mummy case form bizarre and eerie images of a civilization run amuck in violence and self-destruction. Yet little images of love and beauty are interspersed in dream-like flashes, such as a radio that plays only when kissed, making Foreman's private vision a compelling plea for contemplation in a world of frenzy.

Equally involved with visual images, but aiming more toward serenity and meditation in an anxious world than emphasizing the anxiety itself, is Robert Wilson's Byrd Hoffman Foundation. Wilson first gained attention in 1971 with *Deafman Glance*, built around the fantasies of a deaf boy he befriended, who joined the company to play himself. Not a word was spoken, and Wilson's theatre was sometimes called the theatre of silence. But Wilson had learned that the deaf boy responded to certain sounds as though his body itself could hear, and so the show included vivid sounds throughout—owls screeching, animals howl-

Modern science and mathematics on trial. The judges, looking like Einstein, arrive in a spaceship Dancers turn in figures based on the circle. Robert Wilson's *Einstein on the Beach*. Music by Philip Glass, choreography by Andy de Groat.

ing. Continued work with brain-damaged and autistic children showed similar patterns, the child responding directly to images and sounds, rather than to the indirect abstractions of words. The boy would laugh at a joke before the punch line, as though he had grasped the entire incongruous situation as a unit rather than in connected steps.

Wilson came to believe that all people see and hear on two different levels, first through the "exterior screen" of eyes and ears, but also through "interior screens," which we usually are aware of only in dreams or daydreams. The blind and deaf see or hear only on the interior screens, while the autistic child daydreams for hours at a time. For those of us whose frenetic pace of living has blocked out the interior screens, long durations of time, sustained visual and audio images, and a meditative, hypnotic atmosphere can stimulate a mingling of the interior and exterior images, creating a harmonious balance.

Einstein on the Beach, an opera Wilson created in collaboration with the American composer Philip Glass for the 1976 Avignon summer festival, is a meditation on the impact of science and mathematical abstraction on the modern world. *On the Beach* is the title of a book and movie about survivors of an atomic blast awaiting their own destruction. Einstein himself was a gentle man who played the violin and liked boats and trains, yet his calculations made possible space ships and the atomic bomb.

The main performers are dressed like Einstein. The opera begins with a single Einstein in the orchestra pit playing the violin, an image that reverberates throughout the stage space—one Einstein figure appearing like a mad scientist, one like a comic Charlie Chaplin, one like a demonic Hitler. Another Einstein draws mathematical figures and equations on an invisible blackboard while dancers echo his gestures. To suggest the square, the dancers move briskly on straight lines that turn sharp right angles; for triangles they move on diagonal lines; for circles they whirl like dervishes, as clocks and compasses float through the air and a dark disc eclipses a round moon, until finally a crowd below watches a solitary figure high on a building still solving mathematical riddles.

Elaborate equipment moves trains and space ships in an out, floats objects and people through the air, like dreams of beautiful images—many recognizable from well-known paintings. A trial scene suggests that modern science is on trial, but there is no accusation. Pain and evil—and the dreaded atomic holocaust—are indicated, but the sustained intensity and the slow motion of the performance create an awesome spell, a new state of consciousness that is religious and mystic, beyond morals and indignation.

In the movies, montage effects of moving objects, floating symbolic images, or variations on a theme can be presented so easily that they make only a slight impression. In the physical presence of real bodies and objects in the theatre the effect is far stronger. Will this become a new genre of theatre, or will it be absorbed into the mainstream, as expressionism and many other experiments have been absorbed?

Several theatres have not identified themselves with any particular style, but rather have opened their doors to experimental groups and plays of all types. Most notable among these are Ellen Stewart's Cafe La Mama, opened in the 1960s, home to countless playwrights, designers, and directors who found a sympathetic hearing in its creative atmosphere, and Joseph Papp's Public Theatre, with its seven different auditoriums suited to varying styles of production. As one of the many parts of the New York Shakespeare Festival, with its free, open-air Shakespeare productions in Central Park, the Public Theatre has seen the first performances of such long-run hits as *Hair* and *A Chorus Line,* while at the same time providing a home for the experimental work of The Mabou Mines Company or staging Richard Foreman's *Egyptology.* The Manhattan Theatre Club produces largely new plays and exciting foreign imports. The New Federal Theatre is a major home for young black theatre artists. And on Theatre Row, a renovated section of historic 42nd Street, The Lion Theatre and Playwrights Horizons provide intimate, unthreatening atmospheres for new young theatre artists to get their feet wet in the turmoil of commercial theatre. In 1983, Stephen Sondheim, one of America's foremost writers of musicals, decided to forgo the glitter and the tensions of Broadway to develop his newest musical, *Sunday in the Park with George,* in the nurturing atmosphere at Playwrights Horizons.

Among the most enduring of the theatre groups that grew to importance in the 1960s and 1970s is the Bread and Puppet Theatre. Under the guidance of a former German sculptor, Peter Schumann, the group makes its home on a communal farm in Northern Vermont. As implied in its title, two elements characterize all Bread and Puppet performances: puppets—some human-sized, some giant figures up to sixteen feet tall, more like moving sculptures, requiring two or more people inside to operate them, others only inches tall, pulled by strings or wires; and bread—rich, coarse homemade bread with thick herb butter, ritually offered to the audience at the end of most performances. Schumann has said that theatre "is not like commerce . . . where you pay and get something"; it is "more like bread, more a necessity." But people do "not live by bread alone," and so his theatre builds on myths and fairy tales, Biblical stories and contemporary familiar material—a recent prison riot, Hiroshima, modern warfare, food lines. The puppets, constructed to give the simplest, most direct expression of a character type, give a mythic, larger-than-life quality to the actions, as masks no doubt did for ancient Greek tragedy. Uncle Fatso, with a huge ring on his finger, suggests the archcapitalist, while a towering somber, madonna-like female, with a single tear emerging from her eye, reflects the eternal pathos of mothers who lose their children to violence or the deceptions of materialistic success.

Like their bread, homemade from grains they raise themselves, Schumann and his group wish to inspire a return to simple values: humility, charity, love. Nothing in their work is wasted; theirs is a theatre of use. Puppets as well as props are constructed of found materials—scraps of wood, old clothes and fabrics, garbage pails—transforming the ordinary into the magical, and anyone who wants to be a part of the show will be given a necessary function to perform. The performances are celebrations of life, and most begin with a parade.

Preferring to work in the open air, Bread and Puppet is often seen at peace or antinuclear rallies, but exploitation and cruelty are what its members oppose and basic Christian values what they advocate, rather than any specific political cause. Like Peter Brook, Joseph Chaikin, and Jerzy Grotowski, Peter Schumann tries to get at the most elemental communication in a ritual-like "holy" theatre that tries to bring audience and performer as well as production artist together into a total and utterly simple communal experience. They have brought the theatre full circle to a new theatre of exaltation for the modern world, a theatre that affirms humanity's intrinsic capacity for both destructive and creative action and the capacity of human beings to interact significantly with other human beings through the affirmation of values larger than themselves.

DANCE IN CONTEMPORARY THEATRE

Among the most significant developments in contemporary theatre is the increasing importance of dance. As performance is freed from the text, movement becomes all-important and approaches dance. Actors are now expected to work in a number of styles, many of them close to dance. At the same time the two great traditions of dance, ballet and modern dance, have moved closer together and both have come close to the theatre, while post-modern dance, often done without music or choreography, has attempted to redefine both dance and performance.

Modern Trends in Ballet

The modernization of ballet began in Paris in 1909 with the Russian impresario Sergei Diaghilev. He loosened the classic techniques in order to give distinct styles to a variety of short ballets. Many of the best modern painters—Bakst, Rouault, and the young Picasso among them—made designs for him, and many of the best modern composers—Debussy, Ravel, the young Stravinsky, and others—wrote music for him. More than any person of his time, Diaghilev brought into the theatre the creative forces of twentieth-century literature, art, and music.

Ballet came slowly to America, but beginning in 1939 with the founding of the American Ballet Theatre it came to stay, and it moved in new and distinctively American directions. It continued the eclectic, international trends of Diaghilev's Ballet Russe, using folk idioms and theatrical characters, but more important were Anthony Tudor's psychological ballets, and Agnes de Mille's search for an American idiom in the movement of athletes—and for *Rodeo*, her ballet of the American West, in the masculine vigor of cowhands.

Equally important has been the development of an American classicism in ballet, the achievement of George Balanchine and the New York City Ballet. Starting with a school in 1933 and a ballet company in 1946, Balanchine created one of the world's top ballet companies by returning to strict classic form. He made less use of story, pantomime, and gesture than is found in romantic ballet, depending more on the abstract form of music than on the narrative form of literature. Where the simpler romantic ballets presented a fairy story of a dreamer trying to capture the dream, the newer ballets, even in their charm, show the surrealist nightmares, anxieties, and fears of the twentieth century.

Anthony Tudor and Jerome Robbins have gone even further in creating psychological and surrealist ballets, with images of alienation, dread, fear, and flight, or strange gardens haunted by memories, missed opportunities, and frustrations, of Freudian shapes, masks, and monsters, of dark journeys and phan-

American movement in ballet. *Rodeo.* American Ballet Theatre, choreographed by Agnes de Mille.

tom corridors—just the subjects that fascinate modern dancers. On the other hand, Arthur Mitchell, who has done more than anyone to foster ballet dancing among America's blacks, has moved freely between the classical style of Balanchine and traditional story ballet, and into both of them he has injected startling effects of ethnic, African, and Latin American movements in his work at the Dance Theatre of Harlem.

New Relationship of Ballet and Modern Dance

By the 1950s musical comedy had helped to break down the strong barriers between modern dance and ballet, as dancers with different training met together and discovered each other's techniques. A few dancers surreptitiously studied some of the techniques of the other camp. In the sixties an American trained in both forms, Glen Tetley, became director of the Stuttgart Ballet and in a short time made it one of the best in Europe. Soon, mixing the two kinds of dance became common.

A trampoline incorporated into the setting combines ballet with athleticism in *Manifestations*. Danced by Mel Tomlinson, choreographed by Arthur Mitchell. Dance Theatre of Harlem.

Peter Martins in a patriotic pop ballet, *Union Jack*. New York City Ballet. Choreographed by George Balanchine.

This new relationship was celebrated in 1975 when Margot Fonteyn, the English ballerina, and Rudolf Nureyev danced *Lucifer*, a new dance drama by Martha Graham. In the same year Mikhail Baryshnikov danced with the American Ballet Theatre in Twyla Tharp's *Push Comes to Shove*. Both Nureyev and the younger Baryshnikov had been top dancers in Russia and defected to the West because they saw no chance in Russia for experiment in dance. Established in this country, they wished to try American modern techniques—a crossover Margot Fonteyn called a wedding celebration.

Meanwhile, in the theatre, as actors were brought nearer the audience and freed from illusionistic scenery, they could become more rhetorical, lyric, assertive in body movement. They were coming closer to opera and dance. When they formed a choral group, they became less individualized. While the realistic actor presents a specific character with a name and address, the dancer presents an emotion or intention. Music, which is even more abstract, uses its basic patterns of progress, development, opposition, interruption, suspense, statement and response, venture and return, change and continuity, tension and response,

Dance drama with individual characters, strong story, and elaborate setting for action on two levels. Martha Graham's *The Scarlet Letter*, with Nureyev as Dimmesdale. New York, 1975

climax and resolution to express directly all types of emotions, to give shape to all experience. As the elements of dance and music became increasingly important in the "new" theatre, the actor came to need formal training in voice and movement.

Not only were ballet and dance moving closer to each other, they were also moving closer to theatre. The Joffrey Ballet was exploring multimedia lighting and projections, while Jerome Robbins was exploring jazz dance, musical comedy dance, and, with the help of Japanese actors and musicians, the sustained, slow power of the Japanese Noh drama. Modern dance, as austere in its first decades as the "poor theatre" of Grotowski, found Martha Graham in the 1970s and 1980s using a sizable orchestra, elaborate costumes, and spectacular settings.

Post-Modern Dance

Modern dance, like the theatre, developed a rebellious avant-garde starting in the 1950s. Alwin Nikolais exploited elements of the theatre, especially costumes and properties. His performers seemed grotesque animated forms as they moved about encased in geometrical shapes, flexible cords, wrappings, and balloons. But at other times Nikolais let the human element emerge in exciting movements and groupings, with stunning costumes and settings and dynamic lighting. Or he used actors' bodies as screens for patterned projections, setting the human form and its patterned costume against changing shapes of light images. Most theatrical of all was the Nikolais sound track on tape, made up of actual sounds combined with electronic sounds that had never been heard before.

Some avant-garde dancers carried the reaction against romantic emotions and neat compositions much further. Like the theatre avant-garde, they wanted to wake up their audiences, who were passively accepting all the old conven-

Projected patterns of light pulsate with the movement of the dancers in *Scenario*. Choreographed by Alwin Nikolais. New York City Center Theatre.

tions. Why not let the performer dance among the seats, or suddenly look at the audience and imitate their reactions? Put many things on the stage and let the audience choose what they want to watch. Bring back spontaneity for performers and audience. Set a dozen musicians playing anything they want to play, mix in a few radios, electronic sounds, and a siren or two. Or give the audience moments of rest with nothing whatever to see.

The leader of this dance theatre of the absurd, this antidance, was Merce Cunningham, who had danced for years with Martha Graham. With the avant-garde musician John Cage, and later with the experimental artist and sculptor Robert Rauschenberg, he presented programs designed to shock the conservative, amaze the young, and perhaps now and then point out a step beyond nihilism. He used emptiness not for Zen harmony and peace but for the shock of discontinuity, with the impudent effrontery, for instance, of having a dancer stand still for several minutes and then make one jump. The wonderful leaps Cunningham had done with Graham's company were now used for violent kinetic contrasts, as he began by suggesting what dancing he could do, then interrupted himself and threw away the expectation he had created. In his addition of electronic sounds, Cunningham was the first to explore the use of music and dance as independent entities. A standard procedure in his company is to rehearse without music, so that the dancers hear the music for the first time in performance. To Cunningham, the subject of dance is dance itself. He is a formalist exploring pure movement and how it interacts with space. In his "dance by chance" method, he charts each move and then flips coins to determine the order of the moves. The method is not improvisation. Once set, the choreography remains firm. Rather it is a technique to free the imagination, to discover new relationships of movements to each other and to space. Cunningham has remained the acknowledged inspiration of post-modern dance, but the impact of his work on mainstream dance was acknowledged in 1982 when Mikhail Baryshnikov and the American Ballet Theatre danced his "Duets" on the stage of the Metropolitan Opera House, New York's citadel of traditional opera and ballet.

While Cunningham opened the doors, a group of young dancers called the Judson Group, working in the Judson Church in New York City in the 1960s, chased the horses from the stable. The Judson dancers, most of whom had studied with Cunningham, worked with nondancers, "found" movements (ordinary movements of daily living), and contact improvisation, often with nonmusical sounds or no music at all. Yvonne Rainer sought functional, natural movement in relation to objects, and to her "movement itself became like an object, something to be examined coolly without psychological, social, or even formal motives." To Steve Paxton, a simple activity like brushing teeth might take on its own aesthetic significance. David Gordon used dance, by means of repeated movements, to comment on dance itself, often in comic ways. One description of his work which he himself praised is that Gordon "accumulates and organizes multiple views of a single phenomenon into one composition." Like the pheno-monologists of post-World War II philosophy, the post-modern dancers often presented objects or movements, not for technique, not for expression, but for themselves, to be set out where they could be seen and grasped on their own terms.

Recent Dance Blends

The old and the new, the serious and the humorous, the classic and the popular, blend in the work of the black dancer and choreographer Alvin Ailey. He belongs partly in the tradition of modern dance, for he studied with Martha Graham, Charles Weidman, and Hanya Holm, but, in choreographing for the Alvin Ailey City Center Dance Theatre, he also uses ballet and jazz steps—in fact, whatever suits his wide range. His early work, designed to express through dance the black experience, reached a climax in 1960 with *Revelations*, a composition set to traditional Negro music, with singing. It remains a favorite in his repertory. *Revelations'* range of expression gave the dancer Judith Jamison the chance to display her remarkable versatility, from majestic elegance in a scene where she skims on stage wearing a long ruffled dress, holding up an immense white para-sol, to a more earthy comic style when she becomes someone's affable aunt in a church congregation, bustling on stage in a Sunday-go-to-meeting hat. More recently Ailey has created striking works set to the music of the jazz band leader Duke Ellington. One of these, *The Mooche*, has an elaborate setting and costumes to create a nightclub atmosphere. In one movement, men and women perform a jazz routine, counterbalanced by six women following behind them with precise ballet steps. Ailey's company has achieved world renown, traveling extensively for the State Department. He has choreographed for the Metropolitan Opera, and he includes in his repertory dances set not only to Negro spirituals, blues songs, and folk music but to works of most of the important modern compos-ers.

The most striking new dance figure in the seventies was the comic chore-ographer Twyla Tharp, who began her career doing improvisational movement in open environments with nondancers on a college mall and with football play-ers on the gridiron. Her own dancing won such audience enthusiasm that by the mid-seventies she was in demand all over the Western world. She dances with her own small group, but some of her best work has been for other companies, such as the Joffrey Ballet. She is more interested in individuals than the group. Often her characters, each one different, wander on or burst on stage as though completely surprised to find anyone else there. Like Charlie Chaplin, her char-acters meet the fragmented, disjointed world with a cocky defiance or a flippant shrug. They may do the opposite of what is expected: a woman does what a man is expected to do, or a domineering woman easily handles two men. Her dancers wear casual sports clothes and usually sports shoes, and dance to a wide range of

Meredith Monk's House Company in a "composite theatre" that blends dance, acting, singing, lights, films, costumes, and environment into a plotless, surrealistic opera. *Quarry*, created by Meredith Monk.

popular music. She uses movements from ballet, modern dance, tap, ballroom dancing, and sports. We are not surprised that she was a prize-winning baton twirler or that she choreographs for ice shows. After the dream magic of the ballet and the anguish expressed in much modern dance, it is a joy to see brave flippancy or a robust sense of humor.

Out of post-modern dance, Meredith Monk rose in the seventies moving toward a new exploration of theatricality in expressive movement. Her pieces incorporate the fullest use of space, of both found and choreographed movement, music, singing of operatic quality combined with chanting, speech, and invented vocal sounds, story, individualized characters, juxtaposition of costumes and images from different periods or contexts, slides, film, and mythic people and symbols from a variety of cultures. So broad-based are her works that one has difficulty knowing what to call them—dance, theatre, or just performance events—though she herself calls many of them operas.

Monk's 1976 opera, *Quarry*, whose immediate theme is the holocaust, starts as the story of a child in pain, lying in the center of a large rectangular performing space. At the four corners, four separate households vie for our attention, perhaps suggesting the multiple consciousnesses of the child, quarrying through memory and experience to account for the pain. Three modern households, a family of women at dinner, a scholar telling his wife about his research, and an actress rehearsing lines, are inundated with 1940s radio broadcasts, are contrasted with each other and with a fourth household, an Old Testament family sifting grain and reading scrolls. First dictatorship, then victimization form the thematic content in each household. A thirty-member chorus moves through the space, and with their chanting and movement seem to wash away each action of the households as it is transformed into a new action. Then, halfway through the piece, a film is shown in which tiny people emerge among tiny rocks, until, as the perspective changes, we realize that the rocks are huge, the people hunted out both by enemies and by the camera. As the mind of the child in pain has evoked the images of families, of history, and of the world, the film, with its changing perspective, suggests how action itself becomes more or less intense as the scope of it changes in our view.

Monk's pieces do not proceed by narrative but by association, evoking moods, textures, and meanings through multi-level images and variations. Her mixture of the real and the theatrical, the everyday with the cosmic, the actual with the mythic, visual metaphor with dramatic action, music, voice, radio, dance, film, and space makes her work some of the richest of today's liberated theatre.

LIBERATION THROUGH *Spell #7*

A spirit of liberation has characterized the work of Ntozake Shange throughout her career. In her 1976 Broadway hit, *For Colored Girls Who Have Considered Suicide When the Rainbow Is Enuf,* a series of poetic monologues by seven young black women about growing up and facing adult problems in a big city, one of these women liberates herself from apologies:

> one thing i dont need
> is any more apologies
> i got sorry greetin me at my door
> you can keep yrs
> i dont know what to do wit em
> they dont open doors
> or bring the sun back
> they dont make me happy
> or get a mornin paper
> didnt nobody stop usin my tears to wash cars
> cuz a sorry

Liberation from "sorries" is one small indication of the kinds of liberation that

Shange has worked for in her art, most of which are brought into focus in her 1979 theatre piece, *Spell #7: geechee jibara quick magic trance manual for technologically stressed third world people*. First, she calls the work a "theatre piece" and herself a poet, rejecting the terms "play" and "playwright" as representing the "artificial aesthetics that plague our white counterparts." Her theatre piece does not follow the traditional plot structures of character and action but is a unique structure, more akin to modern poetry than plays.

Second, she wants a blending of art forms. Music and movement are part of black people's lives, their cultural reality, far more than mere verbal communications: "we can use with some skill virtually all our physical senses/ as writers committed to bringing the world as we remember it/ imagine it/ & know it to be to the stage/ we must use everything we've got." So *Spell #7* is a mixture of songs and dances, minstrel show and cabaret, magic and reality, poetic choral chants, narrative story telling, direct address to audience, and intense dramatic monologues. It blends the best of two theatre traditions—the European story-telling tradition and the African ritual tradition. The one entertains its audiences; the other transforms or rebuilds them.

Third, the subject of *Spell #7* is liberation, the liberation of black people, especially black women, from debilitating attitudes—self-hatred, envy, anger—and from the minority world mind sets—suicidal, paranoic, escapist, destructive, sycophantic—that plague a people who have survived generations of living by the rules and values of a majority culture they have never been allowed to fully share. Her characters require liberation from misplaced envy toward whites (one young woman dreams of brushing her hair into long flowing tresses), as well as from unrealistic beliefs in black superiority (a naive young girl celebrates black people's little victories: that blacks aren't susceptible to polio or sclerosis or mental illness, because only whites are shown to have such terrible diseases on the evening news). "Spell #7" is a magic spell, a black magic spell, by which Lou, a kind of minstrel master-of-ceremonies magician in the traditional tuxedo, bow tie, and top hat of "Mr. Interlocutor," sets out to liberate his audience of black actors who wear minstrel-show-like masks of frightened blackface:

> all things are possible
> but aint no colored magician in his right mind
> gonna make you   white
> i mean
>   this is blk magic
> you lookin at
> & i'm fixin you up good/ fixin you up good &
> colored
> & you gonna be colored all yr life
> & you gonna love it/ bein colored/ all yr life/

colored & love it
love it/ bein colored. SPELL #7!

The show, in a way, has begun already when the audience enters, for hanging from the ceiling, looming overhead, is a huge black-face mask, a "grotesque, larger than life misrepresentation of life" that will color the "pre-show chatter." The house lights dim, concentrating even greater attention on the looming mask, when Lou, in his minstrel magician outfit, enters to a catchy soft shoe. He confidentially tells the audience about his father, who retired from being a magician when a third-grade boy made the outlandish, politically dangerous request to be made white on the spot. Now the other actors enter in black-face masks and field-hand clothes, while Lou invokes his black magic that sets them dancing through a medley of black dance styles, ending with "hambone, hambone" and a Bert Williams bow. Then, from the circle of kneeling figures with hands outstretched as if to sing "Mammy," he challenges his audience to do some of the dangerous and degrading actions that come with being black in white America.

The performers, fearfully—then boldly—remove their masks and become a group of actors in an after-hours bar, joking, chatting, drinking, complaining about theatre directors who always cast the black actress as the whore. Just as quickly they become a choral dance group in community celebration, because no matter what tawdry place they might find themselves in, when someone special arrives, "in such a place i've seen miracles." Into a bar like this might come someone special, might come "the commodores" or "muhammad ali," and when they come, they

dahlia. make this barn
lily. this insult to good taste
bettina. a foray into paradise
dahlia, lily, alec, natalie, & ross (in unison). we dress up
bettina, eli, & lou (in unison). we dress up
dahlia. cuz we got good manners

. . .

bettina. cd you say to muhammad ali/ well/ i just didnt have a chance to change/ you see i have a job/ & then i went jogging & well, you know its just madison square garden
lou. my dear/ you know that wont do
natalie. we honor our guests/ if it costs us all we got

. . .

lily. we fill up where we at
bettina. no police
natalie. no cheap beer

dahlia. no nasty smellin bano
ross. no hallways fulla derelicts & hustlers
natalie. gonna interfere wit alla this beauty

. . .

lily. we simply have good manners
ross. & an addiction to joy
female cast members (in unison). WHEE . . .
dahlia. we dress up
male cast members (in unison). HEY . . .
bettina. we gotta show the world/ we gotta corner on the color
ross. happiness just jumped right outta us/ & we are lookin good

The celebration over, the performers relax at their tables in the bar, and now the ritual takes a new turn. One actress takes on the character of Fay, a lonely Brooklyn woman out to find excitement on the town. An actor joins her to tell the story that brings Fay from her front gate, all dressed up, all the way from Brooklyn, to "have me a goooooooood ol time." The rest of the performers slip easily

The actors in Ntozake Shange's
Spell #7 unmasked in the bar.
Directed by Oz Scott.

from being an audience for this story to patrons in the bar that Fay invades. One by one, through the rest of the show, the performers assume a range of roles that capture the multiplicity of the black experience, the pain, the yearning, the self-deception, the joy. Eli, the bartender, insists that "i am a poet . . . not a part-time poet . . . not a amateur poet," however impractical that may be. Lily luxuriates in brushing her hair. The company of men become a chorus of gay lotharios, strutting among the skeptical women and repeating the heart-winning come-on, "aw babee/ you so pretty," until it becomes a laughable refrain. Conflict in some vignettes is carried to the point of excruciation. Sue Jean, wanting a baby she calls "myself," goes through the agonies of labor, then kills the baby when it becomes a separate being outside her womb. Natalie pretends to be a white woman for a day—mocks the white woman's imaginary problems, organizing her day around shopping, the beauty parlor, sunlamps, and giving orders to the colored maid. She imagines with sympathy that grows to contempt and then to pain the civil-rights conscious white lady whose whiteness prevents her from sharing the black experience:

> i'm still in my house/ having flung my hair-do for the last time/ what with having to take 20 valium a day/ to consider the ERA/ & all the men in the world/ & my ignorance of the world/ it is overwhelming. i'm so glad i'm colored. boy i cd wake up in the morning & think abt anything. i can remember emmett till & not haveta smile at anybody.

Watching Natalie's pain, Maxine takes over and tells how as a child she celebrated little victories for colored people, then discovered that blacks aren't better than whites, that they get the same diseases and are just as vicious to other colored people as are the whites. And so, each time she hears of blacks doing something beneath them, each time she hears of black people being humiliated, she buys gold pieces, because gold comes from the earth, maybe from South Africa, from pain. Flashing her gold pieces, she announces in an unabated crescendo of rising pain:

> i wear all these things at once/ to remind the black people that it cost a lot for us to be here/ our value/ can be known instinctively/ but since so many black people are having a hard time not being like white folks/ i wear these gold pieces to protest their ignorance/ their disconnect from history. . . . i buy gold/ & weep. i weep as i fix the chains round my neck/ my wrists/ my ankles. i weep cuz all my childhood ceremonies for the ghost-slaves have been in vain. colored people can get polio & mental illness. slavery is not unfamiliar to me. no one on this planet knows/ what i know abt gold/ abt anything hard to get & beautiful/ anything lasting/ wrought from pain.

Her final line both culminates her passion and provides a kind of purging for her own soul, for the other actors frozen by the horror of her relevation, and for the audience who have come to share her pain at the most personal level: "no one understands that surviving the impossible is sposed to accentuate the positive aspects of a people."

Lou, once again the magician, waves his hand and freezes the whole company, and repeats his black magic promise from the opening: "i'm fixin you up good/ fixin you up good & colored . . . & you gonna love it/ bein colored/ all yr life." Then he beckons the actors to join in chanting "colored & love it" and the ritual mood now reaches its epiphany, "a serious celebration, like church/ like home." The actors who came on at the beginning in the degrading masks and slave costumes that are part of black history, have shared celebrations, conflicts, confessions, and purgings; but now, having survived the impossible, they become as one in affirming "the positive aspects of a people." Once more the actors freeze and Lou addresses the threatre audience; the final epiphany must be theirs:

> crackers are born with the right to be
> alive/ i'm making ours up right here
> in yr face/ & we gonna be
> colored & love it

The theatre piece comes to an end with the huge minstrel mask descending once again above the audience's heads, and the performers continue to chant and sing "colored & love it being colored" as the audience makes its exit.

In *Spell #7*, Ntozake Shange has taken all the "kinky" and radical experimentation of the 1960s and 1970s and out of it created a remarkable piece of theatre art for our time. It is a work that is truly liberated from the traditional conventions of the "successful" commerical play. But unlike so much of the negative experimentation that simply protested the inherited models, Shange's liberation has not just rejected the old and outworn. Like Peter Shumann, Jerzy Grotowski, Joseph Chaikin, and Peter Brook, Shange has gone to other traditions, richer sources of creativity: to the ritual motifs of her African heritage, to the revivalist patterns of gospel churches, to the songs, the dances, and the traditional characters of Negro showbiz, to the sounds of her people in joy and in pain, and even to the hated minstrel show, a symbol of white exploitation of the blacks. True liberation has come not from shunning the past and creating in a vacuum, but from the artist who hears the voices and needs of the present, who commands a rich understanding of her historical, social, and cultural roots, and who, out of these, creates a unique blend that is liberated in its own artistic form and liberates its audiences by its vision and by its power to help us rediscover who we are.

And so liberation may finally be the inspirational source for all true theatre experience. All the theatres we have looked at in the preceding chapters, as they sought to find new forms to express their times and to reach their audiences, were attempts to liberate the theatre from conventions that had become encrusted through the years. From Sophocles to Shakespeare to Stanislavsky to Shaw to Schumann and Shange, each has helped to resurrect "the fabulous invalid," the living theatre, to make it once again a place of vitality and of import, a place to invite living audiences to share in the joy and inspiration of creative and recreative art. New theatres yet unbuilt and new artists yet unborn, though they inherit our traditions, will not simply copy them, for they will also inherit the need to liberate themselves and the audiences they invite to share the liveliest of all the arts—the living theatre.

THE PLAY
IN PRODUCTION
III

THE PLAY IN PRODUCTION

When we go to the theatre, we expect to see a play. We can read the play, of course, but that is not theatre. A reader is unlikely to experience all the appeals to ear and eye that are part of a production and even less likely to imagine the action occurring on a stage with an audience watching. For a play in the theatre is a composition not merely of a story in words (sometimes there is neither story nor words); it is a composition also of color, line, space, and light, a composition of images and ideas that move in rhythmic order toward a definite goal, constantly interacting with the thoughts, emotions, and sometimes even the live responses of the audience.

Theatre, a complete art in itself, uses the living presence of actors to create human action in the composite medium of time and space. Yet theatre artists take elements from all arts. They use story like the novelist, language like the poet, three-dimensional structures like the sculptor or architect, pattern and color like the painter, fashion like the couturier, music like the composer, voice like the singer or orator, body movement like the athlete or dancer; then they add light and sound to highlight the dramatic progression of the action. But in the theatre, none of these many arts works alone. The setting may be pleasing to look at, but it needs the living, moving presence of actors to fill its space with the unfolding drama, and the costumes, no matter how dazzling, serve mainly as clues to tell about the characters who wear them.

At the beginning of this century, the English director-designer Gordon Craig was hailed as a prophet when, in his book *On the Art of the Theatre*, he argued that a single artist should be sole creator for each production—designing lights, sets, and costumes, directing the play, interpreting each role, training the actors to carry out his interpretation, and, ideally, writing the script. Until the modern era, beginning in the nineteenth century, the theatre had no real need for the kind of artist Craig described. Each previous era had its own set of conventions to be used for all plays. A company of actors, with thirty to forty plays ready to perform at all times, rarely played any show more than two or three times running. Staging had to be simple; settings had to be interchangeable; actors had to play what was called a "line" of roles (one specializing in juvenile parts, another in the ingenue roles, a third playing the "heavies," and so forth), making for stock patterns of character development. The playwrights in the company wrote for the talents of specific actors and also did what little directing was needed. After a few short rehearsals, the new play was added to the repertory where it remained, virtually unchanged, for years. On stage, the leading actors and actresses, whom the audiences had come to see, dominated the play. In the mid-nineteenth century, the star simply took center stage and all the supporting cast found their own appropriate places to support the grandeur of the star's performance.

"Realism" changed all that, demanding a new aesthetic of theatre. First, it called for authenticity. The realist wanted audiences to see life itself directly represented on the stage. If the scene was in a working-class kitchen, audiences came to expect stoves, cupboards with dishes, working doors and windows, and perhaps even real food being prepared and eaten. If the scene was Venice, vistas of actual Venetian buildings and a canal with a real gondola completed the authentic touch. Second, in keeping with the new theories of evolution, the realist believed that people's actions were influenced by their surroundings. Leading actors were no longer stars, but part of an ensemble, subtly affected by their physical environment as well as by all the characters whose lives interacted with their own. Thus each action had to be carefully planned, each element of the stage setting had to be carefully designed to show this complex interplay of influences. Third, because of the passion for authenticity and because of

the emphasis on environment, each play demanded its own unique setting and staging. No longer would just any interior do; no longer could the star simply take center stage; no longer would a few short rehearsals suffice.

Further, with all the departures from realism that followed in the early twentieth century, each play began to demand its own style as well as its own unique setting. Audiences might find new conventions every time they went to the theatre and would only be confused unless each production had a carefully controlled unity. Into this theatre of diversity came Gordon Craig's "artist of the theatre"—the director—the central artist who coordinates the work of all other members of the producing team, making sure that everyone—actors, designers, technicians—are all guided by the same idea of what kind of play they are creating.

The audience sees primarily the actors, but they are only part of a large team of workers who bring many different skills to the theatre. In the next chapters, we shall look at the specific contributions of each of the theatre artists, and we shall examine some of the ways they collaborate with each other to create the synthesized work of living art, ready for the invited audience to share.

à mon ami
Louis Legal

Cambo. Avril · 1903

Edmond Rostand

THE
PLAYWRIGHT
11

Costume and scenery sketches by Edmond
Rostand for *Cyrano de Bergerac*.

*T*he playwright is the primary artist of the theatre, the one who initiates the entire process from which the other artists then build. The playwright defines the action, creates the characters, invents the plot, composes the dialogue, and shapes all these materials into a unified whole. In Part II of this book, we saw how playwrights in different times and places created their plays from a variety of impulses. From ancient Greece we saw Sophocles create a stately and dignified tragedy about Antigone, honoring her brother with the rites of burial though it meant her own death, thus giving his civic audience the chance to explore relationships between human and divine law. From eighteenth-century London we saw Richard Brinsley Sheridan create a sparkling high comedy around Lady Teazle, trying so hard to make her place in fashionable society that she almost destroys her reputation and her marriage, thus giving Sheridan's Age of Enlightenment audience a chance to laugh at a society obsessed with being in fashion. From nineteenth-century Norway, we saw Henrik Ibsen create a domestic tragedy about a woman whose hopes for her son's future are corrupted by the "ghosts" of her husband's profligacy and her own fear of public opinion, thus helping his scientifically disposed audience to explore the subtle relationships between heredity and environment. And from our own time, we have seen Samuel Beckett create a haunting tragicomedy about two tramps at the side of a road waiting for a "Godot" who will never come, thus helping his audiences to come to an existential awareness of life, where goals are meaningless and where neither people nor events are predictable or reliable.

In this most communal of arts, the playwright is the loneliest figure. Though some playwrights work in the midst of actors, sometimes creating out of the actors' improvisations, that is the exception. Playwrights immerse themselves in life itself. There is where they find the stuff of their dramas—the actions, the characters, and the unique vision that gives them form. Sitting alone at their desks, they fill the blank sheets of paper with the scenes, the characters, and the dramatic speeches that their imaginations have wrought out of their contact with life in the raw.

From Aeschylus and Sophocles to Beckett and beyond, playwrights have been the ones to look with a penetrating eye at their society, to express in drama the vision of their own eras. When the script is done they often disappear from the process, while the producing artists (directors, designers, actors, and technicians) take over. Even a new play usually finds the playwright only an embarrassing adjunct, not personally involved in rehearsals, but merely providing rewrites for the director. But it is the playwright's work that remains after the final curtain has closed, after the sets are dismantled, and the actors have gone on to other plays. The script remains to initiate many more productions in the years and even the centuries to come. So what has the playwright done? How does the playwright's creation enable other theatre artists to collaborate on the performance of the play?

THE PLAYWRIGHT AT WORK

No two playwrights work alike, and their individuality, above all, is to be prized. Nevertheless, all playwrights of any merit must keep in mind at least three facts of production as they sit in front of their blank sheets of paper:

1. What they create must be performable. Actors working with other actors must be able to breathe life into the lines and characters in some kind of physical space.
2. What they create must be loaded with implied meanings. Audiences will have only what they see and hear to build their own involvement in the drama, and only those meanings and emotions they can infer from the dialogue and from their visual experience can be part of the play.
3. What they write must inspire the creative energies of the collaborative artists who will bring the play to its completeness in the living medium of time and space called the theatre.

For the above reasons, *playwright*, not *playwriter*, is the term we use. The playwright is a maker of plays, as a shipwright is a maker of ships, and when the play is made, others must make it fulfill the promise of its design.

Cyrano de Bergerac: A Play Wrought for Production

When Edmond Rostand created *Cyrano de Bergerac* in 1897, it was at the request of the famous French actor Coquelin. "I am a comedian," Coquelin said to him, "but I am a romantic actor first: I can read poetry, I can make love and fight and die. Make me a play of all these things." So Rostand made a particular play for a particular actor. What better way to look at the playwright's craft than to imagine ourselves as the playwright, making *Cyrano de Bergerac!*

Creating an Action

Since Coquelin wants to speak poetry, to love, fight, and die, we have to find a character capable of all those things. There he is, an actual person right out of seventeenth-century Paris, a swaggering Gascon with an enormous nose and a penchant for writing poetry. Give him a love to conquer and he will do it grandly, but make his love Roxane, the most beautiful woman in Paris, and his ugly nose is now an obstacle. If he were only beautiful, he could tell her of his love. But suppose Roxane has already fallen for a handsome man, Christian, a new recruit in Cyrano's own company—a rival—a complication—a love triangle. Having such a nose, Cyrano cannot compete, and so he promises to support her love for his rival. Now we have an internal conflict as well. But add one more complication. Suppose Roxane expects her true love to have a poetic soul to match his beauty, while Christian is terrified even to speak to her for fear of exposing how dull he is. There it is, Cyrano's opportunity! No, he will not show

Benoit Coquelin, the first Cyrano de Bergerac.

up his rival; he is too devoted to Roxane's happiness for that. Since he is too ugly to be loved, he will teach his rival eloquence, to be worthy of the love he cannot have. Thus, when Christian wishes for Cyrano's wit, our hero's course is set:

> Borrow it, then!—
> Your beautiful young manhood—lend me that,
> And we two make one hero of romance!

Now he can pour out his love freely, and his words spoken by the handsome Christian will win the heart of Roxane.

Here is an action to be played. Each character has a goal, something to strive for, with an obstacle standing in the way. To remove the obstacle they create an overwhelming complication. The greater Cyrano's success, the more likely he is to lose Roxane to his rival; the closer Christian comes to winning Roxane, the sooner she will find out his eloquence is not his own. So each actor enters each scene with a clear goal for his character and a secret subtext. The audience, knowing the secret, can share the subtext with the characters at the very heart of the dramatic action. The secret has been "planted," and like a plant it will grow and bloom in the complications of the plot and in the audience's fertile imagination. As it grows, so will suspense and intrigue. Ironies will multiply. The audience will begin to anticipate what's coming next; they will sit on the edge of their seats waiting for the inevitable discovery that will finally unmask the characters, bringing about a reversal of fortune—the climax of most plays.

Building the Scenes Through Loaded Events

We could tell this story as a continuous narrative but to dramatize it, the playwright must build it in scenes or segments. Rostand must select the high spots, the crises and turning points, the moments of conflict, contrast, and ironic power, and most of all the moments that make both characters and audience look toward the future. In short, each scene must be an event. An event gives the characters a reason to be there; it causes them to make decisions, to take sides, to try to influence other characters—that is, it causes them to act. It is through such scenes that the audience comes to know the characters, to share their action, and to care about what happens to them.

Cyrano first needs an event where he can show his most remarkable qual-

José Ferrer, a dashing Cyrano of stage and screen.

ites. He must be heroic as well as poetic. Heroism demands individuality, skill, and above all admiration, so he must stand out from the crowd, perhaps even defy it—a good chance to exercise his skill. For admiration we need a public event. Since Cyrano is a swaggering, poetic character, why not a theatre for the opening scene? There will be a crowd come to admire. Now if Cyrano can outshine the actors, what a chance for admiration! That's it! He will quarrel with the leading actor; he will stop the play. There is action, conflict, and individuality.

So we bring in the crowds: lackeys and cavaliers, guardsmen and flower girls, citizens, cutpurses, and courtiers—a cross-section of Parisian society—each coming to see the play, and each coming with personal motivations, some to admire the actor, some to flirt, some to be seen, some to hear the latest gossip. Christian comes to get a glimpse of Roxane and perhaps to meet her; Ragueneau, the pastry cook, comes to see whether Cyrano will carry out his threat to close the play. We see them gather; we watch them prepare for the play.

Notice how the whole world of the play has been set before us—except for Cyrano. Yet his is the action we are waiting to see: Will he close the play? The actor, Montfleury, takes the stage, and for the first time, all eyes are directed toward the same spot. All attention goes to Montfleury, and then a voice rings out from the crowd, interrupting the event: "Wretch. Have I not forbade you these three weeks?" Tumult breaks out as Cyrano intimidates the actor over the objections of the crowd and then, in a grand gesture, pays for everyone's admission from his own threadbare purse. But so far his actions might be those of any bold cavalier. What may we expect next? We haven't long to wait. One arrogant young nobleman insults Cyrano's nose, but so ineptly that Cyrano, in one of the most famous speeches from all of drama, bombards him with all the insults he might have used had he been clever enough. At last they duel, and Cyrano dispatches his opponent while composing a ballad in rhyme, suiting the words of each verse to the actions of the duel, culminating in the one line he had prepared us for in advance: "Then as I end the refrain, thrust home!" Cyrano has not just stopped the play, he has *become* the play—its chief character, its leading actor, and, to top things off, its playwright and director as well.

Cyrano's role is clearly performable, but do all those other characters merely stand around? Even when one character dominates the stage, the others must have actions of their own. One speech where Cyrano silences the crowd will show how a skillful playwright suggests a constant interplay between the speaking and the listening characters. Notice how each line provides clues to the other actors and the director on how to react and stage the scene.

> I offer
> One universal challenge to you all!
> Approach, young heroes—I will take your names.
> Each in his turn—no crowding! One, two, three—

The entire theatre crowd looks on as Cyrano fulfills the promises of his refrain to the duel in rhyme: "Then as I end the refrain, thrust home!" University of Michigan.

> Come, get your numbers—who will head the list—
> You sir? No— You? Ah, no. To the first man
> Who falls I'll build a monument! . . . Not one?
> Will all who wish to die, please raise their hands? . . .
> I see. You are so modest, you might blush
> Before a sword naked. Sweet innocence! . . .
> Not one name? Not one finger? . . . Very well,
> Then I go on.

Now Cyrano must engage audience sympathy, not merely admiration. That requires a quiet scene where he can confess that he loves Roxane but is afraid to tell her so because of his ugly nose. He feels inadequate. How very human! Still, he needs some hope, and so a message from Roxane to meet her early the next morning. Perhaps she loves him! The excitement is too great to bear. It needs some monumental release: "I feel too strong to war with mortals— . . . BRING ME GIANTS!" And then comes word: A poet friend being ambushed by a hundred ruffians in the streets needs his help. That's it! He will fight the hundred men—alone—and the whole crowd follows, actors and all. Cyrano is not just the play; he is now the theatre. Where he is, there is the action. Thus ends Act I.

For Act II we need the complications, a major source of irony. Roxane will meet with Cyrano, of course, and confide that she's in love. She lists her lover's

Christian (Dennis Cooney) climbing up to claim the kiss from Roxane (Suzanne Grossman) after Cyrano (Robert Symonds) has won her with his words. Repertory Company of Lincoln Center.

attributes, and each one fits Cyrano perfectly—What a moment for the actor! Then she comes to the word "beautiful." All hope is shattered as she names Christian, a new recruit in Cyrano's company. The irony mounts as she asks for Cyrano's help. Next, the meeting with Christian, where this new recruit proves his mettle by a most dangerous ploy; he attacks Cyrano's nose. And Cyrano must hold his temper and his sword—more irony, more rich subtext for the actor. Then the compact, the secret union of Cyrano's poetic wit with Christian's beautiful looks; together they will win Roxane.

Act III must be the wooing—and further complications. We only need to know that Cyrano's words on Christian's lips have enthralled Roxane, but another rival, a powerful nobleman, Le Comte de Guiche, also wants to marry her. Christian cannot wait. He tries to woo her on his own—and fails. Cyrano comes to the rescue in the famous balcony scene, prompts his inept pupil from the shadows with his own ardent words, and, at last, pushes Christian aside.

Under cover of the darkness, he pours out his own love, pretending to be Christian. He wins Roxane's heart; she promises him one kiss. But Christian claims the prize while Cyrano fumes below. Just in time, too, for a priest arrives to marry Roxane to Le Comte de Guiche. We must waste no time in the theatre, and Roxane wastes no time persuading the priest that Christian is the one she is to wed, leaving Cyrano to stall Le Comte de Guiche until the ceremony is complete.

Roxane must not learn the secret, so a call to war interrupts the wedding night. Act IV is at the battle front, where Cyrano has daily crossed enemy lines to send her letters in Christian's name. Separated from her lover's beauty, Roxane has responded to his words alone, Cyrano's ardent letters, and she has come to love his soul. She arrives at the front lines, ready to die with her true love. Now we have the big discovery scene. But not too soon. Let's let Christian learn the secret first. Roxane loves him passionately. It would not matter if he were ugly; she loves his soul—but the soul is that of the letters—Cyrano's letters. We join in sympathy with Christian as he sees his own hopes fade even as Roxane pours out her love. We admire his supreme sacrifice as he sends Cyrano to claim the love he's earned. But what about Roxane? She cannot simply be told. We're on a battlefield. That's it!—one irony resolved with a new complication. A shot rings out, wounding Christian just as Cyrano is about to reveal his love. He cannot now betray his dying friend, so Cyrano steps aside as Roxane finds his last tear-stained letter clasped to her husband's heart.

Act V is many years later in a convent where Roxane has retreated from the world to mourn Christian's memory, and Cyrano has devoted himself to a weekly rendevous. The final visit is all we need on stage. What happens in that final scene? Well, we must leave some surprises for when you read or, better yet, see the play. Cyrano remains an individual, of course. Though his body may have been ugly, neither life nor death could cheat him of his incomparable pursuit of beauty and the ideal, which he takes with him to the end, unspotted and unsullied. He has loved, he has been poetic, he has fought, and he has challenged death itself. A hero's role if there ever was one—a role for an actor to glory in!

Writing for the Other Theatre Artists

Throughout the previous section we have seen again and again how the role of Cyrano and the contrasting roles of Christian and Roxane are written to be performed. Compelling actions guide the characters from the time they first appear and motivations are built into each event, growing and developing with each obstacle and complication. A rich subtext is evident even for the members of the crowds who speak no lines but react with obvious motivation to Cyrano's deeds. Without usurping the designers' or director's jobs, notice how Rostand has also been attentive to their roles. The show requires five different sets: a theatre, a bakery shop, the exterior of a house with a balcony, a battlefield, and a convent. A huge job for any stage designer, you say? But the locales are drawn in the broadest strokes. A designer with unlimited resources may choose to give full detail, but there is no need. The theatre scene requires a platform for the actor, Montfleury, which can easily become an Act IV battlement; it requires boxes above for the ladies and nobility (Roxane's balcony for Act III); and it requires an open space for the crowds to gather, a space required for every scene. Mainly the script identifies different playing areas, delineating them by the functions they will serve. A few well-chosen details, together with the actors' lines, will set the time and place. The lighting designer may take us from the candle-glow of the theatre, to the morning sunlight of the bakery shop, to the shadows of the balcony at night, to the stark exterior of a battlefield, to the dusky twilight of the convent for the final scene.

The costumer may have the biggest job in telling us that this is seventeenth-century Paris. Here, too, Rostand provides some help as one of Cyrano's enemies describes him with contempt: "A clown who—look at him—not even gloves! / No ribbons—no lace—no buckles on his shoes—" If Cyrano's lack of finery is so obvious, the other characters must be richly dressed indeed. Cyrano describes himself "trailing white plumes of freedom, garlanded / With my good name." The contrast is set in the lines, and the designer can take it from there.

With such events to stage and such varied playing areas and sets in which to stage them, with such well-drawn character motivations for the actors, and such color and contrasts in the costumes, the director's job will be an easy one. Each scene gives ample chance to create dynamic stage pictures, to shift focus, to accent ironies, to build to a climax, and to plant the ideas and the actions that propel the play from one scene to the next.

A Form for the Playwright's Vision

In Part II, we saw the various impulses from which drama grows, because theatre always expresses and celebrates a vision of life. *Cyrano de Bergerac*, as we saw in Chapter 5, celebrates the "romantic" view. A few brief reminders will show how completely romantic Rostand's play is.

One ingredient of romantic drama is variety of experience. In *Cyrano*, this variety occurs in many ways. First, the range of characters includes everything from servants and orange girls to soldiers and cavaliers, from gentlemen and noblemen to pastrycooks and musicians, from actresses and poets to nuns and monks and thieves. The activities include dueling, courting, acting, starving, declaiming high ideals, preparing for battle, and, of course, dying. Public as well as private scenes occur in the theatre, in a cafe, on the battlefield, in a convent, and in the quiet of a private garden at night. The moods take us from laughter to pathos to heroic admiration.

The romantic notion that truth is experienced through the feelings is an idea that defines Cyrano himself: "To sing, to laugh, to dream, / To walk in my own way and be alone, / Free, with an eye to see things as they are." His feelings, expressed in poetic words, win the feelings of Roxane to the beauty of his soul, but only when she is free from seeing merely physical ugliness and beauty. With feelings as his source of truth, the romantic hero can soar above the limits of his body. A grotesque nose inspires him beyond mere looks to find true beauty in the soul, expressed in poetic language and heroic deeds.

To experience true feeling, Cyrano must be "free," an "individual." The public's way must not be his. He alone will attack an incompetent actor, protect a friend against the multitude, or sacrifice himself to his mistress's happiness and a dead friend's honor. "My soul, be satisfied with flowers, / With fruit, with weeds even; but gather them / In the one garden you may call your own." The romantic Cyrano has dedicated his life to a truth higher than the pragmatic one the world esteems, a truth that achieves intensity through freedom, variety of experience, individuality, and an unremitting faith in his feelings as his guide.

Credibility and Astonishment

"It was so real!" That is often the height of praise the average theatregoer awards to a play, and the modern theatre is filled with plays about the reality of the everyday, the here and now. With equal enthusiasm, however, audiences apply the term to fantasy or romance, and some of the most popular plays of our time are far removed from what we normally call reality. Witness the recent popularity of *Cats* on stage or *Star Wars* at the movies; notice the recurring popularity of *Peter Pan* in the theatre and *The Wizard of Oz* on film. Nor need we look to fantasy. Supernatural characters have walked the stage from the gods of ancient Greece, to the Ghost in Shakespeare's *Hamlet*, to the Stage Manager in *Our Town* or the fiddler of *Fiddler on the Roof*. Dramatic language until modern times was almost always poetry, and in the musical and opera characters sing their lines and their emotions right to the present day. Sets and costumes may be authentic reproductions of the real world, but more often than not a few select and stylized details or even a bare stage and leotards will serve the play best.

Credibility is what the audience really wants. They ask that the world of the play be internally consistent, that the laws of that world, once set down, be followed, and that what happens in Act II follow sensibly from what Act I began. Poetic language may be credible, but the poetry and what is said must both appear to rise from the character's individual intentions and interests. Characters who appear to act or speak as the playwright's mouthpiece are not believed. No matter how fantastic the situation, they must appear to act with human thoughts and feelings within the world they occupy. It is the human factor that attracts us to plays, and in *Cats* even T. S. Eliot's feline characters appeal because we keep recognizing how very human they are. Animals can talk, and in *Peter Pan* characters can fly. These are conventions of the play that we readily accept. Once the conventions are set, however unreal they may be, they are credible so long as they remain consistent—that is, so long as the characters behave as humans would behave, if humans had the motivations, the qualities, and the abilities found in the world of the play.

Credibility is basic, but playwrights want far more; they want *astonishment*, they want to make their audience sit back and take notice. Credibility requires careful plotting, skill in working out the details so that all the groundwork is laid, skill in creating motivated characters that each actor can develop step by step, skill in building one scene on another so that a director can tie the threads together for the audience. But astonishment requires audacity and imagination. The playwright must dare to do the unexpected, the seemingly impossible. Sophocles wrote about Antigone, a young princess, happily engaged, with everything to live for. Yet she defies her uncle and dares death itself to bury her brother. Shakespeare chose an eighty-year-old King Lear who gives away his kingdom, disowns his favorite daughter, and then is cast out to fend for himself against the elements. Arthur Miller caught the spirit of his age in a morally bankrupt failure of a salesman. And Cyrano—well, what about Cyrano? An ugly romantic hero courts his own love for his handsome rival. That's audacity. For stories like those we go to the theatre again and again. Not only the dramatic situation, but the building of events must astonish. Mere credibility just makes things predictable, and if the audience can predict every outcome and event, they have no reason to watch the play. That is not to say that all plays are built on a "what happens next?" motif of suspense. In fact, some playwrights let us know the outcome from the start. When we go to see a play about Joan of Arc, we know that she will die at the stake. Yet the playwright must surprise us, perhaps with the process leading to her death, perhaps with the motives that cause both her and her accusers to act, perhaps with the similarities we start to notice between her world and our own.

In *Cyrano de Bergerac*, we may expect Cyrano to fight a duel, but to compose a cleverly rhymed ballad while he does so is astonishing. We may expect him to befriend Christian once he has given Roxane his promise, but who would expect him to help Christian to win her? Scene after scene is an event to astonish, each one topping the one that came before.

As playwrights find new visions, new actions to present, new relationships to express, they will be at the heart of a continuous revolution. They will discard last year's methods when they no longer serve, but they may resurrect some methods buried long ago, giving them new life with a new vision. Most of all, they will rewrite the rule-book to find new ways to show us how to see ourselves, "suiting the word to the action, the action to the word." Both audiences and other theatre artists will continue to look to the playwright as the playwright looks to life itself.

Note: For another view of the playwright's skills in *Cyrano de Bergerac* see Anthony Burgess's provocative introduction to his 1970 adaptation and translation of the play (Knopf, 1971), in which he attempted to make the play more suited for a modern audience.

THE ART
OF THE
DIRECTOR

12

The director steps in to coach the actors in the
midst of a *Romeo and Juliet* dueling scene.

*T*he next three chapters will show how directors, actors, and designers transform the playwright's work into living productions. Just as we used *Cyrano de Bergerac* to show how playwrights work, we'll choose a play to highlight the work of each theatre artist. To pick the best plays for the job is the responsibility of the *producer*. Producers are not so much theatre artists as theatre business managers, an indispensable role. They are most conspicuous in the commercial theatre, where they organize the whole endeavor: selecting and securing the rights for the play, seeking out the "angels" to finance the production, renting the theatre, hiring the director and designers, arranging for auditions, employing the actors, usually in consultation with the director, arranging rehearsal space, publicizing the production, selling the tickets, and, of course, paying the bills.

Permanent companies, such as America's many regional theatres, often divide the producer's function between a managing director and an artistic director. The managing director takes charge of the company's business affairs, while the artistic director oversees all artistic matters. In college and university theatres the producer may be a single "Director of Theatre," the entire theatre staff working as a committee, or a faculty and student group of "Collegiate Players" organized together as a producing organization. Like their professional counterparts, they determine company policy, select the season, distribute directing and design assignments, plan and allocate the budget, organize publicity and ticket sales, and arrange for the necessary support staff for each production.

In picking the plays for the imagined productions of these three chapters, a producer need not worry about such problems as budget, casting, or available space, since we will produce the plays in a theatre of the imagination. Mainly the plays in our imagined season must showcase the work done by the different theatre artists and, secondarily, correlate with some of the basic theatre impulses discussed in earlier chapters. For the playwright, we have already used a romantic heroic play, *Cyrano de Bergerac*. To highlight the work of the *director*, our second play should require that its director have to choose among several possible ways of doing the play and also coordinate a complex organization of actors, designers, and technicians. What could be more complex and more open to varied approaches than a Shakespearean tragedy? And since Shakespeare's tragic prince, Hamlet, is a student and even does a bit of play directing himself, what better tragedy than *Hamlet* to explore the job of the director in this student text?

To highlight the role of the *actor*, the third play of our season should be a realistic play, since several modern trends in acting grew out of the realistic movement. Let's use a realistic comedy (to keep the season from getting too heavy), George Bernard Shaw's *Pygmalion*, the story of a young flower girl learning to be a lady. To round out our season with a play for the *designer*, we should select from modern nonrealistic plays, since the many departures from realism inspired modern concepts of design in the theatre. *The Elephant Man*, already discussed in Chapter 2, offers variety in place and mood, presents problems of both period and locale, and demands a theatricalized style of presentation. The scene designer, the lighting designer, and the costume designer will all find it a challenge. Thus we have a varied and appropriate season: *Cyrano de Bergerac,* a romantic heroic play for the playwright; *Hamlet, Prince of Denmark,* an Elizabethan tragedy, for the director; *Pygmalion,* a realistic comedy, for the actor; and *The Elephant Man,* a contemporary, multi-scene, nonrealistic history play, for the designers.

The producer's job is now done. Before setting an imaginary director loose on *Hamlet,* however, we need to outline some of the basic functions and techniques of play directing.

THE DIRECTOR AT WORK

In Chapter 2, we defined the *production format* of the play as the counterpart of plot: selecting and organizing the production elements of the show so as to bring the play's action into focus for an audience. The American director Harold Clurman, in his article "In a Different Language" *(Theatre Arts,* January, 1950, pp. 18–20), called this process one of translation:

> The dramatist's conception—his story-line and plan of action conveyed through descriptive words and dialogue—serves the other theatre craftsmen as the *raw material* from which they make the thing we finally witness at performance. . . . On the stage the dramatist's language must be translated; his spirit must be made flesh.

The chief translator is the director, and as with a novel or poem, when the translation is done well, the audience should be least aware of it, confident that what they see is the play with its conception fully realized in performance. They may be enchanted by the costumes, stirred by the actors, and dazzled by the sets and lights, but the hand of the director should work subtly and imperceptibly, calling attention, not to itself, but to the unfolding drama.

The Director's Concept or Vision

Like the playwright, the director has a unique relationship to the play. While the play script is the written expression of the playwright's vision, the production completes the play through the director's vision. That is not to say that directors arbitrarily manipulate scripts to serve their own ends; rather they discover and illuminate that in the play which expresses something important for themselves and their audience. This expression is called the director's concept, and it is, quite simply, the director's inspiration for translating this play to the stage at this time for this particular audience. When a director takes on a show just to do a job and isn't committed to some artistic vision of the play, the production is doomed to mediocrity from the start, and mediocrity in the theatre means failure. Theatre must be exciting, and excitement comes from the vision the director brings to the show. The play does not just speak for itself. The English director, Peter Brook, said it best: "If you just let a play speak, it may not make a sound. If what you want is for the play to be heard, then you must conjure its sound from it."

Most plays of any depth readily support several production concepts. To produce *Cyrano de Bergerac,* one director might treat the play as a realistic portrayal of a degenerate society, underscoring the corruption and cynicism of its characters, while a seedy-looking Cyrano makes comically pathetic attempts to challenge its phoniness. Another director might see the play as a heroic stand for individualism in a world of conformists. Yet another might depict Cyrano as a comic knave who impetuously gets himself into bad situations, brashly improvises his way through them, and then is as astonished as anyone by the results. These three concepts would create widely different productions of the play. Not only would the actors, in each case, use different subtexts for the playwright's words; the settings, costumes, and the entire tone of each production would appear to be from altogether different plays.

The Production Conference

The director's next step is to collaborate with the designers, usually a process of much give-and-take. A stimulating director's concept can fire the creative imaginations of the designers, while their visual sensitivity and technical knowledge often enrich the director's vision in turn. Out of the collaboration comes the basic style of production.

The broadest style choice might come simply from the play's being tragedy rather than farce, calling for deep colors and rich fabrics, stately architectural features, dignified costume lines, and large expanses of space for movement and stage groupings. For a period play, the design-director team will have to choose what period to set it in. The period in which the play was written does not always serve the concept best. While the Richard Burton–Elizabeth Taylor film of *The Taming of the Shrew* was a completely realistic portrayal of Renaissance Italy, William Ball, in his American Conservatory Theatre production of the same play, wished to emphasize not its realism but its theatricality. He chose a style from theatrical history, commedia dell'arte, presenting the play on a simple stage, with makeshift curtains on poles, stylized makeup and costumes, and rough-and-tumble action suggestive of the circus. In the realism of the film, director Franco Zefferelli constantly based the wild fights and comic chases in realistic motivation of the characters and the environment; William Ball was free to remind his audience at every stage that all the nonsense was just good fun.

Once a style is established, the design-directing team can work out such details as a floor plan for the stage, the number of sets and costume changes, and the lighting needs. This done, the designers temporarily go their own ways to create their designs, while directors proceed to their next step: casting the show.

Casting and Rehearsals

In the past, theatre companies usually cast according to established "lines" for which actors had been hired: one to play comic servants, another the romantic youth, another the mature woman, and so forth. Directors today commonly hold auditions, where each actor and actress presents a prepared audition piece or reads assigned scenes from the play. From these readings the director selects the actors most appropriate to each role, working out an ensemble best suited to the production concept.

Many directors consider casting their single most important job. No matter how good the play or how brilliant the director's concept, the actors make the play happen for the audience, and many a production has misfired when actors failed to project the appropriate energy or image. Clear, rich voices and expressive bodies are fundamental considerations. From there the director often looks for certain physical types. The play may require actors who are mature as well as youthful, rugged and imposing as well as delicate and refined. Actual physical size for an individual character is usually less important than the ensemble effect. Variety and contrast are the key words. Distinctive looks can do more than words to help an audience know a character, but a short pudgy body may create the appropriate distinctiveness just as well as a tall angular one, depending on the rest of the cast. Even more important is the energy level that an actor conveys. Cyrano must be played by a high-energy actor; Willy Loman must be able to project moodiness; and Mama, in *A Raisin in the Sun*, must exude strength and self-confidence. To choose an ensemble, directors mainly have to know how each character contributes to the drama and what contrasts and similarities among the cast will create the most effective dramatic development. Then they will be able to recognize those qualities in the actors that can be nurtured during rehearsals.

Working with the Actors

Before actually starting rehearsals, directors carefully examine the play's structure. They know where the climaxes occur, where the audience must grasp important information, where new complications are introduced, and where the direction of the action reverses itself. They notice patterns of repeated behavior; they notice the flow between relaxed scenes and scenes of tension, between comic scenes and scenes of conflict or terror, between short abrupt scenes and long sustained scenes, between intimate scenes, unruly mob scenes, and more formal crowd scenes; and they notice how these scenes build on, contrast with, or parallel each other. Each scene takes on a tone and purpose of its own, but a purpose that fits into a larger pattern. Now the director is prepared to guide the actors in creating the appropriate rhythm or mood for each scene, to bring the larger pattern into focus through the staging, and to help the actors with their interpretations. This is particularly important for those actors who appear only in brief segments of the play and can never sense this overall flow on their own.

The initial rehearsals may serve several different functions. When a show presents special problems for the actors, such as learning a dialect, directors often devote the first rehearsals to teaching the dialect so that the actors will have an idea how the play should sound even before they begin to work with the playwright's words. Most commonly, directors begin by *blocking* the play—that is, visualizing it in space. They go through each scene speech by speech, telling the actors when to enter, where to stand or sit, on what lines to move or carry out such "stage business" as picking up a package, bowing, turning, or shaking hands, and how to perform many of the small reactions that go with their lines. The actors write all the blocking into their scripts so that they can memorize the movements with their lines.

Some directors prefer to put off blocking until they have explored the script with the actors, helping them find their characters and their relationships to each other through the clues the playwright provides. Sometimes this is done sitting around a large table, though actors quickly get impatient with just talking. They want to act. Thus, many directors get the actors on their feet, improvising movement as they explore relationships with one another. Then later on, the blocking

Gary Charm (left) interprets by means of signing as Gordon Davidson directs John Rubenstein and Phyllis Frelich in *Children of a Lesser God.* The Mark Taper Forum, 1979.

Actors studying the script in rehearsal of *The House of Cards*. O'Neill Theatre Center.

seems to come naturally, since the actors have already discovered the relationships and motivations that the blocking supports. This method works well for amateur actors doing Shakespeare, in that it helps them overcome a tendency toward phoniness often associated with Shakespearean acting. The actors have never been allowed to treat their lines as set speeches. From the start they have had to search the lines for the motivations that cause them to move and interact with other characters as they would with real human beings. The words are their own, not just beautiful speeches to impress audiences.

Controlling the Action in Space

No matter what method is used in the first rehearsals, eventually the director must block the play. Comfortable and motivated actors are not enough to make good theatre. The audience must be able to follow the story visually: which characters dominate and which ones threaten? which ones like each other and which are in conflict? when do characters change, and when are the conflicts resolved?

Movie and television directors use the camera to select and control what the audience looks at, but the stage director uses living actors and the dynamics of stage space to guide the audience's attention, while still leaving them free to take in the rest of the picture as well. By placing and moving actors around the areas of the stage, the director can change the picture in many ways to give different meanings and to shift attention from one character to another. One character may become subordinate by turning away from the audience, while another can "open up" (turn toward the audience), stand up, step out from the group, or move to a stronger area of the stage to achieve dominance. Or the director can throw emphasis to a stationary character by moving others around her (to give her more space and contrast) and by having them direct their eyes toward her. In deploying actors on a proscenium stage, directors divide the stage into six areas and label them *up right, up center, up left, down right, down center, down left.* Stage left and stage right indicate the sides as viewed by the actor facing the audience; upstage is away from the audience and downstage is toward it. For more than three centuries, upstage was actually higher than downstage, since the old picture stage had a sloping floor to give a forced-perspective effect to the wing-and-drop setting. On an arena stage, directors often divide the stage like the face of a clock, directing the actors' movements by the clock face: move to three o'clock or stand at twelve o'clock.

The audience is seldom aware of the composition itself, unless it is cluttered or confused. What is seen is the story in the picture, told through the action and interrelation of the characters. This story-telling "picturization of emotional relations" is a visual language, a medium as powerful as words, by which the director communicates with the audience. It is one means by which a play, so short in comparison with a novel, can make as strong an impression, sometimes even stronger. The actor, designer, and the director can show to the audience, at a glance, complexities and qualities of relationship that would require many pages of description in a novel. In a well-directed scene of an accident in the street, for instance, the audience can tell, from the positions of the actors, which is the wife of the victim, which the friend or the wife's friend, which were the witnesses, and which are mere passers-by adding their own groupings and emotional reac-

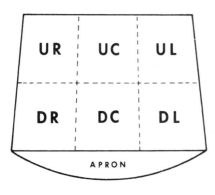

Stage areas. The director divides the stage into at least six areas, which vary in quality and strength from the soft up left or up right to the very emphatic down center.

A view of the center stage at the Metropolitan Opera House in New York, which is surrounded by three stages of equal size. The main stage is in seven sections, any of which can be raised or lowered. The auxiliary stage at right is in sections, permitting the most difficult change of scenery in less than two minutes. The auxiliary stage at left rakes and has an elevator that can move a unit as big as the house in *Madama Butterfly*. The rear stage has a turntable 58 feet in diameter. The cyclorama at the left is one of a pair, one white and one blue—the largest curtains ever manufactured.

tions in the background. Characters on stage, as in real life, naturally turn toward and stay near those they like or trust and keep at a distance from those they dislike. They approach those they want to challenge or relate to and retreat from those who threaten or alienate them. They stand back from action that repels them and hover around that which attracts them. In short, directors arrange stage pictures in the same way people arrange natural relationships in life.

Moving the Action in Time

Moving the play in time is even more important than visualizing it in space, for the dramatic power of a stage picture comes from the way it suggests potential action. To illustrate this idea, imagine one character sitting upstage center, facing

Strong formal lines focus attention on the body at center in this scene from Miller's *A View from the Bridge*, while the narrator (J. Carrol Naish) has secondary focus in the orchestra pit.

front, while all the other characters stand or kneel, spaced around the stage with their body positions and eyes directed toward him. Audience attention will go to the sitting character because of contrast, symmetrical balance, and eye focus. The picture also communicates the power of the focal character and the various levels of subordination that the others feel toward him—the least subordinate character standing at his shoulder, and the most, kneeling abjectly at his feet. The drama in this picture comes, however, from the body language of the seated character, who may be pointing accusingly at the kneeling figures, preparing us for an impending threat, or may be ignoring them, in which case we expect the kneelers to rise to make a more direct appeal or else retreat. If all the standing characters now turn to look at the kneeling figures, this new focus on them seems to demand that they act, either to slink away from the unwanted attention or to rise and turn to the group to take control. Now let's add to this dramatic picture another figure, down right, isolated from the group and leaning casually against a pillar or door jamb. Here is new dramatic potential. The new character appears neither subordinate nor involved. His very posture challenges the order of the rest of the stage picture, and audience attention goes to him expectantly. Will he be drawn in and complete the orderliness, or will he disrupt it? The

Informal scene in naturalistic style in another production of *A View from the Bridge*. Curved lines hold the compact group together. Though the characters are emotionally isolated, the grouping indicates many potential loyalties and conflicts. University of Oregon production, directed by William R. McGraw.

seated figure invites him to approach. No reaction. He repeats the invitation, this time rising. The isolated figure, with surprising energy, straightens up and almost dances halfway in, then abruptly stops and slouches once again. This time the central figure moves grandly toward the defiant one, with arms outstretched in welcome. Suddenly, the defiant figure grasps and shakes the outstretched hands with overzealous gusto, then drops them a shade too quickly and starts circling the entire stage, shaking hands and slapping backs with much too much enthusiasm, working his way up to the now vacated chair, where he flops down, throws one leg over the arm, lights a cigarette, and invites the kneeling figures to come join him in a smoke.

Notice how this little scene, without a word being said, using only stage groupings, posture, and movement, communicates a little drama in itself. The moving picture constantly informs the audience of the changing patterns of relationships and alerts them where to watch for the next action. Notice also how the movement begins slowly, cautiously, becoming quicker and more complex as the scene develops, giving the scene a rising intensity as it builds to its climax. Notice, finally, how the scene comes back to a state of relative calm, with the displaced person now down among his subordinates, perhaps reassessing his position before making an assault upon the usurper or maybe abandoning the field. In either case, the visual patterns have led the audience to expect another encounter between these antagonists, either immediately or in the future, thus helping to move the play in time.

While guiding these larger movements and reactions of the central characters, the director must see to it that all the other characters on stage respond appropriately to the moving scene, by readjusting to the changing picture and by creating little pantomimic reactions. A change in posture, a facial expression, a shake of the head, a knowing smile, the tension of the body, can be more vivid language than speech. When the usurper of the scene just described circles among the crowd shaking everyone's hands, some may pull away with embarrassment or disdain, some may turn their backs, some may look toward another character in confusion, and others may scurry away to avoid contact. Not only will these reactions tell what each character is feeling; they will also add to the energy that is building toward a climax. No actor on stage moves in isolation. The actors are bound in one web of interrelationships as if invisible rubber bands were stretched among them, and each movement is part of a readjustment that affects everyone.

In a scene from Synge's *The Playboy of the Western World*, Christy is reviled by his father, but each actor finds his own way of relating to the dispute between father and son. Brown University, 1982. Directed by Don B. Wilmeth.

The Director as Coach

Just as directors work with many different characters in the play, they work with a wide variety of actors in the rehearsals. The actors begin as separate individuals who often don't even know each other before the first rehearsal. Yet the director must weld them into an ensemble by opening night. Beginning each rehearsal with warm-up exercises helps free the actors from tensions and outside distractions and directs their concentration toward the group effort. But it is in the coaching sessions where the work is done. Directors differ widely in their ways of stimulating the actors' creativity in these sessions. Those who follow the Stanislavsky or Actors Studio methods spend a great deal of time exploring the characters' motivations and searching for experiences from the actors' lives that will evoke appropriate feelings for the characters. American directors acquired a reputation in the 1950s and 1960s for endless discussion sessions about motivation. Many explore motivation, however, by improvising scenes that aren't in the script, to help actors understand the emotions they must bring into the stage scenes that follow. The English director Joan Littlewood used such improvisation to help two actresses feel the weariness of a mother and daughter arriving at their squalid lodgings for the opening scene of *A Taste of Honey*. Miss Littlewood had the two actresses spend an hour dragging heavy suitcases around the stage, trying to get on buses, arguing with landladies, struggling with rain, even imagining they were dragging the suitcases down long, dark, filthy tunnels. They learned how to feel worn out and fretful.

Other directors believe there is nothing like simply rehearsing the play itself. Laurence Olivier expressed his impatience with the American method in an interview for The New York *Times:*

> I'd rather have run the scene eight times than have wasted that time in chattering away about abstractions. An actor gets the right thing by doing it over and over. Arguing about motivations and so forth is a lot of rot. American directors encourage that sort of thing too much. . . . Instead of doing a scene over again that's giving trouble, they want to discuss . . . discuss . . . discuss. . . .

While working the scene, some directors get up on stage with the actors, demonstrating, encouraging, suggesting the effects they want with their own bodies and voices. Others remain out in the auditorium, firing the actors' imaginations with suggestive words or images or barking out commands like a drill sergeant.

Whatever the director's individual method may be, all good directors quickly discover the individual needs of their actors. Some need to be told precisely what to do; others need only the slightest suggestion; still others need to be cajoled, flattered, or even browbeaten to stimulate them to a creative level. The important thing is that during the working rehearsals the director must inspire an atmosphere of high creative energy, where actors and director learn from each

Rehearsing the Hamlet-Laertes fight in Ophelia's grave. *Hamlet*, the Young Vic Company, London, 1979. Directed by Michael Bogdanov; fight director, William Hobbs.

other and feel free to explore, experiment, even fail, as they discover and grow with the play, always guided by the director's vision.

Special rehearsals are needed when scenes require special performance techniques. For a musical, there will be dance rehearsals for the *corps de ballet* and singing rehearsals for the soloists and chorus. Many plays call for activities that, without special training, are dangerous. Learning how to do a believable stage fall while also working on character or memorizing lines is asking for trouble. Even more dangerous are stage fights. Whether for a single punch, a full-blown wrestling match, or a general brawl, the actors must be taught the methods to make the combat believable, yet safe, before staging the scene. Both Cyrano de Bergerac and Hamlet have to fight with swords, and until the actors are well trained in the use of these lethal weapons, they dare not bring them on stage, and then only after they have completely memorized the choreographed fight. Even in the best of circumstances, accidents happen. In a combat scene in one recent professional production, a broadsword suddenly broke loose from its hilt, flew into the audience, and put two people into the hospital. Skimping on the quality of weapons is a dangerous practice.

The Director as Ideal Audience

During the final rehearsals, sets, costumes, lights, properties, and sound effects are added. If the play 's in a period style, the actors have probably been practicing with long rehearsal skirts, fans, walking sticks, and capes for several weeks, but adding new performance elements always creates unexpected problems for actors and technicians alike. The timing of lighting and sound cues, the handling of a door that wasn't there before, the shifting of scenery, the costume and makeup changes, the mustache that suddenly stiffens the upper lip, the wig that covers the ears and muffles the other actors' voices, the heavy boots that have replaced the comfortable sneakers are all new problems to deal with in the technical and dress rehearsals. During these strenuous coordinating rehearsals, the director's eye will be alert to the smallest details of a makeup job that is too ruddy or too pale, a spotlight that is misplaced, a sound effect that is too late or too loud, as well as to the combined effects of the acting with the design elements.

As the technical bugs are worked out, the director takes on the role of the ideal audience member, responding to the uninterrupted flow of the whole play, looking for the overall effect. Is the style maintained consistently? Is the plot clear? Are the characters believable? Do the important ideas come through in words and actions? Is the texture rich and controlled, not too soft or too harsh? And, finally, do all the elements—settings, lighting, movement, tone, words—move together to carry the play to its big climaxes and give it structure and shape? By this time the actor is free to follow without interruption the secret life of the play in the hundred and one little reactions that give the play vitality, ready for one final spark that will set the performance aflame—direct contact with a live audience.

DIRECTING *HAMLET*

With this background in what directors do, let's see how they might apply these skills to *Hamlet*. But first, a little about the play. *Hamlet* was first performed in 1601 by William Shakespeare's company at the Globe Theatre, an open-air theatre with a thrust stage. The play consists of twenty scenes, most of them set in various halls and chambers of the Danish royal court at Elsinore Castle, with two scenes on the castle's battlements, one in a graveyard, and one on the seacoast. It has about two dozen speaking roles, plus lords and ladies of the court, actors, soldiers, sailors, ambassadors, messengers, and attendants.

The story concerns the young Prince Hamlet, who has returned from school at Wittenberg for the funeral of his father, the late King Hamlet, only to be shocked when his mother, Gertrude, remarries, this time her husband's brother, Claudius, the newly crowned king. To make matters worse, Hamlet's father appears to him as a Ghost to tell Hamlet that he had been murdered—by Clau-

A nineteenth-century production of *Hamlet* shows the play-within-the-play. Hamlet (center) watches as King Claudius reacts with guilt to the reenactment of the murder he has done, while a painted scene in the background shows the Player Queen leaving the Player King to his sleep and to his fate.

dius—and he charges Hamlet to avenge his death by killing Claudius. Not only is Claudius now Hamlet's stepfather, he has quickly become a powerful and popular king. Hamlet must act in secret, and so he pretends to go mad.

Madness in a prince, however, cannot be ignored. Soon the whole court is seeking out its cause. The king and queen send for Hamlet's schoolfellows, Rosencrantz and Guildenstern, to observe him and draw him out. Claudius's chief advisor, Polonius, "looses" his daughter, Ophelia, on Hamlet, where he and the king can spy and overhear. Perhaps Hamlet had gone mad when she rejected his love. When that ploy does not work, Polonius hides in the queen's private chamber. Hamlet might tell his mother what no one else can learn.

Meanwhile, Hamlet has done nothing about the revenge, and he doesn't know why. Perhaps he doesn't really believe the Ghost. With all the spying going on, Hamlet decides to do some of his own. He has a troupe of players act a play that parallels the Ghost's story of the murder, and the king's reaction to the play convinces Hamlet that the Ghost was honest. Now he can avenge his father. Alone with his mother, he hears a spy behind the curtain, and thinking that it is the king, he runs him through with his rapier, only to discover that he has killed Polonius instead.

Starting with Sarah Bernhardt in 1899, several women have taken on the role of Hamlet. Here in a New York Shakespeare Festival production, a female Hamlet sits at Ophelia's feet to watch the play within the play.

The king now knows that Hamlet knows he's guilty, so he sends him to England to have him killed. Ophelia, having lost her father at the hand of the man she loves, goes mad and commits suicide. Now her brother, Laertes, plans to kill Hamlet to avenge his father's and his sister's deaths. His chance comes when Hamlet, having escaped his captors, returns to Denmark, and Laertes and Claudius together plot Hamlet's death. They plan a fencing match, but Laertes will use an unbaited sword dipped in poison, and if that plot should fail, Claudius will use a poisoned drink to finish Hamlet off.

Hamlet agrees to the match, believing that Laertes' vengeful cause is a mirror of his own. When it looks as though Hamlet is winning, the queen, elated at her son's success, drinks to his health—from the poisoned cup. Laertes seizes on the distraction and wounds Hamlet when he's not looking. Instantly suspicious, Hamlet disarms his assailant, switches swords, and wounds Laertes with the poisoned tip. Laertes suddenly repents and reveals the plot to Hamlet, who, taking the poisoned sword, runs Claudius through and then pours the remaining drink down Claudius's throat. But Hamlet's wound is fatal, and he dies amidst the carnage in the arms of his friend, Horatio, just as the young Norwegian prince, Fortinbras, arrives to claim the now vacant throne for himself.

The Director's Concept

Though the story is complex, its plot appears on the surface to be simply Hamlet trying to get revenge. Vengeance can be thrilling, but will a modern director and audience find true theatrical excitement in a 400-year-old revenge by a Danish prince? Is that a vision to inspire a production? If we look at the stage history of *Hamlet*, we will find almost as many production concepts as there have been productions, each director finding a new vision in the complex patterns of the play.

One director might start with the famous line, "There's something rotten in the state of Denmark," and see the play as a cleansing process, in which Hamlet is finally sacrificed in order to purify the state. This production would emphasize the revelry, drunkenness, and lust of the characters whenever possible. Another director might decide that Hamlet cannot kill Claudius until he has worked out a conflict with his mother, whom he subconsciously desires, giving special emphasis to Hamlet's jealousy when he sees Claudius and Gertrude together and to his strong attraction to her in their private bedroom scene. Yet another director might want to emphasize the constant "seeming" of the characters, whether it be Claudius seeming to be a good king, Ophelia seeming to have a private conversation with Hamlet, Rosencrantz and Guildenstern seeming to be Hamlet's friends, or Hamlet seeming to be mad. To emphasize the way characters constantly stage events for some effect on other characters, John Gielgud, in the 1960s production that starred Richard Burton, costumed the characters in rehearsal clothes to remind the audience that these were actors playing roles.

Yet another director might look to Shakespeare's own time and notice how Hamlet describes man in terms of the Renaissance ideal: "the paragon of animals . . . how noble in reason, how infinite in faculty, in form, in moving, how express and admirable in action, how like an angel in apprehension, how like a god." But this Hamlet is a disillusioned Renaissance man who concludes by calling this paragon of animals, a "quintessence of dust. Man delights not me." This director will call special attention to Hamlet's searching, particularly in his soliloquies, where he pauses to examine the world around him, as well as his own actions and failure to act, to try to understand this universe that he always thought was orderly and good and now appears to him disorderly, "nothing but a foul and pestilent congregation of vapors." Since even the best-intentioned actions seem to breed corruption, Hamlet must come to understand action itself before he can act. He will at last find for himself an existential answer, in his own internal nature: "The readiness is all."

Still another director might notice that when the play was first produced, in 1601, Elizabeth I was an elderly lady, in poor health, and without an heir. Was

Jon Voight as Hamlet suggests a grieving, disillusioned prince. University of California at Northridge, 1976.

the play speaking to an audience worried about a new power struggle for the English throne? Claudius secretly murders the king, grabs the power while Prince Hamlet is away at school, and then maintains it through incest and spying, while Fortinbras challenges Denmark's borders from abroad. A recent London production depicted Claudius as a crude, power-hungry usurper, more like a mafia chief than a king, playing on the fears of a peace-craving populace to secure his base of power, while Hamlet, without a power base, did nothing but mess things up for the kingdom and himself, leaving the country vulnerable to any petty prince with gall enough to seize the vacant throne.

This production, which was in modern dress, called special attention to the military buildup referred to in Act I, creating the feeling of a police state where any deviation from accepted state policy was dangerous. Soldiers in battle uniform were everywhere; cassette recorders took down what people said; and the women remained politely ignorant of the evil their power-mad husbands and fathers were engaged in, until matters got so bad that Ophelia went mad and Gertrude defied her husband and drank the poison intended for her son. Hamlet, a student and an intellect, had never had to face corruption until the Ghost broke through his philosophical shield and immersed him in reality. By operating secretly, he finally destroyed Claudius, but not without destroying all his loved ones and himself as well. His books, his acting skill, his clever wit failed to equip him with a power base for protection. Thus, Fortinbras, a princely Norwegian opportunist, instantly filled the power gap with a new set of soldiers at the end of the play, just as Claudius had quickly grabbed the crown from his scarcely dead brother when the play began.

This *Hamlet*, altogether different from the earlier ones described, pits a man of thought against a man of action, and in the world of power politics, the man of thought loses—even when he seems to win. This play does not result in the cleansing we often find in theatre of exaltation; a power-mad tyrant is simply replaced with an opportunist, and the innocent are wasted by Hamlet's futile attempts to purify the rotten state.

Perhaps it is now clear why directors cannot simply let the play speak for itself. All the above directing concepts of *Hamlet* are drawn from the same script and all use the revenge structure as central to the play. Yet they take vastly different, sometimes contradictory, views of what the play is saying. Moreover, these concepts of *Hamlet* are only a few among many possible approaches. Each director, in fact, will find a concept unique for each production.

The Production Conference

The design-directing team will work out together such practical details as a floor plan for the stage, the number of sets and costumes, and so forth. But mainly they will devise a style of production that will bring the director's concept to life. For the power-struggle concept just described, they might choose a modern style of formal clothes and institutional structures to suggest to the audience how the characters are controlled by official policy rather than by free choice. If these characters are then surrounded by combat-ready soldiers, the power of official control becomes more formidable. But why a modern style? Would not Elizabethan sets and costumes do the job as well and be truer to the play? Not necessarily. When a modern audience sees combat troops guarding public places with rifles and bayonets, they know instantly that these are extraordinary security measures; whereas Elizabethan soldiers with swords and bucklers might appear to a modern audience simply to be the way things were back then. For the visual to be meaningful, it must be in the visual vocabulary of the audience, and that vocabulary is modern.

For the concept of Hamlet as a disillusioned Renaissance man, the design-directing team might set the play in a Tudor castle, but make that castle into a maze of arches, pillars, and platforms, with specific areas occasionally defined by a throne, a bed, an altar, only to shift and disappear once more into the maze. With this approach, the two scenes that occur away from the castle achieve a clarity that contrasts sharply with the bewildering world of the maze: the open seacoast shows Fortinbras moving toward decisive action; and the empty grave-yard reveals to Hamlet how useless are his efforts to control the world through his actions. Mostly, this maze metaphor reinforces how much the characters need to find some solid base for their actions and beliefs, only to be thwarted constantly by a world shrouded in mystery and secrecy. Each style is a kind of visual metaphor for the action. Each concept requires a different visual experience, and each visual experience gives dimension to the concept and to the play. But now we need actors to give the play its life.

Casting and Rehearsing *Hamlet*

The director's concept also guides the casting, for it is actors who make the show live in the theatre, and each concept has different casting needs. For the power struggle, the actor playing Claudius need not be likable, but he must appear decisive and ruthless, someone you wouldn't want to cross, while Hamlet may appear intellectual and refined, but out of touch with reality and, finally, inef-fectual. Claudius must appear the stronger of the two or the concept will be lost.

The roles will be more evenly matched for those concepts which emphasize the characters' "seeming" to be what they are not, since the action may become almost a cat-and-mouse game between Claudius and Hamlet. For the actor play-ing Hamlet, physical qualities are less important than his ability to draw the audience's natural sympathy while appearing to be a defiant and even somewhat spoiled intellectual brat. An actor with a sense of contained energy about to erupt might give the right combination of brooding thoughtfulness and impetuous behavior. The actor playing Claudius, on the other hand, must instill confidence as a responsible and generous leader, yet make the audience aware of how devi-ous and truly dangerous he is when anyone gets in his way. A beautiful and innocent Ophelia should also convey a strong need to please, while her father, Polonius, instead of simply being old and senile, might be the best character to express the humorless attitudes of officialdom. Laertes is a devoted son, but as a headstrong youth he can provide a better contrast to Hamlet's indecision.

Staging *Hamlet*: The Use of Space and Time

Before actually staging the play, the director carefully analyzes the play's struc-ture in relation to his concept. The analysis will tell where the builds and cli-maxes occur, where tension is relaxed or pace increased, but mostly it will tell how each scene or dramatic unit contributes to the overall effect and how each relates to the others. In *Hamlet* the scene division calls attention to the rhythmic patterns of the dramatic units. A director will notice, for example, how three big court scenes, spaced evenly through the play, bring Hamlet and Claudius into public confrontation: Claudius's very orderly first court is disrupted by Hamlet's

Sword play in *Hamlet* as Hamlet (George Grizzard) takes on Laertes in their final match, while the Queen (Jessica Tandy) looks on. The Guthrie Theatre, 1963, directed by Sir Tyrone Guthrie.

dissension early in the play; then in the middle of the play everyone comes to see the supposedly mad Hamlet present a play that annoys the king and shakes up the whole court; at the very end, Claudius arranges a fencing match and Hamlet's murder, which destroys himself and all his allies. In contrast to these big court scenes, Hamlet's soliloquies, his private attempts to understand and come to terms with his own feelings and his revenge, are spaced neatly through the play. These are interspersed with many intimate scenes where characters try to influence another person's actions: Polonius and Laertes warn Ophelia about Hamlet; the Ghost urges Hamlet to avenge his death; Polonius sends Reynaldo to spy on Laertes in France; Hamlet urges his mother to abandon the king; Claudius contrives with Laertes to murder Hamlet; and so on. Each scene has its own rhythm, its own mood, even its own sound, while together they create an overall rhythm that eventually brings the antagonists into direct conflict in the final scene.

Now the director is ready to block the play, to control its action in time and space. One scene from *Hamlet* will serve to demonstrate the effects that can be achieved from different blocking patterns. Act I, Scene 2, the first court scene, provides a good example. Let's first imagine the stage to be a large open space surrounded by huge arches and pillars. Down right a wide curved staircase descends through an archway to the stage floor, and up center, slightly to the left, two thrones stand on a raised dais. As the scene opens, the stage fills with members of the court gaily greeting each other, but with no one taking focus. Two trumpeters at the top of the staircase play a fanfare, drawing everyone's attention to them, then step aside, revealing the new king with his bride. Though they are not at stage center, the royal pair, announced and then framed by the trumpeters, command atttention, but they keep attention by their elevation above everyone else and by the eye focus directed toward them by all the other characters. From this position, Claudius thanks the court for approving his marriage. Only then do he and the queen move down among the crowd, amiably passing among their subjects toward the thrones. Now Claudius takes the sceptre of office from the hand of Polonius and gives his "state of the union" address from the throne, explaining the threat to their borders from Fortinbras and dispatching two ambassadors to take care of the problem, while all the court focus on him, come to him when bidden, and leave when dismissed. All action revolves around this central focus.

Meanwhile, someone else has taken secondary focus. As Claudius and Gertrude descend, a young man appears on the staircase, his black clothing in sharp contrast to the brilliant array of the assembled court. Instead of sharing the enthusiasm of the crowd, this brooding youth leans against a pillar near the top of the staircase, challenging the mood by his very presence. Though he has no lines, stands in a weak stage position, unnoticed by the other characters, this new figure commands attention because of his elevation, his isolation, and his demeanor, so different from that of the rest of the court. This new character, of course, is Hamlet. Nevertheless, the attention he commands would be a mere distraction unless it were dramatically important, that is, unless it caused the audience to anticipate some action from his defiant appearance. But long before he joins the action, the audience senses his dramatic importance from the staging alone and waits expectantly for the disruption his presence portends.

When at last he is spoken to, Hamlet descends the stairs, but not to approach the throne. Instead, the king and queen, in order to put on a good show of family unity, have to come to him. So the anticipated conflict between the king on his raised throne at up left center and Hamlet mounted on the staircase down right finally comes to a head when the two meet at floor level midway between their two points of vantage. Then, if Hamlet moves right past the king toward his mother, he may even force Claudius to pursue him. But, no! After a moment's reflection, Claudius steps back up onto his dais to lecture this upstart in a kingly manner, forcing the prince to listen, though he chooses to remain apart. If Gertrude joins her husband, the reprimand will appear even stronger. In this way, the moving picture continuously keeps the audience alert to the changing patterns of relationships among the characters. At last the king and queen get Hamlet to agree not to return to school, then quickly break up the court and depart amidst great fanfare, leaving Hamlet alone in the vast emptied space to feel the loneliness in his first soliloquy. Nothing has been resolved by the conflict, for the king with his entire court retreats to sustain the illusion of a Pyrrhic victory, and Hamlet, though he holds the stage, appears lost and abandoned in its vast space. Thus, the physical action combined with the emotional content of the scene prepares the audience to look toward the next encounter between these adversaries, helping to move the play in time.

All the other characters on stage also contribute to the flow of the moving scene, by readjusting to the changing picture and by creating their own pantomimic reactions. Polonius may nod approvingly as Claudius returns to his dais and then emulate his king's stance in opposing the prince; various courtiers may move discreetly out of the way when Hamlet comes too near, not wanting to appear to share his defiance; Ophelia may move toward him sympathetically, only to be restrained by Laertes, preparing us for the warning he is to give her in the next scene; and all the crowd will remain tensely hushed, awaiting the hoped-for reconciliation between the uncle-king and the defiant prince. When Claudius declares that it has happened, they will relax, smile, clasp hands, chatter happily, perhaps even applaud, and follow the royal couple lightheartedly from the room.

For a second staging of the scene, let's place a large banquet table at center stage, with the thrones up center in the place of honor and a conspicuously empty chair beside the queen's throne. As the curtain opens, the celebration is in full swing. Toasts with goblets of wine, rousing fanfares, and cheering from the crowd greet Claudius's introduction of his bride. The ambassadors are dispatched with another toast and more cheers, showing a drunken confidence in their mission. Hamlet, when he appears, will enter from the side, but without the staircase elevation, he will not command attention; he will simply look out of place in his black clothes and solemn mood. Gertrude will whisper to Claudius that Hamlet is present, and Claudius's first words to him will be another toast, as a servant offers Hamlet a goblet of wine. Instead of leaving his throne, Claudius will use the festive spirit of the crowd to try to draw Hamlet into the party atmosphere, always smiling and amiable, always inviting the court to share his jovial mood. At last, when everyone leaves, Hamlet will use the leavings from the banquet table to point up his disgust at his mother's corruption and the world he now inhabits.

Now let's try a third approach. The thrones will be directly up center once again, but this time high above the crowd, with steps descending in all directions to the floor below. Two formal doorways, with armed guards, flank the thrones. Through one doorway Polonius enters and silences the crowd. Then the king and queen make their formal entrance through the other door and take their place before the thrones. When any contact need be made with those below, Polonius takes the dispatch from the king, hands it to a guard, who conveys it to the waiting character. Only the royal party and the guards may approach the upper level, and soldiers spaced formidably around the stage are a stern reminder of the rules. No one but the king and queen sit down, except for one lone figure down left, Hamlet, sitting on a stool almost out of sight, his head resting against a pillar as though he is very tired. Even when spoken to, he does not rise, not until his mother speaks to him. Then it is in anger, and he starts up the steps accusingly. The guards are suddenly alert, but Claudius stops them with a gesture and invites Hamlet to approach. That stops Hamlet. Gertrude takes a step down toward her son, and Claudius rises to demonstrate his concern, but only leaves the area of the throne to draw Gertrude back toward him. Hamlet remains stranded, resisting the invitations, unable to launch an attack, disruptive but ineffectual, finally subdued by his mother's request to stay with them in Denmark. At the end of the scene, he remains on the steps, neither up nor down, hopelessly bewildered by his lack of power.

Pulling It All Together

During the final run-throughs, the costumes, makeup, lights, and sound will spur the actors to new energy, as they begin to feel the rhythm of the play and sense the sustained building of the action toward its climax. The director remains in the auditorium, taking scrupulous notes on all the little details still needed for final polishing. But mainly he notices the overall effect—where things are too drawn out, where they are rushed, where more energy is needed. He knows that pacing a show is not a matter of speed; it is precision in each important moment and the anticipation of the next; it is the variety of impressions reaching the audience and a clear connection between those impressions and others already received. The director's notes to the actors and technicians will help them learn where to accelerate, where to slow down, where to intensify, and where to mute, until they are ready to share their joint creation with an audience. At that point, the director's job is done. Though he may continue to make suggestions and even major changes between performances, once the stage lights come up each night, the show is no longer his. It is a living experience between the audience, the actors, and the play. It will end each night with the final curtain, but if the director's job was well done, it will be ready for a rebirth for each new audience, night after night for its entire run.

For an entirely different approach to directing *Hamlet*, several sources exist, but none more complete than *Minneapolis Rehearsals: Tyrone Guthrie Directs "Hamlet,"* by Alfred Rossi, University of California Press, 1970. The book is a record of the production that opened the famous Guthrie Theatre in 1963, with George Grizzard in the title role. Rossi, who played Rosencrantz as well as serving as assistant to the director, kept a complete rehearsal log. The book includes the log, a complete prompt script, excellent photographs, costume drawings, and reviews.

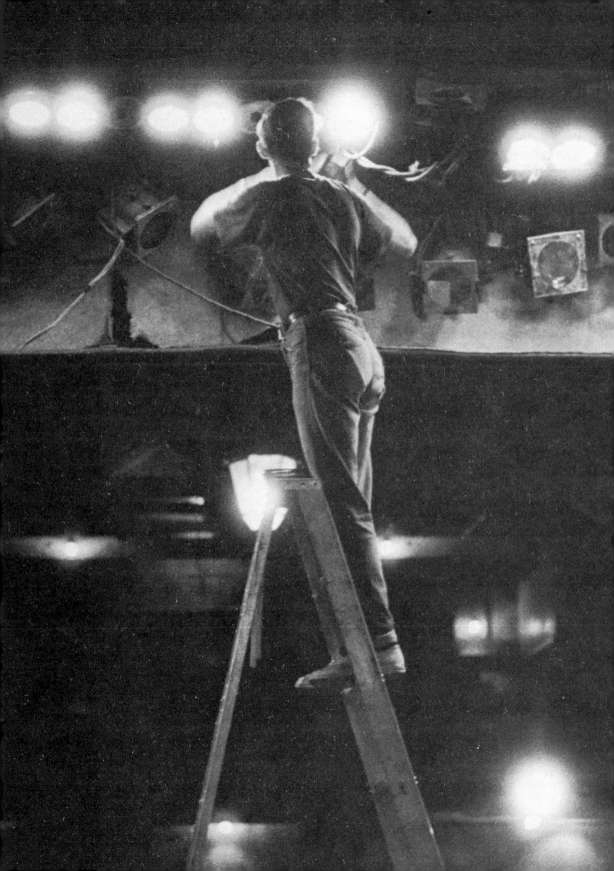

DESIGNING
THE PRODUCTION
13

The illusion on stage is created as much by the
spotlights which audiences never see as it is by
the visible setting.

*T*heatrical productions, especially in the commercial theatre of Broadway, are often lavish affairs, with glittering costumes, moving scenery, modulating lights, stereophonic sound, and special effects that range from breakaway furniture, lightning bolts, and thunder crashes to flying bats, moving trains, actual rain and fog, and—for the mountain-climbing play *K2*—an avalanche. At the other extreme, actors may create the play in street clothes, under natural sunlight on the "bare boards" of an "empty space." In either case, the choice is "by design," a conscious effort to provide an appropriate environment for the action of the play.

People create environments in life also, businesslike for the office and "homey" for the house or apartment. Every dormitory resident immediately sets out to add that personal touch to make the room "livable." To study, we surround ourselves with background music and comfortable cushions or else clear the desk, adjust the lamp, and purify the space of all distractions. To relax, we may seek a quiet spot beside a brook, a dimly lighted coffee house, or a noisy disco. We choose our clothes for the event, for our age and sex, and to comply with or defy the conventions that fashions dictate.

STAGE DESIGN AND THEATRICAL ILLUSION

All of these design choices, common to daily living, are much like design choices in the theatre, but with one fundamental difference. The stage design, like the stage character, is illusion. The mountain vista is a painted backdrop; the stately marble columns are constructed out of styrofoam and end just above the proscenium opening; the intimate bedroom atmosphere is actually lit by several thousand watts of light to make actors' faces visible to the upper balcony; and the Dior original wedding dress is held together by velcro seams so that the actress can make a 45-second costume change into a tennis outfit for the honeymoon scene that follows. All the audience sees is the illlusion of atmosphere, not atmosphere itself. So we have the first principle of theatrical design, one that is taken so much for granted that designers rarely speak of it. Theatrical designers don't create real atmosphere for those who inhabit the stage; they create the illusion of atmosphere for those who view it from the audience. Theatregoers on a first visit backstage will be instantly startled by the contrast from the magical illusion out front to the tawdry reality of the frayed drops, the makeup-stained costumes, and the chipped paint on the set, and even more startled behind the set by the stage braces propping up the canvas-covered light wooden frames that appeared from out front to be the heavy stone walls of a castle. Like the little child who goes behind the movie screen to see where all the people are, backstage novices will hunt in vain on that empty set for the atmosphere they had experienced from their seats in the auditorium. It isn't there; what's more it never was—only the illusion of the atmosphere was there, shaped by the set, enhanced by distance, dressed out by props and costumes, transformed by light, and animated by the skills of actors.

The style of any particular design is determined by the kind of illusion that is sought, and the history of design reflects the different kinds of illusions that different periods believed important. In Shakespeare's open-air theatre, for example, no lights could be used to adjust the mood. The few props (a throne, a spear, a bed, a lantern) simply suggested place and time, and the costumes, though often very grand, were mostly the fashions of Shakespeare's own time, even when the play was about ancient Greeks or Romans. The illusion was frankly a thing of the imagination created through the playwrights' words and the actors' skills. By the nineteenth century, theatrical fashion had gone to the opposite extreme. Permanent indoor theatres, gas lights, perspective painting, and the general fascination of the nineteenth century with industrial inventions and historical study made the stage a place to create pictures of life in the romantic theatre or reconstructions of life in the naturalistic theatre. Elaborately painted backdrops (often of actual places) and authentic costumes told the audience they were in ancient, medieval, or modern times, in Spain or China, prince's palace or peasant's kitchen, summer garden or winter snow. Whether the play was a comedy or tragedy, satire or fantasy, the designers brought on stage the "accu-

Painted backdrops help place the audience in an enchanted woodland in Charles Kean's production of *A Midsummer Night's Dream* at the Princess Theatre, 1856.

racy" of careful research. Going to the theatre was as important a way of learning facts as a guided tour through a museum or a social survey of how the other half lives. The designer was glad enough if the illusion included mood, but mood was a byproduct, secondary to the illusion of actual time and place.

The Expressive Function of Design

In the modern theatre, "environment" is the key word. Design is not decoration: it is an integral part of the movement of the play. The illusion often includes specific details of a period or locale, but mood and atmosphere, spaces for moving actors, and the visual progression of an idea assume at least equal importance. Many modern designs do not indicate place at all but present imaginative atmospheric abstractions or arrangements of pipes, ramps, platforms, and steps. In 1899 Adolphe Appia, in one of the most influential of all theatre books, *Music and the Art of the Theatre*, distinguished the "expressive" from the "symbolizing" functions in theatre art. He maintained that the symbolizing details that indicate a particular locale should be kept to a minimum—just enough to orient the audience, as a signboard might—in order to allow the expressive functions of open or interrupted space to have free play. By 1919 Kenneth MacGowan had defined the aims of this "new stagecraft" as simplification, suggestion, and synthesis: simplification to get rid of all ornament that might distract attention from the actor; suggestion to evoke a mood by simple means—"a single Saracenic arch can do more than a half dozen to summon the passionate background of Spanish *Don Juan*"; and synthesis to create a unity and consistency whereby actor, setting, lights, and action would express the essential quality of the play and would change as the play progressed.

Theatre Space and Illusion

From 1900 to 1930, the German director Max Reinhardt popularized the notion that the desired illusion, different for every play, could be enhanced by the total environment of actors and audience. He built several theatres of different sizes and shapes to provide the proper atmosphere, ranging from a chamber theatre (Kammerspiele) that seated three hundred to the Grosses Schauspielhaus, called the "theatre of five thousand," for vast productions of Greek and Shakespearean tragedies and German romantic dramas. He also experimented with non-theatre spaces, doing the medieval morality play *Everyman* on the steps of the Salzburg Cathedral and the Greek trilogy *Oresteia* in the Circus Schumann in Berlin. Others sought the desired illusion by reconstructing theatres of the past or by redoing theatre interiors to simulate the audience-performer relationship that may have existed in Shakespeare's Globe Theatre, a Greek amphitheatre, or a commedia dell'arte street performance.

Two different results grew out of the experimentation with audience-actor relationships. First, the rediscovery of old forms of theatre popularized the *thrust* or *apron* stage and the *arena* or *theatre-in-the-round*. Second, in the period of exper-

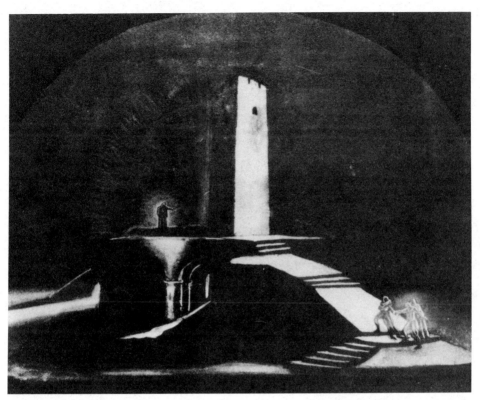

Lee Simonson's design for *Hamlet* shows an abstract structure of ramps, stairs, planes, and vertical shapes designed for actors' movement and molded by plastic light.

imental liberation of the 1960s, many young rebels found their greatest adventures in using a "found" place for their productions. No matter if there were no comfortable seats—the adventurous audience could stand or sit on the floor or on part of the platforms and steps used by the actors. All the better if the place were a run-down warehouse or garage. The environment could unite audience and actor in one room. Though the novelty of "slumming it" quickly wore off, the flexibility of the found space has been incorporated into our theatre institutions through an experimental room, sometimes called "the little black box," where playing structures can be built and chairs for the audience rearranged in many different ways, as in the photos on pages 291 and 387. It can have good sound and lighting equipment, and best of all a floor cut up in modules which can be lowered or raised to different levels by the touch of a button, between scenes or even during the performance.

One great advantage of the *arena stage*, with audience on all four sides, is that if brings the actor and the audience very close together, contributing to the illusion of intimacy. The ground plans on page 370 show that the last row of an

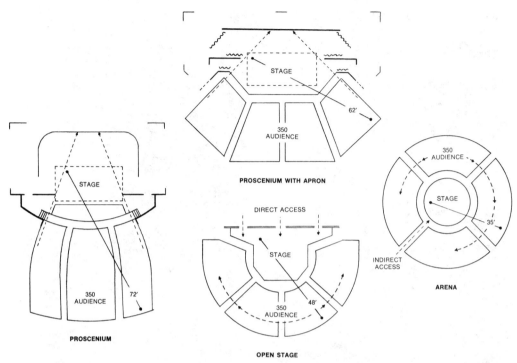

Ground plans showing the relative distance of the last row of an audience of 350 from the actor in four kinds of theatre—regular proscenium, proscenium with apron, thrust or open stage, and arena. Drawn by Don Creason after a drawing by James Hull Miller.

audience of 350 will be more than twice as close to the actors in an arena theatre as in a proscenium type. When Glenn Hughes started the in-the-round movement for college theatres at the University of Washington in the 1930s, he planned his arena primarily for drawing-room comedy, with only three rows of seats—170 in all—and a playing area little larger than a 12-by-18 foot carpet. Today varying sizes of arena theatres across the country are used to create intimacy for almost any kind of play ever written. Though it has four times the seating capacity of Hughes's tiny Penthouse Theatre, the splendid Arena Stage in Washington, D.C. still has only eight rows seats.

Though no walls may come between the acting area and the audience, a surprising amount of scenery is possible in theatre-in-the-round. Low hedges, fences, or fireplaces can give a touch of local color below the line of sight, as on page 372, and lightweight scenic elements may hang from above. At the side or corner entrances, realistic segments of walls, windows, and doors may be used when the action requires them, and light frames or columns, arches, and pavilions can be outlined in the center, yet not interfere with the audience's vision.

The Penthouse Theatre at the University of Washington, one of the first theatres designed for arena staging.

The *thrust stage*, with audience on three sides of the playing area, retains the illusion of intimacy because nothing separates actor from audience, but more elaborate scenic effects are possible than in the arena. It may be used almost like an arena, as the Guthrie Theatre in Minneapolis did for *The Three Sisters*, with both the living room and dining room furniture in place on the forestage, while window seats suggested walls. But the most interesting challenges in designing for a thrust stage come in the possibilities offered by the relationship of the playing space to the wall that rises behind it. The wall may be nothing more than a set of drapes or a painted backdrop that suggests a story-telling quality to the action in front of it; it may be a complex structure of permanent-looking columns, arches, doors, windows, or balconies, which give the characters a solid sense of place yet allow them to move out onto the open platform and relate directly to the audience for asides, soliloquies, and monologues; or it may be a three-dimensional structure of steps, platforms, and arches, or of plastic shapes that extends out into the playing area, tying everything together as one architectural unit for the actors to walk on, around, under, or through in ever-changing patterns of pictures and movement. The Guthrie Theatre's 1976 production of *King Lear* used plastic forms of stonelike levels and terraces, which, combined with the

A thrust stage used like an arena, with a fence defining the yard of the shanty home in O'Neill's *A Moon for the Misbegotten*. Dirt on the floor, a working pump, and a front porch actually taken from a dismantled house lend the realistic touches while the fence, bench, and tree stump provide seating spaces out on the thrust as in an arena theatre. Directed by Fred R. Miller, designed by Junius Hamblin.

costumes of animal skin and homespun, created the illusion of a primitive world that matched the raw emotional power of Lear's passion. The upper terraces and niches commanded a sense of power and control, while the lower levels thrust the characters out into the midst of the audience, exposed and vulnerable.

The *proscenium* stage, the standard Western form since the early Renaissance, gives the designer the most control over the entire illusion. It puts the actor within or directly in front of a framed picture. The setting, lights, and costumes within the picture create both mood and style, while shaping the movement and action of the whole play. The proscenium stage was invented to create a picture-like setting. It conceals the machinery for changing scenes and frames the picture, enhancing the illusion that the world of the picture is a complete world of which the audience sees only the portion set off within the frame. But over the years, almost every kind of theatrical style has found a home on the proscenium stage. Platforms or runways have been extended out into the house to give the feeling of a thrust stage, as was done in the 1980 Broadway production of *Pirates of Penzance*. For *Equus,* audience were seated on the stage behind the acting area to give the feeling of an arena, while *Evita* achieved something of an environmental effect with huge murals of Argentinian workers surrounding the audience area, though no actors came into the audience or invited the audience onto the stage, as was done in *Hair* a few years earlier.

Hence designers today must consider four possible patterns of scenic environments for the illusion they want to create. Their problem differs according to whether they are putting the audience in the same space as the actor, seeking the intimacy of an arena theatre, striking a combination of direct contact and theatrical illusion of the thrust stage, or building a complete scenic picture back of a proscenium.

THE DESIGNER AT WORK

The first step in creating any design is total familiarity with the play script, so that the designer can enter the first production conference ready to share ideas and to respond creatively to the director's concept. The designer is often as influential in determining the production concept as the director. Though directors usually know the kinds of effects they want their production to achieve, the designers are their main resource for the visual means to create those effects. So the first production conference is usually to share ideas, identify problems, and propose possible solutions to those problems.

Let's say the play we're doing is Shakespeare's *Troilus and Cressida*, a play that is set during the Trojan war. The director wants to draw a sharp contrast between the rough, uncouth Greek warriors in their encampment outside the walls of Troy and the sophisticated but decadent Trojans in their banquet halls

The elegance of the Trojan courtiers with their gracefully draped costumes contrasts with the rudeness of the short, stark tunics of the Greek soldiers in Shakespeare's *Troilus and Cressida* at the University of Texas. Directed by B. Iden Payne, costumes by Paul D. Reinhardt.

and bed chambers. At the same time she wants a fast-flowing pace that moves quickly between the two contrasting groups and at last joins them in violent battle. The rapid movement of the action back and forth does not permit a change of sets each time, and so a single set must be designed which can be transformed by lights and costumes. The set designer proposes a downstage neutral area on a flat floor, behind which stark-lined leaning columns and angular platforms recede in criss-cross patterns toward the rear of the stage, creating a labyrinth of arches and passageways. The costume designer suggests costuming the Greeks in leather armor, with short tunics and capes of dark heavy fabrics trimmed in animal hair and fur, while the Trojans wear white and pastel silks and linens, with full-length robes and capes trimmed delicately in gold and silver. Their armor should be metallic, perhaps jeweled, with helmets topped by bright feathers. The lighting designer now describes how the Greek encampment can be staged in the downstage neutral space and the lighting confined to a campfire-like color in that area, while the upstage illumination creates huge angular shadows among the leaning columns to suggest the imposing walls of the enemy city. For the Trojan scenes, bright lights flood the whole stage from the front, highlighting the bright costumes and creating a feeling of confident superiority among the Trojans. For the famous battle scene, the frontal lights are killed and side lighting cuts across and behind the columns, as multiple groups of soldiers are seen battling, running, carrying the wounded in a criss-crossing pattern that now makes it almost impossible to distinguish Greek from Trojan, lost in the maze of war's destruction. The red lights of a burning city begin to glow amid the most distant arches as smoke starts to fill the space. At last, the smoke settles, and harsh white lights from overhead show the Trojan survivors, their spirit crushed and their beautiful costumes filthy and in tatters. Director, lighting designer, costumer, and set designer have joined their creative imaginations in putting together a production concept that can bring *Troilus and Cressida* to life, one very similar to that used in the Royal Shakespeare Company production at Stratford-on-Avon in 1976.

Working Out the Details

With a production concept settled, the design process now begins. Rather than looking at the steps of the process, which will vary from one design and designer to the next, we might better look at the functional needs of production that the designers are trying to satisfy.

Meet the technical demands of the production. Unless a design is, first of all, *functional*, it is not a good design. An architect designs an office building for its functions, with an appropriate ratio of offices to conference rooms to supply closets, rest rooms, and lounges, and clear access to the areas of most traffic. A designer of sporting goods studies the kind of activity that the sport involves, providing padding where violent contact is expected, extra fabric or stitching in areas of stress, and a loose or snug fit for the freest movement of the limbs.

Similarly the theatre designer determines the functional needs of the play. How many sets or costumes are needed? Will the changes be made during an act break, or must the sets be changed in full view of the audience during a musical bridge, while the costume change occurs backstage with less than a minute before the actress's next entrance? If twenty dancers have to appear on stage while the orchestra plays two measures of music, a single narrow entrance will not do. If a scene calls for three separate entrances, a stairway, and a window-box, the designer has to include all those in the design. If an actor is to conceal a weapon on his person, fall down a flight of stairs, appear in a later scene as a different character, take off or put on part of a garment on stage, the costumes must be designed with those needs in mind. Similarly, the lighting designer must know whether there will be night scenes as well as daylight scenes, indoor as well as outdoor scenes. Will the entire stage be lit uniformly or must parts of it be in darkness while other areas are brightly lit? What practical lights are on stage—such as candles or fireplaces—or what special effects, such as moonlight shining through a window or a character in silhouette?

For the answers to such questions, the designers have two resources: the play script, which they study with careful attention to all the technical needs revealed in the lines, the action, or the stage directions, and the director, who lets them know about any special staging methods or bits of business that depend on the design. Perhaps the director has worked out a bit of business where a character hides behind a door while she overhears a plot against her. Not knowing about this plan, the set designer may have built the door to open out, away from the stage, rather than on stage. Either the business must now be abandoned or the door rebuilt, wasting precious time and money. Or during rehearsals, an actor decides it would be funny for his character to hide under another character's cloak. If no one bothers to tell the costumer about this business, the cloak, if there is one, might be too small.

Provide information to the audience. Audiences often depend on visual details for such basic facts about the play as historical period, nationality, time of day, weather, and social status of the characters. Architectural detail will help set the play in rural Ireland or in southern California, in a fifteenth-century Danish castle, or a 1920s New England farmhouse. Lights can indicate late afternoon, dawn, or night, besides suggesting the gloom of a rainy day or bright sunshine. Costumes remind us if a character is a servant or a lady, a medieval knight or a 1950s rock-and-roll singer, but give a character raincoat and galoshes or an overcoat and muffler and the costume also suggests the weather or time of year. In order to provide such detail, designers devote the early stages of design to research, reading about fashions and fabrics, looking at paintings, old catalogues, the architecture and decor of old buildings, and studying the construction of period furniture, garments, tools, and weapons. In a completely realistic production, these are the details that give the play authenticity, and some sharp-eyed audience member is sure to notice any oversight, such as a 1920s American boy wearing long pants instead of knickers or a modern hardware store broom in a colonial kitchen. A careful designer also acts as a conscience for the director in such matters of detail. In rehearsal it may have seemed like a great idea to hide one character under another's cloak, but the costumer is likely to say "no," because that kind of character would never have worn a cloak in that period or country. The really inventive designer may come up with an alternative idea, equally funny, and in period. Even nonrealistic productions often use selected details from a period or country as suggestive clues for the audience. A Grecian column, a Tudor throne, or a Japanese kimono may be just the kind of detail needed to set the period and locale.

Reinforce the mood of each scene or the play as a whole. The ancient Greeks and Romans are said to have costumed their tragic heroes in long robes and buskins (high leather boots) and their comic characters in short tunics and socks or slippers. Any costume designer today also distinguishes between the line and weight of a tragic or comic costume. A long flowing line to the costume, deep colors, and fabrics that drape well lend dignity, whereas crisp fabrics, pas-

Two costumes for women in mourning. Based on the same period, one is designed for tragedy and one for romantic comedy. Soft flowing lines and heavy corduroy convey the dignity and sorrow of Lady Anne in Shakespeare's *Richard III*, while the shiny taffeta bodice and skirt, the crisp glittering sleeves, and the low decolletage suggest that bright energy is more important than mourning for Lady Olivia in Shakespeare's *Twelfth Night*. Costumes by Paul D. Reinharhdt.

tels, and fussy detail suggest comedy to the audience. Color, weight, and line are equally important to the set designer. For comedy, curving lines, delicate decorations, and bright colors are the norm, while tragedy calls for stark lines, sharp angles, deep or muted colors, and simple decoration. For the quick action of farce, many pieces of furniture help to create lots of short abrupt movements, as well as circular patterns around, over, and under the furniture, while a serious scene may require the dignity of long straight movements, uninterrupted by objects that get in the way. The lighting designer in comedy will often flood the stage with pinks and yellows, and for tragedy, use strong accents of blue shadows or pools of colorless light that isolate one character from another. Within the play, whether in comedy or tragedy, some scenes may call for light or heavy moods, and so the designs must allow for variation in mood as the show moves from scene to scene.

Early in this century, Gordon Craig, in a famous passage from his book *On the Art of the Theatre,* suggested how one might go about creating mood in a scene design for *Macbeth:*

> I see two things. I see a lofty and steep rock, and I see the moist cloud which envelops the head of this rock. That is to say, a place for fierce and warlike men to inhabit, a place for phantoms to nest in. Ultimately the moisture will destroy the rock; ultimately these spirits will destroy the men. Now then, you are quick in your question as to what actually to create for the eye. I answer as swiftly—place there a rock! Let it mount high. Swiftly I tell you, convey the idea of a mist which hugs the head of this rock. . . .
>
> But you ask me what form this rock shall take and what color? What are the lines which are the lofty lines, and which are to be seen in any lofty cliff? Go to them, glance but a moment at them: now quickly set them down on your paper; *the lines and their direction,* never mind the cliff. Do not be afraid to let them go high; they cannot go high enough; and remember that on a sheet of paper which is but two inches square you can make a line which seems to tower miles in the air, and you can do the same on the stage, for it is a matter of proportion and nothing to do with actuality.
>
> You ask about the colors? What are the colors that Shakespeare has indicated for us? Do not first look at Nature, but look in the play of the poet. Two; one for the rock, the man; one for the mist, the spirit.

Craig completes his description by warning that it is no mere picture independent of actors. "You have to consider that at the base of the rock swarm the clans of strange earthly forces, and that in the mist hover the spirits innumerable . . . clearly separate from the human and more material beings."

Slight variations among the design elements can swiftly alter a mood. In the first London production of *Waiting for Godot,* a flat, featureless landscape with a forlorn stick of a tree jutting from it left the two tramps in their shapeless suits and bowler hats desolate, alone in an empty universe. In a University of Iowa production, bright-colored puffs of smoke from behind the earth-banks punctuated every pause. That universe was not empty at all: a bright demon was just out of sight, laughing at mankind.

Assist the actors in projecting their characters. Though all the designers help the actors project their characters, the costumer has the most obvious role in this function of design. The costume, more than any other element, helps many actors get into character. Looking in a mirror, the actor gets a vision of what he is supposed to be; he must live up to that vision. The costume and makeup are like a mask that the actor puts on, not to hide the identity, as sophisticated socialites might do going to a masked ball, but to embody the identity, as in primitive societies. Like the primitive tribesman, the actor must put on his *persona*, or mask, before he can become the personality to play his role.

After long hours of perfecting a character's gestures, stance, and movement, the actor dons the costume as the final embodiment, confident that the audience will believe the character to be a dashing lover, a beggar, a brassy barmaid, or a kind old grandmother. Costumes also help the actor change and grow through the show. The shabby, hard-working clerk of the first act becomes a well-dressed corporation president in the second. Audiences love the sudden transformation of Miss Gooch in *Mame*, from a dumpy secretary in a plain gray suit, horn-rimmed glasses, a bun hair-do, and sensible shoes to a flamboyant sparkling woman in a red flaring dress, dancing pumps, and flying hair. Her next appearance in a maternity smock simply adds to the comedy. It plays ironically off from the earlier images and seals Gooch's character for actress and audience alike.

In movement the actor soon learns why the designer gave him a cape or a long sleeve. As he turns his shoulders, lifts an elbow, or raises an arm, the cape or sleeve sweeps on beyond, extending the movement and accenting it. The longer and heavier the cape, the slower the sweep. That extra material is not a hindrance but a tool. The actress learns to give her full skirt a swing that expresses the character and just what she is thinking. A cane, a pipe, or an umbrella in the hand becomes a telling extension of the personality, and no one has exhausted the possibilities of the fan for indicating changes of thought or feeling. Nothing pleases costumers more than watching an actor or actress find the many possibilities for expression that the costumes afford.

Scene and lighting designs are equally helpful in projecting character. Whether realistic or abstract, every good design is a kind of machine for action, and all good actors quickly learn how to play the hot spots and the angles of the lights, how to use the platforms, doors, and furniture to point a line or to express emotion, and how to take command in the open spaces or seek the shelter of a quiet niche. An open arch or doorway becomes a frame for an important announcement or for surprised bewilderment, a soft divan a place to recline in luxurious idleness or invite a friend for a cozy chat, a staircase a machine for effecting a grand entrance or a bumbling exit. A pillar can give strength to the hero who stands boldly beside it in a shaft of light, or it can overwhelm Eliza Doolittle, crouched in the shadows at its base.

Lowly Eliza Doolittle (Julie Andrews) sits at the base of the pillar, while Henry Higgins (Rex Harrison) leans on it with authority in the first scene of *My Fair Lady*.

Provide a visually pleasing and interesting design. In one sense, the designer is like the painter working with the principles of spatial composition. The setting should be pleasing to look at, unified and in balance. Except in very special cases, perfect symmetry is not recommended, but rather the more interesting patterns of asymmetrical balance, with a stage-right staircase balanced by a stage-left pillar, or a piano placed up left balanced by a fireplace or a set of French doors down right. If the stage must be split down the middle, with two separate sets on either side, as in Neil Simon's *Chapter Two*, some architectural feature such as a roof line or complementary color schemes or balanced placement of furniture in the decor should tie them together. The costumes also give unity and harmony to the visual picture through color, line, and texture. They relate closely to the setting yet must stand out from the background. The costumes must look good together, and they must be so planned that in large scenes the colors are well distributed. Yet they must control the spread of attention, indicating which are subordinate characters and which important, which ones relate to each other and which are in conflict. Balanced lighting must give depth

An extended roof line, balanced placement of pictures and complementary alcoves, as well as parallel action, tie two strikingly different apartments into a single set in Neil Simon's *Chapter Two*. The Indiana University, directed by Jay Stephens, designed by Wes Peters.

to the set and make the actors stand out from the background by the angle of the light sources and by the use of complementary colors in the lights to give the illusion of highlight and shadow while fully illuminating the actor from all visible sides.

Spatial composition creates pleasing pictures, but a play is not a picture. Even more important is the temporal composition of the design. In many plays, the sets and lights change from scene to scene and even within a scene. One setting following after another gives variety and interest to the show, while repeated colors or architectural details give a sense of unity. In a musical or an epic play, the rapid shifting of scenery adds to the rhythm of the play and can do as much as the action to build excitement. The whole set might revolve, revealing an entirely new scene on the other side. One scene may rise out of sight into the fly loft, while another set is rolled on stage on a wagon. On a large unit set, space staging is often used. Pools of light are brought up independently on different parts of the stage, dimming out one scene on the forestage while cross-fading to a new scene on a balcony, while different colored lights or projected images on the big sky cyc at the rear of the stage accent the changing moods of the scene.

Adolphe Appia, the great Swiss prophet of stage lighting, saw light as the major factor in the temporal design of a show. In his book, *Music and the Art of the Theatre*, trying to find a method of staging the operas of Richard Wagner, he called for light to express the soul of the drama. "Light is to production," Appia wrote, "what music is to the score: the expressive element in opposition to the literal signs; and, like music, light can express only what belongs to 'the inner essence of all vision!'" He wanted settings of sculptural forms with very little painted detail and little color; the form, the intensity, and even the color were to be created by the mobile, focused light.

Even for a single-set show, the setting is designed so that actors can move in ever-changing patterns that give variety and interest to the visual picture. The American designer Robert Edmond Jones described the challenge of temporal composition in an inspired book called *The Dramatic Imagination:*

> A setting is not just a beautiful thing, a collection of beautiful things. It is a presence, a mood, a warm wind fanning the drama to flame. It echoes, it enhances, it animates. It is an expectancy, a forboding, a tension. It says nothing, but it gives everything. . . . The designer creates an environment in which all noble emotions are possible. Then he retires. The actor enters. If the designer's work has been good, it disappears from our consciousness at that moment. . . . The actor has taken the stage.

Since the most obvious temporal element on the stage consists of costumed living actors, the costume designer would seem to make the final design contribution to the visual movement of the production. Each new costume that a character wears adds interest and variety. Each new combination of characters, each new arrangement, changes the picture and the flow, and the costume designer will be aware of how the changing costumes help the audience keep track of the characters, follow the plot, and feel the changing moods of the characters and the story.

Fulfill the needs of the production concept. "Design is not mere adornment," points out the American designer Howard Bay; "it is the visual progression of a dramatic event." To fulfill the needs of the production concept is the overriding design function, and when designers seek ways to meet the technical demands of the play, provide information to the audience, reinforce the moods, assist the actors in projecting characters, and make the show visually interesting, they do so within the framework of the production concept. In our description of *Troilus and Cressida* earlier in this chapter, we already saw a production concept taking shape. The director wanted to contrast the decadent Trojans with the invading Greek warriors but, at the same time, wanted to create the feeling that the total destruction at the end resulted as much from internal corruption as from outside attack. Costumes, which told the audience that the play was set in ancient times, also provided the major visual contrast between the two civilizations, with pastel silks and linens versus dark leathers and animal skins. The tiny Greek encampment occupied a small spot downstage and seemed almost overwhelmed by the dimly lighted shapes of the city towering behind it. In the Trojan scenes, that same tiny space formed the center of activity, but now the towering shapes, brightly lit from the front and above, provided an opulent space for luxurious Trojan living. Multi-leveled platforms and intricate patterns of arches created opportunities for characters to be in separate groupings, move easily from one group to another, to hide, to eavesdrop, to appear unexpectedly. Intrigue, isolation, conflict, carefree camaraderie were all made possible on this machine for action. With each new appearance of the Greeks, the space of their encampment grew, largely through the use of added light, suggesting a cancerous growth within the Trojan citadel, but also adding to the space in which the actors played, and building interest in the visual movement of the action. The leaning pillars, while they helped inform the audience that the scene was an ancient city, also suggested the decadence of the people who occupied the city, preparing the audience for the destruction that was to come. At last lights and smoke, the staging of multiple battles within the labyrinthine arrangement of pillars and arches, and the reduction of costumes to filthy rags combined all the design elements and the directing to create the illusion of the final collapse of the Trojan civilization.

A contemporary production concept of the same show might set the play in a steel and glass office-recreational complex, with cocktail-sipping Trojans in

This production of Shakespeare's *Troilus and Cressida* at San Francisco State College shows the Greek encampment surrounded by the towering walls of Troy.

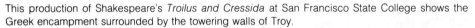

Another production of *Troilus and Cressida* shows the decadence of the Trojan civilization in a modern context. London, The Old Vic Theatre, 1956.

lightweight business suits and golf shirts amiably mixing politics and pleasure, while the militaristic Greeks wear no-nonsense browns and blacks and imposing army uniforms. In either case, the designers create a visual atmosphere to complement the action and mood of the play, providing space to move and group characters appropriately for the action, providing a decor that reinforces the ideas of the play and points up ironies, providing a flow of space and visual stimuli for the right rhythm and tempo, and, above all, providing visual information that clarifies the developing relationships among the characters in the movement of the plot.

DESIGNING *THE ELEPHANT MAN*

The Elephant Man, written by Bernard Pomerarnce in the late 1970s, has a relatively simple plot, but its fragmented structure, its mixture of styles, its almost cinematic movement across time and place, and its distribution of twenty-one roles among nine actors make it a particularly interesting problem for designers. The play is set in London and Belgium from 1884 to 1890, but its point of view suggests the disruption of contemporary theatre more than the realism of that period.

Since *The Elephant Man* was treated in detail in Chapter 2, a brief reminder here of the plot should suffice. Two characters are at the center of the action: John Merrick, the elephant man, and Dr. Frederick Treves. Merrick is a highly intelligent and sensitive young man, but with a grotesquely deformed body, causing severe ambulatory problems and an unusually repulsive appearance. The most notable feature is his enormous head with spongy protuberances and a deformed shape, making both facial expression and normal speech impossible. Thus, people also assume he is mentally deficient. As one might expect, at the beginning of the show Merrick is at the mercy of a freak-show manager, Ross. The second central character, Dr. Treves, an up-and-coming young physician at the London Hospital, rescues Merrick from his freak-show tormentors and maintains him in a private ward. Once Merrick is settled in his new hospital-ward "home," his qualities of inner beauty begin to emerge: his human compassion, his intelligence and artistic sensitivity, as well as religious aspirations, love of beauty, and a highly developed set of ethical values. In trying to help Merrick live as normal a life as possible, Treves tutors him in the rules of his new home and provides him with books to read and visitors to converse with. Mrs. Kendal,

John Merrick (David Bowie) with his model of St. Philip's Church, central to the design of any production of *The Elephant Man.*

one of London's leading actresses, is the first of these visitors, but she is so astonished by Merrick's mind that she soon brings the best of London society to visit him, including royalty and the Bishop of London.

Merrick's action is to be a man like other men. For this he shares the pleasures of society; he creates, by building a model of St. Philip's Church, whose spires are visible from his garret window; he aspires toward the joys of Heaven where he will not be physically impaired; he strives for the experiencing of beauty, both in the church model and in his association with Mrs. Kendal; and most of all he tries to have explained to him the contradictions in the rules society and Dr. Treves impose on him, rules that are supposed to bring happiness because they are "for our own good."

The main action of the play is that of Frederick Treves. He is success incarnate by all standards of Victorian society and, at the beginning of the play, by his own as well: a scientist and an Englishman in an age when both are universally admired, a successful doctor and teacher at London's most important hospital, a published author, and a happy family man. As the play moves on, Treves' success multiplies, bringing with it knighthood, and royalty as clientele. But Merrick's penetrating questions soon begin to challenge the glory of the Victorian social order and morality. One incident that shocks Treves' Victorian sensibilities forms the turning point. Mrs. Kendal, responding to Merrick's ingenuous desire to experience the full beauty of womanhood, delicately exposes her body for his view. Just then Treves walks in. Appalled at such moral outrage, he breaks off further contact between the two. When he later realizes the innocence of the event, he begins to doubt his own moral values.

By this time, however, scientific success has begun to raise even greater doubts. Even as he helps his patient achieve greater normality, Treves also knows that Merrick is edging closer to death, and, with all his scientific skill, he is helpless to prevent it. Treves finds himself unable to cope with the mockery of that contradiction.

Early in the play, Treves had used Merrick as a specimen for a scientific lecture to his colleagues on physical abnormality. Toward the end of the play Treves has a dream that Merrick uses him as a specimen to give a scientific lecture on moral abnormality. At the beginning of the play, Merrick begs help from Treves the scientist. By the end of the play, it is Treves, the scientist, who begs for help from the Bishop. At the end, Merrick, the artist, dies, having completed his image of beauty, the model of St. Philip's Church, while Treves, the medical scientist, lives on in indecisive uncertainty, unsure even what human touch to add to a coldly objective obituary prepared for the press by the hospital administrator, Mr. Gomm.

Developing a Production Concept

In developing a production concept, the first thing we notice about *The Elephant Man* is its fragmented style. Twenty-one brief scenes make up the play. Each one quickly zeroes in on an incident in the Treves-Merrick relationship, makes its point, then abruptly ends—no elaborate development, no transitions, no winding down—just the incident itself, terse and simple. In Scene 3, when Treves delivers his anatomy lecture, he illustrates his points with projected slides. The abrupt rhythm, as slide replaces slide, suggests a motif for the entire show— scene replacing scene to illustrate each important incident in the action.

Second, we notice that the actor playing Merrick does not wear costume or makeup to depict the grotesque deformity of the historical original. Instead, a normal-looking actor appears; then, while Treves delivers his lecture, the actor begins to contort his body to approximate the real Merrick the audience sees in the projected slides. This technique also suggests a demonstration format: Show what is needed to make the point and don't attempt to simulate actuality. Add to this the fact that, except for the portrayal of Merrick, all the actors play anywhere from two to five roles, and the idea of demonstration becomes more pronounced. Third, we notice how frequently the characters either spend their time observing others or are on display themselves. Merrick is first a carnival freak, then a specimen for a lecture, and even in his "home," hospital workers try to get a peek. Ross points out that Merrick's high-and-mighty visitors are merely there to stare at him so that they can feel better about themselves. Treves observes his patients and lectures on their abnormalities with scientific objectivity, and in his dream he is the object of equally dispassionate observation. Mrs. Kendal is an actress, used to concealing her true feelings and assuming others for the public, but she points out ironically that she differs from other women in this skill only in being famous for it. In this Victorian showcase, it is all right to operate on a naked woman, but to view a naked body for its beauty is obscene. One must follow society's rules, and over and over John Merrick is asked to repeat the lesson: "Rules make us happy because they are for our own good."

From these details, a production concept begins to emerge. We will want an atmosphere of institutional observation, but with quick shifts from one scene to the next. Within that framework, we must also depict the subjective world of Dr. Treves' dream, and the warmth of human passion must cut through the cool objectivity from time to time. The world the characters inhabit is strongly Victorian, so both costumes and sets must suggest that period. But the audience must not feel that the play is merely a history lesson; they must be drawn into the same feeling of objective observation that we find in Dr. Treves, not to make them feel that they are in the Victorian world, but rather that they share Dr. Treves' desire for scientific inquiry, in contrast to the idle curiosity seekers of the side show.

Working Out the Details

An environmental structure in a "black box theatre" could serve the concept very well. One main stage area at one end of the room is needed, since the slides for Treves' lecture and Merrick contorting his body must be seen simultaneously by

A rehearsal of *The Elephant Man* in an environmental setting, showing acting areas surrounding audience positions in the center. State University College at Oneonta, N.Y. Directed by Edward Pixley, designed by Junius Hamblin.

the entire audience. That space can also serve as Merrick's "home," framed by a Victorian institutional structure of bricks and iron, with a balcony above, where the slide lecture can occur. Three smaller stages can be placed out in the midst of the audience with access between them. The stage directly opposite the main stage could serve as the anteroom where people prepare to enter Merrick's home, as well as the Belgian carnival scene. The two side stages could serve as places for doctors to watch Treves' lecture, and all spaces, including the main stage, might be filled with curiosity-seekers at the carnival, giving them the same point of view as the audience. The side stages might also serve for the railway station where Treves finds Merrick abandoned, and for the scenes Treves has with the Bishop, where his own inadequacies are exposed. We might even go one step further and have the actors sit there and watch the show as part of the audience, when they are not in the action and when these spaces are not in use. Moreover, if live music is used to form bridges from scene to scene, a musician, perhaps a cellist, in modern concert dress should be seated in a position visible to all.

Such an approach will meet all the technical demands of the set, and with lighting quickly taking us from one spot to the next, it will provide both the abruptness that the many short scenes suggest and a fast flow of action from scene to scene. The main stage area with its institutional Victorian decor, combined with costumes of the period, will set the play in 1880s London, without creating a Victorian world separate from the audience. White and cool lights and the institutional decor support the mood of cool objectivity against which Merrick's and later Treves' passionate questioning of values can occur, while the rich tones of the cello support the depth of the ideas the play evokes. The different locations of the action in the playing spaces will provide interesting patterns for the audience, but will also help the actors project the feeling of observing or being on display, in that it will tend to separate and isolate them at key moments in the action.

More than any other element, costumes will tell the audience the period and location of the play. A policeman, a railway conductor, a nurse will be distinguished by their uniforms. The rule-bound doctors will be dressed in conservative black suits, while Merrick's socialite visitors may be dressed in more elegant daytime wear, with spats and gold-tipped walking sticks, bustled skirts and parasols. With the actors playing multiple roles, often less than a minute apart, all costumes must be designed for quick changes. Two characters' costumes present special problems. Mrs. Kendal must be able to remove enough of her costume on stage to expose her body to Merrick, though not necessarily to the audience, and she should also be able to let her long hair fall down around her shoulders. Her costume must be so constructed that it can be undone, but it must also include undergarments of the period, and if the actress has short hair, a good-quality wig must be prepared to accomodate the action.

Merrick's costumes also require special attention. For the early scenes in the hospital, a simple loincloth will allow the actor to display his contorted simulation of the elephant man's disorder, while for traveling, his clothing should conceal the disorder, even to a sack-like head-covering with holes cut out for the eyes. By the time he starts receiving guests, he obviously must be fully clothed in proper Victorian fashion. The costume should be designed, however, so as to accentuate the contorted body rather than conceal it, as the conservative fashions of the time would do. Since he is in his own home, perhaps we can break with Victorian authenticity enough to dispense with a coat in most scenes, and have him only in a shirt and vest. Thus, the contrasting colors and textures of shirt, trousers, and vest will set off the different parts of the actor's body and help him project the illusion of the elephant man. The more colorful costume will also be an effective contrast to Treves' conservatism, calling audience attention to the central conflict that their different temperaments create.

A bed, a bathtub, and a table for the model of St. Philip's Church must be on the main stage area. The table can also serve as Gomm's desk in the opening scene and for Treves' projector in Scene 3. Nondescript benches should do for the other stages. Anything else that is needed can be brought on and taken off by the actors.

Thus we have a design concept that fulfills all the functions of an *Elephant Man* production. The theatre space provides an environment that should make the audience share the observers' point of view; the sets suggest the time and place of the action, provide the spaces for quick and varied flow from scene to scene, and enhance the objective scientific mood and the characters' need to observe or be on display; the lights help set the coolness of the mood and reinforce the rhythm and the objectivity by abruptly shifting audience focus from one space to another throughout the show; the musician helps set the moods for the series of actions in each scene, while his or her physical presence reminds the audience that they are part of the mood-setting experience; and costumes help the actors project their characters, give information about the time and place, and contrast characters by class, profession, and temperament, and in Merrick's case also support the changes he undergoes during the action. Though this is one way the show might be designed, it is not the only way. As with any other play, a new design-directing team will create a new production concept each time *The Elephant Man* is done. For another design concept, read the excellent description of the New York designs (lighting by Beverly Emmons, set by David Jenkins) in the January/February 1980 edition of *Theatre Crafts*, beginning on page 24.

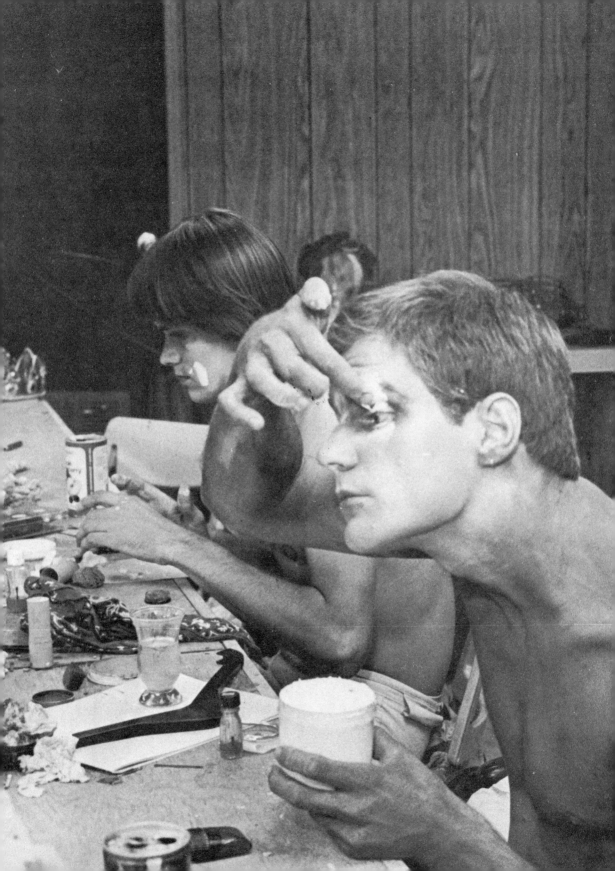

THE ART OF THE ACTOR

14

The actors begin to get into their characters
while getting into their makeup for *A Midsummer Night's Dream*.

For all that modern theory calls for the domination of the director, the actor (man or woman) is still the center of the theatre. For all that modern theory calls for subordinating the actor to the overall mood of the play, the best actors are remembered even more than the play. For all that many modern directors have been fascinated by the choral group, the individual who possesses the magic of a primitive shaman still emerges as the great force in the theatre. "Star" is a word reserved for that special actor or actress who shines forth from the stage or screen.

THE MYSTERY OF THE ACTOR

In our daily lives, all of us do things that might be called acting. We imitate and we play roles. From earliest childhood, human beings learn by imitation. Skills like walking, talking, swimming and dancing, carpentry and cooking are learned largely by watching and doing. We learn social graces by emulating the style of those we admire, perhaps adopting a role model, such as a teacher, an aunt or uncle, an older cousin, or even some famous person.

Role-playing is more complex than imitation. By playing dolls or house or school, children learn intricate social interactions, trying out the roles of a scolding Mommy, a tired Daddy, or a demanding teacher in little dramas. Later on in life, in the privacy of our rooms or our cars we may enact in our minds the upcoming job interview, the excuse for missing an exam, the hoped-for conversation with an attractive boy or girl, some new ideas to propose to the boss, thus helping ourselves prepare for untested situations. Not only do we role-play to become familiar with strange situations, we play the many different roles expected of us in our daily lives. A college student may start her day as a motherly roommate, rousing her sleepy "roomies" before heading for an early class, where she becomes the enthusiastic student, discussing and taking notes. Between classes she consoles a friend who just blew a test, then for two hours files and types on her work-study job. After classes she tutors another student in basic math, goes to a paste-up session for the school paper, and then home for the weekend, dinner with her parents, and a quiet evening with her boyfriend. During her rather ordinary day, she has moved gracefully from one role to the next—roommate, student, friend, employee, teacher, fellow worker, daughter, and girlfriend—in each role adapting her manner, her objectives, probably her clothes, and even her vocabulary to what others expect of her in each role. Such role-playing largely occurs unconsciously, but when we are faced with a new role, we consciously imitate its outward aspects. We dress up for the job interview and try to assume a relaxed confidence we don't feel. We assume a hushed dignity in a funeral parlor, a cheerful warmth with the sick, a boisterous enthusiasm at the football game, a stoic determination in the dental chair, a business-like efficiency in the lawyer's office. Such behavior suggests the stereotyped expectations people bring to conventional situations, and people are alternately shocked and amused at those who don't know how to "act," who carry efficiency to the football stadium, cheer to the dental chair, or boisterousness to the funeral parlor.

But is all this really acting? When children consciously imitate their elders, they do what actors do, but with one big difference. Children imitate to learn the skill, whereas actors imitate to create an illusion. Let's take an example from a play. In Lanford Wilson's *Fifth of July*, the invalid character, Frank Talley, has had to learn to walk with artificial limbs. To do this, he may have watched others who had already mastered the process, observing how they move the hips and shoulders in order to propel the legs forward, to become independently mobile. When Richard Thomas or Christopher Reeve rehearsed the role of Frank Talley, they very likely watched and imitated paraplegics, but not so they could become mobile. They imitated the technique so that on stage they could create the illusion of moving artifical limbs rather than organic ones. Frank Talley imitated to

Richard Thomas as Kenneth Talley walking as though he had artificial legs, while Gwen (Swoosie Kurtz) gives him a hand, in Lanford Wilson's *Fifth of July*.

master a skill; Richard Thomas and Christopher Reeve imitated so as to make it look to an audience as though they had mastered a skill—but the skill they mastered was not the walking; it was the imitating itself, the creating of a theatrical illusion. To master the skill, they would have to have their own legs amputated—ridiculous, of course, and also in total contradiction to the art of acting. More complex comparisons also apply. An actor cast in the role of a doctor does not enroll in medical school to acquire a doctor's skills. He observes doctors at work, notices their manner with patients, their style of giving diagnoses, their way of handling instruments and notes. These are the details an actor must master to create the illusion of being a doctor.

We might also note that actors imitate solely to be observed, not for any practical end. That's why the illusion is enough. Imitating to learn a skill requires no audience, but the actor's imitation would be pointless without an audience. Role-playing, on the other hand, whether in life or on stage, is done for an audience. Let's look at a life situation—a teacher worrying about a sick child home in bed. In her teacher role she must be alert and responsive. Is she acting? Not really. She genuinely enjoys helping her students learn. As she assumes a helpful attitude and concentrates on her students' questions, this very real aspect of her personality takes over, temporarily suppressing her worry. When class is over and she gets to a telephone, her worry as a mother becomes dominant. She is not faking in either case. She is both mother and professional woman and can move gracefully between these two aspects of her person as the situation demands. Of course, some people do fake the roles they play in life. A politician on the campaign trail may hate fried chicken, yet will eat it with a down-home gusto that suggests it's his favorite meal. But the success of real-life role-playing depends on its appearing genuine. The observer who sees through it makes a moral judgment, labeling it hypocrisy, and it destroys the credibility of the exposed phoney. On seeing through an actor's performance, we make an artistic not a moral judgment. It is not the actor's veracity, but his skill that is in question. In fact, one of theatre's pleasures comes in admiring a skillful actor assume a variety of widely different roles.

Our admiration, however, reflects one of the paradoxes of acting. The actor, like the singer, is both the instrument and the one who performs on the instrument. While the painter and the instrumental musician stand outside the thing they create and are involved only indirectly and symbolically, actors identify with their characters and seem to be living the emotions they show to the audience. But it is only a seeming, a pretense, an illusion. The actor in private life is one person, but the well-toned voice and body of the actor, on command, can assume all the physical and emotional characteristics of another person, in fact many other persons, as different from each other as they are from the actor, while the artist inside the body is always watching, guiding, criticizing, adjusting the performance to the tension of the audience. When asked whether they

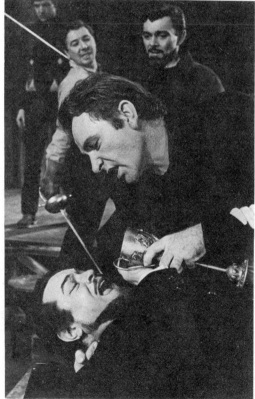

Richard Burton playing the role of a psychiatrist in Peter Shaffer's *Equus*, while in *Hamlet* he plays the impetuous young prince bent on revenge.

actually feel the emotions they express, most actors answer yes—and no. They are never sure just what combination of warm heart and cool head may give the best performance.

ACTOR TRAINING

Whether actors are in cool control of every technique or whether their voices and bodies are trained to respond to the inspiration of each dramatic situation, somewhere they have learned the techniques. For many years this training occurred in the theatre itself. A young man or woman who showed promise would be hired for little pay to play small parts in a provincial stock company. There the elder actors would criticize the novice's work and prescribe voice and body exercises handed down for generations. With this kind of training actors developed voices to be heard in large theatres and learned how to build long speeches to ringing climaxes. They learned to move in the aristocratic deportment of bows and curtsies, to develop skill in singing, dancing, and fencing. In high or "genteel" comedy, actors expected to play with elegance, pride, and teasing insinuation, and in low comedy with exaggerated anguish or glee.

A few actors trained in this method, such as England's David Garrick in the eighteenth century, achieved a naturalness that was widely acclaimed, but far more common was the oratorical grandeur of his rival, James Quin, or the emotional fervor of such stars as Edmund Kean a half century later. By the end of the nineteenth century, smaller theatres and the growth of realism changed audience expectations, and the large style of acting came to seem exaggerated and empty, calling for a radically new approach to actor training.

The Stanislavsky Method

As co-founder of the Moscow Art Theatre in 1898, Constantin Stanislavsky began to formulate a radically new system that was to influence actor training methods throughout the Western world. It came to be known as "the method" in the United States. Stanislavsky assumed that his students were working long hours at the traditional techniques of movement, dance, fencing, voice placement, singing, and diction, so he concentrated on the inner preparation of the actor, which he has described fully in *An Actor Prepares,* the most admired book on acting in modern times.

Stanislavsky's primary aim was to free the actor (man or woman), to teach him to relax each part of the body from unnecessary tension, but especially to free him from the false actions inherent in the conventional techniques of the nineteenth century. Instead of trying to convey to the audience a big general emotion, the actor had to concentrate on such details as his feelings about another character, his relation to the furniture around him, and, especially, to small properties and pieces of business, the specific details of everyday living. Give an actor something to do and a reason for doing it—hold a teacup, move a chair, hand something to another character—and both body and voice would come alive. The immediate triumphs of naturalistic acting are in the little pantomimic dramatizations—the unconscious snarl on the lips, the half-clenched fist, the flinching shoulder—that give color to the spoken phrases and are a visible expression of the character's inner life.

Second, the actor had to work on creating a consistent role in depth by analyzing the character's "objective" in each scene and defining the "superobjective" or "spine" of the character for the whole play. When actors have clear-cut objectives to play in each scene—picking a quarrel, cheering up a downcast friend, concealing a secret—they have a focus for everything they do in the scene, giving clarity and truth to the performance. The superobjective gives continuity from one scene to the next, because it expresses what the character wants most from life. An actor playing Willy Loman in *Death of a Salesman* might define his character's superobjective as proving that his dream of success is the best dream for himself and his sons. Within this larger spine, his objective for individual scenes may be to encourage his son, Biff, in a million-dollar business

Laura under the spell of the Gentleman Caller in Williams' *The Glass Menagerie*. Suzanne Collins and Gary Dantzig, Seattle Repertory Theatre, 1978–79 season.

scheme, to conceal his failure from his wife, Linda, or to blame his failure on changes in society or on Biff's spite.

Most important to Stanislavsky's system was the actor's discovery of the power in the little word "if"—the "magic if," Stanislavsky called it. That little word can unlock the imaginative power to create truth in the most intense situations for the most complex dramatic characters. But the actor does not simply ask, "What would I do in this situation?" The actor may be a twenty-year-old honor student who has played three leading roles in the past year. If she were in Laura Wingfield's position in *The Glass Menagerie,* with a gentleman caller offering her chewing gum and extolling the benefits she could gain from a night-school course, as herself she would probably tell him to get lost. Her "magic if" must include the physical and emotional conditions that Laura brings into the scene: a world of semi-poverty, a lifetime of feeling inferior and dependent, a limp that has made her self-conscious, and a high school crush she once had on this young man who had forgotten she existed. "If" the actress can imagine all this as part of her background, the proffered chewing gum achieves power to provide undreamed-of social contact, the night-school course becomes the sharing of a dream. So actors would immerse themselves in the biographies of their characters, perhaps visit the kinds of houses and streets associated with the characters, absorbing the sights, sounds, smells, and moods of the environment, and improvise scenes with the other actors, so that together they might begin to think, feel, act, and speak *as if* they actually were the characters.

Training for such acting is to stimulate the power of the unconscious mind through "psychotechniques." Stanislavsky found that actors had several ways of calling up deep feelings, of searching for the "inner flow" or "subtext" that lay hidden behind the words of the play. He recognized, as Freud did, that although the subconscious would not release its secrets directly, indirect methods might unlock its treasures. Most important of the psychotechniques was the appeal to emotional memory. If the actor thought back to a personal experience that had created a feeling similar to that of his situation in a play—a childhood experience, for example, perhaps trivial in itself but important to him at the time—he might rediscover the tone and texture that accompanied the original experience. Another psychotechnique was improvisation. The actor might go beyond the written scenes, imagining other moments in the character's life and improvising appropriate actions and words for them. Returning then to the play itself, the actor possesses the inner flow, the hidden life, of the character and thus can present a whole person.

Training for Nonrealistic Acting

The realistic "method" of actor training dominated the American theatre for more than three decades after New York's Group Theatre first espoused it in 1931, but many plays and productions make nonrealistic demands on actors that

Acting in *Godspell* calls for simplicity in characterization as well as simplicity in settings. Eastern Illinois
University, directed by E. G. Gabbard, settings by C. P. Blanchette.

are often far more important than realism, and even Stanislavsky abandoned
some of his methods in later years. For Shakespearean roles, no amount of inner
preparation will help the actor deliver a sentence seven lines long on one breath,
while building it toward a climax and still keeping all of its parts clear for an
audience, nor will it help perfect the animal-like stylization of voice and movement for a modern play like *Cats*. Attention to pantomimic little details has no
place in the grand movements and unison chanting of a Greek chorus, nor for
that matter in the rapid shifts of style from "cowboy" to "calypso" that the
brothers do in *Joseph and the Amazing Technicolor Dreamcoat*. The parables in *Godspell* do not require deep subtext but vivid, quickly drawn caricatures, nor will
emotional memory help actors play horses in *Equus*.

Since the 1960s, actor training in America has worked for more freedom,
flexibility, and control in the actor's entire instrument—voice, body, imagination, and emotions—as well as spontaneity, coordination, and trust among
groups of actors working in ensemble. Voice training has worked to create
relaxed, free sounds that seem an extension of the body itself and resonate from

the actor's whole being. Movement training has absorbed the traditional techniques of ballet and modern dance and several of the traditional Oriental techniques. By the 1960s The Actors Studio, the shrine of devotion to Stanislavsky's method, had added classes in Tai Chi Ch'uan, the traditional Chinese training for defense.

Central in recent training is group work, often combined with sensitivity training, to increase the actor's awareness both of himself alone and as part of an ensemble. Theatre games are used in groups to develop spontaneity through improvisation and also to provide the discipline of group coordination.

Any teacher of acting finds suggestions in the work of such directors as Peter Brook, Joseph Chaikin, and especially Jerzy Grotowski. Grotowski developed a more complete system of training than most of the other directors of the avant-garde groups described in Chapter 10. His actors achieved a wild, almost terrifying intensity that seemed the opposite extreme from the quiet, subtle underplaying of the Stanislavsky school. They developed techniques for extending the range of body and voice: exercises to explore opposing movement patterns (rapidly circling the hand in one direction while the elbow circles in the opposite direction, or suggesting rejection with the legs while accepting with the hands) and exercises for locating and focusing resonances for the voice in unexpected parts of the head and body.

Besides both new and old Western techniques, Grotowski borrowed training methods from the Kathakali dance dramas of India, from Chinese opera, and from the Japanese Noh. Each actor was encouraged to seek the "root impulse" of any action in order to integrate his own inner being with the outer expression. And, like Peter Brook and other contemporary idealists who seek a "global village" and communication among people of all races and languages, Grotowski hoped to achieve an objective expression so basic that it could appeal to the collective unconscious of all people without depending on the audience knowing the words—acts and gestures as specific as ideograms or hieroglyphs. Grotowski's theory and practice, though still uniquely his own, have inspired many teachers seeking new approaches to the problems of acting.

ACTING IN *PYGMALION*

George Bernard Shaw's *Pygmalion,* written in 1910, requires realistic acting. Yet its realistic characters get themselves into situations that sometimes demand nonrealistic techniques from the actors, and in the musical version of the play, *My Fair Lady,* they sing, dance, and create some group effects that are completely stylized.

Pygmalion centers on two characters, Eliza Doolittle, a low-class, ill-mannered, but independent London flower vendor, and Professor Henry Higgins, an upper-class linguist, who takes pride in his skill at labeling people's upbringing by their vocal sounds and speech patterns. When he encounters Eliza in the rain outside the Covent Garden opera house, he claims that in three months he could train her to speak well enough to pass for "a duchess at an ambassador's garden party" or even get her a job in a shop, "which requires better English." The prospect of moving from the gutter to a flower shop appeals to Eliza; so the next day she arrives in her Sunday best at Higgins' apartment to enroll for lessons in proper speech.

Higgins had no plans to actually teach Eliza, but his friend Colonel Pickering makes a wager to pay for the lessons if Higgins can make good his claim. The challenge is irresistible. Higgins packs Eliza off with his housekeeper, Mrs. Pearce, to get her scrubbed up and presentable. No sooner is she gone, than her father, Alfred Doolittle, shows up, shocked that Eliza has gone alone to a rich

Eliza Doolittle practicing her vowel sounds with her tutor, Professor Higgins. Cheryl Kennedy and Rex Harrison in the 1980 Broadway version of *My Fair Lady*.

man's private apartment. Though Doolittle suspects the worst, he has no intention of saving his daughter from a fate worse than death; he simply wants his fair cut. When asked if he has no morals, he confesses that he "can't afford 'em," astonishing Higgins and Pickering with his original argument in favor of a life of pleasant poverty and unabashed imprudence.

We next see Higgins and Eliza in Act III, trying out the first stage of her transformation on a few of his mother's "at-home" guests, Freddy, Clara, and Mrs. Eynsford-Hill, a family of high birth but no money and little fashion. Eliza's fashionable clothes and perfect diction persuade them that she is a remarkable person, and her incongruous choice of words and tidbits of low-class gossip, such as an aunt who was "done in," delight them as examples of "the new small talk." At the beginning of Act IV, Eliza is back in Higgins' apartment immediately following her triumph at the long-awaited Ambassador's garden party. But she sits forlornly by herself, ignored, while Higgins and Pickering congratulate each other on their success, express relief that the whole boring experience is ended, and prepare to go to bed. Higgins sticks his head back into the room to ask Eliza for his slippers. She hurls them at him in a fury.

By Act V, Eliza has run away and found refuge with Higgins' mother. When Higgins shows up in pursuit, she greets him only as a charming acquaintance, which makes him furious. Then she accuses him of having given her the speech and manners of a lady, making her unfit for her old life, and without the money to sustain herself as a lady, she is now fit for nothing. At last she realizes that she does have a skill; she can teach diction using Higgins' methods and she can do it better than he, because she understands people's feelings. So she walks out at the end, not a flower girl, not a useless lady, but an independent woman ready to start her own life.

Creating the Role

The first thing that all the actors in *Pygmalion* must attend to is dialect. The play is set in London, so everyone speaks with English accents, but not all the same accents. Professor Higgins and all the upper-class characters use what is called standard British, but the lower-class characters must use cockney and a variety of other dialects, including at least one from England's rural south. The actress playing Eliza has a special problem. She begins the play with the lower-class dialect of northeast London, moves to an overarticulated and badly inflected standard British in Act III, and in Acts IV and V speaks with the most aristocratic British of anyone in the show, lapsing into lower-class patterns when she gets angry. Before they work on lines or character, the actors work with special dialect tapes to learn the sound changes and the special resonance and inflection patterns that will give their characters authenticity. They might also listen to recordings of English actors or authentic English-speaking people to get a feeling for the accent in conversation. Nothing would more quickly destroy their characters' credibility for an audience than sounding as if they were from Long Island, Dodge City, or Duluth.

Discovering Eliza's Character Through the Play

Most actors begin by researching their character, both inside and outside the play. From inside the play, using what Eliza says about herself, what she does, how others react to her, and what they say about her, the actress begins to get a full picture of the character she is creating. She will notice that Eliza is proud of her independence and her moral character. "I'm a good girl, I am," she affirms repeatedly and sets up a howl at the slightest hint that her actions might be thought illegal or immoral. Eliza also accepts no charity. She comes prepared to pay for her lessons and knows the going rate—from a friend who took French lessons at eighteen pence an hour "from a real French gentleman. Well, you wouldnt have the face to ask me the same for teaching me my own language as you would for French; so I wont give more than a shilling. Take it or leave it." She tells Higgins, "Youre no gentleman, youre not, to talk of such things," when he tells Mrs. Pearce to get rid of her old clothes, but she reacts with delight when Pickering calls her Miss Doolittle.

Other characters provide varying views of Eliza. Higgins first calls her a "squashed cabbage leaf" but later commends her quick ear for all kinds of vocal sounds, while Pickering praises her genius for music. Mrs. Higgins calls her "naturally rather affectionate," and her father says she's "very tender-hearted." These descriptions match her own plea to Higgins that all she wants is "a little kindness, . . . not to want you to make love to me . . . but more friendly like." Higgins rejects such sentimentality: "If youre going to be a lady, youll have to give up feeling neglected if the men you know dont spend half their time snivelling over you and the other half giving you black eyes." Freddy Eynsford-Hill is smitten with her beauty and originality, and Eliza is pleased by his attention.

Bit by bit, a complete picture of Eliza Doolittle takes shape. She is proud and independent, though her job as a flower vendor gives her little to be proud of. Thus she is defensive at insinuations about her morality and crushed by scorn toward her person. Likewise, self-improvement appeals to her. She likes to impress people and flaunts her ability to pay for a cab. But when her pride leads her to seek lessons in speaking and acting like a lady, she enters an unfamiliar world and so becomes dependent on her teachers. Without independence she comes more and more to need approval and attention. The crisis in Eliza's life comes when she gets neither attention nor independence, so she runs away. But with nowhere to run to, she is at last forced to have it out with Higgins and declare a new level of independence.

Notice how this picture of Eliza provides motivations for the actress. Her character has a clear goal: to achieve an independence which will give her the pride and the attention she craves. This might be called her "superobjective" or "spine." Now she has a solid basis for developing reactions to the many different obstacles and complications she will encounter through the play. Let's look at her progress in the first scene. She moves among the late-night crowd, gathered for shelter from the rain, and tries to sell flowers. With each rejection, she grows more desolate. When someone warns her that a gentleman is taking down her words, she jumps on the defensive, assuming that he is taking evidence against her, wailing her innocence to the whole crowd to get their sympathy. Of course, the gentleman is Henry Higgins, transcribing her dialect phonetically for his records, and attention goes to him as he tells everyone who speaks where they were born and raised just by listening to their words. With attention off from her, Eliza bewails her wounded pride to herself until Higgins turns on her:

> Cease this detestable boohooing instantly. . . . A woman who utters such depressing and disgusting sounds has no right to be anywhere—no right to live. Remember that you are a human being with a soul and the divine gift of articulate speech: that your native language is the language of Shakespear and Milton and The Bible; and dont sit there crooning like a bilious pigeon.

This attack so overwhelms her that her only reply is "Ah-ah-ah-ow-ow-ow-oo!" which Higgins instantly jots down phonetically.

Eliza makes one more attempt to sell Pickering some flowers as the two men leave, but Higgins catches Eliza in a white lie, and she flings her flower basket at his feet in desperation: "Take the whole blooming basket for sixpence."

Eliza has one last pattern of motivational change in this scene. Higgins, instead of buying her flowers, throws her a handful of coins. Her pride finds immediate use for this new-found wealth. Freddy Eynsford-Hill, whose mother and sister had sent him into the rain to hunt a taxi, returns to find them gone, leaving him stranded with the cab. But Eliza sails grandly past him to claim the cab for herself and asks to be taken to Buckingham Palace. Then she waves goodbye to Freddy before admitting to the cab driver her real and far less grand destination.

The actress can find in each of Eliza's actions in this scene some variation on her superobjective. With independence threatened and her pride wounded, she defends herself, she wails to get sympathy from others, she retreats into self-pity, or she strikes out in anger. But when she has the chance to impress someone, she flaunts herself with an assumed grandeur beyond her station. As a poverty-stricken flower girl, however, she can never let her pride take over completely until the unexpected money frees her of the immediate need to sell flowers to provide for her lowly but independent living.

One other important internal guide for the actress is the character's language. At first, actors often find that the playwright's words seem unnatural, and beginning actors are tempted to rewrite the lines so that they come more easily off their own tongues. But Eliza's individuality and her development through the play are built into her unique language patterns, which are among the actress's most important clues to creating the role. Not only are Eliza's many variations on the single expostulation "Aaaaaahh-ow-ooh!" important to her dialect, they reveal an impulsive need to express her feelings immediately and directly. By Act III when she has her first test in society, she has acquired elegant diction, but she uses it to tell outrageously inappropriate stories about an aunt being "done in" over a new straw hat, and her father ladling gin down the old woman's throat. Then when Freddy laughs at her stories, she turns impulsively on him:

LIZA: Here! what are you sniggering at?
FREDDY: The new small talk. You do it so awfully well.
LIZA: If I was doing it proper, what was you laughing at?

By Act IV, Eliza has learned to bottle up her feelings and throughout the Ambassador's garden party she has maintained a proper decorum. But at last, having sat quietly listening to Higgins belittle her contribution to the evening's triumph, we wait for the moment when the impulsive Eliza we knew in Act I will burst loose and hurl Higgins' slippers at him in unrepressed fury. This internal character quality has been suppressed, but the actress holds on to it, ready to release it when the action provides the right motivation: "There are your slippers. And there. Take your slippers; and may you never have a day's luck with them!"

The Character Discovered Outside the Play

Actors do a great deal of research outside the play as well. Learning a dialect is one such example. But this teaches techniques of performance, not of character. The actor will read what critics or other actors who have played the role can reveal about the character in journals, interviews, reviews, and books. To get a fuller sense of Eliza's life in the slums of London, the actress might seek out detailed accounts of London life in 1910. Another of Shaw's plays, *Major Barbara*, with its scenes in a Salvation Army soup kitchen, might give her a somewhat different but enriching view of Eliza's world. The popular television series Masterpiece Theatre regularly gives detailed portraits of both upper- and lower-class English life of the period, most notably in such works as *Upstairs, Downstairs* and *Brideshead Revisited*. History and sociology books, paintings and photographs can help immerse the actress in the conditions that Eliza Doolittle faced daily and can help her create a fully rounded character. What would it actually feel like to be an impoverished flower girl in London in 1910? What kinds of pleasures or fears would life hold in store for you? What would it be like to earn your living twopence at a time by catering to the whims of the rich who treat you like dirt, avoiding the perils of the law that could mercilessly destroy you, or trying to stay moral when even your own family assumes that immorality is the path to survival?

Shaw has even written extra scenes intended for his reading audience, and added others for the 1937 movie. An actress can use these scenes to see how Eliza might have experienced important offstage events—a taxi ride, a scrubbing-off-the-slum-dirt scene, a phonetics lesson (which was later adapted into one of the most famous scenes from the musical version of the play, "The Rain in Spain Stays Mainly in the Plain"), and, of course, the long-awaited Ambassador's ball. These are the sort of offstage scenes that a realistic director might have had his actors improvise, but which Shaw has provided ready-made.

Working Out the Details

Having completed her research, the actress playing Eliza understands her basic character: her superobjective through the whole play, her action in each scene, the obstacles and complications that govern her changing motivations, her relation to other characters, and the unique conditions of London in 1910 that can base her character in reality. Now comes the creative part—making her own body and voice animate Eliza into a living being on the stage. Michel Saint-Denis, one of the leading acting teachers of France and England in the mid-twentieth century and a founder of the Juilliard Acting School, compares the actor during this process to a glove:

> Open and flexible, but flat, and remaining flat at the beginning. Then by degrees the text, the imagination, the associations roused by the text penetrate and bring you [the actor] to life. Ways are prepared for the character to creep in slowly and animate the glove, the glove which is you, with your blood, your nerves, your breathing system, your voice, with the light of your own lucid control switching on and off.

As lines are memorized and blocking secured, the actress tries out different ways to emphasize the lines, explores what textures, rhythms, and tones of voice match Eliza's vocabulary and manner of expression, and experiments with different ways of walking and gesturing to point up her personality. One speech from Act II shows how Eliza's lines provide important clues ror voice and movement patterns. Higgins has agreed to take Eliza on as a student, but refuses to worry about what happens to her afterward: "We can throw her back into the gutter; and then it will be her own business again." Eliza's response is instant and vehement:

> Oh, youve no feeling heart in you: you dont care for nothing but yourself. [*She rises and takes the floor resolutely*]. Here! Ive had enough of this. I'm going

[making for the door]. You ought to be ashamed of yourself, you ought.

The sentences are short and direct, and they move quickly, almost abruptly, from unequivocal moral judgment about Higgins to her decision to leave, accompanied by instant action. But Eliza can't quite resist ending with one last thrust at her tormentor. This gives Higgins time to tempt her with chocolates, which she resists until he tosses half a one into her mouth, almost choking her. "I wouldnt have ate it," she announces, "only I'm too ladylike to take it out of my mouth," now revealing an attempt at controlled gentility. Then when Higgins asks her if she came in a taxi, she switches right back into another kind of abruptness: "Well, what if I did? Ive as good a right to take a taxi as anyone else." This series of lines suggests a vocal pattern of strong and quick contrasts, from accusing, to determination, to scolding, then to caution, then to lady-like demureness, and then abruptly to defensive arguing. Within these shifts she alternates between controlled observations about herself and Higgins and impulsive responses to the unexpected. These alternations could be accompanied by equally sharp contrasts in her physical manner. For the controlled observations, the actress might want to pull herself up erectly, holding her head almost haughtily, while the impulsive responses might produce a sudden forward movement, with head thrust out as if in attack. The two contrasting physical actions visually reinforce both Eliza's pretensions toward grandeur and her lower-class upbringing. As the lines supply clues for character mannerisms, movement, and vocal contrasts, the character begins to fill out the "glove-like" actress with its own dimensions and shape.

By Act V, when Eliza has learned to speak and act like a lady, her language patterns are more complex, suggesting that she is now consistently controlled and demure, but she still can't quite resist ending her speeches with a sarcastic dig at Higgins. She describes to Pickering how his gentlemanly manners helped her to become a lady, "things that shewed you thought and felt about me as if I were something better than a scullery-maid; though of course I know you would have been just the same to a scullery-maid if she had been let into the drawing room." She ends the speech, not with a direct attack as in Act II, but with an innuendo that Higgins must overhear: "You never took off your boots in the dining room when I was there," implying that Higgins did. "I am not blaming him. It is his way, isnt it?" The physical and vocal pointing of the sarcasm must be different from earlier in the play, but the same kind of contrast is still there to highlight the consistency of character across the entire play.

While the actress develops her own voice and movement patterns, she also balances them with the patterns being created by the other actors. She can be ladylike with Colonel Pickering, who always calls her Miss Doolittle, intimidated by the no-nonsense behavior of Mrs. Pearse, both annoyed by and superior to her amoral father, arrogant with the easily impressed Eynsford-Hills, and quietly relaxed with the respectful and compassionate Mrs. Higgins. But with Henry Higgins, who is interested only in results and never caters to her whims, she alternates between assertiveness and defensiveness, as though they are in a constant contest of wills. In any case, the actors working together learn how to play off from each other, so that their work is in proportion. They orchestrate their movement and speeches to build together toward the intensity of a climax or to share the tension of a pause, until at last they are working as a unit. Each actor in turn picks up focus on cue and then helps direct it toward the next point of attention. They feel each others' rhythm and intensity and weigh the level of their own responses to build appropriately off from what has gone before. In these final stages of polishing, added details of props and costumes enrich the characterizations. Eliza finds that she can wrap herself tightly in her Act I cape and huddle against a pillar to emphasize her desolation, caress her prize hat of Act II for added security, and swish her Act III skirt like a society lady, while her oversized fashionable hat points every line as she bobs her head for emphasis.

For the sake of brevity, we have confined the acting problems of *Pygmalion* to the character of Eliza. Each actor and actress in the show goes through a similar process to discover and develop his or her role, though the process would not be so involved for the members of the Covent Garden crowd of Act I, who have only one or two speeches and then are not seen again. But even they will have used those one or two speeches to discover an action for their characters that will provide believable motivations as long as they are on stage. Do they feel sorry for the flower girl? Do they resent the busybody professor or are they amused by him? Are they hoping for a good row, or do they wish the rain to stop so they can get home before real trouble starts? Are they on their way home from a pub, a date, an evening with friends, or on their way to a late night job? These are the kinds of questions that each actor can use to give a sense of reality to even the briefest walk-on part.

Though realistic acting has been the basis for creating the role of Eliza, certain nonrealistic techniques would also be helpful in acting *Pygmalion*. For Eliza, the actress would be especially in need of what we call "technique" in Act III, the first test of Eliza's lady-like development. The character has learned only how to stand, to walk, and to pronounce words like a lady. Thus, her manner of speaking and moving must appear out of proportion both to the ideas and feelings she is expressing and to the basic simplicity of the situation. In short, they will appear nonrealistic. As she is introduced, she greets each person she meets with the same "How do you do?" The actress will probably repeat the question with virtually the same mechanical expression and tone each time, suggesting a carefully rehearsed but meaningless phrase. She had been prompted by Higgins to talk about the weather, a "safe" subject, so when asked if it will rain, she is ready: "The shallow depression in the west of these islands is likely to move

The Ascot Race scene from *My Fair Lady*. Eliza may be dressed to the teeth, but her inner nature comes through to shock the society toffs around her.

slowly in an easterly direction. There are no indications of any great change in the barometrical situation." If this astonishing weather report is slightly overarticulated with all the seriousness of a theological pronouncement, but with some difficulty in remembering the exact words, the incongruity will increase the comic effect. In fact, such incongruity between what is said and the way it is said is one of the most important methods of comic stylization.

An even higher level of stylization was achieved for Eliza's first test in *My Fair Lady*, the musical version of *Pygmalion*. Lerner and Loewe chose to set the scene at the Ascot races, where the entire chorus watched the exciting horse race in unified precision, with totally immobile faces, and sang to the lively rhythm of a gavotte, but with crisp expressionless voices, about

> What a smashing, positively dashing
> Spectacle: the Ascot op'ning day.

Cecil Beaton's costumes of uniform white and grey formal dress and Moss Hart's staging, which had everyone raising their opera glasses simultaneously and lowering them with machine-like precision, reinforced the incongruity between the words being sung and the emotionless world that the very human Eliza was entering. But Eliza, under no such constraints, yells to her favorite horse, "Come on, Dover!!! Move your bloomin' arse!!!"—completing the comic incongruity.

The most important stylization in the musical comes in the transitions from realistic prose dialogue into the presentational styles of the songs and dances. When Eliza practices making vowel sounds with her nonsense comment on the weather, "The rain in Spain stays mainly in the plain," her teachers chime in, "I think she's got it!" They break into a tango rhythm, and move into a style more comic and lyric than realistic. In general, the choral numbers permit the actors to use a style more intense and exhilarating than simple everyday acting. Late in the play, Alfred Doolittle leads a cockney chorus in "Get Me to the Church on Time!," a playful celebration of independence that parallels Eliza's more rebellious assertion.

At last the actors are ready for an audience. The dressing room's atmosphere is a mixture of tension and excitement, with some actors quietly starting to get into character as they carefully apply their makeup. Others review their lines or complicated bits of business. Still others do warm-up exercises to get their voices and muscles ready to respond on stage. Some, not wanting to tamper with what they have spent weeks perfecting, relax by making small talk. No one whistles and everyone carefully avoids wishing anyone "good luck," both sure omens of bad luck. At last the Stage Manager calls, "Places!" The actors make their way onto the stage or into the wings to await their first entrances as a hush falls over the company. This is it, the moment they have been preparing for. The work lights are killed. Through the curtains the actors hear the audience chatter die down as the house lights dim, and then the curtain rises, spotlights illuminate the stage, and the sounds of wind and rain penetrate the shadows. Suddenly the stage is the portico of a church in Covent Garden; the actors are pedestrians running for shelter from the rain, shaking off the water a stage hand doused them with backstage moments before, and the play begins. For a few moments, the actors play their roles carefully, making each word clear, each gesture precise, giving the audience a chance to acclimate themselves to this world they have been invited to enter. Will they respond? No matter how much the actors admire the work of the playwright, no matter how much confidence they have in their director, this is the moment of truth. The director and playwright are nowhere around. This moment is between actor and audience. Then, quite unexpectedly, the first laugh rings through the house. The actors hear it with a sense of relief, of joy. The audience has willingly joined them to share in the world they are creating. This is what the weeks of preparation were all about. This is theatre. The laugh energizes and focuses the actors who now have someone to play to. And as the play moves from line to line, from scene to scene, the actors not only play to each other, as they had done in rehearsal, they measure their intensities, their pauses, the timing of their lines to the responses of the audience. So it will be in each performance as the actors recreate the world of the play and invite new audiences to discover and share that world with them.

Note: To get an idea of how Stella Beech Campbell, the original Eliza, approached the role, see *Bernard Shaw and Mrs. Patrick Campbell: Their Correspondence*, edited by Alan Dent (Knopf, 1952). An especially revealing letter from Shaw to Mrs. Campbell is found on pages 179 to 181. In 1960, Jerome Kilty did a highly entertaining stage adaptation of this correspondence in a play called *Dear Liar*.

EPILOGUE: THE PLEASURE OF YOUR COMPANY

The pleasure of audience and performer is a
shared experience with performers like Tommy
Tune leading the way. *My One and Only*.

Our revels now are ended. These our actors,
As I foretold you, were all spirits, and
Are melted into air, into thin air;
And, like the houseless fabric of this vision,
The cloud-capp'd towers, the gorgeous palaces,
The solemn temples, the great globe itself,
Yea, all which it inherit, shall dissolve
And, like this insubstantial pageant faded,
Leave not a rack behind. We are such stuff
As dreams are made on, and our little life
Is rounded with a sleep.

—Prospero in Shakespeare's *The Tempest*

I s the play—any play—a dream? An insubstantial pageant that fades, leaving not a rack behind? As it was in Shakespeare's Globe Theatre, so now, at the end of a good play, the spellbound tension of the audience relaxes in applause and we seem to wake as from a dream. Call it illusion, imagination, willing suspension of disbelief, a higher state of consciousness—it is a transcendent experience, a symbolic journey into a sacred realm, into a world of visions and meanings, of the gods and our ancestors who bequeathed us language and all the arts, who enlighten our path with purpose.

We leave the theatre feeling more friendly than before with the rest of the audience, for these individuals have shared our journey. We have seen deep into the lives of characters so like ourselves yet so different—lives lived more intensely than our own, focused, framed, complete, clear, whole. Our journey has widened our sympathy and deepened our compassion. We are more civilized.

The more literal-minded pilgrim, returning from this journey to the ideal, immediately sets out to reform the world, hoping to build the Kingdom on earth as it is in Heaven. What better tool than theatre? Like the Marxists, who see the world in terms of class warfare, they want the theatre to serve their private revolutions. Such earnestness provokes its opposites: "art for art's sake" or art as entertainment. A more balanced view, of course, is that art reflects in various ways the conditions of the artist's time and place but that the relation between art and action is rarely direct. The greatest satisfaction in art is the understanding of human relations on a symbolic level.

Theatre as Therapy

The psychologically oriented pilgrim sees the theatre journey as a journey into the mind. This is Hamlet's point of view: art as a tool for diagnosing inner guilt—"The play's the thing / Wherein I'll catch the conscience of the King." In Hamlet's view, art may also relieve or purge the guilt.

The therapeutic function of the arts is fully recognized, first of all for the artist himself. The painter Vincent Van Gogh and the playwright Eugene O'Neill held off disaster in their own disturbed lives for decades by relentlessly creating new artistic forms to give order to their feelings. Their paintings and plays have been of tremendous help to other people in meeting the disturbances of the modern age.

Theatre is one of the world's greatest therapeutic agencies, but not in the manner of psychodrama, where mentally ill patients act out personal relationships with partners in order to find and solve the cause of their disturbances. Psychodrama is specifically derived from, and pointed to, a particular person. But theatre offers to cure not the individual quirk so much as a general malaise. All the arts, but especially the theatre, point to the strains in a society and sometimes help avert disaster. Great religious leaders insist that the most ineffable joy is enlightenment, which relieves human beings from the agony of confusion and provides a light in darkness, a path through chaos, a place in time and space.

Theatre as a Connection to Our Past

The modern world offers excellent orientation in space. People can go to, or get a message to, almost any spot on earth. But they are dangerously disoriented in time. They fear the future because they have no past and do not know where they are or how they got there. They try to run a society without reading the minutes of the previous meetings. To the early Christians, who were sure that the Second Coming of Christ was imminent, history was not important. It would cease to exist. After 1945 the promise of the second coming of a nuclear bomb became so paralyzing that history seemed to lose all meaning. But recently such works as *Roots*, the book (and television film) by Alex Haley, who dug deeply into dusty records and traced his family to their African origins and down through the slave years to his own time, have reminded us that the present can be linked to the past. An increased understanding of our place in history and of how our ancestors changed through the years is one of the great healing pleasures of the theatre. Nowhere in our time has this need appeared more clearly than in the numerous dramatizations of the Nazi holocaust, by Germans, French, English, Americans, Poles, and Swiss, among others, as each has tried to reconstruct those terrible years to better understand one of the most emotionally charged eras of modern history. Perhaps therapy for a disturbed society is as important as therapy for an individual. It is supplied in the many forms of theatre.

Theatres in Our Time

The commercial theatre. Of all the types of theatre organizations, the "legitimate" theatre, the professional theatre of the cities, is the most highly touted. Broadway in New York, the West End in London, and the Boulevard theatres in Paris thrive on a fashionable well-dressed audience, who have parties before and after the show and meet friends in the intervals between acts to discuss the play and the actors. Though, in fact, this "fashionable" audience makes up only a small portion of actual theatregoers, the myth is sustained as part of the box-office ballyhoo.

The commercial theatre, theatre that is supported by the box office, started in the sixteenth century a generation before Shakespeare, where, with the expansion of the free-enterprise system, London, Paris, and Madrid grew large enough to support sizable acting companies. For four hundred years the commercial theatre has worked, after a fashion, paying fantastic fees to the great personalities who can draw crowds. But the speculative pressures are intense. A hit comedy or musical may bring in millions of dollars at the box office, and millions may be lost on the flops and near hits. Broadway legend is strewn with spectacular flops, typified by a $2.4 million investment in the 1981 *Frankenstein*, which closed after one performance. Yet starry-eyed investors, or "angels," hoping for windfall gains in the spirit of horse-racing, seem ever ready to pour in more money. Newspaper and television gossips spread the word of the latest

The spirit of commercial theatre is captured in the popular musical *42nd Street*, showing the company dancing in front of the blazing marquees of New York's theatre district.

The Chanhassen Dinner Theatre in suburban Minneapolis specializes in the dinner-and-a-show crowd in a sumputous theatre that seats about 600 people.

success, and out-of-towners want to see what "everyone" is talking about. Patrons, hoping for the magic of the most fashionable hit, stand in line for hours for the unlikely "returns," while a superb production for the perceptive theatregoer performs to empty seats just down the block.

Yet Broadway, despite the chaos and the frightful waste, still puts the final stamp of approval on an American play or actor. Hence thousands of young hopefuls descend on New York each year looking for the big break. Few make it, and even those who do average only a few weeks of work a year. On the other hand, an actor in a Broadway hit may be stuck in the same part for months or years, with no chance for professional growth. It is no wonder there is a strong drive to find a wider base for the top professional talent of the country.

By choosing much more modest goals, two kinds of commercial theatre have made a go of it: the dinner theatre in the smaller cities and the "straw hat" theatre in reach of the summer resorts. Dinner theatre appeals to families and groups of friends, who can hold their own parties at tables around the buffet platform. When the meal is over, the audience knows what to expect: a light comedy, a thriller, or occasionally a musical that can be done with limited cast and scenery, certainly nothing experimental. Summer stock is often of a higher quality, for a featured player of Broadway, film, or television fame may play a summer season, trouping from one playhouse to another, presenting a recent popular success or sometimes a new play announced as "prior to Broadway."

For the winter season in large cities, standards are much higher and theatregoers demand good quality in sets and costumes, a carefully rehearsed cast, and, often, a wider range of both new and old plays than Broadway provides. They regard the theatre as far more than "entertainment," as an art with psychological, social, humanistic, and spiritual values. Such a theatre requires subsidy.

The subsidized theatre. European countries have subsidized the theatre since the sixteenth century. Even before Shakespeare, Italian dukes and French and English kings paid for elaborate productions for the guests at their corona-

In recent years public television has taken a major role in showcasing outstanding productions of America's resident theatre companies for a mass viewing public, as in the 1983 broadcast of the Old Globe Theatre production of Wilder's *The Skin of Our Teeth*.

tion and wedding festivities. When opera and ballet gained wide audiences in the seventeenth century, the typical European theatre became the royal theatre built and partly supported by the king but open to the public. In many European cities the royal theatre is still one of the most splendid public buildings, with spacious setting and an imposing design. An outstanding example is the Paris opera house, built under Napoleon III. In all Western countries theatre is increasingly recognized as a public institution no less important than church, museum, or library, and one that should be no more dependent on entrance fees than those institutions.

Among Western nations, the United States, the richest country in the world, has been the laggard. The first national subsidy for the arts came in the 1960s, but with the austerity of the 1980s, that modest budget was among the first to suffer cuts. Even at their peak, appropriations of the United States government for the performing arts were less than those of the single German city of Hamburg for its opera company.

Yet America has seen major achievements. As early as 1927, with the help of private donations, the Cleveland Playhouse, which had been staffed by amateurs, became a professional company with a beautiful two-theatre building. In the 1960s Minneapolis and Houston took the lead in building regional theatres for resident companies, and in the early seventies New York and Washington each finally finished a splendid center for all the performing arts, Lincoln Center and Kennedy Center. Today performance centers across the land follow the same nonprofit image: a building paid for by private and corporate gifts and by city, state, and federal grants, usually located not in the crowded commercial area but near other nonprofit institutions such as art museums and concert halls.

The repertory system of many resident subsidized theatres is among their most attractive features. Offering a different play every few days, they allow the playgoer on a brief visit to the city to catch several shows. The actors may appear in three or more plays in a season, with a variety of roles and nights off, allowing them to come back fresh to one play after performing in others. Playgoers can subscribe for a whole season at good prices, simplifying the problem of getting tickets and assuring the management of a dependable audience.

Equally important is the resident company's freedom to experiment. Many put together a season of newly acclaimed hits, revivals of important plays of the past, new plays from abroad, and most significantly, new untested plays by both young and established American playwrights. Most of the important American plays and playwrights of recent years began, not in the precarious glow of Broadway, but in the nurturing atmosphere of a professional resident theatre. To enrich their programs and their communities, the companies provide workshops and internships for the young and special programs for senior citizens, as well as for the deaf, the handicapped, migrant workers, and local minority groups.

An efficiency expert might ask, why subsidize local live theatre when most people seem satisfied with television drama? But activities like theatre, which are creative and relate each participant to the community, are worth supporting, whether they are "efficient" or not. Many of our impersonal needs are satisfied with great efficiency by mass production. Such efficiency offers a great opportunity: citizens can afford to subsidize those personal needs, the arts, where there can be local distinction and creative joy. Mass marketing and mass communication tend to make all towns, all regions, all groups, exactly the same. It is worthwhile to foster local art and culture. It develops individual creativity and enriches the society as a whole.

The college and the community theatre. If the United States has been slow in supporting noncommercial professional theatre, it has led the world in public support for theatre in the schools. Most high schools and some elementary schools give opportunity for creative improvisation and dramatic performance. College theatres have expanded from a few dozen in the 1930s to several thousand in the 1980s, many of which have among the best theatre buildings in the world. Colleges usually have a competent trained staff, and some give professional training.

This impressive academic theatre program has several goals. Among these, often more important than the training of actors, designers, and directors, is the creation of knowledgeable audiences who appreciate the varied possibilities for human expression found in the theatre. To this end theatre departments offer courses in theatre appreciation and present a wide range of exciting plays from the world's repertoire. Many students who have never seen a live performance beyond the senior class play are surprised at the quality and artistic stimulation of college productions. Many college actors have considerable experience and training, and, as on the athletic field, youthful zest and enthusiasm go a long way.

The academic theatre for professional training involves not only classroom study of theatre history, dramatic analysis, and artistic theory. It is a laboratory for developing the skills of performance and production and often maintains connections with a resident theatre, an adult, professional extension of the college theatre. Both forms of theatre are planned on concepts delineated at the beginning of this century by Gordon Craig: that the theatre is not a show place for star actors but a creative art uniting many skills, and that workers in the theatre cooperate to see that every detail down to the last button and the last offstage sound makes its creative contribution to the production.

But the majority of students perfecting their skills in college theatre programs, even in prestigious professional schools, go on to use their training in related fields, not in theatre careers. Yet many continue theatre activity after college in a more modest, but no less significant way. These students put to use their considerable theatre knowledge and skill in community theatres across the land. The community theatre is basically nonprofessional and the actors are amateurs, though the director and designer usually are professionals. An "amateur" is one who works without pay for the pleasure of creative activity. Like the musician who continues to enrich his or her life in weekly rehearsals with a local choral society, jazz ensemble, or string quartet, or the athlete who plays weekly with an amateur league team, the trained actor finds both relaxation and creative stimulation in the community theatre group. The college training that these actors bring into the community helps raise the standards of production and performance as well as the artistic expectations and the taste of the audiences for whom they perform.

Theatre makes an ideal community activity: each play lasts just the right length of time for workers with responsibilities outside the theatre. The performers and technicians quickly become a team of comrades. From four to six weeks they work together intimately yet impersonally, with new tasks each day. The tempo gradually increases and leads to a tremendous climax: the performance itself, a gala occasion shared by friends who have heard only hints of the excitement.

For college and community actors, the excitement does not end with the last performance: it must be carried on to a celebration. More than a farewell to the companions of the voyage, there must be some recognition of achievement. More than the applause and curtain calls, the flowers and telegrams, the flutter of friends backstage—more than all these, the actors and backstage crews need a kind master of ceremonies, preferably not the director, who gently and wittily brings up the mistakes and near-disasters and gives awards of praise and recognition. In amateur theatre, as in sports, where love of the activity, not the money, is the chief reward, shining trophies may encourage excellence in everything from acting to backstage help.

The Critic and the Review

Ideally, every theatrical event should be concluded with an objective critic carefully delineating the strengths and weaknesses of the play and performance for the public record. Too often the amateur critic engages in irrelevant literary one-upmanship, meaningless praise of everyone whose name gets on the program, or smart-aleck witticisms that condemn the play to show the reviewer's superior taste. All three types of review put an end to discussion: The most useful criticism is sparing in judgment and lavish in description. A critical review that describes the event sensitively can help the playgoer see the play more clearly, the theatre artists understand what they did or did not accomplish, and somone who has not seen the play know what it was like and join in the discussion.

Students should be warned that no critic, amateur or professional, can write a completely just review. Critics usually write in haste, and, although probably better informed than playgoers, they also have their prejudices and preferences. They often seem to expect a play to be either a triumph or disaster. It is seldom either. The worst sin is to attack a play or production for not being what it was never intended to be. Goethe once said that one should determine what the work is trying to do, then how well it does it. Only then ask why it was or was not worth doing.

The tradition of the skeptic-critic, often a hostile critic, has its home in the commercial, free-enterprise age of theatre. Though it has its value there, where audience members are reluctant to put down forty or more dollars for a single seat without some assurance that it's worth the money, it tends to encourage investors to overlook the fledgling work and to go after the big hit that can produce the rave reviews. The problem is magnified on the Broadway stage, where the damning voice of one reviewer can close a show that hundreds have invested time and money in. The role of skeptic-critic seems even less pertinent to a time when resident, college, and community theatres are considered part of the cultural life of any community. A very naive audience may need the skeptic to sort out the good from the shoddy, but when much of the public is blasé from a glut of television entertainment, as well as bewildered by modern experiments in live theatre, a different kind of critic is needed. An advocate-critic can explain and comment on what theatre artists are trying to do. A national company in Europe regularly has on its staff a *dramaturg*, usually the holder of a doctorate in drama or theatre history, to help select the plays to be produced, prepare translations, and give public lectures. The practice has spread to several American resident theatre companies in recent years, and university theatres have now begun to add programs in the training of the dramaturg.

In the Long Run

In one sense, every play invites us to share an experience complete in itself that ends with the applause, and when we have had the pleasure of its company, we say, "That's that," and return to our daily living until the next play. Yet some plays we like to see a second time, or read at leisure the script we heard in the heat of performance. We like to compare plays by the same author, roles played by the same actor, and films made by the same director. A revival of a play of some years ago, or the autobiography of a famous actor, invites comparison of the attitudes and ideas of an earlier generation with those of our own time. Though we may smile at the outdated manners and morals, we soon get a feeling of history and an understanding of our place in time.

Let the actors return to their spirit world and let the great globe itself dissolve: now we know our true nature. As Shakespeare's Prospero says, "We are such stuff as dreams are made on." The world of dreams is the world of knowledge, imagination, values, understanding—the timeless world that endures after "our little life is rounded with a sleep." The theatre may shock, divert, and entertain us. It may make us look closely at the world we live in and perhaps consider how we can improve it. It may rouse our sense of justice, purify our motives and hopes, and warn us against oversimplification. As we are stirred by compassion for the stage characters, we feel a kinship with all mankind. And in theatre experiences, both as actors and audience, we come to know ourselves— by creating a *persona*, an identity, a role in relation to other people, indeed in relation to the universe. We know who and where we are. May our revels never end.

GLOSSARY

Absurdism. A term used to describe a style of playwriting of the 1950s and 1960s that emphasized the unpredictability and meaninglessness of human activity and the impossibility of true communication. Beckett, Ionesco, and Adamov are the playwrights most often associated with absurdism.

Acting areas. Artificial divisions of the playing space on a stage set, used to facilitate the planning of stage movement.

Action (of characters). The process each character in a play goes through in striving to reach a desired goal. The *action of the play* is the single unified human process that the plot brings into focus, to which all of the character actions are subordinate.

Ad lib. An improvised line or set of lines, often inserted when something unexpected occurs in performance, such as an actor forgetting lines.

Alienation. Also called "A-effect." A process in epic realism that causes audience members to distance themselves emotionally from the events to consider their social implications.

Allegory. A play that expresses its meanings metaphorically. Common in medieval morality plays, where characters are personifications of abstract concepts, such as virtues or vices.

Angel. A financial backer for a commercial production.

Antagonist. The character in a play who forms the major obstacle in the protagonist's movement toward an objective.

Apron. See *forestage.*

Apron stage. See *thrust stage.*

Arena theatre. Also called "theatre in the round." A theatre in which the audience surrounds the playing area on all sides.

Artistic appreciation. The audience's appreciation for the skills of the various theatre artists who help create a production.

Aside. A line of stage dialogue spoken directly to the audience that other characters on stage do not hear. A shared confidence between character and audience.

Audition. A competitive tryout for a performer seeking a role in a theatre production.

Avant-garde. Any group that is in the forefront of artistic innovation—literally, the advance guard.

Backstage. The area of the stage concealed from the audience by the set; the working area for stage crews.

Ballet. A dance form developed originally in the seventeenth-century French court, characterized by grace and precision, and based on standard formal positions and movements.

Black-box theatre. A flexible room for theatre performance in which the audience seating and playing areas can be rearranged in any way that suits the needs of the individual production.

Blocking. Planning the arrangement and movement of the actors on stage throughout the course of a production.

Box set. An interior setting associated with the development of realism, consisting of flats for three interior walls and a ceiling, with the fourth wall represented by the proscenium opening.

Broadway. The theatre district of New York City on and around the street called Broadway; the most concentrated area of American commercial theatre.

Build. A term used to describe any pattern of rising intensity, speed, or volume in a dramatic unit.

Burlesque. 1. A ludicrous imitation of a dramatic form or a specific play, to provoke laughter at the excesses of the form imitated. 2. A variety show that exploits sexuality and broad comedy.

Business. Any detailed activity done by actors to express their characters or to develop the action—lighting a cigarette, twirling a fan, dropping to the knees, and so forth.

Cabaret theatre. Theatre presented to audiences while they enjoy refreshments. Sometimes includes full-length plays, but frequently consists of light comic or satiric sketches.

Casting. The process of assigning roles to actors for a given production.

Catharsis. A Greek term to define the effect of tragedy, often referred to as a purging of the emotions of pity and fear.

Character. An agent for action and thought in the play whose traits and qualities result from ethical belief or deliberation, embodied by the emotional and physical portrayal of an actor. A *simple character* is one dominated by a single motivation. A *complex character* is one with an internal conflict.

Chorus. A group of performers who work as a unit rather than individually. They usually stand outside the main action, supporting it emotionally in their song and dance, but often they comment on it or provide a narrative thread as well.

Classical. Generally refers to ancient Greek and Roman theatre and to later theatre and drama that have used them as models. Suggests formal structures that imitate idealized actions in tragedy and universal follies in comedy.

Climax. The turning point of the action in traditional dramatic structure, the point of no return. Alternatively refers to the emotional high point of the play. See also *reversal*.

Comedy. One of the major forms of drama, with many subcategories. Variously defined as having a happy ending, portraying people of lower and middle classes, exposing the folly of humankind, dealing with regeneration, and taking a point of view that provokes laughter.

Comedy of humours. A form of comedy developed by Ben Jonson in the Elizabethan period in which characters are dominated by obsessive personality traits deriving from the imbalance of the four humours (phlegm, choler, bile, and black bile) that Elizabethans believed to control behavior.

Comedy of manners. Usually refers to comedies of the seventeenth and eighteenth centuries whose characters are preoccupied with social behavior.

Commedia dell'arte. A popular form of comedy that originated in Italy in the sixteenth century. Consisted of plays improvised from scenarios by actors playing stock characters, which reappeared from play to play. Filled with repeated standard bits of comic business called *lazzi.*

Commercial theatre. Professional theatre that depends entirely on ticket sales for its income and is concerned with making a profit.

Community theatre. Amateur theatre, though often professionally designed and directed, done by and for members of a local community.

Complication. In the ascending action of the plot, any new information or development that requires characters to readjust their way of relating to the action or pursuing their goals.

Confidant(e). A character who serves as friend to the hero or heroine, providing him or her the chance to express private feelings. Common in French neoclassical drama.

Conflict. The basic tension that underlies dramatic action, leading to crises and climaxes. *External conflict* results when two or more characters are in opposition to one another. *Internal conflict* is the result when characters have to sort out opposing needs or desires within themselves.

Confrontation. A type of theatre activity, common in the avant-garde movements of the 1960s and 1970s, in which the performers attempt to draw the audience into direct interaction with the performance.

Contact improvisation. A form of post-modern dance in which two dancers, without the use of hands, use direct involvement with each others' bodies and movements as the motivating source for their own movement.

Convention. An agreed-upon method or practice that forms a kind of contract between audience and production as to how things will be done. Examples include the dimming of lights to indicate the passage of time and characters speaking in verse.

Corps de ballet. A company or team of ballet dancers.

Crew. The backstage technicians who are responsible for or assist in the technical aspects of production.

Cross. A term used to indicate a movement of an actor from one section of the stage to another.

Cue. 1. A line, movement, sound, etc., that serves as a signal to an actor or technician to perform his or her next function. 2. Any bit of information, verbal or nonverbal, that signals the audience toward an understanding of the drama.

Cycle drama. Medieval plays that followed the Biblical history of Christianity from the Creation to the Last Judgment.

Cyclorama or **Cyc.** A large curved drop that encircles the back and sides of the stage and masks off the backstage. Used as background for outdoor scenes or, with special lighting effects, used to create a background of mood in presentational styles of production. Also a permanent neutrally painted wall that serves the same function.

Denouement. The part of the play that follows the climax, during which the threads of the action are untangled and the action is resolved.

Determinism. The philosophical position that people are controlled by factors largely beyond their control, such as heredity and environment. The basis for naturalism in the theatre.

Dinner theatre. A popular theatre form where audiences dine together before the play.

Dionysia. In ancient Greece, the City Dionysia and the Rural Dionysia were festivals in honor of the god Dionysus that included dramatic performances. The City Dionysia is considered the birthplace of tragedy, while the Lenaia, a third such festival, was the home of comedy.

Director's concept. The idea that guides a specific production of a play, forming the basis for all artistic choices.

Dithyramb. In ancient Greece, a song of praise to the god Dionysus, sung and danced by a chorus of men. Traditionally the form out of which tragedy grew.

Documentary drama. Drama that records actual events or the lives of actual people. The documentary film uses the people themselves as the performers.

Downstage. The area of the stage closest to the audience.

Drama. 1. The literary essence of a play, sometimes contrasted with its theatrical essence. 2. Any play that is serious in tone but is not a tragedy.

Dramatic irony. See *ironic experience.*

Dramaturg. A member of a theatre company who acts as a script consultant on a production. In the European theatre the dramaturg also is responsible for casting and organizing the season of plays.

Drop. A large painted cloth that serves as a background to a stage setting.

Dumbshow. In Renaissance theatre, a pantomimed summary of the plot that sometimes preceded the performance of a play.

Eccyclema. In ancient Greek theatre, a machine that was used to reveal tableaux of objects or people, often the dead. The eccyclema was rolled out from an opening in the skene.

Elevator stage. A stage that can be raised or lowered for quick changing of scenery.

Elizabethan theatre. One of the high points in the history of theatre, usually referring to the time from the beginning of the reign of England's Elizabeth I (1558) to the closing of the theatres during the English Civil War (1642). Important both for its playwrights, such as Christopher Marlowe, William Shakespeare, and Ben Jonson, and for its open-air, thrust-stage theatres.

Emotional memory. In the Stanislavsky system of acting, a technique by which actors relate to deep emotions of their characters by recalling the details surrounding some similar emotions from their own personal experience.

Empathy. One of the many responses that audiences have toward characters in a play, a "feeling with" the character, both emotionally and physically.

Ensemble. 1. A unified group of performers. 2. A term to describe the sense of unity achieved by a group of performers.

Environmental theatre. A modern theatre form in which the audience space and the playing space are intermixed, so that the audience finds the action occurring all around them and may even have to choose where to look as they would in real life.

Epic realism. A form of drama developed in Germany in the 1920s by Erwin Piscator and Bertolt Brecht, appealing to the audience's willingness to make judgments rather than relate to the play emotionally. Using a narrative style and a variety of theatrical devices, it invites the audience to distance themselves from the events so as to consider their social implications.

Epilogue. A short scene or speech that sometimes follows the main action of a play.

Episode. In ancient Greek drama, the sections of the play that develop the dramatic action of the characters, separated by the choral odes. In later times, any discrete unit of dramatic action.

Ethnic theatre. Theatre that is created by a specific ethnic group for members of its own group to express the life of the ethnic culture from their own point of view.

Existentialism. A modern philosophical system that underlies much of the theatre of disruption as articulated by Albert Camus and Jean Paul Sartre. In the absence of any fixed standards or values, each person defines his or her own essence in those situations where choices must be made that lead to action.

Exodos. In ancient Greek drama, the closing choral speech.

Exposition. Those elements of a play that provide background information necessary to the audience's understanding of the action.

Expressionism. In drama, a movement that flourished in Germany immediately before and following World War I, characterized by a subjective view of reality and symbolic presentation of meaning. Typically, an Everyman-like central character would encounter a mechanized world and a dehumanized society presented through distortion to help the audience experience the terrors of modern existence through the eyes of the central character. In the United States, playwrights such as Eugene O'Neill and Elmer Rice experimented with expressionistic techniques in several plays during the 1920s.

Farce. One of the major genres of drama, often classified as a form of comedy. It uses broad visual and sound effects, accelerated speed, and rough-and-tumble action to entertain and provoke laughter, but is played with deadly seriousness by its characters.

Festival. A special time set aside for theatrical performance, such as the ancient Greek festivals devoted to the god Dionysus, the Roman dramas on feast days of the gods, and the medieval Christian festivals, especially the spring festival of Corpus Christi, which were celebrated with religious cycle dramas. In modern times, the religious theatre festival still lives in the Mormons' Hill Cumorah pageant and in the summer festival of the Passion Play at Oberammergau, Germany. The idea has been expanded to include historical pageants and festivals devoted to the works of such writers as Shakespeare and Wagner.

Flat. A standard unit of scenery consisting of a light wooden frame covered with painted canvas.

Floor plan. A diagram of the stage floor in a set design, showing the placement of all walls, doorways, platforms, furniture, and so forth.

Flying. A process in which scenery is raised and lowered, using the area above the stage (*Flyloft*) for storage.

Footlights. A strip of lights (often recessed into the floor) along the front of the stage.

Forestage. The part of a proscenium stage that extends from the proscenium opening toward the audience. Also called *apron*.

Found material. Material taken directly from life and incorporated into the dramatic event exactly as is. In the contemporary theatre, groups have frequently put on plays in such found spaces as a street, warehouse, or gallery. Post-modern dance and avant-garde theatre groups have made use of found movements and found objects as part of the works they create. The art is not in the creation of the object, movement, or space, but in the way it is used in an artistic context.

Fourth-wall convention. A term common in the naturalistic theatre, referring to the idea that the stage setting is like a normal room with the wall toward the audience removed.

Groundlings. In the Elizabethan theatre, the lower-class, rowdy patrons who sat or stood in the yard (the cheap, open-air section immediately surrounding the stage).

Guilds. Medieval religious organizations for professional and trade groups that organized the religious cycle dramas.

Heavy. The role of any solemn leading character, especially the villain of melodrama.

Heroic verse. An idealized style of writing found in neoclassical drama, consisting of rhymed couplets in iambic pentameter or, in French, iambic hexameter (Alexandrines).

High comedy. Comedy of the intricate social maneuverings of characters from the upper classes, with a strong emphasis on witty language and intellect.

History play. A play set in a historical period emphasizing historical themes, usually of a nationalistic nature. Made popular in Elizabethan England where Shakespeare and his fellow playwrights wrote a variety of plays on the themes of English history.

House lights. The lights illuminating the audience portion of the theatre.

Humanism. A philosophy that places human concerns rather than theological concerns at the center of interest.

Illusion. Refers to the audience's way of accepting as real the events and scenic elements they see on the stage.

Impressionism. A style of drama using fleeting details and moods to evoke the deeper truth of a situation rather than simply copying its outward objective form.

Improvisation. Rehearsal or performance technique in which the actors respond directly to the immediate situation without relying on preplanned details.

Ingenue. The role of the sweet, innocent heroine.

Intermezzo. A kind of entertainment, usually musical, that was performed between the acts of plays or operas in Italian Renaissance courts.

Ironic experience. The response an audience has to the ongoing patterns of a play because of its privileged perspective. Because audience members have information the characters do not have, and see connections and relationships that the characters cannot see, they appreciate the action in ways that the characters themselves cannot.

Lazzi. Stock bits of business that could be inserted wherever appropriate in a play. Associated with *commedia dell'arte* and with French and Italian farce of the seventeenth and eighteenth centuries.

Legitimate theatre. A term used to describe professional live theatre, as opposed to film and television.

Levels. The various elevated playing areas—balconies, platforms, stairway landings, and so forth—of which many modern settings are comprised.

Lighting. The special illumination for a play that provides visibility, emphasis, and focus and may suggest time, place, and mood.

Liturgical drama. Drama that takes its form from elements of religious worship, or drama that creates a sense of worship in its structure.

Living newspaper. A type of multimedia documentary drama that focuses on social and political events by interweaving dramatic scenes with actual news accounts of the events.

Magic if. In the Stanislavsky system of acting, the technique that allows actors to imagine themselves in the situations of the characters they play.

Manager. In English theatre, the same as the American producer.

Mansion. In medieval theatre, a scenic structure that indicates a particular place (such as Paradise, or Noah's ark) in front of which the action of the play is staged. Several mansions often appeared on a stage or around a playing space *(platea)* simultaneously. Hence, *simultaneous staging*.

Masque. A spectacular entertainment common in the court theatres of the Renaissance. Emphasis was on lavish costumes and scenic effects with plots from mythology and fantasy.

Melodrama. Literally "music drama," suggesting the use of external effects to heighten emotional impact. Melodramas are plays that emphasize the conflict between good and evil in a morally simplistic universe, with stock heroes and villains, sudden reversals of fortune, an abundance of external conflict, and a resolution that reaffirms the prevailing value system of the audience.

Method acting. The American version of the Stanislavsky system of acting, with an emphasis on the emotional life of the character.

Mime. In modern-day terminology, a style or type of performance in which the story is presented visually, through movement and gesture, instead of with words.

Minstrel show. A light entertainment of the late nineteenth- and early twentieth-century American theatre based on unrealistic imitations of the speech and manners of the American Negro. Performed by whites.

Miracle play. Medieval plays that treat the lives of the saints.

Modern dance. A style of dance that began in the early twentieth century, breaking with the formal idealized patterns of ballet, with emphasis on free movement patterns, flowing costumes, interpretive approaches to the music, and the expression of the full range of human experience.

Morality play. Allegorical plays of the medieval period with characters representing abstract concepts or generalized groups of people, such as Strength, Beauty, Greed, Kindred, and so forth. *Everyman* is a major example. Variations of the morality play continue into the modern nonrealistic theatre.

Motif. A recurring thematic element or a pattern of repetition of design elements in a work of art.

Multiple casting. Casting an actor in more than one role in a given production.

Multiple focus. A stage picture that requires the audience to choose among more than one point of focus at a time, or to shift focus among vying points of attention.

Musical. Also called "musical comedy." A major American form of theatre, though its roots are in nineteenth-century Viennese operetta. Typically it includes a spoken text (or book) interspersed with solos, duets, choral songs and dances, and a great deal of spectacle. Several recent musicals are sung throughout.

Mystery play. Plays of the medieval period based on Biblical stories. The cycle dramas consisted of a series of mystery plays.

Naturalism. An early branch of realism, especially common in France, Germany, and Russia from about 1880 to 1900, that emphasized determinism and the sordid detail of daily living, with special attempts to present objective reality so that the characters could be examined in relation to their heredity and environment. The adherents of naturalism were trying to improve social conditions by scientifically examining the conditions that had brought about the problems.

Neoclassical. Refers to the attempt to model an artwork after the forms of classicism. In theatre, the great periods of neoclassical drama are the Italian Renaissance and the French seventeenth century.

New stagecraft. A movement in scenic design beginning in the early twentieth century that emphasizes suggestion, simplification, and synthesis rather than the imitation of reality to create unity of production.

Objective. In the Stanislavsky system of acting, the goal toward which a character is striving. The *super-objective* (also called *spine*) is the life goal that determines how the character responds in any situation.

Obstacle. Any factor that stands in the way of a character's achieving a desired goal. A basis for dramatic conflict.

Ode. In Greek theatre, a lyrical unit sung and danced by the Chorus that separated and commented on the episodes.

Off Broadway. Small professional New York theatres outside the central theatre district around Broadway and Times Square. Originally noted for their experimental nature, they have come to share much of the commercialism of Broadway.

Off-Off Broadway. Very small professional theatres, often subsidized, which are often set up in lofts, warehouses, or churches and are usually characterized by their experimental scripts and styles of production.

Off stage. Those areas of the stage not visible to the audience.

On stage. Any part of the stage in view of the audience.

Open stage. See *thrust stage.*

Opera. A dramatic musical composition for the stage that is sung throughout.

Operetta. A light dramatic musical composition for the stage that intersperses songs with spoken text.

Orchestra. 1. The dancing circle at the center of the Greek theatre where the Chorus performed. 2. In the American theatre, audience seating area on the ground-floor level.

Oriental realism. A term used to describe the incorporation into Western realistic theatre of the symbolic techniques common in the traditional theatres of China and Japan.

Pacing. Apparent rate of performance. Though speed is a factor of pacing, equally important are intensity, frequency of new impressions, precision, and clarity of the connections between impressions so as to cause anticipation in the audience.

Pageant wagon. In the medieval period, a stage mounted on a rolling wagon for the performance of individual mystery plays within the cycle drama. Used in England, Spain, and parts of central Europe.

Pantomime. 1. In Roman theatre, a story-telling dance done by a solo performer accompanied by a chorus and a small group of musicians. The modern English Christmas pantomime combines traditional folk stories with song and spectacle and a magical scene of transformation. 2. Acting with the body rather than the voice.

Parados. In Greek drama, the section of the play in which the Chorus enters. Also the alleyway between the orchestra and the audience area through which the Chorus enters.

Parody. A performance that imitates another performance for the purpose of comic ridicule.

Parts of drama. Aristotle established what have come to be called the six parts of drama that are fundamental to any dramatic event: plot, character, thought, diction, music (sometimes called rhythm), and spectacle. This book has defined a three-part breakdown: that which is performed, the means by which it is performed, and the audience for whom it is performed.

Perspective scenery. Scenery constructed or painted to simulate the effect of receding distance by manipulating size.

Phenomenology. The study of all the possible appearances of phenomena in human experience, with both objective and subjective considerations temporarily set aside, while things are examined in and for themselves.

Picture-frame stage. A term applied to the proscenium stage to describe the impression that the audience sees the play as through a picture frame.

Picturization. The arrangement of characters on the stage to create balance and focus and to reveal the dynamic relationships between the characters so as to help convey the developing stages of the drama.

Plant. In playwriting and directing, to give special emphasis early in the play to a word, object, action, or idea so that the audience is led to expect some further development from it later on.

Platform stage. A stage raised above the audience area that is not enclosed by a proscenium arch.

Plot. The organizing structure of a play. The playwright selects which elements of the story to show on stage and then arranges the order in which to present them so as to focus attention on the action for the best dramatic effect. In short, the playwright plots the action.

Poetic justice. The idea that reward and punishment are meted out in ways particularly appropriate to the nature of the deed.

Poor theatre. A term popularized by Jerzy Grotowski and his Polish Laboratory Theatre. Refers to a theatre stripped down to what he considered to be its only essential elements—actor and audience.

Post-modern dance. A style of dance in contemporary theatre that has redefined dance to include found movements, improvisation, dance without music, nonhuman animated forms, emotionless movement, and, in some cases, periods of nonmovement.

Presentational. A method of performance and design that frankly displays its theatricality, as opposed to *representational*, which attempts to simulate reality.

Producer. In the American theatre, the person or organization responsible for all the business decisions connected with the production. In Great Britain the producer is the same as the director in the American theatre.

Production format. The production counterpart of plot. The selection and arrangement of all the production elements by the producing artists to focus attention on the action for the best dramatic effect.

Projection. 1. In acting, the technique for making spoken words or movements and gestures clear to all parts of the house. 2. In design, the throwing of an image onto the setting by means of light for optical effects.

Prologue. In Greek drama, the part of the play that precedes the first entrance of the Chorus. In later drama, a speech or a scene preceding the main action that entertains, defends the play, sets a mood, sets the scene, or warms up the audience.

Promenade theatre. A style of theatre production, most common in England, where the audience has no designated seating space but moves to whatever position allows them to follow the action, which is also moving. Designed to create a feeling of drama as a community experience.

Prompt book. A script of the play that contains a record of all production details, such as actor movements, sound and light cues, and call cues for actors. The stage manager works from the prompt book during performance.

Props or properties. Portable objects used on stage to complete the picture or the action—furniture, letters, telephones, wall hangings, and so forth.

Proscenium stage. A stage that is separated from the audience by a framing unit, called the proscenium arch, which conceals backstage operations and helps create the illusion of a complete world of the play beyond the proscenium.

Protagonist. In Greek theatre, the first or major actor. In later times, the leading character of a play.

Realism. In the broadest sense, realism in theatre is the dramatic treatment of the day-to-day problems of ordinary people, usually presented so as to simulate the actual living conditions of the characters. Though realism can be found throughout theatre history, it became a major movement in the late nineteenth century with the rise of the middle class and new developments in science and social thinking that made theatre a tool for improving the human and social condition.

Regional theatre. Also called *resident theatre*. A term applied to permanent nonprofit professional theatre companies that have established roots outside the major theatre centers. Besides bringing first-rate theatre to their region, they often have special programs to nurture local talent and to encourage new plays of special regional interest.

Repertory. A set group of productions that a theatre company has prepared for performance. Also, the practice of alternating performances of the different plays of the repertory.

Representational. A style of production that strives to simulate or create the illusion of reality on stage. See *presentational*.

Reprise. A repetition of a song or dance with variation. Common in musicals.

Resident theatre. See *regional theatre*.

Restoration. 1. The period in England dating from the restoration of the English monarchy in 1660 to about 1700. 2. Plays written in the Restoration period, usually characterized in tragedy by elevated expression of feelings, and in comedy by wit, social intrigue, a fascination with social manners, and a cynical view of human behavior.

Reversal. A sudden change in fortune or knowledge for any of the major characters of a play, resulting in new expectations and a new direction for the action. The climax is the major reversal of a play in traditional structures.

Review. A descriptive and evaluative public report on a production.

Revolving stage. A large turntable built into or mounted on a stage on which different settings can be constructed, so that by revolving the turntable, a new setting or a new view of the setting will emerge.

Rigging. The system of ropes, pulleys, counterweights, pipes, and so forth that is used backstage in the manipulation of scenery.

Road company. A company of performers who travel with a show that they present in essentially the same way it was originally created in a theatre center such as New York.

Romantic comedy. A type of comedy developed in the Renaissance in which knights and idealized ladies engaged in the loves and intrigues of an aristocratic court, surrounded by a variety of colorful comic characters whose escapades are viewed tolerantly and even lovingly. In the modern theatre, any comedy that centers on a love interest.

Romanticism. A style of theatre that began at the end of the eighteenth century, emphasizing inspiration as the major creative force, freedom of expression as the creative method, and individualism and the infinite variety of human experience as subject matter.

Romantic love. A concept of love invented in the Middle Ages that idealized woman as the inspiration for knightly prowess. The knight was transformed by a glimpse of his lady and then worshiped her from afar, while performing difficult tasks that she would set for him.

Satire. A form of comedy that uses wit and irony to poke fun at social institutions, ideas, public figures, or general human traits.

Scenario. In *commedia dell'arte* the plan of the plot or action from which the actors improvised the performance. Speaking generally, a narrative description of a plot.

Scenery. The stage settings for a play.

Script. The written version of a play. The text from which the theatre artists work as they create the produced play.

Selected realism. A modification of realism that has become the most common approach to realistic drama, in which careful selection of realistic detail creates the illusion of reality, as opposed to filling the stage with all the details that might be present in the actual environment represented.

Sensory experience. The audience response to the visual and sound effects of the play as well as to its rhythmic flow.

Setting or set. The scenery for a particular scene or for an entire production.

Shutter. A large flat slid on from the wings to form a scenic background when paired with a second shutter that is joined with it at center stage. A variant form of the backdrop. See *wing and drop*.

Simultaneous staging. A stage arrangement in which more than one set appears on stage at once, often with a neutral playing area (platea) in front that can be used as part of whichever set is being used at the time.

Situation comedy. Often called "sitcom" in television. A type of comedy in which immediately recognizable character types provoke laughter because of the ways that their character qualities are played against unexpected or incongruous situations.

Skene. The scene building in Greek theatre.

Slapstick. 1. A comic sword made of two strips of wood that provides a maximum of sound and a minimum of pain when applied to the rump. 2. A type of comedy or comic business that derives its humor from violent but ridiculous physical conflict.

Slice of life. A style of drama associated with naturalism, in which playwrights attempted to create plays as though they were lifting actual segments out of life and placing them on stage intact, with no attempt to build toward climaxes or to tie up all the loose threads at the end.

Soliloquy. A speech delivered by a character alone on stage to explore the character's private thoughts. Often lyric in style and highly emotional.

Space staging. A style of production in which the acting areas are defined by separately lighted spaces against a dark background.

Spectacle. One of Aristotle's six parts of drama, and the one that most clearly distinguishes theatre from other forms of story-telling. Refers to the visual and sound elements in a production. Hence, a theatre piece that appeals largely to the sensory experience is often called a "spectacle."

Spine. In Method acting, the dominant motivation or goal of a character that connects all aspects of the character's behavior and attitudes.

Stage directions. In a play script, the nondialogue sections that describe the design elements or the techniques of performance. Often written by someone other than the playwright.

Stage left. The area of the stage to the left of an actor when facing toward the audience.

Stage manager. The theatre staff member who coordinates all elements of the production from back stage during performance.

Stage right. The area of the stage to the right of an actor when facing toward the audience.

Stanislavsky method. A system of acting devised by the Russian director and actor Constantin Stanislavsky, in which the actor finds and expresses the inner truth of the character by defining the character's objectives, developing a subtext for every moment on stage, exploring the character's emotional life through emotional memory and improvisation, and applying the "magic if" during rehearsal and performance.

Star system. A producing structure in which all minor and supporting roles for a season are played by resident actors, while stars are brought in to play the leading roles. Common in nineteenth-century theatre, and still prevalent in opera and in summer stock.

Stereotypes. See *stock characters.*

Stock characters. Clearly defined character types (stereotypes) that appear repeatedly in many different plays.

Straw-hat theatre. Loosely describes theatre companies organized to appeal to the recreational interests of summer audiences.

Street theatre. Theatre that tries to attract spontaneous audiences in open-air spaces, often for the purpose of social activism.

Stylization. Any systematic production method that departs from realistic representation.

Stylized realism. Plays that keep the central character realistically intact, but surround him with abstract and distorted effects and break the environment into fragments to show the violence of his subjective conflict with reality.

Subtext. 1. In the Stanislavsky system of acting, the thoughts that accompany the lines, implied but not spoken in the text. The actors invent the subtext appropriate to their characters and situations to help achieve the sense of immediate truth. 2. The continuing dialogue that audience members carry on with the drama as they imaginatively interact with the events of the play.

Summer stock. Professional or semiprofessional theatre companies organized for the recreational interests of summer audiences.

Surrealism. An antiformalist, antirealist movement in the arts that developed after World War I in Europe and sought to transform society through total liberation of the unconscious.

Symbolism. A style of theatre developed in the 1890s that strives to reveal deeper spiritual truths through suggestion rather than by direct representation. Emphasis on myths, moods, and symbols that can evoke subjective and spiritual truth.

Sympathetic experience. The feeling an audience experiences when they find themselves sharing the concerns and point of view of one or more of the characters in a play.

Synthesizing experience. The response of an audience that draws connections from the play into the world they know outside the play, causing them to reaffirm or readjust their view of reality. Identified with *theme.*

Tableau. A living picture presented by actors without motion or speech.

Theatre in the round. See *arena theatre.*

Theatre of cruelty. A term made popular by Antonin Artaud to describe his vision of a theatre that would pierce through the veneer of civilized humans to release their basic primitive nature and purge them in the process. To do this he wanted to redefine theatre space so as to merge audience with performers and to use sound, light, rhythm, and symbolic movement and gesture to assault the senses of the audience.

Theatre of disruption. Theatre that is designed to call attention to the unreliability of order and universal values.

Theatre of exaltation. Theatre that is designed to inspire its audiences with an awareness of their relation to higher powers, such as a divine being or the forces of history.

Theatre of fact. A form of realism usually meant to teach or persuade by presenting documented factual material or by trying to recreate an actual event, such as a court trial, by using the characters and often the actual words from the event. See also *documentary drama; living newspaper.*

Theatre of liberation. Used in this text to describe theatre activity of recent decades that (1) has tried to free theatre of encrusted tradition and return it to its basics or (2) has used theatre forms to liberate its practitioners and audiences from stultifying conditions in society.

Theatrical. Refers to any device or style which calls attention to the fact that the event is a performance and not real life.

Theme. The central thought or idea that the play evokes, producing the audience's synthesizing experience.

Thrust stage. Also called *apron stage* and *open stage.* A stage that extends into the audience, with the audience surrounding it on three sides, and scenery or some kind of formal facade on the fourth side.

Tony Award. Awards given annually by the directors of the American Theatre Wing for outstanding contributions to the current season of Broadway theatre. Named in memory of actress/producer Antoinette Perry.

Tragedy. Among the most honored of theatre forms. Popularly conceived as any play that ends unhappily for its protagonist. As defined by Aristotle, tragedy imitates an action of an essentially admirable hero who goes from good fortune to bad fortune. Though the hero is partially responsible, the punishment is out of proportion so that the emotions of both pity and fear are aroused in the audience. Traditionally, the choice the tragic hero makes is an ethical one, raising moral and philosophical questions of universal significance, and the punishment of the hero affirms the triumph of cosmic or moral order over individual fate. Modern plays called tragedies tend to focus more on personal and social responsibility and ethics rather than on questions of cosmic import.

Tragicomedy. In the Renaissance, a form of play that joined a comic and a tragic plot. In the modern theatre tragicomedy, like comedy, often laughs at folly in human behavior, but, like tragedy, it depicts the characters suffering the fruits of their folly or traps them in a world where laughter fails to provide an antidote for their suffering.

Trap. An opening in the stage floor which, when uncovered, can be used for special effects, such as a grave or a stairway leading to a lower level.

Trilogy. Three plays (usually tragedies) intended to be performed as a unit, tied together by either a continuous story thread or by theme. Tragedies in ancient Greece were commonly written as trilogies.

Trope. A dramatic interpolation into a religious text or service. Medieval drama is believed to have evolved from tropes.

Turntable. See *revolving stage*.

Unities. In the Italian Renaissance theatre and the French neoclassical theatre the ideal play form followed the "three unities"—the unities of time, place, and action—so that the entire play centered on a single action occurring in a single day in one place.

Unit set. A single setting designed to accommodate all the scenes of a multiple set show, sometimes by rearranging the basic units of the set. The lighting, the words of the text, and the way the actors use the various spaces tell the audience where the action is occurring.

Upstage. The area of the stage farthest from the audience.

Vaudeville. A variety show of family entertainment, popular in the nineteenth- and early twentieth-century American theatre. Consisted of skits, specialty acts, short plays, and song-and-dance numbers.

Wagon stage. A large rolling platform on which scenery is placed, so that a new setting can be rolled into view while another is being removed.

Well-made play. A formulistic play structure popular in the nineteenth and early twentieth centuries. The formula consisted of the illusion of cause and effect, a secret withheld from the characters but known to the audience, a pattern of reversals of fortune throughout the play building to the scene where all information is finally revealed, and heavy reliance on props to provide complications and bring about reversals.

Wing. 1. The right and left offstage areas. 2. A flat adjacent to other scenic units, used for masking. 3. Scenic flats parallel to the apron along the sides of the stage.

Wing and backdrop. A style of setting popular from the Renaissance until the development of the box set in the nineteenth century. The scenic elements are painted on wings and on a backdrop or back shutter, and scene changes occur when one set of wings and drop is removed to reveal another set behind them.

Work lights. The lights that illuminate the stage and backstage as working areas whenever a performance is not in progress, or used while the curtain is down for the convenience of technicians.

BIBLIOGRAPHY

GENERAL WORKS

Applebaum, Stanley (ed.). *The New York Stage: Famous Productions in Photographs.* New York, 1976.

Blum, Daniel. *A Pictorial History of the American Theatre, 1860–1980.* Revised edition by John Willis. New York, 1977.

Brockett, Oscar G. *History of the Theatre.* 4th ed. Boston, 1981.

Clark, Barrett. *European Theories of the Drama.* 3rd ed. New York, 1965.

Dukore, Bernard. *Dramatic Theory and Criticism: Greeks to Grotowski.* New York, 1974.

Eidsvick, Charles V. *Cineliteracy: Film Among the Arts.* New York, 1978.

Esslin, Martin. *The Encyclopedia of World Theatre.* New York, 1977.

Gascoigne, Bamber. *World Theatre: An Illustrated History.* Boston, 1968.

Gassner, John, and Ralph S. Allen (eds.). *Theatre and Drama in the Making.* Boston, 1964.

Gassner, John, and Edward Quinn. *The Reader's Encyclopedia of World Drama.* New York, 1969.

Hartnoll, Phyllis. *Oxford Companion to the Theatre.* 4th ed. New York, 1983.

Hewitt, Barnard. *Theatre USA, 1668–1957.* New York, 1967.

Nagler, Alois M. *A Source Book in Theatrical History.* New York, 1959.

Nicoll, Allardyce. *The Development of the Theatre.* 5th ed. New York, 1966.

Oenslager, Donald. *Scenery Then and Now.* New York, 1936.

Roberts, Vera Mowray. *On Stage: A History of the Theatre.* 2nd ed. New York, 1974.

Southern, Richard. *The Seven Ages of the Theatre.* New York, 1961.

CHAPTER ONE   THE AUDIENCE IN THE THEATRE

Burns, Elizabeth. *Theatricality.* New York, 1973.

Cole, David. *The Theatrical Event: A Mythos, a Vocabulary, a Perspective.* Middletown, Conn., 1975.

Goldman, Michael. *The Actor's Freedom: Toward a Theory of Drama.* New York, 1975.

Jellicoe, Ann. *Some Unconscious Influences in the Theatre.* Cambridge, 1967.

Jones, Margo. *Theatre in the Round.* New York, 1951.

Lahr, John, and Jonathon Price. *Life-Show: How to See Theatre in Life and Life in Theatre.* New York, 1973.

Langer, Susanne K. *Feeling and Form.* New York, 1953.

McNamara, Brooks, Jerry Rojo, and Richard Schechner. *Theatres, Spaces, Environments: Eighteen Projects.* New York, 1975.

Mielziner, Jo. *The Shapes of Our Theatre.* New York, 1970.

Southern, Richard. *The Open Stage.* New York, 1959.

CHAPTER TWO   THE PLAY AND THE CREATIVE AUDIENCE

Beckerman, Bernard. *Dynamics of Drama: Theory and Method of Analysis.* New York, 1979.

Bentley, Eric. *The Life of the Drama.* New York, 1964.

Clay, James H., and Daniel Krempel. *The Theatrical Image.* New York, 1967.

Esslin, Martin. *An Anatomy of Drama.* New York, 1977.

Gross, Roger. *Understanding Playscripts: Theory and Method.* Bowling Green, Ohio, 1974.

Styan, John L. *Drama, Stage and Audience.* Cambridge, England, 1975.

————. *The Elements of Drama.* Cambridge, England, 1960).

CHAPTER THREE   THE THEATRE OF EXALTATION

Greek Tragedy

Aristotle. *Aristotle's Poetics.* Tr. by S. H. Butcher. New York, 1961.

Arnott, Peter D. *The Ancient Greek and Roman Theatre.* New York, 1971.

————. *Greek Scenic Conventions in the Fifth Century,* B.C. New York, 1962.

Bieber, Margarete. *The History of the Greek and Roman Theatre.* 2nd ed. Princeton, 1961.

Butler, James R. *The Theatre and Drama of Greece and Rome.* San Francisco, 1972.

Corrigan, Robert W. *Tragedy: Vision and Form.* 2nd ed. New York, 1981.

Fergusson, Francis. *The Idea of a Theater.* Princeton, 1968.

Hamilton, Edith. *The Greek Way.* New York, 1964.

Kernodle, George R. "The Fifth-Century Skene: A New Model." *Educational Theatre Journal,* XX. December, 1968.

Kitto, H. D. F. *Greek Tragedy.* New York, 1961.

Kott, Jan. *The Eating of the Gods: An Interpretation of Greek Tragedy.* Tr. by Boleslaw Taborski and Edward Czerwinski. New York, 1973.

CHAPTER FOUR   THE THEATRE OF EXALTATION

Medieval Drama

Chambers, E. K. *The Medieval Stage.* 2 vols. Oxford, 1903.

Kahrl, Stanley. *Traditions of Medieval English Drama.* Pittsburgh, 1975.

Nelson, Alan H. *The Medieval Stage: Corpus Christi Pageants and Plays.* Chicago, 1974.

Potter, Robert. *The English Morality Play: Origins, History and Influence of a Dramatic Tradition.* London, 1975.

Salter, F. M. *Medieval Drama in Chester.* Toronto, 1955.

Southern, Richard. *The Medieval Theatre in the Round.* London, 1957.

Wickham, Glynne. *The Medieval Theatre.* New York, 1974.

Tragedy: Elizabethan to Modern

Adams, John C. *The Globe Playhouse: Its Design and Equipment.* 2nd ed. New York, 1961.

Beckerman, Bernard. *Shakespeare at the Globe, 1599–1609.* New York, 1962.

Berry, Ralph. *On Directing Shakespeare: Interviews with Contemporary Directors.* New York, 1977.

Campbell, Lily Bess. *Scenes and Machines on the English Stage During the Renaissance.* New York, 1960.

Chambers, E. K. *The Elizabethan Stage.* 4 vols. Oxford, 1923.

Gurr, Andrew. *The Shakespeare Stage, 1574–1642.* Cambridge, England, 1980.

Heilman, Robert B. *Tragedy and Melodrama: Versions of Experience.* Seattle, 1968.

Hewitt, Barnard (ed.). *The Renaissance Stage: Documents of Serlio, Sabbatini, and Furttenbach.* Coral Gables, Fla., 1958.

Hodges, C. Walter. *The Globe Restored: A Study of the Elizabethan Theatre.* New York, 1968.

Kernodle, George R. *From Art to Theatre: Form and Convention in the Renaissance.* Chicago, 1964.

Kott, Jan. *Shakespeare Our Contemporary.* Tr. by Boleslaw Taborski. New York, 1964.

Krutch, Joseph Wood. *"Modernism" in Modern Drama.* Ithaca, N.Y., 1953.

Lancaster, H. C. *A History of French Dramatic Literature in the Seventeenth Century.* New York, 1966.

Lawrenson, T. E. *The French Stage in the XVIIth Century: A Study of the Advent of the Italian Order.* Manchester, England, 1957.

Miller, Arthur. *The Theatre Essays of Arthur Miller.* Ed. by Robert Martin. New York, 1978.

Turnell, Martin. *The Classical Moment: Studies in Corneille, Moliere, and Racine.* New York, 1948.

Yates, Frances A. *Theatre of the World.* Chicago, 1969.

CHAPTER FIVE   THE THEATRE OF LAUGHTER

Corrigan, Robert W. (ed.) *Comedy: Meaning and Form.* 2nd ed. New York, 1981.

Felheim, Marvin (ed.). *Comedy: Plays, Theory and Criticism.* New York, 1962.

Grawe, Paul H. *Comedy in Space, Time, and the Imagination.* Chicago, 1983.

Heilman, Robert B. *The Ways of the World: Comedy and Society.* Seattle, 1978.

Hume, Robert D. *The Rakish Stage: Studies in English Drama, 1660–1800.* Carbondale, Ill., 1983.

Kernodle, George R. "Excruciatingly Funny; or, the 47 Keys to Comedy." *Theatre Arts,* XXX. December, 1946.

Kronenberger, Louis. *The Thread of Laughter.* New York, 1952.

Lea, Kathleen M. *Italian Popular Comedy.* New York, 1962.

Lever, Katherine. *The Art of Greek Comedy.* London, 1956.

Nicoll, Allardyce. *The World of Harlequin.* Cambridge, England, 1963.

Segal, Erich W. *Roman Laughter: The Comedy of Plautus.* Cambridge, Mass., 1968.

Sypher, Wylie (ed.). *Comedy.* Garden City, N.Y., 1956.

CHAPTER SIX   THE THEATRE OF THE ROMANTIC

Romance and Melodrama

Carlson, Marvin A. *The French Stage in the Nineteenth Century.* Metuchin, N.J., 1972.

_____. *The German Stage in the Nineteenth Century.* Metuchen, N.J., 1972.

Disher, Maurice. *Melodrama: Plots That Thrilled.* New York, 1954.

Moody, Richard. *America Takes the Stage: Romanticism in American Drama and Theatre, 1750–1900*. Bloomington, Ind., 1955.
Rowell, George. *The Victorian Theatre*. Oxford, 1956.
Vardac, Nicolas A. *Stage to Screen: Theatrical Method from Garrick to Griffith*. Cambridge, Mass., 1949.

Opera and the Musical

Engel, Lehman. *The American Musical Theatre*. New York, 1967.
Kerman, Joseph. *Opera as Drama*. New York, 1956.
Smith, Cecil M., and Glenn Litton. *Musical Comedy in America*. 2nd ed. New York, 1981.
Williams, Stephen. *Come to the Opera*. Greenwich, Conn., 1961.

Dance

See bibliography for Chapter 10.

CHAPTER SEVEN   THE THEATRE OF REALISM

Antoine, Andre. *Memories of the Theatre Libre*. Tr. by Marvin Carlson. Coral Gables, Fla., 1964.
Clurman, Harold. *The Fervent Years: The Story of the Group Theatre in the Thirties*. New York, 1957.
DeHart, Steven. *The Meininger Theater: 1776–1926*. Ann Arbor, 1981.
Marker, Lise-Lone. *David Belasco's Naturalism in the American Theatre*. Princeton, 1974.
Munk, Erika (ed.). *Stanislavski and America*. Greenwich, Conn., 1968.
Stanislavsky, Constantin. *My Life in Art*. New York, 1948.
———. *Stanislavski's Legacy*. Ed. and tr. by Elizabeth Reynolds Hapgood. New York, 1968.
Stone, Edward. *What Was Naturalism? Material for an Answer*. New York, 1959.

CHAPTER EIGHT   THE THEATRE OF DISRUPTION

Bentley, Eric (ed.). *The Theory of the Modern Stage*. Baltimore, 1976.
Brockett, Oscar G. and Robert R. Findlay. *Century of Innovation: A History of European and American Theatre and Drama Since 1870*. Englewood Cliffs, N.J., 1973.
Esslin, Martin. *The Theatre of the Absurd*. 3rd ed. New York, 1980.
Gorelik, Mordecai. *New Theatres for Old*. New York, 1975.
Meyerhold, Vsevolod. *Meyerhold on Theatre*. Edited by Edward Braun. New York, 1969.
Pronko, Leonard. *Avant-Garde: The Experimental Theatre in France*. Berkeley, 1963.
Roose-Evans, James. *Experimental Theatre: From Stanislavsky to Today*. New York, 1970.
Rosen, Steven J. *Samuel Beckett and the Pessimistic Tradition*. New Brunswick, N.J., 1976.
Sartre, Jean-Paul. *Sartre on Theatre*. Tr. by Frank Jellinek. New York, 1976.
Simonson, Lee. *The Stage Is Set*. New York, 1932.
Taylor, John Russell. *Anger and After*. Baltimore, 1963.
Willett, John. *Expressionism*. New York, 1970.

CHAPTER NINE   REALISM TRANSFORMED

Oriental Theatre

Alley, Rewi. *Peking Opera.* 1957.
Arnott, Peter D. *The Theatres of Japan.* New York, 1969.
Brandon, James R. *The Theatre in Southeast Asia.* Cambridge, Mass., 1967.
Ernst, Earle. "The Influence of Japanese Theatrical Style in Western Theatre." *Educational Theatre Journal,* XXI. May, 1969.
Keene, Donald. *No: The Classical Theatre of Japan.* Palo Alto, Calif., 1966.
Pronko, Leonard. *Theatre East and West: Perspectives Toward a Total Theatre.* Berkeley, 1967.
Scott, A.C. *The Classical Theatre of China.* London, 1957.
_____. *The Kabuki Theatre of Japan.* London, 1955.

Transformations of Realism

Appia, Adolphe. *The Work of Living Art* and *Man Is the Measure of All Things.* Miami, 1960.
Bentley, Eric (ed.). *The Theory of the Modern Stage.* Baltimore, 1976.
_____. *Theatre of War.* New York, 1973.
Brecht, Bertolt. *Brecht on Theatre.* Tr. by John Willet. New York, 1964.
Gorelik, Mordecai. "An Epic Catechism." *Tulane Drama Review,* T5. Autumn, 1959.
Houghton, Norris. *Moscow Rehearsals: An Account of Methods of Production in the Soviet Theatre.* New York, 1962.
_____. *The Exploding Stage: An Introduction to Twentieth Century Drama.* New York, 1971.
Ley-Piscator, Maria. *The Piscator Experiment: The Political Theatre.* New York, 1967.

Ethnic Theatre

Cohen, Sarah Blacher. *From Hester Street to Hollywood: The Jewish-American Stage and Screen.* Bloomington, Ind., 1983.
Hogan, Robert G. *The Modern Irish Drama: A Documentary History.* Atlantic Highlands, N.J., 1975.
Kavanagh, Peter. *The Story of the Abbey Theatre.* New York, 1950.
Kennedy, J. Scott. *In Search of African Theatre.* New York, 1973.
Lifson, David S. *The Yiddish Theatre in America.* New York, 1965.
Mitchell, Lofton. *Black Drama: The Story of the American Negro in the Theatre.* New York, 1967.
_____. *Voices of the Black Theatre.* Clifton, N.J., 1975.
Schiff, Ellen. *From Stereotype to Metaphor: The Jewish Contemporary Drama.* Albany, N.Y., 1982.
Seller, Maxine Schwartz. *Ethnic Theatre in the United States.* Westport, Conn., 1983.

CHAPTER TEN   A LIBERATED THEATRE

Artaud, Antonin. *The Theatre and Its Double.* Tr. by M. C. Richards. New York, 1958.

Blau, Herbert. *The Impossible Theatre: A Manifesto.* New York, 1966.

Croyden, Margaret. *Lunatics, Lovers, and Poets: The Contemporary Experimental Theatre.* New York, 1974.

Foreman, Richard. *Richard Foreman: Plays and Manifestos.* Ed. by Kate Davy. New York, 1976.

Grotowski, Jerzy. *Towards a Poor Theatre.* New York, 1970.

Heilpern, John, *Conference of the Birds: The Story of Peter Brook in Africa.* New York, 1979.

Kirby, E. T. (ed.). *Total Theatre: A Critical Anthology.* New York, 1969.

Kirby, Michael. *Happenings.* New York, 1965.

Lesnick, Henry. *Guerrilla Street Theater.* New York, 1973.

Marranca, Bonnie (ed.). *The Theatre of Images.* New York, 1977.

Pasolli, Robert. *A Book on the Open Theatre.* Indianapolis, 1970.

Sainer, Arthur. *The Radical Theatre Notebook.* New York, 1975.

Schechner, Richard. *Environmental Theatre.* New York, 1973.

———. *Essays on Performance Theory.* New York, 1977.

Schevill, James (ed.). *Break Out!* New York, 1977.

Shank, Theodore. *American Alternative Theatre.* New York, 1982.

Dance (Ballet, Modern, and Post-Modern)

Banes, Sally. *Terpsichore in Sneakers: Post-Modern Dance.* Boston, 1979.

Cayou, Dolores K. *Modern Jazz Dance.* Palo Alto, Calif., 1971.

De Mille, Agnes. *The Book of the Dance.* New York, 1963.

Horst, Louis, and Carroll Russell. *Modern Dance Forms in Relation to Other Modern Arts.* San Francisco, 1961.

Kochno, Boris. *Diaghilev and the Ballets Russes.* New York, 1970.

Kriegsman, Sali Ann. *Modern Dance in America: The Bennington Years.* Boston, 1981.

Lawson, Joan. *Classical Ballet: Its Style and Technique.* New York, 1960.

———. *History of Ballet and Its Makers.* New York, 1964.

Siegl, Marcia B. *The Shapes of Change: Images of American Dance.* Boston, 1979.

Taper, Bernard. *Balanchine.* New York, 1963.

CHAPTER ELEVEN   THE PLAYWRIGHT

Cole, Toby (ed.). *Playwrights on Playwriting.* New York, 1960.

Lawson, John Howard. *Theory and Technique of Playwriting.* New York, 1960.

Wilder, Thornton. "Some Thoughts on Playwriting" in *The Intent of the Artist.* Ed. by Augusto Centeno. Princeton, 1970.

CHAPTER TWELVE   THE DIRECTOR

Brook, Peter. *The Empty Space.* New York, 1968.

Clurman, Harold. *On Directing.* New York, 1972.

Cole, Toby, and Helen Krich Chinoy (eds.). *Directors on Directing.* Rev. ed. Indianapolis, 1963.

Craig, Gordon. *On the Art of the Theatre.* New York, 1925.

Dean, Alexander, and Lawrence Carra. *Fundamentals of Play Directing.* 3rd ed. New York, 1974.

Gorchakov, Nikolai. *Stanislavsky Directs.* Tr. by Miriam Goldins. New York, 1954.

Hodge, Frances. *Play Directing: Analysis, Communication, and Style.* 2nd ed. Englewood Cliffs, N.J., 1982.

Hornby, Richard. *Script into Production.* Austin, Tex., 1978.

Langley, Stephen. *Producers on Producing.* New York, 1976.

Mitchell, Lee. *Staging Premodern Drama: A Guide to Production Problems.* Westport, Conn., 1984.

CHAPTER THIRTEEN   DESIGNING THE PRODUCTION

Appia, Adolphe. *Music and the Art of the Theatre.* Tr. by Robert W. Corrigan and Mary D. Dirks. Miami, 1962.

Bablet, Denis. *Revolutions of Stage Design in the Twentieth Century.* New York, 1977.

Bay, Howard. *Stage Design.* New York, 1974.

Bowman, Ned. *Handbook of Technical Practices for the Performing Arts.* Williamsburg, Pa., 1972.

Burian, Jarka. *The Scenography of Josef Svoboda.* Middletown, Conn., 1971.

Corey, Irene. *The Mask of Reality: An Approach to Design for Theatre.* Anchorage, Ky., 1968.

Corson, Richard. *Stage Makeup.* 5th ed. Englewood Cliffs, N.J., 1975.

Gillette, Arnold S. *An Introduction to Scenic Design.* 1967.

Hainaux, Rene (ed.). *Stage Design Throughout the World Since 1935.* 1956; *Stage Design Throughout the World Since 1950.* 1964; *Stage Design Throughout the World Since 1960.* 1973; *Stage Design Throughout the World, 1970–1975.* 1976.

Jones, Robert Edmond. *The Dramatic Imagination.* New York, 1941.

Larson, Orville K. *Scene Design for Stage and Screen.* East Lansing, Mich., 1961.

Mielziner, Jo. *Designing for the Theatre.* New York, 1965.

Parker, Oren, and Harvey K. Smith. *Scene Design and Stage Lighting.* 4th ed. New York, 1979.

Rosenthal, Jean, and Lael Wertenbacker. *The Magic of Light.* Boston, 1972.

Russell, Douglas. *Stage Costume Design: Theory, Technique and Style.* 1973.

_____. *Costume History and Style.* Englewood Cliffs, N.J., 1983.

CHAPTER FOURTEEN   THE ART OF THE ACTOR

Benedetti, Robert. *The Actor at Work.* 3rd ed. Englewood Cliffs, N.J., 1981.

Burton, Hal (ed.). *Great Acting.* New York, 1967.

Chaikin, Joseph. *The Presence of the Actor.* New York, 1972.

Chekhov, Michael. *To the Actor: On the Technique of Acting.* 1953.

Cole, Toby, and Helen Krich Chinoy (eds.). *Actors on Acting.* Rev. ed. New York, 1970.

Funke, Lewis, and John E. Booth (eds.). *Actors Talk About Acting.* New York, 1973.

Kernodle, George R. "Style, Stylization and Styles of Acting." *Educational Theatre Journal,* XII. December, 1960.

Linklater, Kristen. *Freeing the Natural Voice.* New York, 1976.

Saint-Denis, Michel. *Theatre: The Rediscovery of Style.* New York, 1969.

————. *Training for the Theatre: Premises and Promises.* Ed. by Suria Saint-Denis. New York, 1982.

Spolin, Viola. *Improvisation for the Theatre.* 1963.

Stanislavsky, Constantin. *Creating a Role.* Tr. by E. R. Hapgood. New York, 1961.

EPILOGUE: THE PLEASURE OF YOUR COMPANY

Atkinson, Brooks. *Broadway.* Rev. ed. New York, 1974.

Conolly, L. W. (ed.). *Theatrical Touring and Founding in North America.* Westport, Conn., 1982.

Farber, Donald C. *From Option to Opening: A Guide for the Off-Broadway Producer.* 3rd ed. New York, 1977.

Gard, Robert E., and Gertrude Burley. *Community Theatre, Idea and Achievement.* New York, 1959.

Jacobs, Susan. *On Stage: The Making of a Broadway Play.* New York, 1972.

Larson, Gary O. *The Reluctant Patron: The U.S. Government and the Arts.* Philadelphia, 1983.

Morison, Bradley G., and Kay Fliehr. *In Search of an Audience: How an Audience Was Found for the Tyrone Guthrie Theatre.* New York, 1968.

Novick, Julius. *Beyond Broadway: The Quest for Permanent Theatres.* New York, 1968.

Price, Julia. *The Off-Broadway Theatre.* New York, 1962.

Young, John Wray. *The Community Theatre and How It Works.* New York, 1957.

Zeigler, Joseph Wesley. *Regional Theatre: The Revolutionary Stage.* New York, 1977.

PICTURE CREDITS

Theatre, 1898–1917; 208, Schomburg Center for Research in Black Culture, The New York Public Library, Astor, Lenox and Tilden Foundations; 209, The Museum of Modern Art/Film Stills Archive.

Chapter 8

P. 216, Elliot Erwitt/Magnum; 220, Eugene Cook; 223, The Museum of Modern Art/Film Stills Archive; 225, 226, Billy Rose Theatre Collection, The New York Public Library at Lincoln Center, Astor, Lenox and Tilden Foundations; 236, Gerry Goodstein; 239, Schomburg Center for Research in Black Culture, The New York Public Library, Astor, Lenox and Tilden Foundations; 240, Bill Reid.

Chapter 9

P. 250, 252, top and bottom, 269, 271, 274, © 1984 Martha Swope; 255, Billy Rose Theatre Collection, The New York Public Library at Lincoln Center, Astor, Lenox and Tilden Foundations; 256, Peter A. Juley and Son; 260, Van Williams; 263, Actor: Robert Boles, Photo: Ken Klingenmeier; 265, 273, Robert Burroughs; 278, © 1984 Bert Andrews; 279, Gerry Goodstein.

Chapter 10

P. 282, HBJ Collection; 287, 305, 306, 307, 308, 316, © 1984 Martha Swope; 291, *The New York Times*; 293, Photo courtesy of Richard Schechner; 295, Governors of the Royal Shakespeare Theatre, Stratford-Upon-Avon; 297, © 1971 Fred W. McDarrah; 300, 301, © 1976 Babette Mangolte; 309, Photo by Susan Schiff-Faludi from the choreographed piece "Scenario" by Alwin Nikolais; 312, Johan Elbers.

Chapter 11

P. 324, from Philip G. Hill, *The Living Art*, published by Holt, Rinehart and Winston, 1971; 329, Billy Rose Theatre Collection, The New York Public Library at Lincoln Center, Astor, Lenox and Tilden Foundations; 332, © 1984 Martha Swope.

Chapter 12

P. 338, Clifford Baker; 345, A. Vincent Scarano; 347, Metropolitan Opera Association Press Department; 348, Gordon Parks, *LIFE Magazine*, © 1955, Time Inc.; 352, Donald Cooper, London; 354, Billy Rose Theatre Collection, The New York Public Library at Lincoln Center, Astor, Lenox and Tilden Foundations; 355, © 1984 Martha Swope; 357, Jeffrey Levy; 360, The Guthrie Theatre.

Chapter 13

P. 364, Alfred Wertheimer; 367, Crown Copyright Victoria and Albert Museum; 371, University of Washington Archives; 372, 387, Josef Elfenbein; 379, HBJ Collection; 380, Courtesy Indiana University Audio-Visual Center; 382, Robert Segrin; 383, Houston Rogers, from J. L. Styan, *The Shakespeare Revolution*, Cambridge University Press; 384, © 1984 Susan Cook

Chapter 14

P. 390, Bill Reid; 393, 401, 409, © 1984 Martha Swope; 395, top, Van Williams; 395, bottom, Billy Rose Theatre Collection, The New York Public Library at Lincoln Center, Astor, Lenox and Tilden Foundations.

Epilogue

412, 416, © 1984 Martha Swope; 417, Betty Engle LeVin; 418, Robert Burroughs.

Color Section

Plate 1, Bill Reid; 2, 4, 10, 14 © 1984 Martha Swope; 3, © 1984 Susan Cook; 5, © 1982 George Lange; 6, 13, Michael Schoenfeld; 7, Courtesy of Bill Hektner; 8, Courtesy of Eastman Kodak Company; 11, Courtesy Education Department, Metropolitan Opera Guild/Curt Kaufman.

INDEX

Note: Page numbers in italics refer to illustrations or captions.

Poor theatre, 294
Porgy and Bess, 179–80, *179*
Porter, Stephen, *137*
Poulenc, Francis, *color*
Presentationalism, 222
Prince, Harold, *250, 271*
Private Life of the Master Race, The, 267
Producers, 340
Production concept
    design and, 381–83
    of *The Elephant Man,* 385–86
Production conference, 342, 358–59, 373
Production format, 46–50, 341
Promenade theatre, 20
Proscenium, 94
Proscenium stage, *18,* 19–20, 372
Provincetown Players, *255*
Provincetown Playhouse, The, 197
Public Theatre, The, 303
Purpose, 65
Push Comes to Shove, 307
Pygmalion, 146, 254, 400–11

Q

Quare Fellow, The, 253
Quarry, 312, 312–13
Quartermaine's Terms, 272–73

R

Rabe, David, 228–29, 274
Racine, Jean, *107,* 107–108
Radio, 4–5
Rado, Ted, 177
Ragni, Gerome, 177
Rainer, Yvonne, 310
Raisin in the Sun, A, 23, 24, 25, *204,*
    204–209, *208,* 278
Randall, Tony, 7
Rashomon, 261
Rauschenberg, Robert, 310
Realism (realistic movement), 188–215,
    323
    comedy and, 251, 253
    directing and acting and, 198–200
    documentary, 200–202
    epic, 262–71
    ethnic theatre and, 275–80
    factual, 200–209

impressionism, 192–96
    intimate theatre and, 196–98
    in movies, 209–13
    naturalism, 189–92
    Oriental influences on, 257–62
    romance and, 248–51
    selected, 253–54
    stylized, 254–57
    on television, 213–15
    theatre of fact, 202–204
Rebel Without a Cause, 118
Recitative, 166
Reds, 212
Regional theatre movement, 289
Rehearsals, 343–44, 359
Reinhardt, Max, 266, 368
Reinhardt, Paul D., *373, 376*
Religious cycle dramas, 91–92
Religious drama, 85–86, 90–94
Renaissance comedy, 127–29
Reprise, 176
Restoration comedy, 141–42
Restoration drama, 129
Revelations, 311
Reviews, 421–22
Rhoda in Potatoland, 300, *300–301*
Rice, Elmer, 224, 225, 251
Rice, Tim, 270
Richard III, 376
Riders to the Sea, 116, 276
Ring of the Nibelungs, The, 169
Robbins, Jerome, 305, 308
Robertson, T. W., 197
Rodeo, 305
Rodgers, Richard, 175, 177
Role-playing, 392–94
    in theatre of the absurd, 234
Roles, 5
Romance
    in movies, 163–65
    in musicals, 174–84
    as psychological structure, 184–85
    realism and, 248–51
Roman theatre, 90, *90,* 94
Romantic dance, 165, 170–72
Romantic ideals, 152–55
Romantic theatre, 152–63
    birth of the romantic ideals and,
        152–55

A 4
B 5
C 6
D 7
E 8
F 9
G 0
H 1
I 2
J 3